W9-AHJ-951

CRIMINAL JUSTICE IN AMERICA

THIRD EDITION

Developed by

Marshall Croddy
Bill Hayes
Todd Clark

Constitutional Rights Foundation

601 South Kingsley Drive
Los Angeles, California 90005
(213) 487- 5590
www.crf-usa.org

MARJORIE S. STEINBERG
President, Constitutional Rights Foundation

JEROME C. BYRNE
Chairman, Publications Committee
Constitutional Rights Foundation

TODD CLARK
Executive Director

Developed by

Marshall Croddy, Bill Hayes, Todd Clark

Editor

Bill Hayes

Contributing Writers

Bill Hayes, Marshall Croddy, Teri Engler, Sandy
Kanengiser, Carlton Martz, Betsy Salzman,
Coral Suter, Charles Tremper, Eden Kusmiersky

Principal Staff and Reviewers

Todd Clark, *Executive Director*
Carolyn Pereira, *Executive Director, Chicago*
Constitutional Rights Foundation

Board Reviewers

Jerome C. Byrne, Gerald Chaleff, Lee Edmond,
Peggy Saferstein, Marvin Sears, Lois Thompson,
and Carlton Varner.

Subject Matter Consultants

Richard Chrystie, *Former Deputy District Attorney,*
Los Angeles County
Star French, *Deputy Probation Officer,*
Los Angeles County
John Hud, *Criminal Defense Attorney, Bozeman,*
Montana
Daniel E. Lewis, *Wasserman, Comden &*
Casselman, LLP
Robert Mascali, *Director of Claims, New York*
State Crime Victims Board
Julia Rider, *Luce, Forward, Hill, Jeffer &*
Mangels
Richard Simonian, *Superintendent, C.K Wakefield*
School, Fresno County Probation Department
Captain Robert Taylor, *Commanding Officer,*
Juvenile Division, Los Angeles Police Department

Production

Andrew Costly, *Designer and Production Manager*
Navigator Press, *Printing*

Library of Congress Cataloging-in-Publication Data

Criminal Justice in America / developed by Marshall Croddy, Bill Hayes, Todd Clark ;
[contributing writers, Bill Hayes ... et al.].– 3rd ed.

    p. cm.

  Includes index.
  ISBN 1-886253-12-9 (pbk. : alk. paper)
    1. Criminal justice, Administration of–United States. I. Croddy, Marshall. II Hayes,
  Bill. III Clark, Todd, 1933-

HV9950.C745 2000
364.973–dc21

                                  00-060237

© 2000, 1998, 1993, 1991, 1983 by Constitutional Rights Foundation. Third Edition. All rights reserved. No part of this
book may be reproduced, in any form or by any means, without written permission. Printed in the United States of
America.

The development of these materials was financially assisted through the United States Office of Juvenile Justice and Delinquency Prevention, Grant #85-
JS-CX-0007.

CRIMINAL JUSTICE IN AMERICA

Table of Contents

Introduction

No matter who you are, crime affects your life. As a student, your school might be vandalized or your wallet stolen. Statistically, chances are very good that sometime in your life you will be a victim of some crime. As a future taxpayer, you will be forced to contribute money in the fight against crime or to repair the damage it does. As a voter, you will be asked to choose candidates based in part, at least, on their view about solutions to crime. Everyone agrees that crime is a serious problem. Few agree about its causes or solutions.Although the debate over the causes and solutions to crime will probably never end, society has evolved a criminal justice system for dealing with crime. Essential to an understanding of this system are two areas of jurisprudence. These are called **criminal law** and **criminal procedure.**

Criminal Law

Criminal law focuses on defining crime itself. That is, for what conduct or behavior does our society punish people? After all, if society had no standards for human behavior, we would not have any crime, let alone a crime problem.Today, our criminal law is contained in a wide array of statutes and ordinances enacted by federal, state, county, and city government. Each law spells out the ingredients of the crime in question and the punishment for those who break it.The process of defining and applying criminal law never stops. Legislatures repeal out-of-date laws, modify existing laws, and enact new ones. Criminal trial courts interpret the meaning of various laws and apply them to particular cases. Criminal appeal courts check the decisions of trial courts and set precedents for other trial courts to follow. Thus the body of criminal law keeps changing.

Criminal Procedure

Criminal procedure comes into play when the police start investigating a particular crime. It focuses on the steps taken and decisions made in the investigation, accusation, trial, verdict, and sentencing of a criminal defendant. It is the process by which we decide the what, when, where, how, and who questions of criminal justice.

Criminal procedure is also designed to protect a defendant from being falsely accused or convicted of a crime. The U.S. Constitution requires "due process of law," offers protection from "unreasonable searches and seizures," and forbids "cruel and unusual punishment." These, and many other constitutional provisions, have done much to shape our criminal procedure.

Criminal procedure has other functions also. Rules of court attempt to assure an orderly and consistent decision-making process. Rules of evidence are designed to ensure that the facts of the case are relevant, accurate, and not overly prejudicial. There are also rules of conduct for judges, lawyers, and juries.Like criminal law, criminal procedure is ever-changing. Legislators enact new laws, judges and courts adopt new rules, and the Supreme Court interprets and applies the Constitution.

Criminal Justice

This book will have a lot to do with criminal law and procedure. They are important parts of criminal justice. Yet there is much, much more to consider. Criminal justice also involves people, institutions, and important societal issues. Perhaps even more importantly, it raises vital questions in each of us about fairness, security, and rights in a free society.As you explore the selections in this book, you will meet the people who investigate crime and enforce our laws. You will learn about judges and courts and their struggle to protect individual rights while determining guilt or innocence. You will see the darker side of the criminal justice system and find out how society deals with people after they have been found guilty beyond a reasonable doubt. You will visit prisons and prisoners, guards, and parole officers, and in doing so you will discover the problems they face on a daily basis.

The Problem of Crime

Beyond criminal law and procedure and the system that investigates, apprehends, and punishes lawbreakers, you will study crime itself. Social scientists who take this role are called criminologists. They try to find answers to some very difficult questions. Why do people become criminals? How serious is our crime problem? How can crime be reduced? Although you won't be a professional criminologist after studying this book, you will have a much better understanding about some of the important issues of criminal justice.

Criminal Justice in America on the Internet

You can find additional information on every part of this book on the Internet. Go to Constitutional Rights Foundation's web site (www.crf-usa.org), click on Links, and click on *Criminal Justice in America* Links.

Crime

Friday evening, 9:30 p.m. . . .

In an underground parking garage downtown, a young man staggers to a pay phone on the wall and leans against it to hold himself up. Finally he gets the strength to call 9-1-1. A few seconds later, a voice comes on the line.

"Emergency services."

"My name is Sam Peterson," the man stammers. "I've just been robbed."

Meanwhile, in a middle-income residential area, a young husband and wife arrive home from a movie. The wife is the first to notice that the glass in the back door has been smashed in. Inside they find a horrible mess, with furniture tipped over and china broken on the floor. The television and stereo are gone. They both start to tremble. A place that they believed was private and safe had been torn open and violated.

A major crime happens somewhere in America every three seconds. But this isn't just a statistic. Behind each crime are people: victims who are hurt, criminals who often live violent and destructive lives, and those who must deal with the aftermath—the police, social workers, attorneys, judges, and legislators.

In this unit, we will examine crime in terms of victims, criminals, and society. What is it like to have your life changed in an instant by someone else's wrongdoing? Who are the criminals and why do they do it? What acts does our society, through its laws, define as crimes? What must be proved before a person is convicted of a crime? By considering these questions, you will learn a lot about crime and its consequences. And you will be able to take an intelligent part in a great debate going on in our society: What should we do about crime?

CHAPTER 1
Crime and its Victims

Who Are the Victims?

Suzanne Rossetti, 26, was driving home from the theater at Arizona State University in Phoenix. On the way, she stopped at the market, where she accidentally locked her keys inside her car. Two young men got the door open for her with a coat hanger and then asked her for a lift. She agreed, but once in the car, they turned vicious almost immediately.

The young men forced Suzanne to drive them to her apartment. There they beat and raped her for several hours. Then they drove her into the desert and threw her off a cliff. When they heard her moans down below, they climbed down after her. She pleaded with them to leave her alone.

"I'm dying anyway," she begged.

"Damn right you are," one of them growled. He picked up a rock and crushed her skull.

Shocking stories like these have frightened most of us. *The streets just aren't safe at night. I've had my third car stereo stolen. I hate putting bars on my windows, but what choice do I have?* Opinion polls consistently show that Americans express great concern over the crime rate and the effectiveness of the criminal justice system.

Down through the years this concern has sparked many studies of the causes of crime and many proposals for possible solutions. In recent years, attention has shifted to the *victims* of crime. Who are they? How can we help them through the tangle of the legal system? What can be done to protect them? And what can be done to help them recover from the effects of the crime?

First, who are the victims? They come from all walks of life and all age groups. But studies show that the most common victim of violent crime is a black male teenager from a low-income family. And the most common victim of theft is a white male teenager from a low-income family. Most studies show that criminals tend to victimize members of their own race.

Being a victim can be deeply disturbing. It can take years to recover, and some victims never recover. This is not just true of violent crime. Fraud can wipe out a victim's life savings. A bank swindle can take away a home that an elderly couple worked all their lives to pay for.

Crimes against property like fraud, burglary, and theft are the most common crimes in the United States. Violent crimes such as murder, rape, and robbery are less common. But they probably cause more anxiety and fear. Violent crime can leave a victim crippled, physically or emotionally. It's hard to imagine the effect if it hasn't happened to you. Some victims never want to leave the safety of their homes again.

In the following sections, we will examine some victims of violent and property crimes. First we will find out what **victimology**—the study of victims—tells us about victims of these crimes. Then we'll listen to some victims describe the effect crime had on their lives.

Victims of Violent Crimes

Violent crimes, such as murder, rape, robbery, and assault, are also known as **crimes against the person**. In these crimes, the criminal either uses force or threatens to use force against the victim. Below, we will take a closer look at victims of two kinds of violent crime—robbery and domestic violence.

The Robbery Victim

In a robbery, the criminal takes property by force or by threat of force. In this scary crime, victims can lose their property, suffer injuries, and even die. Statistically, the chances of being killed are small: Almost 99.8 percent of all robbery victims survive. About one-third of all victims suffer injuries, mostly minor. Only two percent receive wounds serious enough to stay overnight in a hospital. Strangely, victims are most likely to be hurt by unarmed robbers, probably because these robbers often attack their victims to establish control in the robbery. Victims are most likely to be killed, however, by robbers armed with guns. Victims who resist are more likely to be injured or killed than those who do not resist.

The most likely victim is a male between the ages of 12 and 24. As a person's age increases, the likelihood of being robbed declines. People over 65 make up the age group least likely to be robbed.

What is it like to be robbed? The following is excerpted from a robbery victim's statement.

Harry's Story

"My dad and I were walking to meet my brother at a cafe where we went to lunch a lot. As we walked up, we saw the owner down the street waving and jumping up and down. We waved back. Later, we found out he was trying to warn us not to go in. He had been in the bathroom when the robbery started and had climbed out a window and run down the street.

"When my dad opened the cafe's door, a guy grabbed him and pulled him in. I turned and started to walk away, but a guy came out, pointed a sawed-off shotgun at me, and ordered me into the cafe. I did what he said. Inside, he threw me on the ground and pressed the shotgun against my head. All the customers in the cafe—about 25 people—were lying on the ground. There were seven robbers, all with guns. They went around from person to person grabbing wallets and jewelry. One man didn't like how they had talked to

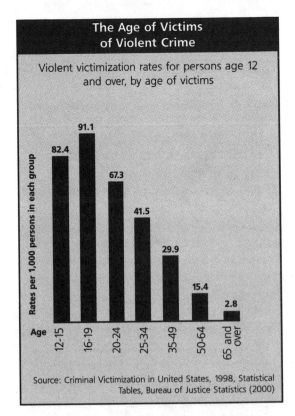

The Age of Victims of Violent Crime

Violent victimization rates for persons age 12 and over, by age of victims

Rates per 1,000 persons in each group

Age	Rate
12-15	82.4
16-19	91.1
20-24	67.3
25-34	41.5
35-49	29.9
50-64	15.4
65 and over	2.8

Source: Criminal Victimization in United States, 1998, Statistical Tables, Bureau of Justice Statistics (2000)

his wife. When he objected, a guy hit him with his gun. I lay there thinking, 'I hope the cops don't come until these guys get outside.' I was afraid of being taken hostage.

"They took my wallet, refused my old watch, and tried and failed to get my ring off. It stuck on my finger. They didn't want to spend any more time in the cafe, so they left. We had come in near the end of the robbery.

"The next day I had a large knot on my head. I don't understand why. The guy had just pressed his gun against my head. He didn't hit me. My dad had lost a ring he had owned his whole life. My brother to this day has never gone back to the cafe. The robbery shook up the owner so much that he sold the cafe to someone else."

The Domestic Violence Victim

Typically, when people use the phrase "domestic violence," they are referring to spousal abuse (also known as intimate partner violence), which can be committed by spouses, ex-spouses, boyfriends, and girlfriends. The term also has a broader definition that includes family violence, child abuse, elder

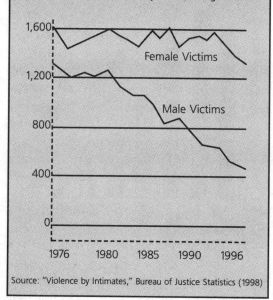

Murder by Intimates

For persons murdered by intimates, the number of male victims has fallen steadily since 1976. The number of female victims has dropped dramatically since 1993.

Note: Intimates include spouses, ex-spouses, common-law spouses, same-sex partners, boyfriends, and girlfriends.

Female Victims

Male Victims

1,600

1,200

800

400

0

1976   1980   1985   1990   1996

Source: "Violence by Intimates," Bureau of Justice Statistics (1998)

abuse, and abuse by residents of the same household.

Much violent crime takes place at home and is committed by family members or intimates. Half of all 911 calls are related to domestic violence. In most cases, however, nobody calls the police and the incident goes unreported. Of the nearly 1 million Americans suffering from intimate partner abuse each year, 85 percent of those victims are women. If victims decide to leave their abusive partners, they remain at risk of suffering serious or lethal violence. One study showed that 65 percent of all murdered female abuse victims were separated from their abusers at the time of death.

Domestic violence is a terrifying crime, violating a person's most basic zone of safety—the home. The following is an excerpt from a statement made by a survivor of domestic violence.

Denise's Story

"When I met Al, he was handsome, polite, and totally charming. I fell for him immediately. He was divorced and had a 4-year-old daughter, who lived with his ex-wife. I didn't know that he had broken his previous wife's jaw and she had a restraining order against him.

"We went out for a year and then we got married. We had a son the next year and a daughter the following year. Al was fine at first. But things gradually grew worse. When he'd get upset, he would tell me I was fat (I've always been thin) or that I was disgusting or stupid. Sometimes when he didn't like the food I'd serve him, he'd throw it out the window or feed it to the dog. At his daughter's 7th birthday party, I had ordered two pizzas. When Al saw them, he got mad. They weren't the right kind. In front of all the kids, he threw the pizzas on the ground and started swearing at me.

"This was just the beginning. I became afraid whenever he got upset. He would often strike out. He'd grab the kids and spank them. Sometimes he would twist my arm behind my back. Other times he hit me. But after hurting me or the kids, he always apologized—sometimes spending lots of money on trips for the family or special gifts. I began to believe his outbursts were my fault and tried harder to be a better wife and mother.

"In the time we were married, I had many broken fingers, a broken arm, and numerous stitches. I wore dark glasses and makeup to cover black eyes. It got so bad that I started missing work. Although I was trying to hide it, people knew what was going on. My boss told me, 'If you don't get help, you're going to lose your job.'

Ask an Expert

There are many rape and domestic-violence crisis centers around the country today. And many police departments have specially trained officers to deal with victims of rape and domestic violence. Invite a representative from one to visit your class. Have the guest speaker explain how rape or domestic-violence victims are treated and what special services are available in your community.

"I started seeing a counselor. This helped. One day, after eight years of marriage, I bundled up the kids, went to a shelter, and got a restraining order. We lived in the shelter for three months. After that, I got a new job in another city. I haven't seen Al in five years."

For Discussion

1. Why do you think many women do not report rapes or instances of domestic violence? Would you if you were a victim of these crimes? Why or why not?

2. What do you think would help victims of violent crimes recover from the crimes? Explain.

3. Victims of violent crimes sometimes report that witnesses do not call the police or try to help them. Why do you think people might not respond when they hear screams or see crimes?

Victims of Property Crimes

Property crimes, such as theft, burglary, and fraud, involve stealing property. They differ from violent crimes because the criminal *neither* uses force *nor* threatens to use force. If the criminal uses force, the crime is a violent crime—a crime against the person—not a property crime.

According to FBI statistics, losses from property crime add up to more than $15 billion a year. Every family in the country suffers—some from direct loss, some from high insurance rates, and some just from fear and insecurity. In the following sections, we will take a closer look at victims of two kinds of property crime—burglary and identity theft.

The Burglary Victim

Burglary is the unlawful entry into a building with the intent to commit a crime, normally theft. More than $3 billion in losses are reported each year. Crime surveys reveal that victims report about half of all household burglaries to the police. Although not a violent crime, burglaries often greatly upset the victims, because the criminal has intruded into the privacy of the home. The following story is excerpted from a statement given by a burglary victim.

Helen's Story

"I was coming home from work on a Monday. My front door was unlocked. I walked in, and the first thing I noticed was the television and VCR were missing. I thought, 'How dare she (my younger sister) take them out of this apartment without asking me!' Then I noticed clothes scattered in the hallway and thought, 'She must be doing the laundry, but why does she have to dump it in the hallway?' It wasn't until I walked into the bedroom that it dawned on me that we had been burglarized. The stuff in our nightstands was scattered on the bedroom floor. I ran into the living room to look for my camera equipment. It was gone. I ran around the apartment—anything and everything of value they took. I was in shock and felt so helpless. When I called the police, I had to repeat everything twice because I was crying and talking at the same time.

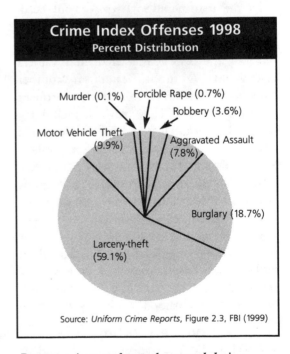

Crime Index Offenses 1998
Percent Distribution

Murder (0.1%) Forcible Rape (0.7%)
Robbery (3.6%)
Motor Vehicle Theft (9.9%)
Aggravated Assault (7.8%)
Burglary (18.7%)
Larceny-theft (59.1%)

Source: *Uniform Crime Reports*, Figure 2.3, FBI (1999)

Property crimes make up the overwhelming majority of crimes committed.

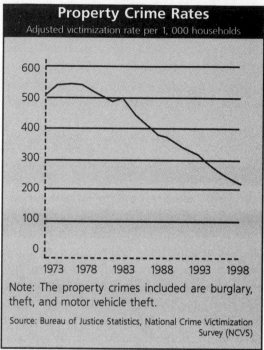

Property Crime Rates
Adjusted victimization rate per 1, 000 households

Note: The property crimes included are burglary, theft, and motor vehicle theft.

Source: Bureau of Justice Statistics, National Crime Victimization Survey (NCVS)

Compared to other countries, the United States has a high rate of violent crime. Its rate of property crime, however, has fallen steadily since 1978 and is comparatively low.

"The burglars had picked the lock to enter the apartment. So I replaced my dead-bolt lock with a new one, which, according to the police, was 'practically unpickable.' I replaced the TV, VCR, stereo, and camera equipment. A month later on another Monday, I came home to find my apartment burglarized again. They had not picked my unpickable lock. They had broken down the door with a crowbar. They took everything I had replaced and looked through places they missed the first time. The police took finger-prints both times and came up with a suspect. But they haven't caught him yet.

"After the second burglary, I no longer felt safe. The thought of being invaded a third time was too much. So within a month, my sister and I moved to a new apartment in a different neighborhood."

The Identity Theft Victim

Identity theft is a new type of fraud. A criminal steals a person's credit card or Social Security number, assumes the victim's identi-ty, and quickly spends as much money as pos-sible. The criminal may pay for goods, get loans, apply for new credit cards, rent houses, get a job, and even declare bankruptcy—all in the victim's name. This crime was rare just a few years ago. Now, hundreds of thousands fall victim to it each year.

Unlike most fraud, the victim never meets the criminal. The victim doesn't dis-cover anything is wrong until it is too late. A credit card company may call asking about unusual activity on the account. Or the vic-tim may be denied credit because of all the bills the criminal has accumulated.

The victim is not responsible for most of these debts. But payment will be demanded. The victim must spend countless hours con-tacting and convincing merchants that the person who ran up the bills was not the vic-tim. Identity theft leaves victims' credit in shambles. It may take years for them to restore it. This is one victim's story:

Maureen's Story

"On a Sunday afternoon we received a phone call questioning an unusual pattern of activity on our credit card. Neither my hus-band nor I had authorized or made the charges to the account. I was told our credit card would be canceled. Two months later we received a phone call from J.C. Penney's cred-it department advising us that an account had been opened using my husband's name and Social Security number. We were advised by J.C. Penney's to immediately contact the three major credit reporting bureaus [Trans Union, Experian, and Equifax] to place fraud alerts on our credit reports.

"In speaking to the three credit bureaus, I discovered there had been 25 inquiries into our credit report in the previous 60 days. I requested that each credit reporting agency send me a copy of our credit reports, and I spent the next three days frantically making phone calls to the merchants who had made inquiries. I also contacted the Federal Trade Commission's Identity Theft Hotline, which assigned a reference number to our case."

[Subsequently, Maureen learned that

several different suspects were fraudulently using their personal information and had gotten a cell phone account, three bank loans totaling $45,000, and two new cars.]

"Our efforts to restore our good names and good credit have been extensive. I have made hundreds of phone calls. I've sent dozens of notarized letters to the merchants. We have submitted numerous affidavits, notarized statements, and notarized handwriting samples. We have filled out over 20 different sets of forms and statements in order to comply with the merchants requests for further information. It's like filling out your income tax return 20 different times, using 20 different forms, and following 20 different sets of instructions.

"I have logged over 400 hours of time trying to clear our names and restore our good credit. The impact of being a victim of Identity Theft is all encompassing. It affects you physically, emotionally, psychologically, spiritually and financially. We now have adverse ratings on our credit reports. We are also receiving phone calls from collection specialists wanting to know why we are overdue on the payments for our two new cars. I try to nicely explain to these collection specialists that we are victims of Identity Theft and we did not purchase these vehicles. Once you become a victim of Identity Theft your life is forever changed. We do not know how many more accounts may still be outstanding, we do not know if a collection specialist is calling when our phone rings, we do not know if our good names and financial reputations will ever be truly restored."

For Discussion

1. Many victims speak of not being the same person after being victimized. Why do you think this is so? What has changed for them?

2. Many victims of burglary describe the crime as an invasion of their privacy. What do you think they mean by this?

3. Have you ever had anything stolen? If so, how did it affect you? Do you worry that it may happen again?

4. States make receiving stolen property a crime. Do you think it should be? Why or why not?

5. What sorts of crimes do you think people are most likely to report to the police? Least likely? Why do you think some people don't report crimes to the police?

Helping Victims of Crime

Some ancient legal codes called for compensating crime victims. The Code of Hammurabi (c. 1750 B.C.), for example, forced the criminal to pay as much as five times the value of the damage caused. If the criminal couldn't be caught, the state would compensate the victim.

Early English and American law forced criminals to make direct payments, called restitution, to victims. Gradually, however, criminal law shifted away from helping victims and focused exclusively on punishing lawbreakers. The only way for a victim to get restitution was to sue under civil law. Unfortunately, this was usually impossible. Either the criminal had escaped or the criminal was poor and couldn't pay the victim.

It was only in the 1960s that we again began looking for ways society could help crime victims directly. In an influential 1964 *New York University Law Review* article, former Supreme Court Justice Arthur J. Goldberg wrote that:

> Government compensation of victims of crime . . . is long overdue here. The victim of a robbery or an assault has been denied the "protection" of the laws in a very real sense, and society should assume some responsibility for making him whole.

In 1963, New Zealand passed the first victim-compensation legislation. This pioneering act set up a board to pay cash awards to crime victims. The idea spread quickly to England in 1964 and then to California in 1965. Today, every state has a victim-compensation program.

One State's Model

- During a street mugging, a man is assaulted and hit several times in the face. The mugger takes the man's wallet with $35 in it and flees. Bruised, scared, and with broken glasses, the man is taken to a nearby emergency room for treatment. The New York State Crime Victims Board would pay for the replacement of the eyeglasses, the lost cash, and the emergency room bill if the man did not have insurance.

- A young woman, age 16, sitting in the park becomes the victim of a random shooting. Rushed to the hospital, she dies after several days. The New York State Crime Victims Board would pay for any unreimbursed medical expenses, funeral costs up to $6,000, and counseling for her parents and brothers and sisters.

The state of New York offers monetary aid to families who have suffered financially from violent crime. This plan is run by the Crime Victims Board, a five-member panel.

Crime victims, their dependents, or immediate family members can apply for compensation. The board will pay for medical expenses, mental health counseling, job retraining, funeral or burial expenses, lost earnings, and loss of support. It will also compensate for losses of cash or essential personal property if the victim has suffered a personal injury. The limits on the amounts of the awards are as follows:

Medical expenses ....unlimited
Counseling...unlimited
Vocational rehabilitation ....unlimited
Funeral or burial $6,000
Lost earnings $30,000 ($600/week)
Loss of support $30,000 ($600/week)
Crime-scene cleanup $2,500
Loss of cash or essential
personal property ....$500 ($100 for cash)
Attorney fees $1,000
Emergency $1,500

The New York plan only compensates for losses caused by crimes of violence, such as assault, rape, murder, and hit-and-run. The board will not pay for losses that have already been covered by insurance.

The New York plan also requires the victim to cooperate with the police and prosecution. And the board checks to make sure that the victim did not contribute to the incident in some significant way. This is particularly important in cases involving drugs or substance abuse.

These are the main standards that the New York Crime Victims Board checks before making an award:

(1) a violent crime occurred, resulting in an injury;

(2) the victim cooperated with authorities; and

(3) the victim did not contribute to the crime.

The main problem with the New York plan and other victim compensation programs is money. Many state compensation boards are behind in the settlement of claims because of lack of funds and inadequate staffing. In fact, many programs would be overwhelmed if every eligible person applied for benefits. With increased public awareness of the programs, more funds will be needed in order for them to meet their goals.

Other Victim Programs

Cash payments aren't the only way victims can be assisted. Government agencies and private organizations offer many other services: shelters for battered women, rape counseling, crisis intervention programs, child-abuse intervention, and medical counseling.

In many cities, the prosecutor's office or a private help organization has a unit to aid victims when they first come into contact with the criminal justice system. This service is aimed at comforting victims, notifying them of court dates, and even helping them find transportation to court.

Many communities have programs that offer crime victims free or low-cost legal advice, psychological counseling, or employment assistance. And some agencies offer help in replacing items stolen or destroyed in crimes. It can be a great comfort to a crime victim to have someone's help in as simple a task as replacing a stolen ID or a broken door lock.

The primary goal of most victim assistance programs is to help the victim get through the crisis with dignity and get back to as normal a life as possible.

Class Activity: Crime Victims Board

Imagine that you are a member of a Crime Victims Board similar to the New York model. It is your responsibility to review applications for crime victim compensation and decide which, if any, should be approved.

1. Form small groups of four students each.

2. Each group should:

    a. Review the standards used for making awards in New York on page 14.

    b. Read each of the cases below and decide, based on the standards, whether compensation should be awarded.

    c. For each case, write down the following:

       (1) the case number

       (2) whether you approve or deny an award of compensation

       (3) reasons for your decision

       (4) the total amount of the award

       (5) the amount of award money allocated to medical expenses, vocational rehabilitation, funeral or burial, lost earnings, loss of support, and loss of cash or essential personal property

    d. Be prepared to discuss and support your recommendations.

Case No. 1

William Hall was at the Shady Oak Bar playing a game of pool with the suspect, Ken Ross. William had a $50 bet on the game. He lost the pool game, and the two men began arguing over the bet. According to witnesses interviewed by the police, William threw a punch at Ken and missed. Ken picked up the pool cue and struck William in the mouth, causing him to lose several teeth.

William claims that he did not try to strike Ken and that they had no argument.

The District Attorney's office refused to prosecute Ken because of insufficient evidence.

William is claiming $1,500 in medical damages and $600 in lost wages.

Case No. 2

Robert Samuelson, owner of the Valley Drug Store, was shot during a robbery of the store. He died as a result of gunshot wounds to his chest. His widow, Ruth, is claiming a wage loss of $50,000 per year for five years due to her husband's death. Funeral expenses totaled $7,000.

Ruth will receive her husband's estate, which is valued at $100,000. In addition, she receives Social Security benefits of $600 per month.

Case No. 3

Rocky Pineda was playing with his two children at Allstone Park when he was approached by two young men. One of them had a gun and demanded money. Rocky attempted to explain that he could not speak much English. He tried to take his children and run when one of the young men shot him in the back. He died a few moments later from the gunshot wound. The suspects were never found.

The funeral expenses were $7,000, to be paid by Maria Pineda, his widow. She is eight months pregnant and has no health insurance to cover her medical expenses. She is claiming a $30,000 wage loss due to her husband's death.

Case No. 4

Susan Jones was sitting in the Whaling Ship Bar with two of her girlfriends. They were listening to music and having a drink. Three men sat down at their table and began to talk. After a while, they all started dancing and continued drinking.

One of the men, Mike, offered Susan a ride home. She accepted. When they arrived at her apartment, she invited him in for coffee. He followed her into the kitchen, grabbed a knife, and then forcibly raped her and cut her several times with the knife.

Her medical insurance covered her hospital bills. She stayed away from work for three weeks because of the psychological trauma. She is claiming $3,000 for seeing a psychiatrist and $1,800 in lost wages.

Debriefing Questions

1. Which claims did groups deny? Why?

2. Are the standards for awarding compensation fair? Why or why not? How would you change the standards?

3. If you could write your state's law regarding compensating victims, what would your laws provide?

4. Although most states do not, a few require serious financial hardship for compensation awards. Do you think the requirement makes sense? Why or why not?

5. What is the difference between state victim compensation and restitution for victims? Which do you think is better? Why?

6. What are the benefits of victim compensation laws? What are their drawbacks? Do you think states should have such laws? Why or why not?

The Push for Victims' Rights

Since the 1960s, concern has grown about how the criminal justice system treats crime victims. Citizens have banded together to form groups to represent crime victims and their families.

These groups have often complained that crime victims are injured twice—first by the criminal and then by an insensitive criminal justice system. They claim that too often victims have been ignored or even subtly blamed for the crime. Many victims have found themselves caught up in police investigations and judicial proceedings that they don't really understand. They have been moved from hear-

ing to hearing at the convenience of attorneys or judges or the police. In the early 1980s, the President's Task Force on Crime said, "Somewhere along the way, the system began to serve lawyers and judges and defendants, treating the victim with institutionalized disinterest."

Advocates of crime victims have pressed for reforms in the criminal justice system. They have been joined by many groups, including women's groups interested in helping victims of rape and domestic violence. They have met with remarkable success.

New Federal Programs

The federal government has passed several acts designed to address the needs of crime victims. In 1982, Congress enacted the Victim and Witness Protection Act. In addition to protecting crime victims and witnesses, the act was meant to serve as a model for legislation for state and local governments and to ensure that the federal government helps victims and witnesses without infringing on anyone's constitutional rights. The following are some specific features of the act:

- The crime's impact on the victim should be considered in deciding penalties.

- Anyone threatening or harming a witness should be punished severely.

- Court orders should be used to restrain anyone from harassing a witness.

- A victim is entitled to restitution from the criminal.

In 1984, Congress passed the Victims of Crime Act of 1984. This act set up a Crime Victims Fund, which provides grants to local victim compensation programs. Today it supplies almost 40 percent of the funds in these programs. The money comes from fines and forfeitures paid by federal criminals. Government payments to individual crime victims now range from $100 to $50,000 or more. The majority of the grant money goes to victims of rape and family violence.

In 1990, Congress enacted the Victims' Rights and Restitution Act. It set into law basic rights for victims of federal crimes. The Victims Rights Clarification Act of 1997 made clear that victims could attend trials and testify at sentencing hearings.

Responses from States

Many states have passed what are called **victims' bills of rights** into law. These laws focus on procedures within the criminal justice system. They attempt to make the victim an important part of the process. Michigan, for example, passed a constitutional amendment in 1988. It gave crime victims such rights as:

- to keep the accused's trial from being unnecessarily delayed.

- to be protected from retaliation.

- to be notified of court proceedings.

- to attend all court proceedings that the accused has the right to attend.

- to confer with the prosecution.

- to make a statement to the court at sentencing.

- to get restitution.

- to receive information about the sentence and release of the accused.

By the year 2000, 33 states had adopted victims' rights amendments to their state constitutions.

Although almost everyone favors helping crime victims, some amendments have drawn fire when they intrude on the rights of criminal defendants. For example, crime victims no longer have to testify at preliminary hearings in California. This was approved by voters in 1990 as part of Proposition 115, California's Crime Victims Justice Reform Act. Investigating police officers may read what the victims said in the police report. This means defendants no longer have the opportunity to cross-examine their accusers at preliminary hearings. (These hearings determine whether the prosecution has enough evidence to hold the defendant for trial.) Some critics argue that denying criminal suspects the right to see and contradict their accusers may well result in unjust prosecutions. They point out that more than 90 percent of all criminal cases end in plea bargains and never go to trial. The preliminary hearing is the only formal presentation of evidence in most cases. They say that the idea of using unchallenged accusers goes against the grain of the entire Anglo-American judicial system. Supporters of the law point out that the police report is only read at the preliminary hearing—not at trial where defendants can still cross-examine their accusers. They believe that it's important to spare the victim from making any unnecessary court appearances. This law was upheld on appeal in California courts (*Whitman v. Superior Court*, 1991).

Another controversy involves victim-impact statements made at sentencing hearings. After a defendant is convicted, courts often conduct sentencing hearings. These are required in death-penalty cases when the court must weigh mitigating and aggravating factors in the crime. Victim-impact statements allow victims (and their families) to tell the court how they suffered from the crime. Critics have argued that courts should not consider these statements. They say that the victim is not on trial and that the victim's character should not be either an aggravating or mitigating factor. The U.S. Supreme Court has grappled with this issue. In 1987 in *Booth v. Maryland*, the court ruled that victim-impact statements in death-penalty cases violated the Eighth Amendment's ban on cruel and unusual punishments. The court said the statements inflamed juries and led to erratic results. But

four years later in *Payne v. Tennessee*, the court reversed itself. The court stated that sentencing hearings had always examined the harm done by defendants. "Victim-impact evidence," said the court, "is simply another method" for the court to get this information.

Proposed Constitutional Amendment

In recent years, support has grown for an amendment on victims' rights in the U.S. Constitution. This would require passage by two-thirds of both houses of Congress and ratification by three-fourths of the state legislatures. The amendment, if passed, would give victims of violent crimes these rights:

- To be given notice of and to attend any public hearing.

- To be heard at the hearings and to submit statements at any hearing determining release from custody, a negotiated plea, a sentence, or parole.

- To notice of any release or escape from custody.

- To not have unreasonable delays in the trial.

- To restitution from the convicted offender.

- To consideration for the safety of the victim in determining any release from custody.

Supporters of the amendment believe it will finally enshrine in the Constitution basic rights for victims of crime. These will be rights that no state may deny. They view the amendment as restoring the balance between the rights of criminal defendants and victims.

Critics of the amendment think it provides nothing that most states don't already guarantee by law. Most troubling to the critics is the amendment's vagueness. Courts, they say, will have to interpret exactly what each of these rights means. Critics worry that the amendment may erode some basic rights of criminal defendants.

For Discussion

1. Do you agree with California's policy of permitting police officers at preliminary hearings to read what the victims said in the police reports instead of having the victim testify? Explain.

2. Some victims' rights groups propose that statements made by victims during post-crime counseling sessions should not be used in court or made available to the defense. Do you agree with this policy? Why or why not?

Ask an Expert

Does your state have a victims' bill of rights? A victims' compensation board? What does your state do for crime victims? Invite a prosecutor to your classroom to discuss these questions.

3. The Supreme Court has ruled that victim-impact statements may be used at death-penalty hearings. Can you see any dangers in doing this? Would you support stronger penalties for killing a nun as opposed to killing a prostitute? Why or why not?

4. Make a list of the problems that crime victims face. How can society address these problems?

5. What is the proposed victims' rights amendment to the U.S. Constitution? What are some arguments in favor of it? What are some arguments opposing it?

Class Activity: Victims' Rights Amendment

In this activity, students role play state legislatures deciding on a proposed amendment to the U.S. Constitution.

1. Ask students to imagine that Congress has passed the victims' rights amendment to the U.S. Constitution described in the article. Three-fourths of the state legislatures must now ratify this amendment.

2. Divide the class into pairs. Each pair will represent a state legislature considering the victims' rights amendment. Each pair should:

   a. Discuss the amendment's pros and cons.

   b. Decide how its state will vote (if the pair cannot agree, the vote is "no").

   c. Prepare to present its position to other "state legislatures."

3. Regroup the class and ask for different pairs to present pro and con arguments on the amendment.

4. Vote and conduct a discussion using the Debriefing Questions, below.

Debriefing Questions

1. What do you think were the strongest arguments in favor of the amendment? The strongest arguments against it?

2. Do you think the amendment, as proposed, is a good idea? Explain.

History of Violent Crime in America: A Look Back . . .

When I was young, I could play in the park at night. Now it's all drug dealers. You could leave all your doors unlocked. Now you can't walk down your own street without getting robbed.

For 30 years beginning in the 1960s, crime rates rose in America. Many Americans may view the dropping crime rates of the 1990s as the start of a return to a normal low rate of crime. Many older people look back on their past as a time when streets were safe and crime happened somewhere far away. Indeed, statistical evidence shows that the decades from the 1930s through the 1950s were less crime-ridden than today. Yet those decades may be exceptions in American history. If you take a careful look back into our history, you will find that violent crime has played a large role in American life.

During the 1700s, robbery and other violent crimes were already troubling the English colonies of America. Land was growing scarce. The English were fighting a series of wars and demanding high taxes from colonists to pay for them. In turn, the colonies suffered high rates of unemployment and poverty. Crime flourished in this environment.

Adding to the crime problem, criminals from England's jails, both men and women, were deported to America as indentured servants. Before the American Revolution, more than 50,000 of these lawbreakers had arrived. Some ran away immediately and joined the growing criminal population.

Philadelphia, one of America's first important cities, was known as the "crime capital of the colonies" during the early 1700s. Robbery, rape, murder, and arson occurred with frightening regularity.

By the mid-1700s, New York City was challenging Philadelphia for the dubious title of "crime capital." Its population was exploding. New immigrants were arriving by the boatload. Along with the increasing population, came a rise in violent crime. A New York newspaper editorial complained, "It seems to have now become dangerous for the good People of this City to be out late at night without being sufficiently strong or well armed."

In the countryside and on the frontier, gangs of thieves and robbers preyed on farmers. Gangs in the North Carolina backwoods provoked citizens to take the law into their own hands. In 1767, citizens formed the first American vigilante group, which attacked and punished gang members.

Crime in the 1800s

During the 1800s, many American cities grew rapidly. Workshops and new industries attracted immigrants from England and Northern Europe. By 1800, New York had passed Philadelphia and Boston to become the biggest city in the country, with 60,000 people. Further waves of immigrants came to escape famines and wars in Europe. With the rise of heavy industry and mining in New England and the industrial Midwest, many companies actively recruited in Europe for laborers.

Many of the new immigrants had to squeeze into crowded tenements in urban areas. Cities like New York gained a reputation for overcrowding and criminal violence. In the decade before the Civil War, more than 3,000 homeless children roamed the streets of New York. Many of them became pickpockets and street robbers. One civic leader wrote in 1842: "Thronged as our city is, men are robbed in the streets . . . . The defenseless and the beautiful are ravished in the daytime and no trace of the criminals is found."

Before the Civil War, few cities in America had anything like a police department to keep order. Boston had a night watch, but it was mainly a fire lookout. Watchmen were afraid to enter many neighborhoods at all. In some places, vigilantes were the only organized resistance to criminals.

More murders took place in New York than London, a far bigger city. One English traveler wrote, "Probably in no city in the civilized world is life so fearfully insecure." The same fear plagued other cities. In Philadelphia

The Whyos	

The Whyos, an urban youth gang of the mid-19th century, even advertised its services. A handbill found on a gang member set the following rates:

Punching	$2
Both eyes blacked	$ 4
Nose and jaw broke	$10
Jacked out (blacked jacked)	$15
Ear chewed off	$15
Leg or arm broke	$19
Shot in leg	$25
Stab	$25
Doing the big job (murder)	$100

during the mid-1800s, bands of robbers began to prey on wealthy citizens, stripping them of their cash.

Out West, men often wore guns wherever they went. Horse and cattle theft became a major problem. Los Angeles was only a sleepy village of about 8,000, but in one 15-month period in the 1850s, 40 murders occurred. In much larger San Francisco to the north, there were entire neighborhoods where no one dared go after dark.

Ethnic Urban Gangs

In many cities, jobless immigrants formed violent gangs in ethnic slum neighborhoods. In Philadelphia, lower-class Irish and black groups formed gangs. With names like the Bleeders, Garroters, Rangers, Tormentors, and Killers, the gangs sometimes fought bloody battles on a spot known as the Battle Ground. Gang members as young as 10 carried clubs, knives, brass knuckles, and pistols. They attacked lone pedestrians, younger children, or members of other ethnic groups.

In New York, well-organized adult street gangs controlled the immigrant areas of Five Points and the Bowery. Made up mostly of young Irish immigrants, gangs called the Dead Rabbits, Plug Uglies, and Shirt Tails grew famous for mugging people. In the nearby Fourth Ward, the Daybreak Boys murdered 20 people between 1850 and 1852. Political parties recruited squads of toughs from these gangs to intimidate voters.

Probably the most violent New York street gang at this time was called the "Whyos." The Whyos came from Mulberry Bend, another slum neighborhood. They robbed people and burglarized homes and stores throughout the city. At one time, the Whyos had more than 500 members, all of whom supposedly had killed at least one person. Dandy Johnny Dolan, the gang's leader, invented a copper device for gouging an eye out and kept an eye as a trophy.

In cities of the Northeast, urban rioting broke out often from the 1830s through the 1850s. The pressures on the urban slums boiled over. There were ethnic riots, labor riots, election-day riots, anti-black riots, and anti-Catholic riots. In that period, Baltimore alone had 12 major riots, Philadelphia had 11, and New York had eight. This burst of lawlessness spurred the development of police forces in most cities.

Post Civil War Violence

The Civil War killed more than 600,000 people, more than any other war in our history. It also left behind enduring habits of hatred and violent revenge. The most vicious and widespread postwar violence targeted blacks. During the period of Reconstruction, freed slaves served in state legislatures in the South. Former slaves educated themselves, voted, and many started businesses or began farming their own small fields. In response to these developments, some Southern whites created the Ku Klux Klan and other groups to terrorize blacks and help end the social changes of Reconstruction. In a reign of terror in Louisiana in the 1870s, a group called the White League killed more than 3,500 blacks, many by **lynching**—a form of mob violence that punishes an accused person without a legal trial. Most lynchings are hangings.

The Klan executed lynchings against poor blacks and their supporters for decades. In incidents all over the country, almost 2,000 African Americans were lynched from 1882 to 1903.

Outlaws in the Countryside

After the Civil War, violence in the West took a new turn. The Reno brothers of Indiana invented train robbery, and dozens of small gangs followed their example. The most famous robbers were the James brothers—Jesse and Frank. They had been Confederate guerrillas and after the war they turned to robbing trains and banks, terrorizing Union states from Missouri to Minnesota. They killed 16 people.

In the 1870s, Billy the Kid, who was born in a New York slum tenement, roamed the West, gambling, killing, and hiring out as a cattle rustler. Sheriff Pat Garret finally tracked him down and shot him. According to legend, Billy the Kid had killed 21 men, one for each year of his life. The actual number was probably smaller.

John Wesley Hardin from Texas killed his first victim at age 15. The victim was a black teen who had beaten him at wrestling. He went on to kill more than a dozen men, including one because he had badmouthed Texas. Hardin was shot and killed in 1895 and became another outlaw legend, though today we would probably think of him as a psychotic serial murderer.

Even more violent were the range wars. Throughout the Western states, cattle and land barons hired armies of gunmen to guard or expand their private empires. In some cases, the cattlemen had the law squarely on their side. But often their gunmen settled scores and fought battles. Texas had the Sutton-Taylor feud, the Horrell-Higgins feud, the Jaybird-Woodpecker feud, and several others. Montana had the Johnson County War, which pitted European immigrant homesteaders against a cattle baron. Arizona had the worst range war of all. In the Pleasant Valley War, the cattle-raising Grahams fought the sheep-raising Tewkesburys with hired armies. The conflict raged for six years and was fought literally "to the last man."

Racial Violence

The end of the century marked the beginning of a long era of race riots. As early as 1871, a white mob in Los Angeles went on a rampage and hanged 20 Chinese workers from street lamps. Near the turn of the century, mobs in Eastern cities began descending on black neighborhoods to lynch any black man unlucky enough to be caught. Major race riots against blacks erupted in Atlanta in 1906, Springfield, Illinois, in 1908, and in many other cities.

Prohibition and Organized Crime

The 20th century saw the rise of organized crime. In 1920, the 18th Amendment to the Constitution made the manufacture, transport, or sale of alcoholic beverages illegal. The era of Prohibition, one of this country's most violent crime periods, extended from 1920 until the 18th Amendment was repealed in 1933. Prohibition created the conditions for thriving illegal businesses.

In Chicago, gangsters set up illegal beer-brewing and distribution businesses, plus a network of bribed police and politicians to protect them. The business proved so lucrative that rival gangs fought for control. Between 1923 and 1926, the Chicago beer wars killed more than 200 people. By 1927, the mobster Al Capone had come out on top. His beer business took in over $60 million a year, which would be well over $1 billion in today's dollars.

During the early 1930s, various crime organizations sought to form alliances to control gambling, prostitution, narcotics, and other illegal money-making activities. Gangster rivalry and greed, however, led to many underworld murders.

Depression and World War II

As the Great Depression began in the early 1930s, violent crimes reached a peak. In 1933, the murder rate was 9.7 murders for every 100,000 Americans. The murder rate would not be this high again until the late 1970s.

A curious thing happened as the Depression worsened and unemployment skyrocketed: The crime rate went down. Despite widespread news coverage of Depression-era bank robbers like John Dillinger, "Pretty Boy" Floyd, and Bonnie and Clyde, violent crime actually declined. The murder rate, for example, dropped 50 percent between 1933 and the early 1940s. Other serious crimes fell by a third.

Why did crime decrease during a time of great hardship for almost all Americans? According to some historians, the Depression brought Americans closer together, because almost everyone was in the same boat. In addition, the birthrate had dropped in the 1920s, which meant that the youth population—15 to 24 year olds—declined in size. Younger people commit the most crimes, especially violent crimes. World War II unified Americans even more.

The Postwar Years

Following World War II, many people started families. The "baby boom," which lasted from 1946-1964, produced a huge increase in the birth rate.

The 1950s stayed relatively calm, but the turbulent 1960s saw an increase in many kinds of violence. A dozen civil-rights activists were murdered in the South, and many tens of thousands of anti-war activists took to the streets in demonstrations that sometimes turned violent. In the mid-1960s, major urban riots exploded in African-American communities in Los Angeles, Newark, Detroit, and other cities where urban problems had been festering.

Street crime also began to increase. The children of the baby boom were growing up. The 15-24 age group grew rapidly. Many crime experts believe that this surge of young people in the population contributed significantly to the increase of crime in the 1960s and 1970s.

In the early 1980s, the sudden appearance of crack cocaine caused a tremendous rise in drug addiction and associated crimes. Drug-dealing gangs plagued many Latino and African-American communities. With unemployment and homelessness rising, reports of street crime skyrocketed. Crime so concerned ordinary citizens that it spawned whole communities barricaded with walls, barred windows, and burglar alarms.

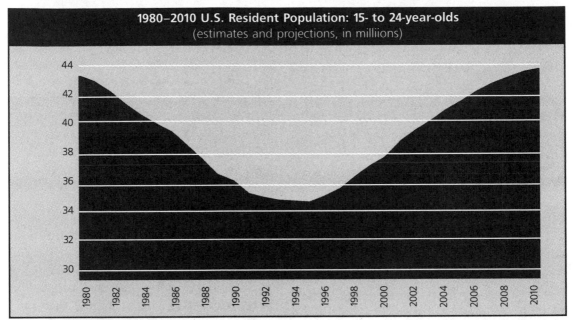

1980–2010 U.S. Resident Population: 15- to 24-year-olds
(estimates and projections, in milliions)

Many criminologists believe that the number of young people in the population influences the crime rate. When the number of 15-24 year olds rises, crime is likely to increase. When the number falls, crime is likely to decrease.

Then in the early 1990s, crime started plummeting. By the end of the decade, the crime rate had dropped to its lowest point in 30 years. This went against expectations, because the number of 15-24 year olds in the population was growing. People have advanced various reasons for the decline: More police on the streets, more criminals behind bars, and better policing. These factors may account for some reduction in crime, but crime fell in parts of the country that didn't have more police, more prisoners, or better policing. Some people believe the booming economy caused the drop, but others point out that the economy and the crime rate both soared in the 1960s. Some experts believe that the dwindling use of crack cocaine produced the drop.

Since the number of 15–24 year olds in the population will continue to grow, some Americans think crime is bound to shoot up. They note that in the first half of the year 2000, the number of murders in New York and Los Angeles increased. They think these murders may be the beginning of an upward trend. Others predict the new century will bring even greater declines in violent crime. No one knows for sure. But one fact remains: Violent crime has almost always existed at a high level throughout American history.

For Discussion

1. Why do you think that violent crime has existed at such a high level throughout American history?

2. Why do you think American outlaws like Jesse James and Billy the Kid have so often been portrayed as heroes? Is there anyone like them today who is portrayed as a hero?

3. How do you account for so much mob violence directed against African Americans throughout our history?

4. Why did the crime rate go down in the 1930s? Why did it go up again in the 1960s? Why do you think it fell in the 1990s? What direction do you think it is heading today? Why?

5. List on the board as many causes of crime in American history as possible. Discuss the list and select the five most important. Explain your reasons.

6. Are there countries that you think have a more violent history, or a less violent history? Why do you think this is true?

Class Activity: Now and Then

The problem of crime in America varies from place to place and from generation to generation. In this activity, students interview a parent or older person and compare this person's experience with crime growing up to their own.

1. All students should:

   a. Read and answer for themselves the Interview Questions, below, on a sheet of paper.

   b. Find a parent or older person to interview. Ask and record their answers to the same questions on another sheet of paper.

   c. Write a two or three paragraph essay comparing their responses to those of the person they interviewed.

   d. Staple all the pages together to be turned in.

2. Before students turn in their papers, ask them to share their findings.

Interview Questions

1. When were you born?

2. As a young person, where (did, do) you live?

3. (Did, do) you feel safe in your neighborhood? Describe crimes, if any, that took place in your neighborhood.

4. (Did, do) you feel safe at school? Describe crimes or major incidents of misbehavior that took place in your school.

5. What crime story from the media most impressed you when you were growing up?

6. Do you think it was safer then or now? Why?

How Much Crime Is There?

How do we know how many murders, rapes, robberies, burglaries, and other crimes there are each year? Where do crime statistics come from? There are two main sources: (1) the Uniform Crime Reports (UCR) and (2) the National Crime Victimization Survey (NCVS).

Since 1930, police departments from across the country have sent crime data to the Federal Bureau of Investigation for inclusion in its Uniform Crime Reports. The UCR lists eight so-called index crimes—four violent crimes and four property crimes. They are homicide, forcible rape, robbery, aggravated assault, burglary, larceny-theft, motor vehicle theft, and arson. Almost every police department in the United States reports its crimes for inclusion in the UCR.

The UCR has at least two built-in weaknesses. First, it does not attempt to account for all crime—only for crime reported to the police. If someone does not report a crime, it cannot possibly get included in the UCR. Second, it relies on police departments to relay the information accurately. This may not always happen.

To get a fuller picture of crime, the Department of Justice started an annual National Crime Victimization Survey in 1973. (Until 1991, it was called the National Crime Survey.) The survey polls 49,000 households, representing about 100,000 persons over age 12. Following a detailed questionnaire, poll takers ask individuals if they have been victims of rape, robbery, assault, larceny, burglary, or car theft. Unlike the UCR, the NCVS reflects both reported and unreported crimes.

But the NCVS has problems also. First of all, it doesn't track some crimes. It cannot count homicides because murder victims cannot be interviewed. It doesn't include crimes against businesses, such as robberies and burglaries, because it only interviews households. It only interviews people over age 12, so it doesn't count crimes against young children. Of the crimes it does count, the interview could be flawed.

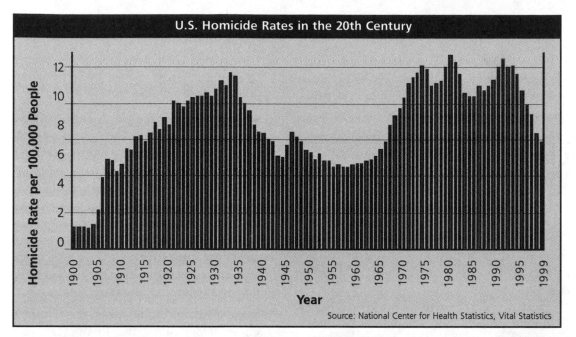

U.S. Homicide Rates in the 20th Century

Homicide Rate per 100,000 People (vertical axis) vs. Year (horizontal axis, 1900–1999)

Source: National Center for Health Statistics, Vital Statistics

The Trend of Crime

Since the UCR and NCVS measure different data, they come up with different numbers for most crimes. As would be expected, the NCVS consistently reports far higher numbers than UCR, except for auto theft. NCVS reports only slightly higher numbers of auto thefts than the UCR.

What do the UCR and NCVS say about the trend of crime? Is it increasing, decreasing, or staying the same? Is it worse than in previous years or better? If 10 years ago, fewer robberies took place than today, would it mean that crime got worse during this period? Not necessarily. The population today is greater than it was 10 years ago. To make comparisons between two different time periods, you need to know the **crime rates**—the amount of crime per person. The NCVS usually calculates these rates as the number of crimes for every 1,000 persons age 12 or older. The UCR calculates them for every 100,000 persons.

According to the NCVS during the period 1973 to 1990, the robbery rate peaked in 1981, dropped rapidly until 1985, rose steadily until 1992, and then dropped dramatically. In 1973, the rate was 6.7 for every 1,000 persons age 12 or older. By 1998, it had fallen to 4.0. In fact, the NCVS shows that the rate of all violent crime followed a similar pattern. In 1973, the rate of violent crime was 47.7 per 1,000. It reached a peak of 52.3 per 1,000 in 1981, declined to 42.0 in 1986, rose steadily to 51.2 in 1994, and then plummeted to 36.0 in 1998.

The UCR paints a slightly different picture. It shows crime rising almost steadily from 1973 to 1992. From that point, the crime rate starts declining.

Most experts tend to trust crime trends from the NCVS over the UCR. But experts also believe the UCR statistics for homicide are highly accurate. The NCVS does not cover homicide. The UCR homicide statistics follow almost the same pattern as the NCVS statistics for other violent crimes. They rise to a peak of 10.2 homicides per 100,000 in 1980, drop to 7.9 in 1985, rise to 9.5 in 1993, and then fall off to 6.3 in 1998. Other homicide studies back up these figures.

For Discussion

1. What are the differences between the Uniform Crime Reports and the National Crime Victimization Survey? Which do you think more accurately paints a picture of crime in America? Why?

2. Why do you think the UCR and NCVS report similar numbers of car thefts each year? Why do you think the other crimes are not similar in number?

3. Why do you think experts believe UCR homicide statistics are so accurate?

4. What do you think could account for the difference in the UCR's and NCVS's trends in violent crime since 1973? Which do you think is more accurate? Why?

Class Activity: Crime Victim Survey

How has crime affected the people who live in your community? In this activity, students survey people to find what experiences members of the community have had with crime.

1. Break up into small teams. Each team should prepare several copies of a Crime Victim Survey following the suggested questions below. Leave room for brief explanations to each answer.

2. Within the team, each student should target a person with a different occupation in the community, e.g., a small storekeeper, homemaker, religious leader, business supervisor, fast-food employee. Survey the targeted person.

3. Summarize and compare the responses within your team. Try to account for any differences, based on different occupations. Then have the teams compare their surveys and list results on the board. Do you find similarities among the answers given by people with similar occupations? Why or why not? Do you find similarities based on other factors?

Crime Victim Survey

1. Have you ever been a victim of a crime such as bike theft, burglary, assault, etc.?

2. Have any members of your family been victims of crime?

3. Have any nearby neighbors ever been victims of crime?

4. Do you feel unsafe alone at night in your own neighborhood?

5. Do you believe a crime problem exists at the local schools?

6. Have the people in your family been forced to change any part of their lives because of crime?

7. Do you think the police in your community are doing an adequate job of protecting you and other citizens from crime?

8. Compared to one year ago, do you think the crime problem in your community has gotten worse, stayed the same, or improved?

Debriefing Questions

1. Were there any surprises in the results? How do you explain the surprises?

2. Make a list on the board of the kinds of crimes reported in the survey. Do you think other areas in your town or other towns would have a different list? Why or why not?

3. Discuss ways your family and neighbors attempt to protect themselves from crime. For example, you might consider special locks, bars on the windows, watchdogs, guns in the home, neighborhood patrols, etc.

4. What crimes occur most frequently at school? What could be done to prevent them?

5. What are the police in your area doing to prevent crime? What should they be doing?

CHAPTER 2
Who Are the Criminals?

Youth, Gangs, and Violence

About 60 percent of all violent crimes are committed by young males under the age of 25. In fact, males commit most crimes. They account for 84 percent of all arrests and 90 percent of violent crime arrests.

One of the most common violent criminals is the street robber. In his book *Criminal Violence, Criminal Justice*, Charles Silberman described the typical street robber as a male minority teenager or young adult from a poor family. This type of robber takes money from people impulsively if the opportunity arises. Rarely does he plan a holdup.

Sometimes street robbers steal because they want money for drugs, food, or goods. Sometimes they just need to impress someone. At other times, the street robber acts out of boredom. The victims of street robbers are often weak or vulnerable. They could be an old person walking alone or a drunk who has passed out on a park bench.

Silberman interviewed many young street robbers and gained some insight into why they apparently enjoyed stealing from people and threatening them with violence. "I get a kick out of it," said one. Another explained, "If I had a .38 right now, I can make you do just about anything I wanted to do." Others told Silberman that robbing people with a gun makes them feel important, like a judge or a king or a god.

Not all criminals who commit acts of violence think this way, but those who do are especially dangerous. For a few dollars, some would maim or kill their victims with little hesitation or feeling.

A disturbing characteristic of many young violent offenders is their apparent lack of feelings. For example, three young Miami boys covered a homeless man with lighter fluid and set him on fire. They told police that it was just a prank.

Some criminologists believe that many young violent criminals have been so brutalized by their own families and surroundings that they cannot feel anything when they maim or kill. With no parental supervision, no education, no skills, and no hope of a job, they find that it is all too easy to lash out. James Galipeau, a veteran probation officer in Los Angeles said, "There are a million kids out there who have no skills other than fighting. They are not afraid of the police or jail or of dying."

Youth Gang Violence

Youth gangs are not new to our cities. Throughout American history, gangs of young men have come together in immigrant and poverty areas of cities. In the late-19th and early-20th century, Eastern cities such as Boston, New York, and Philadelphia saw the rise of numerous gangs. Their members usually came from newly arrived or first-generation groups—Irish, Jewish, and Italian. In the early 1900s, the sociologist Frederick M. Thrasher studied the youth gangs of Chicago and found over 1,000 of them. These early gangs mainly took part in street crime. Later some developed ties to political machines and formed the basis of organized crime in America.

The Latino street gangs of Los Angeles arose in the 1920s during a huge wave of Mexican immigration from poor rural farms. In the 1930s and 1940s, these early gangs solidified into the *pachuco* lifestyle. They wore special clothes called zoot suits, had nicknames, and spoke their own slang called *Calo*. Feeling shut out of American society, they became heavily territorial, each defending a small neighborhood or *barrio*. They acquired names like Los 39s and Clarence Street Locos. Many of these groups have survived in the same area for more than 70 years. Puerto Rican youths in New York formed similar gangs, as portrayed by the Sharks in the popular 1961 film *West Side Story*.

To some degree these gangs were social clubs, but they also took part in street crime, drugs, and long-running turf warfare. In fact, by the 1970s, this turf warfare had given rise to the characteristic gang crime—the drive-by shooting. Gang kids as young as 13 would lean out the windows of cars to avenge some wrong by shooting at an enemy gang member. Often the shots hit the wrong target—a guest at a wedding party or a tiny child playing on a lawn.

Outlaw motorcycle gangs developed in some poor white communities in the 1950s. As shown in the 1950 film *The Wild One*, these bikers were less interested in defending turf than in appearing like a marauding band of pirates. Later, motorcycle gangs became associated with drug trafficking and other crimes.

Outlaw motorcycle gangs were often marked by a vicious anti-black, anti-Latino racism. In the 1970s and 1980s, some impoverished white communities saw the development of similar groups who called themselves skinheads. They modeled themselves on British punk gangs who shaved their heads. Often identifying with punk music and avowing overt racism, the skinhead groups produced an embittered subculture of hatred and violence.

African-American youth gangs had a different history. They arose in the 1950s to protect local turf, much like the Latino gangs. In the period of political protest of the 1960s, some of these gangs turned to radical politics. The Blackstone Rangers in Chicago became Black P. Stone (the "P" stood for power). After the Watts riots of 1965, the Slausons became the nucleus for the Los Angeles Black Panthers. These politicized groups did not survive long into the 1970s. Black P. Stone, for example, changed again and eventually became a drug-dealing gang called El Rukn.

In the early 1970s, Los Angeles saw the beginning of a new federation of gangs called the Crips. Unlike other gangs, the Crips spun

In 1986, two young people look at graffiti about crack near an area known as an open air drug market, in Roselle, New Jersey.

off subgroups called "sets" in many areas around Southern California. An archrival group called the Bloods also developed, spinning off its own sets, until many Los Angeles neighborhoods became a patchwork of gang territories. The two super-gangs sported official colors—blue for the Crips, red for the Bloods—and each set had a hand sign, like a letter of the deaf alphabet, to identify itself. Gang members, known as gangbangers, also used pro football and basketball jackets to announce their identities.

The black gangs might have settled into the pattern of earlier gangs—street crime, turf wars, and petty vendettas. But in the early 1980s, crack cocaine hit the streets. The normal powdered form of cocaine cost about $100 a gram. Crack, however, could be bought as cheaply as $5. This cheap and highly addictive drug instantly transformed cocaine use into a widespread and deadly problem. With millions of dollars to be made overnight, many sets of the Bloods and Crips turned themselves into drug-dealing networks to rake in the profits.

This flood of cash plus ties to Latin American drug suppliers brought along a huge increase in violence. Gang members now used automatic weapons like the Uzi or AK-47. Some sets of the Crips and Bloods started sending out exploration parties to set up business in cities across the country. The drug network spread.

On the Eastern seaboard, Jamaican immigrants formed similar crack-dealing gangs called posses, and they too started to spread outward from Boston, New York, and Washington, D.C. The Untouchables from Miami and El Rukn from Chicago did the same. By the late 1980s, gangs of second-generation Vietnamese, Cambodian, and Chinese immigrant youth were also jumping into the crack trade.

The number of drug- and gang-related murders soared to over 400 a year in Los Angeles county. Even tiny Martinsburg, West Virginia, which had been colonized by a Jamaican posse, went from an average of one murder a year to 20 drug killings in 18 months.

Crack addiction created many social problems. With more addicts searching for small amounts of ready cash to buy crack, reports of street crime and theft continued to rise. Crack addiction also increased prostitution rates and the use of injected drugs like heroin. These were major factors in the spread of AIDS.

In recent years, the crack epidemic has slowed. The number of gang-related killings has dropped. But gangs remain a serious problem.

Young people join gangs for different reasons. For some inner-city youths, it may seem safer to be in a gang (although statistics show that gang members are at least 60 times more likely to be killed than those in the general population). For others, the gang offers a way to make money. For many, gangs provide a substitute for a functioning, supportive family.

One researcher has classified gangs into three types: corporate, territorial, and scavenger. Corporate gangs try to make money. These gangs tend to be highly organized and almost everything they do concerns making money. Territorial gangs are less organized and focus on protecting their turf. They respond with violence to anyone they view as an intruder. Scavenger gangs are the least organized. The members who band together are usually low achievers and violence prone. Their outbursts of gang violence tend to be impulsive and senseless.

Gang Suppression

To stop gang violence, many communities have taken steps to suppress gangs. Four innovative techniques have been tried in recent years:

Directed police patrols. In the 1990s, New York City police adopted a tactic of flooding areas known for gang activity with officers. Police would stop suspected gang members who were committing minor offenses (such as drinking in public). If suspects had bulges in their clothing, they would be searched for guns. These stop and frisks became so common that gang members stopped carrying guns. As a result, the murder rate fell dramatically. The police have drawn some criticism, however, because the directed patrols took place in poor and minority neighborhoods and many people stopped and frisked were not gang members.

Anti-loitering ordinances. In 1992, the city of Chicago passed a Gang Congregation Ordinance, which banned "criminal street gang members" from loitering in public places. The law defined loitering as remaining "in any one place with no apparent purpose." Under this law, a police officer could order people loitering in public to disperse and leave the area if the officer reasonably believed one of them was a gang member. Anyone not promptly obeying the order violated the law. In three years, police dispersed about 90,000 people on Chicago streets and arrested more than 40,000 who refused to move on. The law, however, was challenged in court. In 1999 in *Chicago v. Morales*, the U.S. Supreme Court ruled 6–3 that the law violated due process and was unconstitutional. A basic requirement of due process is that a law must clearly describe what is forbidden. The court found that the crime of loitering was too vague for people to recognize when they were breaking the law. In January 2000, Chicago enacted a new ordinance, which it hopes will pass constitutional tests. It bans "gang loitering" in certain parts of the city. "Gang loitering" is defined as remaining in one place "under circumstances that would warrant a reasonable person to

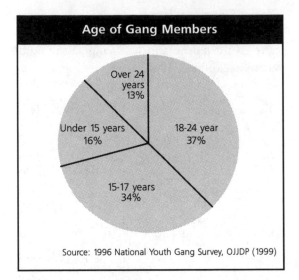

Age of Gang Members

- Over 24 years 13%
- Under 15 years 16%
- 18-24 year 37%
- 15-17 years 34%

Source: 1996 National Youth Gang Survey, OJJDP (1999)

believe that the purpose or effect of that behavior is to":

(1) "establish control over identifiable areas,"

(2) "intimidate others from entering those areas, or"

(3) "conceal illegal activities."

Street-gang injunctions. Beginning in the late 1980s, several California cities got court orders, known as injunctions, against gangs. Under laws in most states, courts can grant injunctions to shut down "public nuisances." A nuisance suit is not a criminal action, but a civil lawsuit. If a court grants an injunction, however, anybody who violates it can be held in contempt of court and fined or jailed. A "nuisance" is something that interferes with people enjoying their property or personal interests. A "public nuisance" affects a whole community or neighborhood and endangers public health or safety. Nuisances are long-running abuses, not single incidents.

In 1993, the city of San Jose got an injunction against more than 30 alleged gang members. Every night for several years, they had allegedly taken over Rocksprings, a neighborhood they didn't live in. They allegedly sold drugs, played loud music, fought with rival gangs, and made the residents virtual prisoners in their own homes. The injunction ordered the gang members not to use certain drugs, carry weapons, destroy property, or trespass.

All these things were illegal. But the injunction also banned the gang members from doing things in the neighborhood that were legal. It ordered them not to gather in groups, wear clothes with certain symbols, or carry a beeper. In the years following the injunction, crime in the neighborhood dropped dramatically. Several of the alleged gang members, however, challenged the injunction in court. They argued it violated due process to penalize them without a criminal trial. They also said the injunction violated their First Amendment right to peaceably assemble and associate freely. In 1997 in *Gallo v. Acuna*, the California Supreme Court upheld the injunction. The court stated: "To hold that the liberty of the peaceful, industrious residents of Rocksprings must be forfeited to preserve the illusion of freedom for those whose ill conduct is deleterious to the community as a whole is to ignore half the political promise of the Constitution and the whole of its sense." One of the justices who disagreed with the opinion argued that the injunction should be limited to illegal acts only. He said in his dissent that the court "would permit our cities to close off entire neighborhoods to Latino youths who have done nothing more than dress in blue or black clothing or associate with others who do so . . . . In my view, such a blunderbuss approach amounts to both bad law and bad policy." The U.S. Supreme Court refused to hear an appeal from this decision.

Zero tolerance for gang violence. Operation Ceasefire was developed as a zero-tolerance part of an anti-gang strategy in Boston. A research group led by Harvard professor David Kennedy looked into the city's problem of gang violence. It found that fewer than 1 percent of all young people belonged to street gangs. Yet this small number accounted for *at least* three-fifths of all youth homicides. The researchers also found that 75 percent of all young murderers and victims had lengthy criminal records, an average of 10 crimes apiece. Because gang members committed so many crimes, most had warrants out for their arrest or were under some form of court

This 1999 photo shows a curfew sign posted on Blythe Street in the Panorama City area of Los Angeles. The city obtained a controversial injunction against 100 members of a Blythe Street gang, banning them from carrying pagers, blocking sidewalks, and gathering in groups of more than two people.

supervision—probation, parole, or pretrial release. This meant that the criminal justice system could greatly impact each gang member. For example, those on probation could have their probation revoked and those with outstanding warrants could be arrested. Personnel from many agencies—local and federal police and prosecutors, probation officers, youth corrections, gang outreach, neighborhood groups—started meeting with gangs and informing them that any violence attributed to the gang would result in a crackdown on all members of that gang. Aside from the warning, gangs were told that the city could also offer services—job training, protection from enemies, but they must stop the violence. The first episode of violence following these meetings led to a crackdown that broke up a gang. At the next meetings with gangs, the crackdown was talked about and gangs were

asked: "Who's next?" Law enforcement did not have the personnel to crack down on every gang, but it didn't have to. Gangs didn't want to be next.

Boston's anti-gang strategy had two other parts. Operation Night Light sent police and probation officers into the homes of young people on probation to check on them each night. The third part was the Gun Project, which cracked down on illegal sales of guns to juveniles. These strategies paid off. By 1995, the number of youth homicides had dropped 80 percent from 1990. In 1996, no young people in Boston died from gun violence.

No one doubts that police must act to suppress gangs. But many doubt that police action alone can have a long-term effect. They point out that gangs flourish in poor, neglected neighborhoods and schools. They believe the best long-term solution is investing in children. This can mean building up the neighborhoods and schools. It can also mean providing special programs for children at risk of joining gangs.

For Discussion

1. List some of the factors that might push a young male toward violence. Do these factors also affect young females? As a group, why are young males more violent than young females?

2. Does gang activity exist in your community? How has it changed in the last 10 years? In the last 20 years?

3. What do you think should be done to stop gangs? Explain.

Class Activity: Take Back the Park

In this role play, students take the role of community members debating what to do about gangs in a community park.

1. Read and discuss "Cowan Park," below.

2. Divide the class into triads. Assign each student in the triads a role as a member of Keep It Constitutional (KIC), Take Back the Park (TBP), or the city council.

3. Regroup the class to consult with one another while preparing for the role play. KIC members should sit on one side of the room, TBP members on other side, and city council members in front. KIC and TBP members should think up their best arguments and city council members should think of questions to ask each side.

4. Reassemble as triads and begin the role play. TBP members will present their case first. Each side will have two minutes to make its presentation. The city council member can interrupt to ask questions. After both sides present, each council member should return to his or her seat at the front of the room.

5. The city council should discuss and vote on the ordinance.

6. Conclude the activity using the Debriefing Questions on this page.

Cowan Park

Once a haven for young children, Cowan Park has slowly changed into a hangout for rival gangs. Several gang-related shootings have taken place there in the last three months. Two weeks ago, a stray bullet killed four-year-old Monica Hines, who had been playing on the swings. Since that time, mothers have kept their young children away from the park.

Several community members have banded together to form a group called "Take Back the Park." Members of TBP want to rid the park of gang members and make it safe again for ordinary citizens. They have proposed the city adopt the following ordinance:

No person who is a member of a criminal street gang may enter any city park. A criminal street gang is any organization whose members have committed two or more of any the following crimes: murder, voluntary manslaughter, assault with a deadly weapon, robbery, or selling narcotics. Any person found guilty of this ordinance shall be subject to a $350 fine.

While this proposal has garnered support, it has also drawn criticism from a citizens group called "Keep It Constitutional." KIC believes that the ordinance violates the First Amendment to the U.S. Constitution. This amendment protects everyone's right to assemble in peace. KIC says this even includes gang members, because being in a gang is not against the law. If gang members break any laws, says KIC, they should be arrested. Otherwise, KIC believes, they should enjoy the same rights as everyone else. KIC also fears the police will use the law to pick up anyone who looks like a gang member. KIC believes the park problem can be solved by stationing police officers there.

TBP does not believe the ordinance violates the Constitution. According to TBP, gang members do not meet in the park to assemble in peace. They commit acts that keep others from the park. As things stand, law-abiding people are currently banned from the park. Police will have no trouble telling who are and who are not gang members. Gang members practically advertise who they are—with tattoos and gang colors. They flaunt their membership to intimidate others.

Debriefing Questions

1. What were the strongest arguments for the ordinance? Against the ordinance? Why?

2. Do you think the ordinance violates the Constitution? Why or why not?

3. Do you think it might sometimes be necessary to violate the Constitution to control crime? Why or why not?

4. What do you think could be done to reduce gang violence in parks? Explain.

Swindlers and Con Artists

The average loss from a street crime—a burglary or mugging or theft from a car—is less than $500. White-collar criminals, however, take far more from their victims. White-collar crime refers to acts like bank fraud, selling worthless stocks and bonds, and even taking people's homes through illegal mortgage schemes.

Swindlers don't rely on violence or breaking and entering—they rely on the victims' trust. And in the process, they steal not only money and property, but often they destroy the victims' self-respect. They leave people fearful and less willing to trust others in the future.

One notable swindle that cost people hundreds of millions of dollars took place in the 1980s. It was part of the savings-and-loan collapse, brought on by junk bonds, corporate wheeling and dealing, and shaky investments.

Charles Keating

In 1984, an Arizona home builder named Charles H. Keating Jr. bought Lincoln Savings and Loan in Irvine, California. Keating immediately began funneling bank loans into gigantic high-risk ventures, land deals, luxury resorts, and junk bonds. He also set up a plan that moved profits and loans around from Lincoln to his own American Continental Corporation and to 55 subsidiaries, using land swaps and phony loans.

As the scheme got shaky, he needed more and more cash to hold his empire together. Keating directed his high-pressure sales force to begin selling another $200 million in nearly worthless investments to small investors, including many retired people. These people often wanted safe, government-insured investments. The sales force was instructed to tell the investors that the new junk bonds were "just as good" as insured deposits.

This scheme, too, began to come apart, and federal regulators started investigating. Keating appealed to friends in Washington,

Charles Keating Jr., right, leaves federal court in Los Angeles with his attorney. Keating served 50 months for fraud.

including five U.S. senators to whom he had contributed large sums. He managed to stall the investigation another two years.

The government finally seized Lincoln Savings and Loan in 1989, but it was too late for thousands of small investors. Paying off the insured loans cost the taxpayers over $2 billion, and many thousands of small investors got nothing.

Many victims were elderly, trying to stretch out their incomes during retirement. Some had to return to work. Others were forced on welfare. Several became so despondent from their financial loss that they committed suicide.

Keating, age 69, was convicted in California on 17 counts of state securities fraud and received the maximum sentence of 10 years in state prison as well as $250,000 in fines. In federal court, he was convicted on 73 counts of racketeering, conspiracy, and fraud. He was sentenced to 12 years and 7 months in federal prison and ordered to pay restitution of $122.4 million.

But both convictions were overturned on appeal after Keating served 50 months in prison. The California conviction was reversed because the trial judge gave the jury improper instructions. The federal conviction was thrown out because one juror knew about Keating's state court conviction and had discussed it with other jurors.

In April 1999, Keating made a plea bargain with federal prosecutors. In return for pleading guilty to four counts of fraud, he was sentenced to the 50 months he had already served. The judge did not order that he pay restitution because he faces $3 billion in judgments from lawsuits against him.

California prosecutors appealed to get Keating's California conviction restored, but the appeals court ruled 2–1 in Keating's favor.

Smaller Swindles and Con Games

Not all swindles involve banks and huge sums of money. Smaller swindles—called con games, scams, or buncos—cost Americans billions of dollars each year. Con games can vary from small schemes that take a few dollars from schoolchildren up to elaborate plots to steal large sums from the rich.

P.T. Barnum, the great showman, said, "There's a sucker born every minute." In fact, almost any of us could be suckered at one time or another. Con artists tend to be bright, articulate people. They are clever actors and patient at waiting for the right moment to strike. In addition, they often work in groups to help bamboozle their victims. Often someone called a "shill," who seems to be an innocent bystander, begins the process of drawing in the victim. Complex con games can involve several other people called "cappers" who also pretend to be innocent. In fact, they are all part of the swindle team.

In the end, most con games rely on the victim's desire to get something for nothing. The swindler offers huge rewards at some later date in exchange for some of your money right now. Dallas police investigator W.E. Orzechowski says, "Con men basically are using the same old schemes, time after time, and they still work." The best bet to avoid a con game is to remember: If it seems too good to be true, it almost certainly is. Everyone should say no to schemes suggested by strangers.

The following section describes several classic swindles, and a few new ones developed for the telephone and computer age. To help you keep the bad guys straight, in each case we will call the swindler "Bunco" and the accomplice "Capper."

Pigeon Drop

Mr. Bunco approaches a well-dressed elderly woman named Ms. Green at a bus stop. While chatting in a friendly way, Mr. Bunco spots an envelope on the sidewalk. He peeks into the envelope and says it contains $6,000. Now Ms. Capper arrives and joins the conversation. Mr. Bunco asks both women what they should do with the money. Soon they all agree to share the money, but Ms. Capper recommends that Mr. Bunco go to a nearby lawyer for advice.

Mr. Bunco returns and says the lawyer told him the three should share the $6,000. But Mr. Bunco reports that the law requires a neutral party to hold the money for six months. He says the lawyer has agreed to hold the $6,000 if they will each put up $1,000 to show good faith.

The minute poor Ms. Green adds her $1,000 to the envelope, the swindlers find a way to go off with it. They may even leave her with the original envelope—full of worthless paper.

Ponzi Scheme

Mrs. Bunco guarantees a huge return on an investment of $500. She attracts three investors. Two weeks later, she returns $200 to each investor, saying that each has already earned this amount. The investors tell their friends about the easy money to be made. As

Ask an Expert

Invite a police officer from the bunco squad to discuss with your class different con games and swindles.

more and more investors join, Mrs. Bunco uses some of the newer investors money to pay "dividends" to older investors. The number of investors keeps growing until Mrs. Bunco skips town with all the cash. (This swindle is named after Charles Ponzi, who used this method to defraud people in the 1920s.)

Bank Examiner Swindle

Mr. Bunco visits Maria, a young housewife, and identifies himself as a bank examiner. He picked her out as a victim by watching her fill out a deposit slip at the bank. Mr. Bunco tells Maria that he believes one of the tellers at the bank is embezzling money. He asks Maria to help him trap the teller and offers her a reward of $500. After she agrees, Mr. Bunco asks Maria to withdraw a large sum of money from her account. "Bring the money home," he says. "One of our security people will come by and pick up the bills to examine the serial numbers." Maria withdraws the money, but of course it is picked up by Ms. Capper, who disappears with it.

The Luxury Tax Scam

This is one of the most common telemarketing, or telephone, frauds. Mr. Bunco telephones Henry and tells him he has won a $2,500 cruise to the Bahamas and two diamond-studded Omega wristwatches, worth $500 each. Mr. Bunco promises to send the watches by express mail, but Henry has to pay the tax of $220. Henry mails off his check and either receives two imitation watches worth a few dollars or nothing at all. The cruise tickets never show up.

Other Telemarketing Scams

Telemarketing swindles like the luxury tax scam have become big business, stealing as much as $40 billion a year. Often a room full of callers work these swindles. When authorities begin to investigate, the whole operation can move on easily. Here are some common telemarketing schemes that either steal money directly or offer a service at hugely inflated prices:

- Phony prize or sweepstakes offers, with a fee charged to the "winner"

Some Con Game Slang

big store an elaborate confidence game involving a fake office and many people. The film *The Sting* shows a good example.

blowoff the last move in a con game.

capper an apparent bystander who is actually an accomplice of the swindler. Also, a **steerer**.

fish the victim. Also the **mark**, the **pigeon**, the **customer**.

green a naive victim.

hang paper to write a fraudulent check.

hurrah the point in a con game where the victim is totally committed.

red inking the threat to eliminate the victim from some elaborate scheme just as he or she gets greedy.

salt a mine placing a few real gems in a worthless mine, or something similar.

squeeze a crooked wheel game such as roulette.

stall the point in a swindle where the victim is momentarily delayed in order to increase his or her greed.

touch the money taken from a victim.

- Magazine subscriptions that are overpriced or never appear
- Pseudo charities
- Schemes to fix bad credit or get a credit card for a fee
- Fake offers of loans for a fee paid in advance
- Work-at-home offers that promise huge incomes
- Phony travel and vacation offers

If you are approached by a caller like this, try to get an address or telephone number and then call the police, the district attorney's office, or a local consumer protection agency.

Internet Fraud

It is estimated that retail sales on the Internet will soon reach more than $100 billion. With the growth of e-commerce, many telemarketing scams have moved to the Internet. Scammers set up web sites and telephone banks and send bulk e-mail, known as spam, asking people to contact them. Just like telemarketing fraud, scammers offer phony merchandise, prizes, magazine subscriptions, and investment opportunities. In addition, the Internet offers con artists new opportunities.

Mrs. Bunco offers to sell a new television on an auction web site. She gives a mail drop as her address. When the money arrives, Mrs. Bunco never sends a television. (Auction frauds make up the overwhelming majority of Internet frauds reported to the National Fraud Information Center and the Internet Fraud Watch.)

Mr. Bunco sends spam to customers of a particular Internet service provider telling them their accounts need updating (particularly their credit card information). When customers respond, Mr. Bunco goes on a spending spree with their credit card numbers.

Ms. Bunco buys shares of a cheap stock. She creates a phony web site with an article praising the value of the stock. Ms. Bunco then enters chat rooms and talks about what a great stock Stratosphere is and refers to the phony web site. When the stock price surges, Ms. Bunco sells her stock for a quick profit before the stock crashes.

In more than 90 percent of all Internet fraud cases, payment is made offline—by check or money order. "Requesting cash is a clear sign of fraud," said Susan Grant, director of the Internet Fraud Watch. "Pay the safest way. If possible, pay by credit card because you can dispute the charges if there is a problem."

For Discussion

1. Do you think the penalty that Charles Keating received was appropriate? Explain.

2. Should the criminal justice system treat white-collar criminals like Charles Keating less harshly than violent criminals? Why or why not?

3. Why do victims fall for swindles? How can they avoid them?

Activity: More Cons

There are many more con games and swindles than have been mentioned in this book. In this activity, students find and report on different schemes. Each student should:

1. Research and find a different con game or swindle. To find one, talk to people, go to the library, or research on the Internet. A good place to start on the Internet is at the *Criminal Justice in America* Links on Constitutional Rights Foundation's site (**www.crf-usa.org**).

2. Write a one-page paper describing the con game, how it works, and who its victims are.

CHAPTER 3
Crime and Defenses

The Basics of Crime

Criminal cases differ from civil cases. In most civil cases, individuals sue one another seeking compensation for injuries done to them. In criminal cases, the state prosecutes individuals for injuring *society*. Instead of seeking compensation from defendants, the state seeks to punish them. A criminal case focuses on whether a defendant has committed a crime against society and what sentence is appropriate to punish the defendant for the crime.

But what conduct should society outlaw? In many instances, this question is easy to answer. Almost everyone would agree that murder, rape, and arson should be prohibited. Debates arise, however, over other acts. Should prostitution or the use of drugs be made criminal? What about gambling or private sexual activity? What conduct should society prohibit? These debates raise questions about where criminal laws come from in the first place.

The Sources of Criminal Law

Our criminal laws spring from two major sources: laws passed by legislatures and **common law**. Common law is judge-made. Instead of being created by a legislature, it is based on legal precedents—court decisions—set by judges in earlier cases. English common law is an important root of our current legal system. Originally, the criminal laws in England were mostly unwritten. If a judge heard a case and believed that certain conduct was anti-social, he made it a crime and punished the offender accordingly.

Definitions of crimes and defenses developed in the decisions of the English courts. These later became part of the common law adopted in early America. In turn, American courts began contributing to the common law.

Over the years, a rather unwieldy body of law developed.

Common law has one serious problem. If it isn't written down in some simple way, how do people know if they are breaking the law?

American states are divided on the issue of whether criminal courts can declare an act criminal if there is no specific statute against that act. Some states still recognize the power of the courts to create common law crimes, although this power is rarely exercised. Most states and the federal courts, however, have abolished common law crimes altogether. In these jurisdictions, only conduct that is expressly forbidden by a criminal statute is a crime.

Thus the primary source of criminal law today is legislative enactment. By the second half of the 19th century, legislatures had seen the problems of relying on common law and had begun to enact comprehensive criminal codes. Many of these codes embodied all of the elements of the old common law.

Classification of Offenses

The common law divided crimes into two categories—felonies and misdemeanors. Common law felonies were murder, manslaughter, rape, sodomy, mayhem, robbery, arson, burglary, and larceny. All other crimes were misdemeanors.

Under modern criminal law, the distinction between felonies and misdemeanors is spelled out by statute. Most states make any crime punishable by death or by imprisonment in a state prison a felony. A crime punishable by time in a local jail is a misdemeanor. Other states distinguish by length of imprisonment, not place of imprisonment. For example, a felony is often defined as a crime punishable by one year or more in prison.

For Discussion

1. What characteristics distinguish criminal from civil cases?

2. What are the two sources of criminal law? How are they different?

3. Today, many states have done away with common law crimes. Only acts specifically defined as illegal can be punished. What would happen if some criminal managed to find a loophole? What if an individual did something obviously harmful to others that was not specifically outlawed by statute? Should the courts be allowed to recognize a new crime to fill the gap? Explain your answer.

Class Activity: Felony or Misdemeanor?

In this activity, students evaluate whether certain actions should be crimes, and if so, whether they should be felonies or misdemeanors.

1. Break into pairs. Each pair should:

    a. Read and discuss "Criminal Acts?" below.

    b. Fill out a chart answering the following questions:

    • Should the act described be a crime? Why or why not?

    • If so, should it be a felony or misdemeanor? Why?

2. Then reconvene as a class and share group answers.

Criminal Acts?

a. Margaret tells the police that an officer who stopped her on the street was verbally abusive to her. She is lying.

b. Sam sees a young boy struggling in a pond and calling for help. Sam does nothing and the boy drowns.

c. Dick and Suzanne are living together. They have no intention of getting married in the near future.

d. Robert holds a toy pistol to Ashley's head and demands all of her cash and jewelry. She believes it's a real gun and hands over the goods.

e. Pedro calls a local pizza parlor and orders five pizzas to be delivered to a phony address.

f. Jane's country is at war. She shoots and kills an enemy soldier.

g. John lets his dog run wild around the neighborhood, even though he knows that the dog scares young children and constantly knocks over garbage cans looking for food.

Ingredients of a Crime

The criminal justice system carefully defines exactly what a crime is. The system also takes care in defining what must be proven to show who committed a crime. Almost every crime has four basic ingredients:

1. **A prohibited act.** At common law, this was called the *actus reus*. The act is almost always defined by a statute. The law does not punish people for having criminal thoughts alone. There must be an act. In murder, for example, the act is killing someone. In a few rare cases, *failing to act* is a crime when a person has a legal duty to act. For example, if a parent lets a child die of a long illness without seeking medical help, it can be a crime.

2. **Criminal intent.** At common law, this was called *mens rea*, or a guilty mind. This can be the most difficult ingredient to prove. It will be discussed in more detail below.

3. **Concurrence of the act and the intent.** The person has to intend the act at the same time he or she commits it. For example, Sluggo wants to kill Nancy. Then he changes his mind and forgets all about it. A month later he hits her by accident with a car and kills her. This is not legally murder because the intent to kill and the act did not occur at the same time.

A crime is made up of:			
Criminal Act	**Criminal Intent**	**Concurrence of Act and Intent**	**Causation**
Conduct prohibited by law	KINDS 1. General 2. Specific 3. Criminal Negligence 4. Strict Liability	Act and intent must occur at the same time.	Result must be caused by the act.

4. **Causation.** The act has to cause the harmful result. For example, Marge, intending to kill Homer, puts poison in a doughnut. As he reaches for the doughnut, Homer slips, hits his head, and dies. Marge cannot be found guilty of murder because she did not cause Homer's death.

Criminal Intent

Criminal laws generally punish only those who have criminal intent, a guilty mind. But what constitutes a guilty mind, the so called *mens rea*, depends on the crime. The criminal intent required for most crimes usually falls into one of four categories:

1. **Specific intent.** This is the easiest type to define. It means the person intended just the result that happened. The person did it on purpose. Certain crimes, such as theft, require specific intent. To convict John of theft, for example, the prosecution must prove not only that John took Mary's car, but also that he did not intend to return it.

2. **General intent.** This means that the person either knew the result would happen or consciously disregarded the extreme likelihood that it would happen. For example, John picks up a gun on New Year's Eve and shoots it toward a crowd of people. A bullet hits Mary and kills her. He didn't kill Mary on purpose, but he must have known he would kill, or was likely to kill, someone. This would meet the general intent requirement of second-degree murder.

3. **Criminal negligence.** This means that a person does some act unintentionally but with an extreme lack of care. For example,

John is drag racing down a city street when Mary, a pedestrian, steps in front of his car. Mary is killed.

4. **Strict liability.** This means no mental state is required at all. Anyone doing the act is guilty regardless of intent. Almost all common law crimes required some mental state. But bigamy is an example of a common law crime that required no intent. For example, if John mistakenly believes he has divorced his first wife and he marries Mary, he can be convicted of bigamy. Other examples of strict liability crimes include most health, safety, and traffic offenses.

Class Activity: Did They Commit Crimes?

In this activity, students analyze five cases to determine whether criminal conduct has taken place.

1. Break into groups of four. Each group should:

   a. Read and discuss the five cases that follow.

   b. Refer to the explanations above of the four basic elements of a crime—(1) act, (2) intent, (3) concurrence of act and intent, and (4) causation.

   c. Assign one element of a crime to each person in the group. Have that person say whether that element is present in each case, then discuss whether or not it is. Refer to the glossary if you need a crime defined.

d. When the discussion is completed, assign one case to each student for reporting back to the whole class. Be prepared to explain and discuss them.

2. Reconvene as a class and share the answers.

Case 1: Tim

Marcos and his friends, Tim and Jill, were having a beer together at their local bar. When Tim went to the jukebox to play more music, Marcos asked Jill to dance. Tim became jealous and punched Marcos in the face. Tim has been charged with battery.

Case 2: Karen

Karen told everyone that she hated Emily for stealing her boyfriend. Karen said she wanted to hurt Emily. Two months pass and Karen nudges a flowerpot off her second-floor patio as Emily stands below. The flowerpot hits Emily and gives her a concussion. Karen swears that she forgot all about her threats and didn't mean any harm. Karen is charged with battery.

Case 3: Ray

Mr. Ray Anderson sat on his front porch cleaning his rifle. Many children were playing on the sidewalk in front of his home. When Mr. Anderson turned the gun over it went off, killing one of the children in the crowd. He has been charged with involuntary manslaughter.

Case 4: Gina

Gina was shopping in her favorite department store. She saw a sweater that she liked, stuffed it into her book bag, and ran out of the store. A security guard caught her. Gina has been charged with shoplifting.

Case 5: Gayle

Gayle shoots Mary in the big toe. Mary goes to the hospital to have her toe examined and treated. One week later, Mary dies of blood poisoning that she got from an unsterilized medical instrument. Gayle is charged with murder.

Murder Most Foul

Murder most foul . . . most foul, strange and unnatural.

    —Shakespeare, *Hamlet*

No crime seems to fascinate people more than murder. Religions teach the basic tenet, "Thou shalt not kill." Yet throughout the ages, storytellers have told and retold tales of murder—Cain and Abel, the Greek tragedies, Shakespeare's *Macbeth*, thousands of mystery novels, crime TV shows. In our country, the most severe penalty our society can inflict—death—is reserved for those who commit murder under certain conditions.

Like all crimes, murder is made up of particular elements. These must be proved before a person can be convicted. Let's examine some of the specific elements of murder and those of some other important crimes.

Murder at common law and under many modern statutes is the unlawful killing of a human being with *malice aforethought*. Malice aforethought is the intent, or *mens rea*, element of this crime. It doesn't mean what you might expect it to. Malice aforethought is sometimes defined as an *actual or implied intention* to kill with no provocation by the victim.

Actual intent is found when the defendant consciously meant to cause another's death. Implied intention exists when the defendant *either*:

(1) intended to cause great bodily harm *or*

(2) should have known that the act would result in death or great bodily harm.

Consider some examples:
- If Barbara hates Michael, decides to kill him, and picks up a knife and does so, malice aforethought is present. In this case, Barbara's malice aforethought was an *actual* intent to kill Michael, and she could be charged with murder.

- If Barbara decides to hurt Michael badly, stabs him in the chest, and kills him, malice aforethought is also present. This time the intent to kill is *implied*, because she did not specifically intend to kill, but only cause great bodily harm.

- If Barbara hates Michael, decides to scare him, pushes him in front of oncoming traffic at a street corner, and Michael dies as a result, malice aforethought is also established. In this case, though Barbara didn't intend to kill or even seriously injure Michael, she should have known her actions would cause him to die or suffer great bodily harm. Under the law, Barbara had *implied* intent to kill Michael.

Degrees of Homicide

Over the years, the law has developed several degrees of criminal homicide. The punishment a convicted person may receive depends on the degree of the homicide. The worst degrees of homicide are commonly called murder and the lesser degrees, manslaughter.

First-degree murder is a deliberate and premeditated killing done with malice aforethought. This is a cold-blooded murder. "Deliberate" means it was done with a cool mind, capable of reflection. "Premeditated" means the person actually reflected on the murder before committing it. And "malice aforethought," of course, means that the killer had the intent to kill. It takes all three elements—deliberation, premeditation, and malice aforethought—to establish the *specific intent* for first-degree murder.

Second-degree murder is a killing done with malice aforethought, but without deliberation and premeditation. This covers all murders that are not in the first degree.

Felony murder is any killing done while a person is committing a felony. If the killing is done while committing certain felonies, such as robbery, rape, arson, or burglary, it is classified as first-degree murder. Killings done while committing other felonies are considered second-degree murder.

Voluntary manslaughter is an intentional killing committed without malice aforethought. The killer must:
- be seriously provoked by the victim,

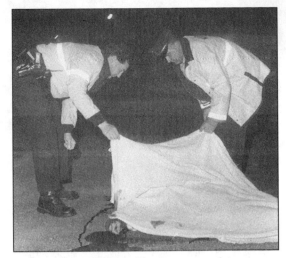

Police examine a body found at a murder scene.

- act in the heat of the anger, and
- not have had an opportunity to cool off.

The provoking act does not excuse the killing, but it makes the crime a lesser degree than second-degree murder.

Involuntary manslaughter is an unintended killing that takes place during a crime that is not a felony. It can also be a killing caused by criminal negligence.

Vehicular homicide is a crime recognized by many states. It covers killings from automobile accidents when the driver is criminally negligent.

For Discussion

1. The penalties for these forms of homicide in every state are increasingly harsh: *Involuntary Manslaughter—Voluntary Manslaughter—Second-Degree Murder—First-Degree Murder.*

   If one person is killed in each of these cases, why do you think the punishments get harsher? Is this fair? Explain.

2. Howard attempts a first-degree murder but fails and harms no one. Fred is guilty of involuntary manslaughter when he accidentally kills a person. Which person should be punished more harshly—Howard or Fred? Why?

Class Activity: Death in the School Halls

In this activity, students examine a hypothetical killing and determine what crime was committed.

1. Break up into groups of four, and read the following case:

   One day in gym class, Adam made fun of the way Rick was shooting a basketball. Rick told Adam to shut up or else he would take care of him. Adam couldn't help making another comment on the way Rick was shooting. Rick grabbed Adam and beat him up.

   Adam ended up with a broken nose and a black eye, and he decided to get even. He dug his father's pistol out of the attic, loaded it, and headed off to school to find Rick. He waited at Rick's locker for almost an hour, but Rick never showed up. Adam became impatient. Nervously, he checked the gun again to make sure that all the chambers were loaded. Just then the school bell rang out, startling Adam into firing the gun by accident. The bullet ricocheted off a locker and hit a student who was walking out of class. She was killed instantly.

2. In each group, assign one person to each of the following crimes: murder, felony murder, voluntary manslaughter, and involuntary manslaughter. Each person should:

   a. Decide whether the crime described above fits the crime assigned to him or her.

   b. Be prepared to explain why or why not.

3. Discuss the case in your group. Go through the crimes, one by one, and the person responsible for that crime should explain whether the case fits that crime or not. Discuss why or why not.

4. Reconvene the class and compare your findings.

No Honor Among Thieves

Stealing is one of the most commonly committed crimes. The law recognizes many forms of stealing. The differences depend on how the stealing is done.

Larceny is the usual legal word for theft. It means taking without permission someone else's property and intending not to give it back. For example, if someone walks by your desk and takes your wallet, that person has committed larceny. There are usually two categories of larceny or theft:

1. **Grand theft** means stealing property worth over a certain amount. The amount varies from state to state, but it is usually around $500. Grand theft is a felony. If your wallet contained $1,000, stealing it would be grand theft.

2. **Petty theft** means stealing property worth less than the grand theft amount. Petty theft is a misdemeanor.

Burglary is the unlawful entry into any building with the intent to commit a crime, usually theft. At one time in common law, burglary meant breaking into a home at night to steal. That definition has been expanded to include illegally entering any building at any time of day to steal or commit any crime. Some states have expanded it to include breaking into cars. If a thief broke into your office to steal your wallet, the crime would be burglary.

Robbery, unlike burglary, is a crime against the person. It is forcible stealing—the taking of a person's property by violence or by threatening violence. If someone grabs you, demands your wallet, and then takes it and runs away, that person has committed robbery.

Armed robbery means using a dangerous weapon to take something from a person. Even pretending to have a weapon is considered armed robbery. If someone pulls a knife on you and steals your wallet, that person has

committed armed robbery. Armed robbery is a more serious offense than simple robbery, and it carries a stiffer penalty.

Other Forms of Stealing

Larceny, burglary, and robbery are the three main categories of laws against stealing. But as the common law developed in England and America, courts and legislatures added additional categories.

Embezzlement is when people take property they have been entrusted with. For example, you lend John your car and he decides to keep it. He has embezzled the car. Embezzlement differs from larceny in that the person takes possession of the property legally.

Fraud is knowingly misrepresenting a fact to get property from another person. For example, John tells you a worthless coin is gold (which he knows is false) and sells it to you for $100. John has defrauded you of $100. Fraud is sometimes a crime in itself and more often an element of other crimes, such as larceny by trick, false pretenses, forgery, and writing bad checks.

Extortion is making a threat with the intent of getting property (usually money) from another person. One form of extortion is blackmail. For example, Elsa threatens to tell your friends that you spent time in jail unless you pay her $1,000. She is extorting money from you.

Ask an Expert

Invite a criminal lawyer to your class to explain the elements of different crimes.

An extortionist can threaten violence. For example, if Elsa says she will kill you unless you give her $1,000 by Friday, she has committed extortion. But if the threat is of immediate harm, the crime is robbery. For example, if she points a gun at you and demands money, she is committing robbery, not extortion.

Receiving stolen property is against the law in every state. The crime requires that the person know or should know that the property is stolen. For example, Sam goes over to his neighbor Ed's house, sees five brand-new color televisions in his garage, and Ed generously gives Sam one of them. Sam is guilty of receiving stolen property even if Ed never told Sam the television was stolen. Sam should have known they were stolen.

Today, a number of states have classified embezzlement, fraud, extortion, and receiving stolen property under a general law against theft. Others retain them as separate laws against stealing.

For Discussion

1. The penalties for these forms of stealing in every state are increasingly harsh: *Theft–Burglary–Robbery–Armed Robbery*.

   If a wallet containing only $20 is stolen in each of these cases, why do you think the punishments get harsher? Is this fair?

2. What is the difference between robbery and extortion? Between larceny and embezzlement?

3. Why do you think states outlaw receiving stolen property? Do you think they should? Explain.

Activity: What's the Crime?

In this activity, students analyze a hypothetical to determine what crimes have been committed.

1. Divide the class into pairs.

2. Each pair should:

   a. Read "Thievesville, U.S.A.," below.

   b. Imagine that the state in which Thievesville, U.S.A., is located has laws against **larceny, burglary, robbery, armed robbery, embezzlement, fraud, extortion, and receiving stolen property.**

   c. Determine which of these crimes, if any, each person broke. Review the article for information on each crime.

   d. Write down the offender's name, which law the offender broke, and why.

   e. Prepare to report the answers to the whole class.

3. Have the pairs report and the class discuss the answers.

Thievesville, U.S.A.

Amy, Bob, Carol, Dave, Eden, Frank, and Gina all live in separate houses in the same neighborhood. Determine which laws, if any, each of these persons broke.

Early every morning, Amy goes from house to house stealing newspapers. She gets about 20 every day. She takes them to the corner newsstand run by Bob and sells them to him for a nickel apiece. She takes the dollar she earns and deposits it in the bank. She always goes to her favorite teller, Carol. Carol has a policy of taking 5 cents of every deposit for herself. She only makes a few dollars a day (all in nickels), but over the years the money has added up to $1,200. She doesn't dare put it in the bank. She keeps it at home under her mattress. One day Dave is out searching for his newspaper when he sees that Carol has left one of her bedroom windows open. He seizes the opportunity, crawls in, finds the bulging mattress, and steals her money. As Dave crawls out the window, Eden sees him. She writes Dave a note, "I saw you. If you don't pay me $1,000, I'll tell the police." Dave thinks he better pay Eden off. Late at night, he takes $1,000, puts it in a bag, and walks toward Eden's house. But Frank is lurking in the bushes. Frank sneaks behind Dave and jabs his finger in Dave's back, saying, "I've got a gun. Just drop the bag on the ground and leave. Don't turn around." Dave does as he's told. When he gets home, he realizes he has to raise some cash fast to pay off Eden. He calls his neighbor Gina, who he's heard is an investment wizard. He tells her he only has $200 and needs $1,000 soon. She says, "No problem. I've got an investment paying 5–1, guaranteed. It's a sure thing." Dave gives Gina $200. She puts it with all the other "investments" she's received recently and flies to Rio to live where none of her "investors" can find her.

Hate Crimes

- In 1999, a gunman sprayed bullets into a Los Angeles Jewish community center wounding three children and the center's receptionist. After he left, the gunman shot and killed a Filipino-America mailman. The attacker selected his victims because he hated Jews and other minorities.

- In 1998, three white men murdered James Byrd Jr., a black man, by dragging him for three miles behind a truck until his body was literally torn apart. The men, all sworn racists, targeted Byrd because he was black.

- In 1998, a young, gay college student, Matthew Shepard, was brutally beaten and left to die entangled in a fence. His murderers chose their victim because of his sexual orientation.

- In 1994, a white man in Lubbock, Texas, was murdered by two African-American men. The father of three, the victim was chosen because he was white.

Each of these brutal crimes had one thing in common: They were motivated by hate. These incidents and others around the country have drawn increased attention to the problem of crimes motivated by prejudice, or so-called hate crimes.

Currently the federal government and almost every state have hate-crime laws. Some of these laws define a hate crime as any crime committed against a person or a person's property motivated because of the person's race, religion, nationality, or ethnicity. Others also prosecute crimes motivated by bias against gender, sexual orientation, and disability as hate crimes.

In 1998, according to the U.S. Department of Justice, almost 8,000 hate crimes were reported around the United States. More than half were motivated by racial bias. Prejudice against religion, sexual orientation, and ethnicity or nationality accounted for about 1,000 incidents apiece.

Crimes against persons, such as assault or threats and intimidation, made up about 70 percent of the reports. Making threats or intimidating people was the most common hate-crime report and accounted for about 40 percent of all hate crimes.

From 1996–1998, hate-crime reports decreased slightly, even with more jurisdictions reporting. Each of the previous six years had shown an increase in hate crimes. Still, experts disagree whether hate crimes are increasing or decreasing in the United States. Part of the problem comes from the hate-crime statistics themselves. The federal government has only been collecting them since 1991. Some places do not report hate crimes as a separate type of crime, but each year more agencies have started reporting them. This makes it difficult to accurately compare one year with another or to study trends.

Compared to all other types of crime, the overall number of hate crimes is small. But some experts claim that many hate crimes are not reported. They also point out that most crimes in the United States target property, but most hate crimes are directed against people.

According to a 1999 Gallup Poll, one out of eight Americans is worried about being the victim of a hate crime. Among non-whites, however, one in four worry about being victimized.

R.A.V. v. City of St. Paul

Some critics of hate-crime legislation argue that these laws violate the First Amendment's protection of free speech. This gives every American the right to express opinions or hold ideas even if they are racist or bigoted.

"Some states have special laws that provide harsher penalties for crimes motivated by hate of certain groups than the same penalties for the same crimes if they are not motivated by this kind of hate. Would you favor or oppose this type of hate crime law in your state?"

Favor	Oppose	No Opinion
70%	25%	5%

"If a hate law were enacted in your state, which of the following groups do you think should be covered?"

	Yes, should be covered	No, should not	No opinion
Racial minorities	85%	11%	4%
Women	83	13	4
Homosexuals	75	20	5
Religious and ethnic minorities	84	12	4

Source: Gallup Poll (1999)

On several occasions, the U.S. Supreme Court has been asked to determine whether hate-crime laws violate the Constitution.

In 1989, St. Paul, Minnesota, passed a city ordinance making it a crime to place on public or private land a hate symbol, such as a burning cross or Nazi swastika. About a year later, police arrested a group of white juveniles for a series of cross burnings. In one instance, the youths taped chair legs together into a crude cross and set it ablaze inside the fenced yard of a black family.

In an appeal that reached the U.S. Supreme Court, attorneys for the juvenile defendants argued that the St. Paul law violated the First Amendment. The city responded that by prohibiting such acts as cross burnings, the ordinance served "a compelling governmental interest" to protect the community against hate-motivated threats.

In June 1992, a unanimous Supreme Court agreed with the juvenile defendants. Writing the opinion for the court, Justice Antonin Scalia stated that although government may outlaw activities that present a danger to the community, it may not outlaw them simply because they express ideas that most people or the government find despicable.

Scalia also pointed out that other laws existed to control and punish such acts as cross burnings. In this case, the city could have prosecuted the juvenile offenders under laws against trespassing, arson, vandalism, and terrorism. (*R.A.V. v. City of St. Paul.*)

Wisconsin v. Mitchell

Other hate-crime laws are different. Instead of creating special hate crimes, these statutes add extra penalties for any crime committed out of hate. For example, Wisconsin's hate-crime statute increases the maximum penalty for an offense whenever a criminal "intentionally selects the person against whom the crime . . . is committed . . . because of the race, religion, color, disability, sexual orientation, national origin or ancestry of that person. . . ."

On October 7, 1989, Todd Mitchell, 19, and a group of other young black men violated the law in Kenosha, Wisconsin. After seeing the movie *Mississippi Burning*, which concerns Ku Klux Klan terrorism against blacks in the South during the 1960s, they decided to attack a 14-year-old white boy, Gregory Reddick. Mitchell asked his friends, "Do you feel hyped up to move on some white people?" He then pointed to Reddick and said, "There goes a white boy. Go get him!" About 10 members of the group, but not Mitchell himself, ran across the street, beat up Reddick, and stole his tennis shoes. Severely beaten, Reddick remained in a coma for four days and suffered permanent brain damage.

As the instigator of the attack, Mitchell was tried and convicted of aggravated battery, which normally carries a penalty of two years in prison. But the jury found that Mitchell had selected his victim because of his race. Consequently, the judge applied Wisconsin's hate-crime enhancement law and added two more years to Mitchell's sentence.

Mitchell appealed his sentence, claiming that the state's enhancement law violated the First and 14th amendments. Since the enhancement law is based on a criminal's motives, Mitchell argued that motives are based on thoughts and beliefs, which are protected by the First Amendment. Mitchell further argued that the law violates the 14th Amendment because it treats criminals who are motivated by prejudice differently from criminals not so motivated, even though their crimes are identical.

Attorneys for the state argued that the law in this case differed from the one in *R.A.V. v. City of St. Paul.* This law did not prohibit specific speech, symbols, or beliefs. It only applied to criminal acts (i.e., selecting a victim), which are not protected by the First Amendment. They pointed out that during sentencing, judges commonly consider many things, including a criminal's motives. Further, they claimed that the state had a "compelling governmental interest" in eliminating prejudiced criminal behavior.

In June 1993, the U.S. Supreme Court upheld the Wisconsin hate-crime penalty-enhancement law. Writing for a unanimous court, Chief Justice William Rehnquist ruled that a criminal's prejudiced motives may be used in sentencing, although "a defendant's abstract beliefs, however obnoxious to most people, may not be taken into consideration by a sentencing judge." The chief justice also stated that "the statute in this case is aimed at conduct unprotected by the First Amendment." (*State of Wisconsin v. Todd Mitchell.*)

As the Wisconsin and Minnesota cases show, the line between punishing hate and protecting speech and free thought can be difficult to draw. On one side, our Constitution seeks to assure tolerance and equal protection for all citizens no matter what their race, ethnicity, religion, or gender. On the other hand, our Constitution contains protections for individual beliefs, no matter how distasteful they might be. As the U.S. Supreme Court has determined, the state may not make the expres-

sion of hate a criminal matter, but it can punish criminal acts motivated by hate more harshly.

Hate Crimes, Pro and Con

Now that the Supreme Court has set guidelines for hate-crime legislation, states and the federal government are considering adopting more such laws. A federal Hate Crimes Prevention Act has been proposed. The U.S. Code already outlaws violence based on the victim's race, color, religion or national origin. The new act proposes expanding the law to include gender, sexual preference, and disability.

Supporters see these laws as extremely important in our diverse society. They believe hate crimes deeply hurt all levels of the community—individuals, families, groups, and society at large. Hate crimes intentionally send a message that minorities are unwelcome and unsafe. Supporters argue that hate-crime laws will help prevent much violence and will convey our society's intolerance for these crimes.

Opponents view hate-crime legislation as well-meaning but unnecessary and even counterproductive. They argue that anyone who commits a serious crime is already punishable under current state laws. These laws protect everyone equally. They see no reason to pass laws that set up special classes of victims. Further, they contend that hate-crime laws will primarily affect those who commit lesser crimes by sending more of them to prison. They believe that sending someone into our overburdened and racist-filled prison system is likely to make them more racist. Thus, they say, the law may actually increase hate crimes.

In addition, opponents see no need for federal intervention into an area of law that states have traditionally handled. In recent years, the federal government has enacted much crime legislation. Opposition has grown to this federalization of criminal law. Opponents have taken heart by recent Supreme Court decisions striking down federal crime laws.

The Constitution limits the powers of Congress. Congress can only enact laws based on those powers given to it in the Constitution. Federal crime laws are usually based on Congress's power to regulate interstate commerce. For most of the 20th century, the Supreme Court liberally interpreted what constituted "interstate commerce," allowing laws to be passed regulating the environment, the work place, and civil rights. In recent years, however, five members of the court have refused to go along with this liberal interpretation. They have started overturning federal laws based on the commerce clause if they find the law is only remotely related to interstate commerce.

In 1995 in *U.S. v. Lopez*, a 5–4 majority of the Supreme Court struck down the Gun-Free School Zones Act of 1990. The law made it a federal crime to have a gun near a school. In his opinion for the court, Chief Justice William Rehnquist found that possessing a gun near a school had nothing to do with interstate commerce. His opinion therefore ruled that Congress had exceeded its powers in enacting the law.

In 2000 in *U.S. v. Morrison*, the court by the same 5–4 majority struck down part of the Violence Against Women Act of 1994. Created to stem "gender-motivated violence," this law permitted rape victims to sue their rapists in federal court. Congress had based the law on the commerce clause and the 14th Amendment, which prevents states from denying people equal protection under the law. In an opinion by the chief justice, the court ruled that Congress did not have power to enact this law. The commerce clause, the court said, did not permit Congress to "regulate noneconomic, violent criminal conduct." Under the 14th Amendment, Congress can only pass laws against actions by states or state officials, not actions by private individuals. The court ruled that the law was therefore unconstitutional.

These opinions by Rehnquist leave doubt as to whether the court will find federal hate-crime legislation constitutional. In Rehnquist's words, the "Founders denied the National government and reposed in the States . . . the suppression of violent crime and vindication of its victims."

For Discussion

1. What are hate crimes? Why is it difficult to determine if they are increasing or decreasing?

2. Do you agree with the court's decision in *Wisconsin v. Mitchell*? Why or why not?

3. How serious do you think the problem of hate crimes is in the United States? Explain.

4. Do you think the federal government should pass hate-crime legislation? Explain.

Class Activity: Hate-Crime Bill

In this activity, students role play a legislative session on a proposed hate-crime law.

1. Ask students to imagine that the following law is being proposed in their state:

   Anyone who intentionally selected the victim of the crime because of the victim's race, religion, color, disability, sexual orientation, national origin, or ancestry shall have his or her sentence increased by 30 percent over the normal sentence.

2. Divide the class into groups of three. Assign every student in each triad one of these three roles: state legislator, supporter of the bill, opponent of the bill.

3. Have all the legislators, supporters, and opponents meet separately to prepare for the role play. The supporters and opponents should think up their best arguments and the legislators should think of questions to ask each side.

4. Regroup into triads and begin the role play. The legislator should let the supporter speak first and then have the opponent speak. The legislator should ask questions of both. After both sides present, have the legislators move to the front of the room, discuss the proposed law, and vote. Each legislator should individually state his or her opinion on the bill.

5. Debrief by asking what were the strongest arguments on each side.

Cybercrime

During the 1990s, the Internet grew popular. More and more people from around the world went online every day. People sent e-mail, chatted, played games, and conducted business with people on the other side of the world. People also committed crimes.

In many ways, the Internet provides a perfect place to commit a crime. Criminals can remain anonymous and prey on victims far away. Police have no crime scene to search for clues and they may have to track criminals halfway around the world.

If police do manage to find the criminal, problems may arise. Although many traditional crimes like fraud and theft occur on the Internet, new crimes, exclusive to the Internet, also take place. The United States has developed laws against these crimes, but many places haven't. No international treaty against cybercrime yet exists. Thus a person could work at a computer in a faraway place, hurt many people around the world, and not have committed a crime if the country does not outlaw what the person did.

Hacking

Hacking is electronically breaking into or disrupting computer systems. Once inside a system, hackers do different things.

Some hackers steal. The thefts can involve almost anything—from money to credit card numbers to intellectual property like books, music, and art. Two hackers in Russia electronically entered an American bank and transferred $10.5 million to accounts in other banks. Another hacker stole thousands of credit card numbers from a music company. The hacker posted the numbers on the Internet when the business refused to pay $100,000 in ransom money for them. When best-selling author Stephen King offered a new e-book for sale on the Internet, hackers broke into the publisher's site, stole the book, and posted it on the Internet for free.

Other hackers vandalize and destroy. Some spread computer viruses, worms, and Trojan horses, which can erase files on computers. For

example, the "IloveYou" virus appeared on people's computers as an e-mail attachment from someone they knew. When a person opened the attachment, the virus erased files on the person's computer and sent the "IloveYou" attachment to everyone in the person's e-mail address book. In this manner, the virus quickly spread to computers around the world, causing millions of dollars in damage. Other hackers vandalize by breaking into web sites and leaving "graffiti." For example, hackers changed the Department of Justice's web site to read "Department of Injustice" on a background of swastikas. Still others try to shut down web sites. Using so-called "denial of service" attacks, which overload a site's computers, hackers have managed to shut down such popular sites as Yahoo, e-Bay, and E*Trade.

Other hackers do nothing except enter the site and look around. Even this, however, is illegal. The federal government's Computer Fraud and Abuse Act outlaws entering without authorization any computer system run by government, banks, or those involved in interstate commerce, such as those on the Internet. It also bans viruses and computer attacks. For a first offense, an unauthorized person entering a computer system without intending to cause harm can get one year in prison. Those intentionally damaging computers or stealing information for commercial gain can get five years. Every state has similar laws.

Hackers fall into three categories—often

called "white hats," "black hats," and "gray hats." The white hats do nothing illegal. They are hired by companies to improve computer security. They try to infiltrate a company's computer system and expose security lapses. "A white hat does it when asked, under contract, with a 'get out of jail free' card," explained Charles Palmer, manager of network security and cryptography at IBM Research. "We'll do the job, evaluate it, and tell the customer what we're doing." On the other extreme are the black hats, who are clearly criminals. They steal, vandalize, and disrupt.

In the middle are the gray hats. These are the hackers of computer folklore. They follow a so-called "hacker ethic." This ethic bans stealing and vandalism. But it allows accessing computers without permission, which is illegal. They also push the borders of illegality by publishing on the Internet hacking programs and security holes they find in computer systems. In fact, the denial-of-service attacks that shut down Yahoo and other sites used a program called Tribal Flood created by a gray-hat computer hacker in Germany nicknamed Mixter.

Mixter and other gray hats believe they are performing a public service by posting such programs on the Internet. They say that they are exposing security flaws and giving everyone an equal chance to come up with countermeasures. Mixter argued: "It would be unfair to provide them to just a small circle of security experts who would possibly only consult some few elected companies. The only fair way is getting the information out to everyone, because generally, everyone on the Net can be affected by security issues." He criticized those who used his program to shut down the sites, calling the attacks "stupid and pointless." But he also thought the attacks were "an inevitable price to pay to be able to develop countermeasures and fixes."

Many disagree that gray hats are performing a public service by breaking into computer systems or posting hacking programs, like Mixter's Tribal Flood, on the Internet. John C. Dvorak of *PC Magazine* compares a web site to a business and the Internet to "a road leading to that business. My business unlocks the doors during the day and keeps them locked at night. If people break in at night, they are considered burglars and are prosecuted as such. Breaking into computer systems is similar, and people are now prosecuted for breaking into them. In many states you can also be prosecuted for owning burglary tools" (like lock picks). Dvorak compares posting hacking programs to designing and giving away a new lock pick that can open most door locks. Few, he says, would consider this a public service.

Fraud

The FBI estimated that people lost almost $400 million to computer fraud between 1996 and 1998. As the Internet grows, so does the variety of scams online. Two of the most common involve stock trading and auctions.

The Securities and Exchange Commission gets more than 300 complaints per day about stock scams. Many are "pump and dump" schemes. Criminals either buy cheap stock or create a phony company. They send e-mails to chat rooms talking up the stock. As people buy the stock, the price rises and the criminals dump their shares for a big profit.

The Federal Trade Commission reports more fraud from auctions than anywhere else on the Internet. Criminals either sell worthless items or just take the money and run without even a pretense of selling something. One man offered rare stuffed animals for sale on auction sites, never delivered a single piece of merchandise, and pocketed about $200,000. He did this by posing as satisfied customers to give himself high ratings on auction sites, using different postal drops as addresses, and insisting on cash payments from auction "winners." He even taunted his victims, posting a message on the web saying: "All you people are really quite ridiculous. You make a deal via e-mail, never see the person, never speak with the person and then get upset when you get ripped off. You must be a bunch of morons." His bravado was short-lived. In 1999, he was arrested and charged with multiple counts of fraud.

These are just a few examples of crime on the Internet. Other current concerns about the Internet include hate crimes, child pornography sites, and chat rooms in which men lure underage children into sex. As the Internet grows, the list of crimes will also grow. The web may be a virtual world, but the crime on it is real.

For Discussion

1. What are the differences between white-, gray-, and black-hat hackers? Do you think that what gray-hat hackers do should be against the law? Explain.

2. What are some common frauds on the Internet? What do you think people can do to protect themselves from fraud?

Class Activity: Free Speech?

Some people think that the Internet should be a bastion of free speech and that anything should be allowed. Others agree that free speech is important, but say that it has limits. They point out that the U.S. Supreme Court has upheld some limits on freedom of speech. In this activity, students look at some examples of material on the Internet and decide whether they think it is free speech that should be allowed on the Internet.
1. Divide the class into small groups.

2. Each group should:

a. Discuss each of the "Six Examples of Material on the Internet."

b. Decide for each whether it should be protected as free speech.

c. Prepare to report its decisions and the reasons for them to the class.

3. Regroup the class and have groups report back.

4. Debrief the discussion using the questions below.

Six Examples of Material on the Internet

1. Instructions for making a bomb

2. Racist remarks

3. Sexually explicit photographs

4. A threat to kill a person

5. The code for a highly destructive computer virus

6. Downloadable, illegally made copies of a new movie

Debriefing Questions

1. Why is freedom of speech important?

2. Do you think some speech should not be protected by the First Amendment? Explain.

Legal Defenses to Crime

In our criminal justice system, persons accused of a crime are innocent until proven guilty. In our system, defendants do *not* have to prove they are innocent. The prosecution must prove that defendants are guilty.

During a trial, the criminal defendant and the defense lawyer do everything they can to prevent the prosecutor from proving guilt. They introduce their own evidence, they examine and cross-examine witnesses, and they make arguments. If they keep the prosecution from establishing every element of the crime beyond a reasonable doubt, the defense wins.

Defendants in our society have even a further protection. Our criminal law recognizes some special legal defenses, known as **affirmative defenses**. The three most common affirmative defenses involve issues of **insanity, self-defense,** and **entrapment.** If the defendant successfully establishes one of these defenses, it does not matter whether the prosecution can prove the elements of the crime or not. The defendant is not guilty. These affirmative defenses have raised many controversies.

The Insanity Defense

Defendants will be acquitted if they can prove that at the time their crime was committed, they were legally insane. This defense has always been controversial. But public debate intensified after President Ronald Reagan was shot in 1981 and his attacker was found not guilty by reason of insanity. The defendant in that case, John Hinckley Jr., purchased a gun and stalked the president for some time. He wrote a letter to a famous actress telling her what he planned to do. Millions of Americans watched in horror as videotapes of Hinckley shooting straight at the president played over and over again on national television. "How could this person be found not guilty?" they demanded.

For criminal law, "insanity" has a special meaning. Even in this context, legal scholars and lawmakers have disagreed about what constitutes insanity for a defense to a criminal charge. Over the years, several different legal tests for determining insanity have been developed, but none has been universally accepted as valid. These different standards are currently used at the federal and state levels:

1. The *M'Naghten* **Rule.** Under this traditional approach, defendants must show that because of their mental illness, either they did not know what they were doing or they did not know it was wrong. (*M'Naghten Case,* 1843.)

Critics of the *M'Naghten* rule point out that it does not protect defendants who cannot control themselves. Thus defendants can be convicted under the *M'Naghten* rule even if they cannot avoid committing the crime because of mental illness.

2. The Irresistible Impulse Rule. In some states, defendants will be acquitted if they can prove that the crime was committed because of an insane impulse that controlled their will. This test of insanity often supplements the *M'Naghten* approach. (*Parsons v. State,* 1887.)

3. The *Durham* **Rule.** To prove insanity under this rule, defendants must show that the crime was "the product of mental disease or mental defect" of some sort. Because of the vagueness of this rule, it has a limited following today. (*Durham v. U.S.,* 1954.)

4. *Model Penal Code* **Test,** also known as the substantial capacity test. A much stricter rule than Durham, this test is used in about half the states. Another third and the federal courts use the *M'Naghten* rule. Under the *Model Penal Code a*pproach, defendants are insane if because of a mental disease or defect, they:

- lacked substantial capacity to appreciate the criminality of their conduct, or

- lacked substantial capacity to conform their conduct to the requirements of the law. (*Model Penal Code* Sec. 4.01 [1].) Some jurisdictions omit this part of the test.

Under any of these tests, defendants who prove their case will be found not guilty by reason of insanity. Often this means the defendants will be committed to mental hospitals. They will not be released in many jurisdictions until they can prove beyond a reasonable doubt that they are sane or that they no longer pose any threat to society.

Some jurisdictions have developed a new verdict—**guilty but mentally ill.** The meaning of this verdict varies from jurisdiction to jurisdiction. In some jurisdictions, it *replaces* the verdict of not guilty by reason of insanity. In these jurisdictions, a jury must return one of three verdicts—guilty, not guilty, or guilty but mentally ill. The latter verdict means that the defendant was legally insane when committing the crime.

In other jurisdictions, "guilty but mentally ill" means the defendant was *not* legally insane, but was mentally ill when committing the crime. It means that the defendant's defense of insanity has fallen short, but the jury recognizes that the defendant has mental

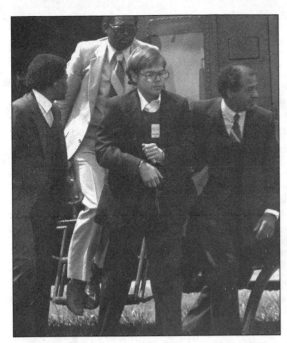

John Hinckley Jr. is shown here in custody of federal agents. Hinckley shot President Ronald Reagan in 1981, but a jury found him not guilty by reason of insanity.

problems. These jurisdictions have not replaced the insanity defense. They have added this new verdict—guilty, but mentally ill—to the other verdicts juries may return—guilty, not guilty, and not guilty by reason of insanity.

The effect of the verdict is the same in most jurisdictions. The defendant will receive a standard prison sentence, but may serve it in a mental hospital.

Self-Defense

You're alone in your apartment, asleep at 3 a.m. You wake up all of a sudden with your heart pounding. Then you realize your bedroom window is sliding open inch by inch. Your legs begin to tremble. A tall shadowy figure steps into the room. In terror, you pick up a lamp by your bed and hurl it. The lamp shatters against the man's head, and he slumps to the floor.

Can you be charged with battery? Yes, it's possible, but it's not likely. Even if you were prosecuted for battery, you would have a strong claim of self-defense.

Generally, you have a right to use whatever force is necessary to defend yourself if you feel you face a threat of immediate violence. For a proper claim of self-defense, you must establish that:

- you reasonably believed that the force was required for your own or someone else's protection—even it that belief turns out to be mistaken;

- the threatened harm was about to happen and the attacker was willing and able to injure you; *and*

- the force used in self-defense was reasonable—that is, no more than was necessary to prevent the victim from inflicting harm.

The law is much stricter about using *deadly* force in self-defense. Deadly force may only be used when you reasonably believe, based on the circumstances, that

- the attacker was about to kill you or inflict great bodily harm; *and*

- the deadly force was the only way of preventing the harm.

Entrapment

Several famous trials have featured the issue of entrapment. Entrapment occurs when a police officer, or any agent of the government, lures a defendant into committing a crime. Most people would agree that it is unfair to entice someone into committing an act and then punish the person for it.

But the issue is not always that simple. Under the law, if the defendant would not have committed the crime, except for the government's enticement, then the defendant is not guilty. But if the defendant already had the idea of the crime in mind and an officer only made it possible to commit the crime, then an entrapment defense would fail.

The federal government's **Abscam** operation in the early 1980s is an example of an entrapment defense that failed. The FBI invented a phony Arab sheik, Kambir Abdul Rahmen, to try to bribe one U.S. senator and seven representatives. The FBI filmed the sting operation and used the films as evidence in the

Automobile entrepreneur John Delorean poses with one of his sports cars at a San Francisco beach. In 1983, Delorean stood trial for trafficking in cocaine. He claimed police entrapped him, and the jury acquitted him.

trials for accepting bribes. The defendants argued that the FBI had entrapped them, but this defense failed. Why?

The FBI had received reliable information that these particular congressmen were corrupt. "Sheik Rahmen" did not approach just any congressmen. He chose ones who were reported to show criminal intent already. The FBI, said the courts, had merely given them an opportunity to do something they already had the intent to do.

On the other hand, the **John DeLorean** case (occuring at about the same time) demonstrates an entrapment defense that succeeded. DeLorean was an auto company executive who left Ford in the late 1970s to set up his own sports car company in Northern Ireland. His new gull-wing DeLorean sports car, named after himself, came out in the midst of a gasoline crisis and did not sell very well. It was well known that his company was in deep trouble.

FBI agents claimed that an informant told them DeLorean was searching for illegal ways to keep the company afloat. In an elaborate sting operation similar to Abscam, undercover operators approached him with a scheme to import $24 million in cocaine. They videotaped him accepting the deal and brought him to trial in 1983.

DeLorean's lawyers argued that he had a clean record, that the government's witnesses were unreliable, and that the FBI had lured and entrapped him into the crime. Despite the videotape, the jury found him not guilty. One juror said, "The way the government acted in this case was not appropriate." After the result, many legal experts suggested that the government would probably be much more wary of setting up elaborate sting operations.

In a similar development in 1992, the Supreme Court threw out the conviction of a man they felt had been entrapped. Postal inspectors thought that a Nebraska man named **Keith Jacobson** was predisposed to buying child pornography. They sent him an offer in the mail, and he turned it down. For the next 26 months, they repeatedly sent him offers to buy child pornography. Finally, he bought two magazines and they arrested him. He was convicted, but the Supreme Court on a 5–4 vote overturned the conviction. The court said that the government had "overstepped the line between setting a trap for the 'unwary innocent' and the 'unwary criminal' . . . and . . . failed to establish that [Jacobson] was independently predisposed to commit the crime." (*Jacobson v. U.S.*)

For Discussion

1. What special protection do affirmative defenses offer defendants?

2. What are the differences among the various insanity defenses?

3. What must you prove for a claim of self-defense?

4. In recent years, several victims of long-term child and spousal abuse have claimed self-defense as a justification for killing their abusers. Do you believe this defense is valid if they kill their abusers when they are not being threatened? Why or why not?

5. Do you think the defense of entrapment makes sense? Why or why not?

Class Activity: The Insanity Defense

In this activity, students apply the four insanity tests to a hypothetical case.

1. Break up into groups of four. Each group should:

   a. Assign each person in the group one of the insanity tests described in the preceding section.

   b. Read "Mark's Statement," below.

   c. Have each person apply his or her assigned insanity test to Mark to see if it fits.

   d. Have the whole group discuss whether each test fits.

2. Reconvene and compare the findings from each group.

Mark's Statement

During his trial for murdering a friend, defendant Mark Khasabian made the following statement:

"I knew that it was wrong, but I couldn't help myself. During the night of April 30, Beelzebub, grand duke of Hell, came to me with biddings from the master. He told me to kill my friend. I resisted, but his will was too strong and finally I had to do what I was told."

Debriefing Questions

1. Which insanity tests fit Mark's case? Which do not?

2. If Mark's statement is true, do you think he should be found not guilty by reason of insanity? Why or why not?

3. Which insanity test, if any, do you think is best? Why?

Class Activity: What Defense Is Valid?

In this activity, students apply the elements of the defenses of insanity, self-defense, and entrapment to hypotheticals to determine whether a defense could be raised.

1. Break up into groups of three. Each group should:

   a. Assign each person in the group one of the following legal defenses: insanity, self-defense, entrapment.

   b. Read each of the three hypotheticals below. Have each person apply his or her assigned legal defense to each hypothetical to see if it fits.

   c. Have the whole group discuss why that legal defense might or might not work.

2. Reconvene and compare the findings from each group.

Peter Hope

Peter Hope is charged with assault with a deadly weapon. He was walking down the street. Without warning, a man began hitting him with a rolled-up newspaper. Peter Hope pulled out a gun and shot him.

Martha Heart

Officer Martin, in plain clothes, approached Martha Heart on the street and offered to sell her a "hot" radio for a cheap price. Martha at first refused, but the officer persuaded her to buy it. He then arrested Martha for receiving stolen property.

Karen Sanchez

Karen Sanchez had her home burglarized twice in the last month. One evening, she heard a noise on her front porch. She grabbed her son's baseball bat and flung open the door to discover a man bending forward with his hand on the doorknob. He jumped upright and reached into his pocket. Afraid that he had a weapon, Karen struck him across the face, partially blinding him. As it turned out, the man had come to ask for a charitable donation and had been reaching for his identification card. Karen has been charged with assault with a deadly weapon.

Class Activity: Debate on Insanity

Choose a pro or con position on the following statement:

The insanity defense should be abolished.

Research this issue. On the Internet, a good place to start is Constitutional Rights Foundation's Research Links or *Criminal Justice in America* Links. (**www.crf-usa.org** and click on Links.) At your school or community library, check the computer index to periodicals or the *Reader's Guide to Periodical Literature* for magazine articles on the subject. Write a two-or three-page essay supporting your opinion. These can be used for a class discussion or debate.

Unit 2:
The Police

Police officers do not have an easy job. When enforcing the law, they deal with society's problems—quarreling spouses, drug and alcohol addiction, serious traffic accidents, and senseless violence. They must face danger and make lightning-quick decisions.

To be effective, the police need community support. Many of their contacts with the public help build this support—the police find a child, solve a crime, return stolen property to its owner. But other contacts may erode public support. Some of us have received traffic tickets or had other minor unpleasant encounters with the police. We grumble and go on our way. Others of us report serious problems with the police including harassment, beatings, and other abuses of authority.

When abuses do occur—whether through error, indifference, or overzealous enforcement—the criminal justice system must act to correct them. In a democracy, part of enforcing the law is upholding the constitutional rights of all citizens. Police authority cannot go unchecked. What that authority should be and whether it is properly used in particular situations are issues that can make police work difficult and sometimes controversial.

In this unit, you go behind the badge to explore law enforcement in our society. In doing so, you will encounter some interesting questions: What might it be like to be a police officer responding in the line of duty? What are people's attitudes about the police and how might that affect police work? How do our laws affect police investigations and arrests? What are the proper limits of police authority? This unit will give you a better picture of police in our society.

CHAPTER 4
Police and Society

Question of Attitude

In 1829, when Sir Robert Peel organized the first police force in England, he said: "The police should maintain a relationship with the public that gives reality to the historic tradition that the police are the public and the public are the police." Has this ideal of police-community relations been borne out over time? Does the public believe that the police serve its interests? Do the police think of themselves as public servants?

Studies have shown that people's attitude toward police is shaped by their contacts with police and how safe they feel in society. If a person has had positive contacts, the person usually has a positive attitude toward police. Negative contacts foster negative attitudes.

In America, a great divide based on race exists in attitudes toward police. Many minorities complain of police harassment. They express fear of being pulled over by police for no apparent reason. They even refer to the reason they are pulled over as DWB (driving while black or brown). A November 1999 Gallup Poll asked Americans whether they had a favorable or unfavorable opinion of their local police. Eighty-five percent of whites responded "favorable" compared to 58 percent of blacks. Thirty-six percent of blacks answered "unfavorable."

On the job, police develop their own attitudes. Police work can be risky and stressful. To survive, officers need to be able to take charge of dangerous situations. They are usually highly protective of one another and can be distrustful of outsiders.

Many people today, including police officers, wonder about the role of the police. According to research, young children think police give orders and punish people. They don't envision the police as helping people

Studies have shown that people's attitudes toward police are shaped by their contacts with police.

and enforcing laws. Research also indicates that the police's **power**, not their service to the public, captures the imagination of young people. Similarly, adults often believe that police officers perform their jobs not out of any sense of dedication to the community, but for the pleasure that comes from exercising power over others.

How accurate are these perceptions of the police? One study suggests that the police themselves have a much different view of their motivations. Five hundred officers, from new recruits to veterans, were asked to respond to a form entitled, "I am a policeman because . . ." Given a list of 40 possible responses, they were asked to choose the 10 most important to them. The top five vote-getters were:

- I want to improve the community.
- I want to improve police work.
- I am part of a team effort.
- I feel a civic responsibility.
- My imagination is stimulated.

On the other hand, at the bottom of the list, only about 10 percent of the officers said:
- I can find excitement regularly.
- I can wear a uniform.
- I can order other people around.
- I can carry a gun.
- I can use force legally.

For Discussion

1. Would you ever consider becoming a law-enforcement officer? Why or why not?

2. Do you think it's important for the police to have good relations with the community? Explain your answer.

3. Why might people develop negative views of the police? Brainstorm and list reasons. How can the public develop more positive views?

4. Why might the police develop negative views of the public? Brainstorm and list reasons. How can they develop more positive views?

Class Activity: Sampling Class Opinion

In this activity, students survey and compare their attitudes toward local police.

1. Each member of the class should answer the questionnaire below on a sheet of notebook paper. Write the letters "a" through "j" down the left-hand column of the paper.

2. Next to each letter, write the number that indicates the degree of your agreement or disagreement with the statements below.

    5–strongly agree
    4–agree
    3–uncertain
    2–disagree
    1–strongly disagree

3. After you have marked your responses, average the answers across the whole class. (Add all the numbers for each statement and then divide by the number of students providing answers.)

4. Discuss the statements that show the strongest agreement and the strongest disagreement. Why do you think the class responded most strongly to these statements?

Questionnaire

In my community, police . . .
   a. treat most teenagers fairly.
   b. are doing a good job.
   c. would refuse bribes offered to them.
   d. avoid using too much physical force against people.
   e. generally treat wealthy people the same as poor people.
   f. generally treat all racial groups in the same way.

Activity: Sampling Police Attitudes

To find out about police attitudes, conduct your own survey of police in your community. Use a form like the one from the study described on page 58. How do your results compare with the officers' responses in that study? What might be some reasons for any differences?

Activity: Sampling Public Opinion

To find out about your community's attitudes toward police, construct an attitude survey for your community. You may wish to conduct one survey for the general population or several surveys directed at specific groups (e.g., homeowners, college students, women and men, racial groups, religious groups, business persons, etc.). Here are some additional statements you might consider using in your surveys.

- The community would be better off with fewer police.
- Police in the United States are often criticized unfairly.
- Police in the community enforce drug laws too strongly.
- I would call the police if I saw someone break into a store.
- I would call the police if I saw a friend stealing a car.
- In the past four or five years, my attitude about the police has become more favorable.

From Citizen Volunteers to Professional Police

Nearly every civilization has had some form of law enforcement. Anthropologists have discovered written records of laws and law enforcement more than 5,000 years old.

Citizen Volunteers in England

In early English history, it was considered each citizen's duty to defend king and country from foreign invaders and local lawbreakers. In some cases, citizens received rewards for capturing criminals. Individuals or even entire villages could be fined for not assisting the king in enforcing the laws of the land.

As English towns grew in size, the need arose for regular law-enforcement officers. Able-bodied men began to take turns looking out for the safety of their neighbors. These volunteers, called constables, depended heavily on other citizens to help them.

Over the years, towns were grouped into counties, or shires. Each shire had a shire reeve, or sheriff, responsible for getting the citizens of the shire to enforce the law properly.

During the 1300s, large towns and cities organized citizen-volunteer groups to protect the streets at night. This form of policing,

Police make an arrest in Philadelphia, about 1900. By this time, most major cities had full-time police departments.

called the night watch, was eventually adopted in the American colonies.

City Police Forces in the U.S.

From colonial times until the late 1800s, citizen volunteers enforced the law in most American cities. Often, volunteer night watchmen carried rattles or noisemakers to warn off criminals. According to jokes at the time, the rattling noise was caused by the night watchmen themselves who shivered and shook with fear.

In 1829, Sir Robert Peel organized a force of paid law-enforcement officers, called Peelers or bobbies, to patrol London. About 10 years later, Boston established the first round-the-clock police force in the United States. In 1844, New York City formed a 24-hour professional police department. By 1870, most American cities had police forces patterned after those organized in Boston and New York.

While U.S. cities organized police departments, rural areas were also developing law-enforcement agencies. Rural police forces followed the form of the old English shire-reeve system. In many parts of the country, they evolved into agencies headed by county sheriffs.

The need for law enforcement on the frontier led to the establishment of the first *state* police force, the Texas Rangers. Later, other states established their own statewide police forces. Today, state law enforcement agencies include highway patrols, bureaus of narcotics, fish and game departments, and civil defense bureaus. Each of these agencies responds to different law-enforcement needs.

The *federal* government has developed various agencies to handle its law-enforcement responsibilities. The Secret Service, among its other duties, investigates counterfeiting and protects the life of the president. The Internal Revenue Service investigates tax evasion. The Bureau of Alcohol, Tobacco, and Firearms monitors these products. These agencies fall under the control of the Treasury Department. The Department of Justice, headed by the attorney general of the United States, directs such agencies as the Immigration and Naturalization Service and the Federal Bureau of Investigation (FBI).

The FBI operates throughout the nation. But it may only investigate *federal* law viola-tions. For example, the FBI investigates kid-napings, bank robberies, civil-rights viola-tions, and crimes committed on federal terri-tory and property. Most criminal acts in the United States, however, are handled by state and local police.

Policing Today

Unlike most countries in the world today, the United States does not have a national police agency that enforces the laws through-out the country. Rather, more than 40,000 independent law-enforcement agencies exist at the local, state, and federal levels of govern-ment. Each agency has its own special func-tion and enforces specific laws in a well-defined geographical area. For example, fire inspectors enforce local fire codes, and health department inspectors enforce a city or town's health and sanitation ordinances. Sheriff deputies patrol counties to enforce county ordinances and state law. Local police enforce a state's and city's criminal laws.

Today, the public often views the police primarily as crime fighters. In reality,

Federal Law-Enforcement Officers	
Agency	**Number of full-time officers with authority to carry firearms and make arrests**
Immigration and Naturalization Service	16,552
Federal Bureau of Prisons	12,587
Federal Bureau of Investigation	11,285
U.S. Customs Service	10,539
U.S. Secret Service	3,587
U.S. Postal Inspection Service	3,490
Internal Revenue Service	3,361
Drug Enforcement Administration	3,305
U.S. Marshals Service	2,705
Administrative Office of the U.S. Courts	2,490
National Park Service	2,197
Bureau of Alcohol, Tobacco and Firearms	1,723
U.S. Capitol Police	1,055
GSA - Federal Protective Service	900
U.S. Fish and Wildlife Service	831
U.S. Forest Service	601

Note: Excludes federal agencies employing fewer than 500 full-time officers.
Source: "Federal Law Enforcement Officers, 1998," Bureau of Justice Statistics (2000)

although the police do fight crime, they also spend substantial time on many other tasks within the community. They settle disputes, handle many forms of social work, monitor public protests, control traffic, and respond to medical emergencies.

To understand the police, it helps to consider the pressures and fears officers work under. Their duties have become more dangerous and more complex in recent times. Many factors have contributed to this: the increase in the availability of dangerous weapons, a more critical news media, a more critical general public, and budgetary problems, including a lack of funds to hire enough officers. Police must cope with the realities of law enforcement in a democratic society. Under law, they must protect the constitutional rights of the public. In enforcing the law, they must also obey the law.

For Discussion

1. How does the organization of police forces in the United States differ from most other countries? Why do you think these differences exist?

2. Could our crime problem be better handled if there were one large police agency to enforce all criminal laws throughout the United States? What would be the advantages of having such a force? What would be the disadvantages? Do you think the United States should have this kind of police force? Why or why not?

3. Read the "Police Officer's Oath" on page 63. It describes the ideals of law enforcement. Do you agree with these ideals? If not, what would you change? Why?

Class Activity: Police Call

What is it like to be a police officer responding to a call for assistance? What is police work like? In this activity, students role play interactions between police and citizens.

1. **Preparation:** In preparation for the activity, contact your police department and arrange for an officer to visit your class on the day of the activity. The officer's role will be to observe and help debrief the role plays. You may wish to conduct the activity over a two-day period and have the officer only present on the second day. Also, you may want to hold the activity in a large multipurpose room or auditorium, if one is available.

2. **Form Groups:** Divide the class into four groups of equal size.

3. **Group Selection:** In each small group, select two members to play police officers and one or two members to act as group spokespersons. The remaining members role play citizens. Send the police officers to a circle in the center of the room.

4. **Police Group Assignment:** The visiting police officer should take part in the group's preparations. At the center circle, the students taking the role of police officers should:
    a. Select a patrol partner.
    b. Read and discuss the "Police Officer's Oath" and "Departmental Regulations" to determine how they will conduct themselves on a police call.

5. **Citizen Group Assignment:** Assign one of the Police Calls below to each group. Each should then take about 10 minutes to decide how it will role play the situation. (Group members should try to act as realistically as possible. For example, how would youngsters caught shoplifting react to the store owner and police? Passively and quietly, or loudly and defensively?) Also, one member of the group should prepare to call the police for help by giving a minimum amount of

information about the assigned Police Call. For example, "Come quick . . . there is a robbery in progress at Green's Drugstore."

6. **Role playing:** When all the groups are ready, conduct role plays one at a time in front of the class. In turn, a member from each should call for help based on the assigned Police Call. A team of police officers responds to each call. The role play may begin or be in progress as the police arrive. The visiting police officer should comment after each role play.

7. **Debriefing:** After the activity, conduct a class discussion including the visiting police officer. Use the following questions as a guide:
   a. What have you learned about the kinds of jobs police officers are called upon to do?
   b. How did you feel when you played the police officer's role? The suspect's role? The role of a citizen in need of help?
   c. What different kinds of incidents have you been involved in or heard about that were not included in the simulation? How many involved violent crimes?
   d. What part do you believe fear plays in the interactions between police and community members? When do you think police officers are most afraid? What might cause police to be afraid? What causes others to fear the police? What could be done to reduce fear?
   e. What effect might police officers' fear have on their attitudes toward civil liberties? Politics? Suspects? Explain.
   f. Does fear of the police keep people from breaking the law? Why or why not?
   g. Try to describe the ideal police officer. Use examples from the game, from your own experiences, or from stories you have heard.
   h. Do you believe society might expect too much from the police? Why or why not?

8. **Follow-up:** As a follow-up activity, you might create additional "police calls" based on similar or typical incidents and have groups role play them for the class.

Police Officer's Oath

"As a law-enforcement officer, my fundamental duty is to serve humanity; to safeguard lives and property; to protect the innocent against deception, the weak against oppression or intimidation, and the peaceful against violence and disorder; and to respect everyone's constitutional rights to liberty, equality, and justice."

Departmental Regulations

On patrol, the police must try to enforce society's laws fairly, be polite and courteous to all citizens, follow procedures established by the courts and their superiors, solve many problems not connected with fighting crime, and respond to each call quickly and efficiently.

Cautions:
- Always be on guard to protect yourself, your partner, and other citizens from attack and injury.
- Handcuff anyone you take into custody.
- Be prepared for unusual public reactions when you are present.
- Treat all people firmly and fairly.
- Treat all people equally: The law is blind to race, sex, religion, and status.

Police Call: Group One

The police will be called to investigate a shoplifting incident.

Design an incident in which a shopkeeper has reported catching a youth shoplifting, and the police are called to the scene. Keep in mind the following questions:
1. How do you think a young person feels when caught shoplifting?
2. Should the police arrest the youth or do something less drastic, such as taking the youth home and talking to the parents, etc.? Explain.

3. Should people report all crimes that they know about? Why or why not?

4. What else could the shopkeeper have done instead of calling the police?

Police Call: Group Two

The police will stop a car with a broken tail light. The car, full of young people, is cruising suspiciously in a shopping district late at night.

Design an incident in which the police stop a car cruising suspiciously. Keep in mind the following questions:

1. What would give the police the right to stop the car?

2. Should the police treat the people in the car differently depending on their age, gender, or ethnic group?

3. How do you think innocent people will feel and act when they are stopped by the police?

Police Call: Group Three

The police will be called to calm a domestic quarrel between a husband and wife.

Design an incident in which a husband and wife fight violently enough for the neighbors to call the police. Keep in mind the following questions:

1. Considering that most murders happen in the home between people who know each other well, what special precautions should the police take?

2. How should police draw the line between private family matters and legitimate law-enforcement concerns?

3. Since many homes have at least one gun, how might the police protect themselves?

Police Call: Group Four

The police will be called to a bar on a drunk-and-disorderly call.

Design an incident involving a drunk, disorderly man in a bar who has threatened another person with violence. Keep in mind the following questions:

1. Does it make a difference to the police what neighborhood the bar is in?

2. Since much violent crime involves people who have been drinking, what precautions should police take?

3. If the drunk resists arrest, what should the police do?

4. If the call had said that the drunk was armed with a gun, how differently do you think the police would have reacted to the situation?

CHAPTER 5
Methods and Investigations

Local Police

In an emergency, most people call their local police department. Most communities have one. The departments range in size from one-person departments in rural areas to the almost 40,000 sworn officers that make up New York City's force, the largest in the nation. More than three-quarters of all law enforcement officers belong to local police departments.

Unlike larger departments, those with only a few members cannot offer services around the clock seven days a week. Their members must do work that would be done by special units elsewhere.

Although large cities account for only 1 percent of all police departments, they employ almost a quarter of all officers. The budgets for these large departments reflect their size. New York City spends almost $2 billion annually on its department.

Large police forces have many units and a set of regulations and policies, known as standard operating procedures, for all officers to follow. Most departments are organized with a military-type structure. The chain of command starts with the police commissioner or police chief and runs down through inspectors, captains, lieutenants, and sergeants to the patrol officers on the street. This chain of command can be quite effective in setting policies and operations. But in day-to-day encounters on the street, police do not usually wait for commands from above. They must act using their own discretion. Officers must be well-trained so that when they act, their actions fall within the department's regulations and policies.

Most large departments divide the workload into five basic units:

Traffic stops are normally routine, but on occasion they can turn violent.

1. **Operations** unit patrols the streets and investigates crimes. It is the largest unit in any department.

2. **Services** unit helps support the operations unit by training officers, keeping records, maintaining equipment, and (in the largest departments) running a crime laboratory.

3. **Administration** unit manages payroll, personnel, and finances.

4. **Internal Affairs** unit polices the police. It investigates any reports of wrongdoing by officers.

5. **Community Outreach** unit works on improving police-community relations. In recent years, many police departments have placed greater emphasis on improving relations and have developed special units for this purpose.

With most officers in operations, many departments have specialized operational divisions. As a general rule, the larger the department, the more special divisions it will have. The special divisions include:

Patrol. Most officers belong to the patrol unit. These uniformed officers patrol the streets, keep the peace within their assigned areas, and respond when a crime or other emergency is reported. Their very presence on the street helps prevent crime.

A patrol officer's job can be divided into three functions, which often overlap. The first is law enforcement, activities directly related to catching suspected criminals. A citizen reports a crime. Police respond. They make an arrest. They investigate the crime. These are the things people think police do most. But the other two functions take up much more of a patrol officer's time.

The second function is order maintenance. A person complains that a neighbor's stereo is too loud. Two people are having a dispute on the street. A large group of people are assembled in one place (for a parade, demonstration, or sporting event). An accident is blocking traffic. A homeless person is sleeping on a crowded sidewalk. Patrol officers must take care of these situations.

The final function is service. Someone asks for directions. A mother reports that her small child has wandered off. A motorist is stranded on the highway. Service is large part of the job. Patrol officers are usually the first to arrive at any emergency. They may have to do first aid. They may even take someone to the hospital. When people don't know who else to call, they call the police.

Detectives. After a period of working as a patrol officer, an officer may be assigned to the detective division. Detectives do not necessarily outrank patrol officers. But they have more prestige, they often get paid more, their hours are more flexible, and they work in plainclothes. They are strictly involved in one police function—law-enforcement investigations.

Although patrol officers investigate some crimes and usually initiate all investigations, detectives investigate serious crimes—robbery, rape, homicide. Special detective units may be set up for homicide, robbery, bunco, vice, auto theft, sex crimes, and narcotics.

They investigate crimes by collecting physical evidence, interviewing witnesses, contacting informants, checking criminal files, and talking with lab technicians and forensic scientists. In some cases, police stakeout locations or even work undercover (especially in drug and vice operations).

If a suspect is arrested, detectives help prepare the case for prosecution. If any suspect agrees to talk, they conduct the interrogation.

Traffic. From 3 to 10 percent of many departments consist of traffic officers. They enforce traffic laws, investigate accidents, and keep traffic moving. Most traffic stops are routine, ending with a ticket or warning. Some, however, uncover criminal suspects and can become violent.

Juvenile. Many departments have juvenile units. Officers in these units undergo special training in dealing with juveniles and in laws related to them. Officers exercise great discretion in deciding whether to take a juvenile into custody and whether the juvenile should be processed through the justice system.

On the Job

As most police department remain open around the clock seven days a week, police must work all hours and days. They usually work eight-hour shifts, which rotate week-to-week from day, swing, and graveyard. Officers can expect to work many holidays, especially New Year's and the Fourth of July, which may require the force to be on alert.

Police work is growing increasingly more complex. In the 1950s, an officer needed street smarts, good judgment on using force, and moral strength to resist the temptations that often arise on the job. A good officer today still needs all these qualities. In addition, the officer must know criminal law and procedure, be able to collect evidence properly, be familiar with forensic science, know how to interact with different people, and be able to mediate disputes and analyze crime problems.

Average Base Starting Salaries in Local Police Departments, by Size of Population Served				
Population served	Chief	Sergeant	Officer after 1 year	Entry-level officer
All	**$38,700**	**$32,300**	**$25,600**	**$23,300**
1,000,000 or more	100,700	47,500	34,000	30,600
500,000-999,999	87,600	42,900	32,000	29,300
250,000-499,999	80,900	45,500	33,000	30,600
100,000-249,999	74,700	43,900	33,200	30,500
50,000-99,999	70,600	44,700	33,300	30,500
25,000-49,999	63,000	42,600	32,500	29,200
10,000-24,999	53,200	38,100	29,900	26,400
2,500-9,999	40,000	31,400	25,800	23,500
Under 2,500	25,700	24,300	20,600	18,800

Source: "Local Police Departments 1997," Bureau of Justice Statistics (2000)

All departments require that applicants have at least a high school education. In 1973, the National Advisory Commission on Criminal Justice Standards and Goals recommended that every police agency require police officers to have completed four years of college. Today, about 30 percent of all officers belong to departments that require some college education.

Other requirements are usually a minimum age of 21, good physical condition, and no criminal record. Applicants must also pass an entrance examination and tests for drug use, mental fitness, and physical strength and agility. Most departments also conduct extensive background checks. To attract more women, most departments have done away with minimum height and weight requirements.

Policing has traditionally been a low-paying job, but in the 1960s many police started joining unions. Today about 75 percent of all officers belong to unions. Most states outlaw strikes by police. Even so, a few police strikes have taken place. Job actions like "blue flu" epidemics (officers calling in sick) and "ticket droughts" (officers not writing tickets) have occurred in many cities. Unionization has raised salaries, improved working conditions, and put grievance procedures in place.

Starting salaries average about $23,000. The top salary reaches around $50,000. But most police earn more than their base salary because of overtime work. In addition, many departments pay generous pension and disability benefits.

Minorities and Women

In 1950, only 2 percent of all police were minorities. Many departments openly refused to hire them. No department in the United States had a woman patrol officer.

The civil rights movement helped change this. In 1972, Congress passed Equal Employment Opportunity Act. It banned public employers from discriminating on account of race, national origin, religion, or gender. Most of the largest police departments have been sued under the act. Many cities are under court order to improve their hiring practices.

In addition, minorities in many cities have gained political power. They have used this power to ensure that departments have fair hiring practices.

By 1997, more than one-fifth of all police officers were minorities. The percentage of African Americans on police forces reflected their proportion of the population. Women made up 10 percent of all police. In cities of 1 million or more, they comprised 16 percent of the force.

No one today argues against the ability of minorities to perform police duties. Some, however, express such doubts about women. The main argument is that they are not strong or tough enough for police work. But studies have proved otherwise. They make as many arrests as men, and they do well in work

Local Police Officers

Race and Ethnicity	Male and Female
78.5% white	
11.7% black	90% male
7.8% Hispanic	10% female
2.1% other	

Source: "Local Police Departments 1997," Bureau of Justice Statistics (2000)

evaluations. Some even argue that they may make better officers than men because they're less confrontational and more adept at mediating disputes.

For Discussion

1. Some departments only hire officers who live in the area the police department serves. Why do you think they do this? Do you think it is a good idea? Explain.

2. Do you think police should have college degrees? Why or why not?

3. In 1973, the National Advisory Commission on Criminal Justice Standards and Goals recommended that police departments should try to get a workforce that reflects the ratio of minorities in the community. What are pluses and minuses of such a policy? Do you agree with it? Explain.

4. Do you think police forces should recruit female officers? Explain.

Community Policing

From the 1930s through the 1960s, most police departments in America went through a reform process that left them more disciplined and more professional. They began training programs designed to teach officers the latest policing techniques. They grew independent from political influence and corruption. Their hiring practices required that applicants have more education and go through a battery of psychological tests and background checks.

Also, by the 1950s, the police had come to rely heavily on squad cars, radio, and other technology. Their primary activity was responding to emergency calls. In some cities,

corruption scandals drove this change. Reformers felt that beat cops were too close to local criminals and too easy to corrupt. But economics accounted for much of the change. Through mobility and technology, reformers believed effective policing could be maintained with fewer officers.

The system that developed did away with foot patrols in favor of squad cars. Often called **proactive policing** or **motorized rapid response**, this approach relied on radio to direct cruising police cars to emergency calls. This meant that most officers had little contact with their communities, except when they were arresting suspects or investigating crimes. And what officers did see of a community was often from the window of a car.

By the 1980s, many people were criticizing the shortcomings of rapid motorized response. They felt this system left the police too divorced from the community and created a bitter "us and them" feeling on both sides. Cities began to experiment with different systems. They sent many officers back on beat patrols on foot, horseback, or even bicycle. They set up neighborhood mini-stations. They also tried to develop Neighborhood Watch programs of local residents who would watch over their communities and tell the police of any problems they could see developing.

The point of most of these new programs was to get the patrol officers to think in terms of patterns of criminal activity, not single radio calls for help. Officers would be visible continuously in an area, not just sent periodically into a community. And most of all, the officers would work actively to win local cooperation and look for causes of crime. This new type of policing was called community-oriented policing, or problem-oriented policing. It consists of three basic ideas.

1. Strengthening the community. First, the goal of community policing is to help make the community stronger. In a strong neighborhood, people care about what happens. They know one another and watch out for each other. They may sometimes call the police, but citizens do most of the "patrolling" when they are out and about in the community.

2. "Broken Windows" theory. In 1982, James Q. Wilson and George L. Kelling wrote a highly influential article in the *Atlantic Monthly* titled "Broken Windows." It advocated that police find out what bothers community members and focus on solving these problems. The problems often turn out to be seemingly unimportant things—graffiti, panhandlers, derelicts drinking on the corner—what Wilson and Kelling called "quality of life" issues. They explained this strategy by giving the example of a car left on the street with a broken window. They say that if the car is left in this condition, soon other windows will be broken and eventually the car will be torn apart. The unrepaired broken windows send a signal of neglect. Similarly, they claim that disorderly behavior, when ignored, leads to worse behavior and eventually to violent crime. This is because people view the neighborhood as out of control and stop going out. The street is taken over by drug dealers, prostitutes, and hoodlums.

3. Problem-oriented policing. Community policing stresses problem solving. The police must not just respond to incidents. For example, when residents of a Los Angeles neighborhood complained about graffiti, the police did not merely try to catch the taggers. They helped organize neighborhood groups into painting out graffiti immediately to discourage tagging.

Many police departments across the country have adopted community policing. Its growth was aided by the Violent Crime Control and Law Enforcement Act of 1994, which set up funding for 100,000 community police officers over six years. The methods of community policing vary from city to city.

New York's Emphasis on Accountability

The New York Police Department has a computer system that tracks crime block by block. Precinct commanders are held accountable for controlling crime in their precinct.

Since 1994, the top brass of the New York Police Department has met frequently with precinct commanders, examining the computerized crime statistics for each precinct. Commanders discuss tactics of what has worked and what hasn't. With the hot spots of crime mapped out, commanders send out patrol and plainclothes officers to make arrests on quality-of-life crimes in these areas.

The arrests have paid off. At first police found many people carried weapons who were arrested for drinking in public or other so-called quality-of-life crimes. Fewer people today risk carrying a gun, and fewer guns on street has resulted in fewer murders. Anyone arrested is questioned about other criminals and crimes. Intelligence about what was taking place in the criminal community grown.

With better intelligence, police started focusing on the criminal support system—the fences who sell stolen property, the chop shops that buy stolen cars, the gun dealers who supply weapons to criminals. Without the support system, crime fell.

With its full-scale attack on crime and quality-of-life issues, crime dropped dramatically. Between 1991 and 1998, the number of homicides fell from 29.31 to 8.60 per 100,000 people, a 70-percent drop. In 1999 and 2000, however, the homicide rate rose slightly. Even so, New York today claims to be the safest large city in the United States.

San Diego's Neighborhood Policing

With a much smaller department than New York's, the San Diego Police Department has taken a different approach to community policing. Its Neighborhood Policing program encourages a problem-solving partnership between citizens and police.

Citizens play an active role in crime prevention and detection. The SDPD has revitalized Neighborhood Watch programs, with community coordinators, watch coordinators, and block captains working together. More than 1,000 citizens have volunteered for more active roles. Some serve on citizen patrols, which go through neighborhoods looking for problem areas and suspicious activity. Others

Bicycle patrols are an important part of many cities' community policing.

work at police stations, freeing officers to go out in the community.

The police now have more time to work on solving crime problems. Officers are trained to identify a crime problem, learn as much as possible about it, develop a carefully planned response, and evaluate their response. In one case, officers discovered that the design of a trolley station contributed to the high rate of crime there. They presented the information to the transit board, which agreed to redesign the station.

Crime has since dropped at the station, as it has in San Diego in recent years. In 1990, 135 murders took place. By 1999, this number had dropped to 57.

Critics of Community Policing

Not everyone favors community policing. Some doubt that the drop in many cities' crime rates can be attributed to community policing, because crime has dropped every-where—even in places without community policing. They point to failed experiments such as Houston's "Neighborhood Oriented Policing." Disenchanted officers openly ridiculed it as "Nobody on Patrol." A new mayor was elected who vowed to end it, and it was abandoned in 1992. The mayor and new police chief's answer was more police on patrol. Houston's crime rate has plummeted since 1992.

Critics explain that communities must make a choice. Either they can have police respond rapidly to crime. Or they can have community policing. They cannot have both. It would cost too much. Community policing costs more than rapid-response policing, because more personnel is required than it takes to just respond to 911 calls and other reports of crimes.

Further, many police officers view community policing as social work that detracts from what they view as the real job of the police—to make arrests and solve crimes. They dismiss community policing as a misguided experiment that wastes personnel.

Finally, many in police leadership positions believe they are the experts on law enforcement. They are reluctant to share their power with non-experts in the community. Indeed, some citizens say that police depart-ments only pay lip service to community policing instead of actually getting involved with a neighborhood and its residents.

For Discussion

1. What are the advantages and disadvantages of community policing?

2. What are the advantages and disadvantages of motorized rapid response?

3. Why might some police officers prefer working in a department that uses commu-nity-oriented policing? Why might others prefer a department that uses motorized rapid response?

4. New York and San Diego exemplify two different styles of community policing. Which do you think is best? Why?

5. Which type of policing would you prefer in your community? Why?

Activity: Checking Out Community Policing

In this activity, students research and report on local or national efforts at commu-nity policing.

1. Break up into teams. Each team should

find a police department in your area that is putting into practice at least some part of community policing. (If there is none in your area, choose one of the major plans, such as New York, Chicago, San Diego, or Seattle and use the Internet or library to conduct your research.)

2. Look up articles in your local newspaper or local magazines about the system. Then talk to someone in the police department about their experiences.

3. As a team, prepare a report on the successes and failures of the local strategy. Divide the report so everyone gets to contribute.

4. Have the teams present their reports to the class.

Criminal Investigations

The goal of criminal investigations is not simply to catch criminals. Investigators must also collect evidence that can be used in court to convict them. If investigators don't follow proper procedures, they open themselves up to courtroom attack by defense attorneys. In some cases, if police don't follow proper procedures, the court will not even allow the evidence to be introduced.

Two of the most common investigatory techniques are searches and interrogation, or questioning, of suspects. Courts have set out special rules for these techniques. Chapter 6 will discuss them in detail, but we will touch on them here. We will mainly, however, take a look at some other techniques and issues of criminal investigation.

The Crime Scene
Patrol officers are almost always the first to arrive at a crime scene. They pursue suspects at the scene and make arrests. Or, more typically, they interview victims and witnesses and make a report. For most crimes, they are the only investigating officers. If the crime is serious or if patrol officers believe the case merits further investigation, they will call in detectives.

By the time detectives arrive, patrol officers have already conducted a preliminary investigation and secured the crime scene.

Securing the scene helps preserve the physical evidence. In an 1892 story, fictional detective Sherlock Holmes lamented about a crime scene: "Oh, how simple it would all have been had I been here before they came like a herd of buffalo and wallowed all over it." Today's detectives have powerful tools for combing a crime scene. They, even more than Holmes, place great importance on sealing off crime scenes from spectators and other officers. They cannot risk picking up fingerprints, footprints, and hair left behind by spectators and other officers who enter a crime scene.

The main job of detectives on the scene is to document it. They take statements from witnesses. They note conditions at the time of the crime. Were curtains open or closed? Were the lights on or off? Where was each piece of furniture? Many departments photograph and videotape crime scenes. All documentation goes into the case file.

Detectives must carefully mark all evidence taken from the scene—whether hair, blood, or the suspected murder weapon. They usually place items in special plastic envelopes. They seal each envelope, write the date and time, and sign it. Most evidence either goes to police evidence lockers or to crime labs. Each new person who takes custody of the envelope must also write the date and time and sign it. In this way, a chain of custody is established. When the evidence is introduced at trial, each custodian can be called to testify about what happened to the evidence while it was in that person's custody. The police can prove that the evidence wasn't tampered with. If police cannot establish a chain of custody, the evidence may not be allowed in evidence.

Lineups, Showups, and Throwdowns
If people witness a crime, detectives will try to get them to identify the suspect. They may call out a sketch artist to draw a picture of the suspect, based on descriptions of witnesses. Many departments today use software to create pictures of suspects. They also may call witnesses down to the precinct to look through books of mug shots.

If police catch a suspect, they will want eyewitnesses to identify the suspect. Beyond providing a strong basis for arrest, eyewitness identification resounds in the courtroom. "It's the most theatrical moment of the trial," says UCLA law professor John Wiley Jr. "Everybody in the jury box looks at the witness, looks at the [eyewitness's] finger and follows the line right to the defendant." Eyewitness identifications can make a case.

Yet experts have known for years that eyewitnesses are sometimes unreliable. Innocent people have gone to prison because witnesses wrongly identified them. Even witnesses who express absolute certainty can be mistaken. Our brains are not videotape recorders storing information perfectly. Psychologist Elizabeth Lofthus explained: "Every time we recall an event, we must reconstruct the memory and with each recollection the memory may be changed. . . . Thus our representation of the past takes on a living, shifting reality."

So investigators must be careful when getting identifications. They typically use three methods for witnesses to identify suspects—lineups, showups, and throw-downs. In a lineup, five or six people, one of whom is the suspect, stand on a stage so witnesses can view them. In a showup, the witness is shown a single suspect. In a throw-down, detectives show pictures for the witness to choose from.

All three methods can be highly suggestive. A showup gives the witness no possibility of choosing anyone but the suspect. A lineup can be just as suggestive if only one suspect resembles the description given by the witness or if officers hint who the "right one" is. Throw-downs can be equally as suggestive if officers give hints or fail to offer an array of photographs.

In the late 1960s and early 1970s, the U.S. Supreme Court made several rulings on lineups, showups, and throw-downs. In 1967 in *U.S. v. Wade*, the court held that a person indicted for a crime has the right to have an attorney present at a lineup. The court believed the attorney's presence would help prevent irregularities. Five years later, however, in the court in *Kirby v. Illinois* refused to extend the right to counsel for lineups held prior to an indictment.

The same year as *Kirby*, the court in *Neil v. Biggers* refused to overturn a conviction because the identification was based on a showup. The court stated that although showups were highly suggestive to witnesses, the "totality of the circumstances" showed that the identification was reliable. The court noted that the witness had not identified others at previous lineups, showups, and throw-downs and that the suspect fit the witness's prior description. The court had ruled similarly in the 1968 case of *Simmons v. U.S.* where witnesses made in-court identifications arguably based on previous exposure to a suggestive photographic array. The court held that "convictions based on eyewitness identification at trial following a pretrial identification by photograph will be set aside . . . only if the photographic identification procedure was so impermissibly suggestive as to give rise to a very substantial likelihood of irreparable misidentification." If there is not such a likelihood, then the evidence can be admitted and the jury is allowed to determine whether it is reliable.

Informants

Many police officers develop a network of informants, who give intelligence about what is going on in the criminal community. Most informants are low-level criminals involved in so-called "victimless crimes"—drugs, gambling, prostitution. Known derisively as "snitches," informants can provide information that an officer could get only by going undercover and working for months to gain the trust of criminals. Police can put the word out that they want information about a particular case or person. Informants often supply it.

Police commonly use informants to get search warrants. The Fourth Amendment protects against unreasonable searches and seizures. It requires warrants be issued only on "probable cause." This means that before a judge may issue a warrant, police must produce evidence of criminality that a reasonable person would believe. This is usually done in a sworn, written statement by a police officer.

The statement describes the place to be searched and things to be seized. It also sets forth the evidence of criminality. Often this evidence consists of the officer stating that a reliable informant has told the officer facts about a crime. The U.S. Supreme Court has held that such evidence is enough for a search warrant as long as the "totality of the circumstances" in the sworn statement show a "fair probability that contraband or evidence of a crime will be found in a particular place." (*Illinois v. Gates*, 1983)

Informants usually ask for something in return. Some informants get paid in cash. Police departments often have funds for informants. Other informants get charges against them dropped. Many police agencies agree not to arrest each others' informants as a professional courtesy.

Some critics condemn the use of informants for several reasons. Most informants are criminals, and critics question their reliability. Critics claim that informants often say what police want them to say. In addition, they point out that informants don't make good witnesses at trials because juries tend not to believe them. Informants themselves don't want to testify, because they don't want to be branded as a "snitch" and risk getting hurt by other criminals.

Critics particularly disapprove of jailhouse informants, those already in jail who testify that a cellmate has confessed. The U.S. Supreme Court has ruled that police cannot deliberately elicit incriminating statements from indicted defendants without their attorneys (*Massiah v. U.S.*, 1964). This means that police cannot send informants into cells to get confessions. But if cellmates without prior police contact offer information to police, their testimony can be used in court. Critics point to many celebrated cases of jailhouse informants helping convict innocent defendants.

Most police defend the use of informants as a necessary evil. Most also agree, however, that the practice must be closely controlled to prevent abuses.

For Discussion

1. What is a chain of custody? Why is it important?

2. What are lineups, showups, and throwdowns? Which do you think is the most reliable? Why?

3. What problems might arise from using informers? What can be done to prevent these problems?

Class Activity: Is This the One?

In this activity, students analyze police procedures for identifying suspects.

1. Break the class into pairs.

2. Each pair should:

   a. Read each of the cases below.

   b. For each case, discuss and answer:

      (1) Why might this identification be unreliable?

      (2) What should the police have done to make it more reliable?

      (3) Do you think the identification should be admitted in court? Explain.

3. Have the pairs report back and discuss each case as a whole group.

Case #1: Hospital Visit. An attacker in the victims' home slays the husband and severely wounds the wife. Police bring a suspect to the hospital handcuffed to a police officer. The suspect is the only African American in the room. An officer asks the wife whether the suspect is "the man." After the suspect repeats "a few words for voice identification," the wife identifies him as the attacker. At trial, the wife identifies the suspect. (*Stovall v. Denno*, 1967)

Case #2: Hallway. An undercover officer buys heroin from a dealer in a hallway lit only by natural light. The two stand two feet apart for about three minutes. Afterward, the officer describes the dealer to another officer as "a colored man, approximately five feet eleven inches tall, dark complexion, black hair, short Afro style, and having high cheekbones, and of heavy build." The other police officer thinks he recognizes the suspect from the description. He leaves a police photograph of the suspect for the undercover officer, who sees it two days later and identifies it as the picture of the dealer. In court, the officer identifies the suspect. (*Manson v. Brathwaite*, 1977)

Case #3: Lineups. At an initial lineup, the witness fails to identify the suspect. Police arrange a showup, at which the witness makes a tentative identification. Finally, at another lineup, the witness makes a definite identification of the suspect. (*Foster v. California*, 1969)

Crime Labs

Because of rapid developments in technology, particularly the computer, crime laboratories play an increasingly important role in investigating crimes. Today's computers allow huge amounts of data to be stored, compared, and retrieved quickly. Crime labs across the country are developing databases and linking them to one another.

More than 300 crime laboratories exist in this country. Every state and many large police departments run crime labs. The FBI operates the nation's largest, which examines evidence from other federal, state, and local agencies as well as from FBI cases.

The FBI divides its crime lab into units, each specializing in one area, like firearms, explosives, or hairs and fibers. One piece of evidence may be examined by several different units. All the units work together as a team, sharing their piece of the puzzle and trying to piece together as much information as they can discover about a crime or criminal. The following are some of the FBI crime lab units:

The Trace Evidence Unit. This examines hairs, fibers, ropes, cordage, feathers, plants, woods, soils, glass, and building materials. It usually gets evidence first so that tiny fibers, hairs, or other debris can be collected before they fall off and are destroyed. The evidence is taken to a sealed-off room where the temperature and humidity are controlled. Examiners carefully scrape it off with a metal spatula. Any hairs, fibers, or other debris fall on a clean sheet of paper and examiners mount them on microscope slides for study. The unit maintains huge collections of fibers, wig hair, human and animal hairs, feathers, ropes, woods, and seeds. Using the collections for comparison, examiners can sometimes re-create entire crime scenes. They can figure out what criminals were wearing and the color, length, and style of their hair. In the case of serial killer Ted Bundy, agents matched nearly 100 clothing fibers between Bundy and one of his victims. The match helped the jury connect Bundy to the crime and he was convicted.

Questioned Documents Unit. This examines anything that has to do with paper. The unit has many specialties, from determining what a piece of paper is made of to analyzing handwriting and breaking codes. It deals with machines that use paper, including typewriters, computers, copy machines, and printers. It also handles footprints and tire tracks since they leave marks behind on a surface, much like writing or typing on paper. It maintains collections of anonymous letters, bank robbery notes, fraudulent checks, office equipment, shoe prints, and tire tracks. The unit has solved many cases by studying indentations left by writing. In one case, a suspect had drawn a map to show her accomplice in a murder where to wait for the victim. The map was found, but it had to be connected to the suspect. When her belongings were searched, the police found a blank notebook. Agents studied the marks left by the machine that cut the paper and found that the map fit perfectly between the 12th and 14th pages. On the 14th page, they found indentations showing the map the woman had drawn. This linked the suspect to the crime.

Firearms and Toolmark Unit. This examines guns, ammunition, evidence with residue from gunshots, tools, motor vehicle numbers, and serial numbers. The unit maintains a collection of firearms, ammunition, and their

Identifying DNA Evidence

The list below identifies some common items of evidence police may need to collect, the possible location of the DNA on the evidence, and the biological source containing the cells. Only a few cells are needed to obtain useful DNA information. Just because a stain cannot be seen does not mean there are not enough cells for DNA typing.

Evidence	Possible Location of DNA on the Evidence	Source of DNA
baseball bat or similar weapon	handle, end	sweat, skin, blood, tissue
hat, bandanna, or mask	inside	sweat, hair, dandruff
eyeglasses	nose or ear pieces, lens	sweat, skin
facial tissue, cotton swab	surface area	mucus, blood, sweat, semen, ear wax
dirty laundry	surface area	blood, sweat, semen
toothpick	tips	saliva
used cigarette	cigarette butt	saliva
stamp or envelope	licked area	saliva
tape or ligature	inside/outside surface	skin, sweat
bottle, can, or glass	sides, mouthpiece	saliva, sweat
used condom	inside/outside surface	semen, vaginal cells
blanket, pillow, sheet	surface area	sweat, hair, semen, urine, saliva
"through and through" bullet	outside surface	blood, tissue
bite mark	person's skin or clothing	saliva
fingernail, partial fingernail	scrapings	blood, sweat, tissue

Source: "What Every Law Enforcement Officer Should Know About DNA Evidence," National Institute of Justice (1999)

distinctive markings. Its ballistics experts can tell what kind of a gun fired a bullet. If police have an alleged murder weapon, lab experts fire it into a tank of water. The water stops the bullet without disfiguring it. Experts then compare the bullet fired into the tank to those found at the crime scene. If the bullets match, they have found the murder weapon. Experts can also tell by the pattern of gunshot residue on the victim whether the shooter fired from close range. In addition, the unit examines marks made by tools. Every tool leaves it own distinct marks and can be identified. In one case, the unit showed that a series of bank robberies in Virginia were done by the same criminals because of the tool markings on the safe deposit boxes they pried open. A tip to one of the screwdrivers broke off at one robbery. When the suspects were arrested, police found the screwdriver. From this evidence, they were convicted.

Latent Print Unit. According to specialists, everyone has different fingerprints and they remain the same throughout life. This makes them excellent for identification. Since 1924, the FBI has had a fingerprint unit. Today,

experts have many methods for combing crime scenes for fingerprints, palm prints, footprints, and even lip prints. They can find prints using lasers, alternative light sources, and chemicals as well as dusting for prints with powders. Once they've discovered prints, experts compare them with the known prints of victims and suspects. In October 1993, Polly Klaas, a 12-year-old girl, was kidnaped from her home. Local police worked with FBI crime-scene experts to collect and analyze evidence. Using fluorescent powder, special goggles, and an alternative light source, agents found a partial palm print on the girl's bunk bed. But the print didn't do much good without a suspect to match it to. Two months later, police learned that a car had been stuck on a nearby road on the night of the kidnaping. From a computer, detectives found out that the car belonged to Richard Allen Davis, who had a police record and prints on file. The palm print matched. When Davis read about the match in a newspaper, he called a detective and confessed to kidnaping and killing Polly Klaas. Davis was convicted and sentenced to death. Today, new technology is making automated identification of fingerprints possible. A national database will soon be used to match prints automatically from all 50 states.

DNA Units. DNA (deoxyribonucleic acid) is the genetic code that determines a person's physical characteristics. No two people, except for identical twins, have identical DNA. Each human cell holds the complete genetic blueprint for an individual. Each cell contains 3 billion "base pairs," the building blocks of DNA. Current technology cannot chart all these pairs, but instead charts a few selected areas. From a small amount of blood, saliva, semen, skin, fingernail, or hair, scientists can make a DNA profile, which looks like a bar code. The DNA profile from a suspect can be compared to DNA found at the crime scene. If they don't match, then the suspect is cleared. In recent years, DNA has played a major role in clearing innocent suspects and freeing wrongly convicted prisoners. If the suspect's and crime scene's DNA do match, this does not necessarily mean the DNA at the crime scene belongs to the suspect. Since the profile charts only a few sections of DNA, conceivably other people could share the same DNA profile. Scientists calculate the odds. The odds can sometimes run as high as 1 in 20 billion and make the match almost certain. Contamination can be a problem if people collecting and storing DNA evidence do not follow proper procedures. Once DNA evidence gets to a lab, poor lab procedures can cause mistakes, but today this seems less likely. A National Academy of Sciences report concluded that overall lab procedures were "fundamentally sound."

For Discussion

1. Which unit do you think is most important? Why?

2. Do you know of any other aspects of crime labs not mentioned in the article?

Class Activity: DNA From Everyone Arrested?

DNA would be a more powerful weapon for law enforcement if more people's DNA profiles were available on a database. At present, most people's DNA is not on file. The procedure for getting a DNA profile is simple and non-intrusive. A technician simply brushes a cotton swab against the inside of a person's mouth. The sample is sent to a crime lab, which makes the profile. England now requires everyone arrested to give a DNA sample. This has resulted in more than half a million new DNA profiles since 1995, and police have linked DNA from crime scenes to 70,000 suspects in their database. Some propose that jurisdictions in the United States require everyone arrested to give DNA samples. The American Civil Liberties Union opposes this. Barry Steinhardt, associate director of the ACLU, stated: "While DNA databases may be useful to identify criminals, I am skeptical that we will ward off the temptation to expand their use. In the last ten years alone we have gone from collecting DNA only from convicted sex offenders to now including people who have been arrested but never convicted of a crime. There have even been proposals to store newborns' DNA for future use by law enforcement."

In this activity, students evaluate the pros and cons of requiring DNA from those arrested.

1. Form small groups.

2. Each group should:

    a. Discuss the pros and cons of the requiring DNA from everyone who is arrested.

    b. Decide whether to support or oppose this proposal.

    c. Prepare to discuss its decision and the reasons for it with the class.

3. Have the groups report back.

4. Conclude the activity by having students vote on whether they think this proposal should be adopted in their state.

CHAPTER 6
Police and the Law

Criminal Procedure

There are two areas of law that police officers must study. One is criminal law, which you learned about in Unit One. It defines which acts are illegal. Because police enforce the criminal law, they must know it. The second area of law that police must study is criminal procedure.

Criminal procedure deals with procedures for arrests, trials, and appeals. It sets out the rules for processing someone through the criminal justice system. Because illegal arrest or investigation procedures may jeopardize a criminal case, the police must pay close attention to criminal procedure.

Criminal procedure comes from a variety of sources, including federal and state statutes. Most importantly, it comes from the U.S. and state constitutions. Appellate courts interpret these statutes and constitutions when criminal defendants appeal their convictions claiming that their constitutional rights have been violated. Deciding these cases, appellate courts produce rules that police and criminal trial courts must follow. As the highest appellate court in the land, the U.S. Supreme Court often decides whether particular criminal procedures meet the U.S. constitutional standards of the Bill of Rights, particularly the Fourth, Fifth, and Sixth amendments.

Originally, the Bill of Rights only applied to the federal government. But after the Civil War, the 14th Amendment was added to the Constitution. Its so-called "due process clause" declares that no state shall "deprive any person of life, liberty, or property, without due process of law. . . ." This means that states cannot deprive people of certain rights. But what rights does the 14th Amendment's due process clause include?

In the 1930s, the Supreme Court ruled that the clause **incorporates** those guarantees in the Bill of Rights that are "rooted in the tradition and conscience of our people." (*Palko v. Connecticut*, 1937.) Since that time, the Supreme Court has decided on a case-by-case basis which rights in the Bill of Rights were fundamental and were therefore rights that every state had to grant to individuals.

In a series of landmark cases beginning in the 1960s, the Supreme Court applied almost

Rights Incorporated by the 14th Amendment			
Rights	**Amendment**	**Supreme Court Decision**	**Date**
Freedom of Speech & Press	First	*Gitlow v. New York*	(1925)
Defense Counsel in Capital Cases	Sixth	*Powell v. Alabama*	(1932)
Free Exercise of Religion	First	*Hamilton v. Regents of U.C.*	(1934)
Freedom of Assembly & Petition	First	*DeJonge v. Oregon*	(1937)
Freedom from Establishment of Religion	First	*Everson v. Board of Education*	(1947)
Public Trial	Sixth	*In re Oliver*	(1948)
Protection Against Unreasonable Searches and Seizures	Fourth	*Mapp v. Ohio*	(1961)
Protection from Cruel & Unusual Punishments	Eighth	*Robinson v. California*	(1962)
Defense Counsel for Felonies	Sixth	*Gideon v. Wainwright*	(1963)
Privilege Against Self-Incrimination	Fifth	*Malloy v. Hogan*	(1964)
Confrontation of Witnesses	Sixth	*Pointer v. Texas*	(1965)
Impartial Jury Trial	Sixth	*Parker v. Gladden*	(1966)
Speedy Trial	Sixth	*Klopfer v. North Carolina*	(1967)
Compulsory Process in Obtaining Witness	Sixth	*Washington v. Texas*	(1967)
Trial by Jury	Sixth	*Duncan v. Lousiana*	(1968)
No Double Jeopardy	Fifth	*Benton v. Maryland*	(1969)
Defense Counsel for Crimes with Jail Terms	Sixth	*Argersinger v. Hamlin*	(1972)

all the rights found in the Fourth, Fifth, and Sixth amendments to the states. Not only did the court apply these rights to the states, it also strengthened them. When speaking of the court, it should be noted that not every justice on the court agreed with all of these decisions. Some justices complained that strengthening the constitutional rights of individuals made law enforcement too difficult. But the majority stressed the need for the police to respect rights. The court made so many profound changes that the era marked a revolution in criminal procedure.

Following the 1960s when the rights of criminal suspects and defendants rapidly expanded, the court changed. New justices were appointed to the court forming a new majority. Although these justices did not directly overturn the decisions of the 1960s, they often restricted them. So while the court minority complained that the court was eroding basic rights, the new majority stressed the need for crime control.

This tension on the court reflects the tension between the two, often conflicting, goals of the criminal justice system: protecting society from criminals and protecting the constitutional rights of those being processed through the system. Criminal procedure attempts to achieve both.

For Discussion

1. What is the difference between criminal law and criminal procedure?

2. How do appellate courts create rules of criminal procedure?

3. What are the two, often conflicting, goals of the criminal procedure? How might they conflict? Which do you think is more important? Why?

The Law of Search and Seizure

One of the most important and complex areas of criminal procedure comes from the Fourth Amendment. This amendment affects how police officers investigate crimes and gather evidence, because the Supreme Court has ruled that illegally seized evidence may not be used at trial. The Fourth Amendment provides:

The right of the people to be secure in their persons, houses, papers, and effects, against unreasonable searches and seizures shall not be violated, and no Warrants shall issue, but upon probable cause, supported by Oath or affirmation, and particularly describing the place to be searched, and the persons or things to be seized.

All police searches, seizures of evidence, and arrests must comply with this amendment. Courts have interpreted the amendment's meaning in hundreds of search-and-seizure cases. These interpretations have grown into a full body of law, known as the law of search and seizure. Although the law is complicated, determining whether a search or seizure is legal comes down to two basic questions:

- Has a governmental search or seizure taken place?

- If so, was the search or seizure reasonable?

In the sections that follow, you will learn how to answer these questions for most searches or seizures.

Has a Search or Seizure Taken Place?

To be a search or seizure under the Fourth Amendment, it must be (1) done by a government employee or agent **and** (2) it must fit the courts' definition of a search or seizure. We will examine each of these issues.

Did a government employee or agent conduct the search or seizure?

The first step in analyzing search-and-seizure problems is to determine who conducted the search or seizure. The Fourth Amendment protects citizens from actions by government officials. The Fourth Amendment does not usually cover actions by private

Police do a pat-down search checking for weapons. Every search must conform to Fourth Amendment standards.

individuals. If, for example, your neighbor breaks into your house, finds evidence of a crime, and turns it in to the police, your rights under the Fourth Amendment would not have been violated. If you were prosecuted, this evidence could be used against you at trial. Of course, the police could also arrest the person who broke into your house for burglary, and you could sue the person in civil court.

Note, however, that if the police had requested your neighbor to break into your house, then Fourth Amendment protections would come into play. The neighbor would be considered an agent of the government.

Was it a search or seizure as defined by the courts?

The Fourth Amendment protects people from unreasonable searches and seizures of their "persons, houses, papers, and effects." But what is a "search"? What is a "seizure"? The next consideration is to decide whether a government official's conduct amounted to a search or seizure.

In the landmark case of *Katz v. U.S.* in 1967, the Supreme Court defined a search as any governmental intrusion into something in

which a person has **a reasonable expectation of privacy**. This privacy interest covers places and things such as houses, yards, garages, apartments, diaries, briefcases, and mail.

The court has held, however, that there is no reasonable expectation of privacy in places or things that are in **plain view**. For example, a person growing a four-foot-high marijuana plant in a front bay window cannot claim that a search was conducted if a police officer spots it from the street. But officers who detect things in plain view must do so from places they have a legal right to be in. For instance, if an officer climbs over an eight-foot fence surrounding a yard and spots marijuana growing in some back corner, a search has taken place. Persons normally have a reasonable expectation of privacy in their private property that cannot be seen except by trespassing.

But the court has held there is no reasonable expectation of privacy for **open fields** away from a residence. Even though they are private property, they usually are readily accessible to the public. Thus police walking through open fields are not conducting a search.

A similar rule applies to **abandoned property**. For example, if a person placed letters containing incriminating statements into the trash, the police could retrieve them from the garbage dump without having conducted a search. There is no reasonable expectation of privacy in such items.

The idea of "seizure" is somewhat easier to understand. A seizure is any taking into possession, custody, or control. Property may be seized, but so may people. An arrest is one form of seizure, because in making an arrest, the police take someone into custody. Thus arrests fall under the requirements imposed by the Fourth Amendment.

For Discussion

1. What is the difference between a search and a seizure?

2. The Supreme Court has ruled that the police have **not** conducted a search if the object is in plain view, in an open field, or has been abandoned. Why does the court say this in each instance? Do you agree? Why or why not?

3. Why do you think the Fourth Amendment protects only against intrusions by the government? Are these intrusions more dangerous than intrusions by individuals? Why or why not?

4. For each of the following, decide whether a search or seizure has taken place and explain why or why not. Don't be concerned whether it was legal.

   a. A police officer arrests Mary Clark for shoplifting.

   b. Lois Kindel, a custodian at the Shadyville Police Department, believes her neighbor deals drugs. She tells police but they have no evidence. She agrees to keep a close watch on her neighbor. One day she spots a marijuana plant, which has grown taller than her neighbor's fence.

   c. Officer Sanchez climbs a hill in a public park and spots three stolen cars in a nearby backyard surrounded by a 10-foot-high fence.

   d. On surprising George Meyers, a known narcotics dealer, police observe him swallow several capsules. They take him to the hospital and have his stomach pumped.

   e. The police stop Anna and question her for a few minutes about where she's been and what she has been doing the past few days. (Anna has been arrested twice in the last year for prostitution but has never been convicted.)

Class Activity: Is It a Search?

In this activity, students analyze and research cases to determine whether a search or seizure has taken place.

1. Divide the class into groups of seven.

2. Each group should:

   a. Discuss each of the cases below and decide if a search or seizure has taken place in the following situations.

   b. Assign each group member one of the cases cited to look up. The cases can be found on the Internet or at a law library. A good place to start Internet research is Research Links or *Criminal Justice in America* Links on Constitutional Rights Foundation's web site (www.crf-usa.org). Law libraries can be found at law schools and at county and municipal courts. (The librarian can help you find the cases you are looking for.)

3. After researching, students should meet in one of seven groups according to the case they looked up. In this "expert" group, students should:

a. Discuss the case and prepare to report on it to the class.

b. Assign one person to report on the facts of the case, another to report on what the court majority decided and why, and another on what the court dissenters believed and why. Finally, each member should state how he or she would have decided the case and why.

Cases

a. Unable to see over Mike's 10-foot-high fence, police hire a plane and fly over the house at 1,000 feet and see marijuana plants growing in the backyard. See *California v. Ciraolo* (1986) and *Florida v. Riley* (1989).

b. Police install a device at the phone company office that keeps track of the numbers that Gilbert dials from his home phone. See *Smith v. Maryland* (1979).

c. Suspecting drug dealing, police have the trash collector turn over Bill's trash to them instead of throwing it in the trash truck. See *California v. Greenwood* (1988).

d. The FBI listens to Joe's conversation by attaching an electronic eavesdropping device to the outside of the public telephone booth he uses at 11 a.m. every day. See *Katz v. U.S.* (1967).

e. Investigating a shooting, police legally enter an apartment looking for weapons and the shooter. While inside, an officer spots a high-priced stereo that seems out of place in the rundown apartment. The officer picks it up, jots down the serial number, puts it down, calls headquarters, and finds out the stereo is stolen. See *Arizona v. Hicks* (1987).

f. Oliver posts "no trespassing" signs around his land and locks the gate to his property. Police go onto a highly secluded part of his land about a mile from his house and find marijuana plants growing. See *Oliver v. U.S.* (1984).

g. A Border Patrol agent boards a bus in Texas. As he walks down the aisle, he squeezes the luggage that passengers have stored above their seats. When he squeezes Bond's bag, he feels a suspicious "brick-like" object, which the agent believes to be a "brick" of methamphetamine. See *Bond v. U.S.* (2000).

Debriefing Questions

1. What is the test used by the Supreme Court to determine whether a search has taken place?

2. Do you think this is a good test? Explain.

3. Do you think the Supreme Court has applied this test satisfactorily in these cases? Why or why not?

Is the Search or Seizure Reasonable?

After a court determines that a search or seizure has taken place, then it must determine whether it was reasonable. This section will help you analyze whether searches or seizures are reasonable.

Was the search or seizure conducted pursuant to a warrant?

In general, courts have held that a search or seizure is unreasonable without a **warrant**. A warrant is a court order issued by a judge authorizing a search, an arrest, or a seizure of evidence. Warrants must specifically describe the place to be searched or the person to be seized.

Before issuing a warrant, a judge must receive evidence presented under oath—usually supplied by a police officer. The evidence must show that there is probable cause to believe that:

(1) a crime has been or is about to be committed, *and*

(2) the person, place, or thing to be searched or seized is related to that crime.

Probable cause means that the evidence must be strong enough that an independent, cautious person would have good reason to believe it.

Police prepare to break down a door during a drug raid. To search a house, police normally need a search warrant.

Once the police get a search warrant, they must carry out the search promptly—usually within 72 or 96 hours, depending on the state. Many states allow police to execute warrants only during daytime hours except in special cases. Police must normally announce that they have a warrant. But they can forgo this formality if they have reason to believe that a fugitive is hiding out or that evidence is being destroyed. In most jurisdictions, the police may forcibly enter a place when no one will let them in.

If police do not obtain a warrant, does one of the court-recognized exceptions to the warrant requirement apply?

The courts do not require police to obtain a warrant before every search and seizure (though probable cause is still required in almost all cases). Over the years, courts have created exceptions to the warrant requirement. They have made these exceptions for several reasons:

- to protect the safety of officers and the public.

- to ensure that evidence will be seized before it can be hidden or destroyed.

- to help apprehend suspects or prevent their escape.

In determining whether a warrantless search or seizure is reasonable, courts weigh the need for immediate police action against the invasion of individual privacy involved. Here is one such case.

U.S. v. Ross (1982)

Late one evening, a reliable informant telephoned Detective Marcum and told him that an individual known as "Bandit" was selling drugs. The informant had just seen Bandit complete a narcotics sale, and Bandit had told him that he had more drugs in the trunk of his car. The informant gave the detective a detailed description of Bandit, described his car as a maroon Chevrolet Malibu, and told Marcum the address where it was parked.

Detective Marcum, along with two other police officers, immediately drove to the address and found a parked maroon Malibu. A license check disclosed that the car was registered to Albert Ross. A computer check on Ross revealed that he fit the informant's description and was known to use the alias "Bandit." The officers cruised through the neighborhood, but did not see anyone matching Ross' description.

When they returned to the address, they saw the maroon Malibu going down the street. They pulled alongside the Malibu, saw that the driver matched the informant's description, and stopped the car. They ordered Ross out of the car. While the officers were searching him, Detective Marcum noticed a bullet on the car's front seat. Marcum took Ross' keys and opened the trunk, where he found a closed brown paper bag. He opened the bag and discovered many cellophane envelopes containing white powder.

Later at the police station, the officers thoroughly searched the car again. They discovered a red leather pouch in the trunk. Unzipping the pouch, they found $3,200 in cash.

A teenager is standing on the corner in a high-crime area. Suddenly, he sees a police car. He runs. Can the police chase him just because he ran? Or do they need more evidence that he is involved in criminal activity?

In 2000 in *Illinois v. Wardlow*, the U.S. Supreme Court ruled on these questions. Sam Wardlow was standing in front of a house in a high-crime neighborhood at about noon. When four police cars rounded the corner, he took off running. Officers caught him, patted him down, and found a loaded gun. Arrested, charged, and convicted of a weapons crime, Wardlow appealed. He argued that the police had no right to stop him. A state appellate court agreed, ruling that officers did not have reasonable suspicion to make a stop and frisk. The Illinois Supreme Court affirmed, determining that sudden flight in a high crime area does not create a reasonable suspicion justifying a stop because flight may simply be an exercise of the right to "go on one's way."

In a 5–4 decision, the U.S. Supreme Court upheld the stop and frisk, declaring that the officers' actions did not violate the Fourth Amendment. The court ruled that, given the circumstances, the officers had reasonable suspicion that criminal activity was taking place. (This is the standard for stop and frisks, set by the 1968 case of *Terry v. Ohio*.) Being in a high-crime area is a factor, said the court, but not enough by itself for reasonable suspicion. "Nervous, evasive behavior is another pertinent factor in determining reasonable suspicion . . . and headlong flight is the consummate act of evasion. . . . Such a holding is consistent with the decision in *Florida v. Royer* . . . that an individual, when approached, has a right to ignore the police and go about his business. Unprovoked flight is the exact opposite of 'going about one's business.'"

For Discussion

1. Why might people in high-crime areas run when they see police?

2. Do you think the circumstances in *Wardlow* gave officers reasonable suspicion that criminal activity was going on? Explain.

The police laboratory later determined that the powder in the cellophane envelopes was heroin. Ross was charged with possession of heroin with intent to distribute.

The police had never obtained a search warrant, and Ross claimed the searches were unreasonable. He made a motion to suppress the heroin and the cash from evidence at his trial.

For Discussion

1. What do police officers have to prove before they can get a warrant from a judge?

2. Why do you think courts require police officers to obtain warrants?

3. Did Detective Marcum's opening of Bandit's car trunk constitute a search?

What about the brown paper bag? The cellophane envelopes? Explain your answers.

4. Assume that opening the trunk, brown bag, and cellophane envelopes were searches. Do you think they were reasonable under the circumstances or should the officers have secured a warrant first? Why?

5. Was unzipping the red leather pouch at the police station a search? If so, was it reasonable under the circumstances or should the officers have obtained a warrant first? Why?

The U.S. Supreme Court has ruled that police do not need a warrant to search a vehicle, but must have probable cause.

Motor Vehicle and Other Exceptions

The U.S. Supreme Court decided *U.S. v. Ross* in 1982. In a 6–3 decision, the court ruled that the searches and seizures were reasonable and did not violate Ross' Fourth Amendment rights. Police officers who have legitimately stopped an automobile (as they did in this case) and who have probable cause to believe that contraband is concealed somewhere within it (as they did in this case) may conduct a warrantless search of the vehicle.

In addition, when police have probable cause to search a vehicle, they may conduct a warrantless search of every part of the vehicle and its contents. This includes all containers and packages that may conceal whatever the police are searching for. But it excludes containers that could not hold what they are looking for. For example, probable cause to believe that undocumented aliens are being transported in a van will not justify a warrantless search of a suitcase in the van.

Justice White argued in dissent:

The majority . . . not only repeals all realis-

tic limits on warrantless automobile searches, it repeals the Fourth Amendment warrant requirement itself. By equating a police officer's estimation of probable cause with a magistrate's, the Court utterly disregards the value of a neutral and detached magistrate . . . .

The court simply ignores the critical function that a magistrate serves. And although the Court purports to rely on the mobility of an automobile and impracticability of obtaining a warrant, it never explains why these concerns permit the warrantless search of a container, which can easily be seized and immobilized while the police are obtaining a warrant.

Justice Marshall disagreed with the decision as well. In his dissenting opinion, he warned that the majority ruling would have "profound implications for the privacy of citizens traveling in automobiles."

The *Ross* case removed the warrant requirement for **motor vehicle searches**. The court made this exception because, if the police had to wait to get a warrant, motor vehicles could easily be moved and any evidence in them concealed or destroyed. (Of course, before searching any vehicle, police must still have probable cause to believe it was used in the commission of a crime or it contains evidence of a crime.)

Other Recognized Exceptions

There are other situations in which searches and seizures may be conducted without a warrant:

Searches Incident to Lawful Arrests. In *Chimel v. California* (1969), the U.S. Supreme Court held that searches and seizures incident to lawful arrests may be done without a warrant. The court said: "When an arrest is made, it is reasonable for the arresting officer to search the person arrested in order to remove any weapons that the latter might seek to use in order to resist arrest or effect his escape [and to] seize any evidence on the arrestee's person in order to prevent its concealment or destruction." These so-called "Chimel searches" may extend to everything within the area of the arrestee's immediate control. Questions sometimes arise as to whether the arrest itself was lawful. If it was not, any search conducted along with it would not be valid.

Examples:

Reasonable Search: Didi is arrested outside of Elliot's Department Store for shoplifting. Without a warrant, the police search the book bag she is carrying.

Unreasonable Search: Didi is arrested outside of Elliot's Department Store for shoplifting. The police go to her home, a block away, and search her bedroom. (The search is not *incident* to the arrest. The police could have obtained a warrant if they had probable cause to believe there was evidence of a crime in the house.)

Stop and Frisk. In certain cases, the police may stop and frisk, or pat down, the outer layers of a person's clothing without making an arrest. "[W]here a police officer observes unusual conduct which leads him reasonably to conclude in light of his experience that criminal activity may be afoot and that the persons with whom he is dealing may be *armed*

and *presently dangerous* . . . he is entitled for the protection of himself and others in the area to conduct a carefully limited search of the outer clothing of such persons in an attempt to discover weapons which might be used to assault him." (*Terry v. Ohio*, 1968, emphasis added.) Thus a brief stop and frisk does not require probable cause—evidence strong enough to give a careful person good reason to believe it. A stop or frisk requires reasonable suspicion—evidence that would make an experienced police officer suspicious. Most searches and seizures require probable cause.

Examples:

Reasonable Search: The police see Fritz run out of a dark alley at 3 a.m. They stop him, ask him who he is and what he has been doing, and frisk his outer clothing. In doing so, the officers detect what feels like a large metal object in his coat pocket. They reach inside and pull out a gun.

Unreasonable Search: The police see Fritz run out of a dark alley at 3 a.m. They stop and frisk him. In doing so, the officers detect what feels like a plastic bag in his coat pocket. They reach inside and pull out a small bag of marijuana. (Because of the nature of the object, it could not possibly have been a dangerous weapon.)

Unreasonable Search: Police receive an anonymous telephone tip that J.L., a juvenile unknown to officers, is carrying a handgun. The anonymous tipster describes J.L. and says he is at a bus stop. Police find J.L. at the bus stop, frisk him, and find a gun. (The officers' suspicion was not reasonable because it was not based on any observations of their own

Ask an Expert

Invite a prosecutor, defense attorney, or police officer to visit your classroom and briefly discuss search-and-seizure law with you. Then have the resource expert take part in the class activity "Applying the Checklist." The attorney can help pairs of students and discuss each case when the activity ends.

but only on a call made by an unknown caller. *Florida v. J.L.*, 2000.)

Consent. The police may search without a warrant if the person "knowingly and voluntarily" consents. (But these searches are not reasonable if the police use deception or fraud to get the person's consent.) Sometimes an individual may consent to a search of someone else's property if the consenting party owns or shares the property with the one being searched.

Examples:

Reasonable Search: The police stop Luis on the highway for driving with a broken brake light. They ask him to open his glove compartment. Luis opens it and the officers look inside.

Reasonable Search: Without a warrant, the police go to Meg's house and ask her parents if they can search her room for illegal drugs that they believe she has been selling at school. Meg's parents let the officers in to search.

Unreasonable Search: Mike and Murray are roommates in a two-bedroom apartment. The police go to their apartment and ask Mike to let them search Murray's bedroom and file cabinet. Mike consents to the search. (Though they share the common areas of the apartment, Mike has no right to consent to a search of Murray's private space.)

Hot Pursuit. Police in hot pursuit of a criminal do not need a warrant to enter a place where they saw the suspect go.

Examples:

Reasonable Search: The police see Josie knock down an old lady, hit her with a lead pipe, and take her purse. They chase Josie into a building about a mile away and see her run into apartment #10B. When she refuses to answer, the officers kick down the door.

Unreasonable Search: Mrs. Thackaberry reports that someone broke into her mailbox and stole her Social Security check. The police suspect Josie, a known robber of the elderly. They trail her for a few days and finally follow her into an apartment building where she often goes. The police knock on the door to #10B, but Josie won't let them in. The police kick down the door. (There is no "hot pursuit" in this case. The police were only following a lead and could have gotten a warrant.)

Emergency situations. Police do not need a warrant to conduct a search or seizure in emergency situations.

Examples:

Reasonable Search: An officer on the beat hears a woman's loud screams and the sound of shattering glass coming from a trailer home. He radios for help and then opens the front door to see what is happening.

Unreasonable Search: The police are concerned about gang violence at Jackson High School. Three students have been killed already. The police hear that a fight between two rival gangs is supposed to take place on Friday. The day before, they ask the principal of Jackson High to assemble all students in the gym. Without a warrant, the officers then open all the lockers with a passkey and search for dangerous weapons. (The police are not reacting to an immediate emergency.)

A number of other kinds of searches have been held to be reasonable by the courts. They include:

• **Airline searches** of passengers and carry-on baggage by means of metal detectors, physical pat-downs, or drug-sniffing dogs.

• **Border searches** by immigration control officers within areas reasonably close to U.S. international boundaries.

• **Customs searches** at borders, ports, and international airports by U.S. customs agents.

For Discussion

1. What reasons does the court consider in making exceptions to the warrant requirement? What are the dangers in making exceptions?

2. Why did the court carve out an exception to the warrant requirement in automobile searches? What reasons did the dissenters give in opposing it? Do you agree with the decision in *Ross*? Why or why not?

A Search and Seizure Checklist

This checklist provides a summary analysis of whether the Fourth Amendment has been violated. Use the checklist to help you determine the legality of searches and seizures.

1. Has a search or seizure taken place?
- Did a government employee or agent conduct the search or seizure?
  [If NO, then no violation]
- Was it a search or seizure as defined by the courts?
  - Did the person have a reasonable expectation of privacy?
    [If NO, then no violation]
  - Was the item . . .
    ____in plain view?
    ____in an open field?
    ____abandoned?
    [If YES to any of these, then no violation]

2. Was the search or seizure reasonable?
- Was the search or seizure conducted with a valid warrant?
  [If YES, then no violation]
- If not, does one of the court recognized exceptions to the warrant requirement apply?
  ____Motor Vehicles
  ____Incident to a Lawful Arrest
  ____Stop and Frisk
  ____Consent
  ____Hot Pursuit
  ____Emergency Circumstances
  ____Border Searches
  ____Airline/Security Searches
  [If YES, then no violation]

3. The court has carved out several other exceptions: searches incident to a lawful arrest, stop and frisks, consent searches, searches done in hot pursuit, searches in emergency circumstances, border searches, and airline security searches. Do you disagree with any of these exceptions? Why or why not?

Class Activity: Applying the Checklist

In this activity, students apply the Search and Seizure Checklist to evaluate the legality of some hypothetical search and seizures.

1. Divide the class into pairs.

2. As a pair, do the following:

   a. Review the checklist on this page and what you have learned about search-and-seizure law.

   b. Analyze the following cases and decide if any Fourth Amendment violations have occurred.

   c. Be prepared to explain your answers and discuss any differences of opinion that may arise.

3. Regroup the class and discuss each case.

Case 1: Hans Metcalf. Smith and Houston, special investigators from the district attorney's office, had been following Hans Metcalf, a suspected bookie. They saw him enter a telephone booth with a briefcase in his hand and make a short call. He then left the phone booth, but without his briefcase. Smith and Houston rushed to the phone booth, opened the briefcase, and found several bundles of betting slips. Just then, Metcalf returned to retrieve his briefcase and he was arrested.

Case 2: Vivian Madison. Mary Krensy was angry with her roommate, Vivian Madison. She went to the police and offered to show them where Vivian was hiding 50 stolen holiday turkeys. The police accompanied her to the garage both women shared and discovered 50 turkeys reported stolen from the Henderson Poultry Company. The police confiscated the poultry and placed Vivian under arrest.

Case 3: Dan Lewis. Officer Hanano was on patrol late at night. Suddenly, she spotted a house trailer behind, but not attached to, a car with no license plates. On closer inspection, she noticed a thin wisp of smoke escaping from one of the trailer windows. She walked to the door and knocked a few times. A voice called back, "Go away!" The officer forced opened the door and found a young man preparing a liquid substance in a makeshift laboratory. Officer Hanano arrested the man, whose name is Dan Lewis, for the manufacture of illegal drugs.

Case 4: Betty Kim. Acting on an informant's tip that Betty Kim was receiving stolen property, Detective Drebs went to her apartment to talk to her. She invited him in, but when he started to poke around the living room she screamed, "I said you could talk, not search the place. Get out!" He grabbed, handcuffed, and frisked her. He found a scout knife in her pants pocket and arrested her for disturbing the peace and carrying a concealed weapon. He then searched the living room and found a stolen stereo receiver.

Interrogation and Confessions

Another important area of criminal procedure comes from the Fifth Amendment to the U.S. Constitution. Part of this amendment says "(no) person . . . shall be compelled in any criminal case to be a witness against himself. . . ." This means that unless you agree to talk to the police, they cannot force you to answer questions about a crime they think you committed. Unlike the Fourth Amendment, which balances your right to privacy against the police's need to act, your Fifth Amendment right not to talk to police is absolute. If you invoke it, the police may not legally make you talk.

The Supreme Court did not apply the Fifth Amendment to the states until 1964. But even before this, it struck down cases where confessions were not made voluntarily. The court determined that these cases violated the due process clause of the 14th Amendment. This clause declares that no "State shall deprive any person of life, liberty, or property, without due process of law. . . ." Due process of law guarantees fair procedures and basic liberties. Among the cases that the court struck down as violating due process were:

- *Brown v. Mississippi* (1936). Trying to get a confession, deputies hung the defendant from a tree twice. Then they whipped him. Whipping him a second time, they told him they would not stop until he confessed, which he finally did. Then they took him to jail.

- *Ward v. Texas* (1942). So that no friend or attorney could contact the defendant, the police took him out of the county to three different jails in three days. Questioned continuously, the defendant at one point said he would make whatever statement the police wanted even though he claimed not to have committed the crime. Finally, he confessed.

- *Ashcraft v. Tennessee* (1944). Police put the defendant in an interrogation room on Saturday night at 7 p.m. and questioned him in relays so they would not get tired. On Monday at 9:30 a.m., the defendant confessed. During the 36-hour interrogation, police had given the defendant only one five-minute break.

- *Malinski v. New York* (1945). Instead of taking the defendant to jail, police took him to a hotel room. They told him to remove his clothes. They questioned him for three hours while he was naked. Then allowing him to put on his underwear, they questioned him for seven more hours until he confessed. Then after letting him dress, they took him to jail.

- *Leyra v. Denno* (1954). After questioning the defendant for days and allowing him little sleep, police brought in a doctor trained in hypnosis. The police had wired the room so they could listen in. During his one-and-one-half hour visit, the doctor repeatedly suggested that the defendant confess. Eventually the defendant did. The doctor then brought officers into the room and had the defendant repeat the confession.

- *Spano v. New York* (1959). Although the defendant refused to talk and asked for his lawyer, police continued to question him for eight straight hours. Police sent in a childhood friend, a policeman with four children, who falsely told the defendant he would be fired unless the defendant confessed, which he ultimately did.

- *Lynum v. Illinois* (1963). Police told the defendant that if she confessed, nothing would happen to her, but if she did not, her children would be taken away from her. She confessed.

Finally in 1964 in *Malloy v. Hogan*, the Supreme Court ruled that the Fifth Amendment protection against self-incrimination applied to the states. But courts still faced the difficult task of determining on a case-by-case basis whether confessions were coerced or voluntary. So in 1966 in the landmark case of *Miranda v. Arizona*, the Supreme Court laid down clearer guidelines for police and courts to follow.

Ernesto Miranda, right, had his conviction overturned because police failed to tell him that he didn't have to talk with them. He was retried and convicted a second time without his confession entered in evidence.

Miranda v. Arizona (1966)

In this case, Ernesto Miranda was arrested at his home and taken to a police station. A witness identified him, then two detectives took him into a special room. After two hours of interrogation, the officers got Miranda to sign a written confession.

At his trial, Miranda was convicted of kidnaping and rape and was sentenced to 20 to 30 years in prison. But he had never been told of his right not to talk to the police. He had never been told of his right to a lawyer. These rights are guaranteed by the Fifth and Sixth amendments. When the Supreme Court heard this case, it decided that any interrogation of suspects in custody is unconstitutional unless the police clearly tell suspects before any questioning begins that:

- they have the right to remain silent;
- anything they say may be used against them in court;
- they have a right to a lawyer; and
- if they want a lawyer but can't afford one, the court will appoint one before any questioning.

Also, after giving a suspect these warnings, the police cannot go on interrogating unless the suspect "knowingly and intelligently" waives his or her rights. That is, suspects must completely understand their rights before they can give them up.

This important decision meant that if police did not give suspects in custody these warnings before questioning them, nothing that they said could be introduced as evidence against them at their trials.

The Supreme Court believed that police questioning of suspects in the station house was inherently coercive. In other words, the court believed that the station house surroundings and police interrogation put tremendous pressure on suspects to say what the police wanted them to say. It felt that the only way to prevent coerced confessions was to make sure suspects knew their rights. Thus police need to tell suspects that they do not have to say anything and that they can have a lawyer with them during questioning. The court concluded that if police do not give a suspect this information, they violate the suspect's Fifth Amendment rights.

Miranda's Aftermath

Miranda requires the police to read suspects **in custody** their rights before any **interrogation**. Police do not need to get people to waive their rights if they are not in custody or not being interrogated. Since *Miranda*, the court has clarified its decision by focusing on what "in custody" and "interrogation" mean.

To be in custody, a person's freedom must be significantly restrained. The court has held that most people stopped briefly by police are not in custody, because they will soon be on their way. Thus routine traffic stops and even stop and frisks do not normally require *Miranda* warnings. (*Berkemer v. McCarty*, 1984.)

In *Rhode Island v. Innis* (1980), the high court defined interrogation as "words or actions on the part of police officers that they should have known were reasonably likely to elicit an incriminating response." In that case, police officers talked to each other as they drove the defendant to the police station. One mentioned that it would be too bad if children attending a nearby school for the handicapped found the abandoned shotgun that Innis had supposedly used to rob one taxi driver and kill another. Innis, who had previously requested a lawyer after hearing his *Miranda* rights, spoke

up and directed the officers to the gun (a major piece of evidence in his later conviction for robbery and murder). The court ruled that the officers' remarks did not constitute interrogation so his rights were not violated.

In 1984 in *New York v. Quarles*, the Supreme Court carved out a major exception to *Miranda*. In that case, police chased a rape suspect through a supermarket. Finally catching and handcuffing him, they found he had an empty shoulder holster. An officer asked him where the gun was. Nodding toward some empty boxes, the suspect said, "The gun is over there." The police retrieved a loaded .38 caliber handgun from a box. Since the suspect had not been given any *Miranda* warnings, his incriminating statement and perhaps the gun should have been excluded from evidence. But the court created a **public safety exception** to *Miranda*. It ruled that the police do not have to give *Miranda* warnings when their questions are "reasonably prompted by a concern for the public safety." Since the loaded gun in the store caused reasonable concern for public safety, the court ruled that the evidence was admissible.

Miranda Upheld

In 2000, the Supreme Court decided a case that directly challenged *Miranda*. It was based on a law more than 30 years old. In 1968, two years after the *Miranda* decision, Congress enacted the Omnibus Crime Control and Safe Streets Act of 1968. Section 3501 of this act purports to overturn *Miranda* for federal cases. It permits a confession to be given in evidence "if it is voluntarily given." Section 3501 lists several factors for a court to consider in determining whether a confession is voluntary. *Miranda* warnings are one of these factors, but are not considered necessary for a voluntary confession.

For 30 years, prosecutors and police ignored Section 3501, believing it unconstitutional. They reasoned that Congress cannot overturn a Supreme Court decision on constitutional law.

But a law professor at the University of Utah, Paul Cassell, thought Section 3501 was

Much police work involves questioning people. Before police can question people in custody, however, they must read them their rights.

constitutional and waged a campaign to get it upheld. He noted language in *Miranda* that said Congress or states could adopt substitutes for *Miranda* warnings as long the procedures were "at least as effective in apprising accused persons of their right of silence and in assuring a continuous opportunity to exercise it." Cassell argued that Congress had done this in 1968.

In 1999, a federal appeals court adopted Cassell's argument in *Dickerson v. U.S.* The case involved a defendant who claimed the FBI had not read him his rights before he confessed. The trial judge, although noting that the confession was voluntary, threw out the confession. When the judge refused to hear new evidence that the FBI had given the defendant his *Miranda* warnings, prosecutors appealed. The appeals court reversed the trial judge's decision, reasoning that the confession was voluntary and therefore admissible under Section 3501.

The U.S. Supreme Court, however, overturned the appeals court decision. By a 7–2 vote, the court ruled that *Miranda* was based on the Constitution and that Congress does not have the power to overturn the decision. It therefore ruled that Section 3501 was unconstitutional. It further rejected the argument that Section 3501 provided an effective substitute for *Miranda* warnings. The court stated that Section 3501 was simply a return to the "totality of the circumstances" test of voluntariness,

which existed prior to *Miranda*. This test, said the court, did not adequately protect a defendant's constitutional rights.

For Discussion

1. Supreme Court Justice Arthur J. Goldberg once wrote: "We have learned the lesson of history, ancient and modern, that a system of criminal law enforcement which comes to depend on 'confession' will, in the long run, be less reliable than a system which depends on extrinsic evidence independently secured through skillful investigation." What did he mean by this? Do you agree? Why or why not?

2. According to the *Miranda* decision, why should the incriminating statement in the *Quarles* case be excluded from evidence?

3. The court majority in *Quarles* said that the public safety exception did not give the police the right to coerce confessions from suspects. According to the *Miranda* decision, was Quarles' incriminating statement made in a coercive situation? Why or why not?

4. Both the majority and dissenting opinions in *Quarles* stated that the decision would "lessen the desirable clarity" of the *Miranda* rule. Why is it desirable that the rule be clear?

5. Do you think Section 3501 is constitutional? Explain.

6. When *Miranda* was decided, its critics claimed that suspects would stop making confessions. This claim has proved false. Suspects confess today as often as before *Miranda*. In fact, one commentator has stated that "next to the warning label on cigarette packs, *Miranda* is the most widely ignored piece of official advice in our society." Do you think *Miranda* sufficiently protects suspects' Fifth Amendment rights? Do you think it goes too far? Explain.

Class Activity: Taking the Fifth

In this activity, students use their knowledge of the Fifth Amendment to argue actual cases that have come before the Supreme Court.

1. Divide the class into triads. Assign students in each triad a number—one, two, or three. All ones will role play Supreme Court justices. All twos will role play defense attorneys. All threes will role play attorneys for the government. Assign each triad one of the cases below—a, b, c, d, e, or f.

2. Regroup the class so they can consult with one another while preparing for the role play. Students arguing for the government should sit on one side of the room, students arguing for the defendants on the other side, and the student justices in front. Each group should follow its group's instructions, listed below.

3. Regroup into triads and begin the role play. The defense will present its case first. Each side will have two minutes to make its presentation. The justice can interrupt to ask questions. After both sides present, each justice should stand and prepare to present a decision on the case.

4. When every justice is ready, go around the room and have each justice read the facts of the case and present his or her decision and reasons for it.

5. Conclude the activity with a discussion using the Debriefing Questions on page 94.

Ask an Expert

Invite a prosecutor, defense attorney, or police officer to discuss briefly the *Miranda* decision. Invite your guest to stay and take part in the activity "Taking the Fifth." The guest can help different groups and debrief the class.

Attorneys' Instructions

As attorneys, you are responsible for presenting the court with sound arguments supporting your side.

If you represent the government, you will argue that the incriminating statements should be allowed in evidence at the trial.

If you represent the defendant, you will argue that the incriminating statements should be excluded at trial.

Carefully read your case. Then review the section above on *Miranda* and the cases following it. How do these cases apply to your case?

To prepare your argument, write a clear, brief statement of your position. Include:

- At least one fact from the case that supports your position.

- An explanation of how that fact supports your position.

- One previous court decision that supports your position.

- An explanation of how that decision supports your position.

- One reason why your position is fair to the government or defendant.

- One reason why a court decision in your favor will benefit society.

Make an outline ordering this information so that you can include all of it in a two-minute presentation.

Justices' Instructions

When preparing to hear arguments, Supreme Court justices review the cases and the law with their clerks and develop questions they want to ask the attorneys. Working with other justices, read each case. Take notes while you discuss the following:

- How do *Miranda* and the cases following it apply to your case?

- What questions would you like to ask the attorneys about your case?

Remember: When you decide your case, you must consider the previous Supreme Court cases interpreting the Fifth Amendment, but you are not bound by them.

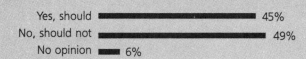

National Opinion Poll on *Miranda*

"When the police arrest someone, do you think the police should or should not be required to inform that person of their constitutional rights?"

Yes, should ████████████████████████████████ 94%
No, should not ██ 6%
No opinion –

"Do you think confessions obtained from defendants who were not read their constitutional rights when they were arrested should or should not be admissible in trial?"

Yes, should ████████████ 45%
No, should not ██████████████ 49%
No opinion ███ 6%

Source: Gallup Poll (2000)

Cases

The issue in each case is the same: **Can the defendant's confession or incriminating statements be introduced in evidence at the trial?**

a. *Illinois v. Perkins* (1990). Police suspect that Perkins, an inmate in jail on another charge, has committed a murder. They put an undercover agent in Perkins' cell. After gaining Perkins' trust, the agent asks him if he has ever killed anyone. Perkins confesses to the murder.

b. *Duckworth v. Eagan* (1989). Duckworth confessed to a crime after receiving *Miranda* warnings from police. Police had deviated from the standard warnings in one way. They had told Duckworth: "You have a right to talk to a lawyer for advice before we ask you any questions, and to have him with you during questioning. You have this right to the advice and presence of a lawyer even if you cannot afford to hire one. *We have no way of giving you a lawyer, but one will be appointed for you, if you wish, if and when you go to court.* If you wish to answer questions now without a lawyer present, you have the right to stop answering questions at any time. You also have the right to stop answering at any time until you've talked to a lawyer." (Emphasis added.)

c. *Arizona v. Mauro* (1987). Arrested for killing his son, Mauro declined to answer any questions without a lawyer. The police let his wife in to talk with him, but they conspicuously placed a tape recorder on the table between them, which recorded incriminating statements.

d. *Fare v. Michael C.* (1979). Police gave *Miranda* warnings to Michael, a 16-year-old boy accused of murder. When asked if he wanted a lawyer during the interrogation, Michael asked if instead he could call his probation officer. When the police told him they would not call the probation officer right away, Michael somewhat reluctantly agreed to talk and eventually incriminated himself.

e. *Oregon v. Mathiason* (1977). Weeks after a burglary, police sent Mathiason a note asking him to call. He called and made an appointment at his convenience to come into the station. On his arrival, an officer informed him he was not under arrest, but led him into a conference room. The officer falsely told Mathiason that police had found his fingerprints at the burglary scene. Mathiason confessed to the crime. The officer then let Mathiason leave without arresting him that day.

f. *Beckwith v. U.S.* (1976). Arriving at Beckwith's house at 8 a.m., IRS agents asked Beckwith if they could ask him some questions. He invited them in and they interviewed him for three hours. During the interview, he made incriminating statements. He was later arrested for tax fraud.

1. Which of the justices' decisions expand the *Miranda* decision? Which restrict it? Why?

2. What were some strong arguments presented by the attorneys for the government for each case? What arguments would have improved their cases?

3. What were some strong arguments presented by the attorneys for the defendants? What arguments would have improved their cases?

4. What were some key questions asked by the justices? What other questions should they have asked?

5. Which decisions do you agree with? Why?

The Exclusionary Rule

After seizing evidence, police must tag and store it for use at trial.

"Criminals always get off on technicalities." You have probably heard this before or even thought it yourself. But do you know what these "technicalities" are? Generally, they refer to the individual rights protected by the Constitution, particularly provisions of the Fourth and Fifth amendments. When these rights have been violated by an illegal search, seizure, or interrogation, an accused person may invoke the exclusionary rule. This is done by making a motion in court to suppress any illegally obtained evidence.

The **exclusionary rule** is a special remedy created by the courts to compel police to respect the constitutional rights of suspects. Under the rule, no illegally obtained evidence—whether papers, objects, or testimony—may be presented in court to convict a defendant whose constitutional rights have been violated. This does not mean that the accused will automatically be set free. But in some cases, this evidence makes up the bulk of the government's case. In such cases, the charges may have to be reduced or dropped altogether.

The exclusionary rule is based upon two theories:

- **Judicial integrity.** Courts are supposed to uphold the law. If they allow illegally obtained evidence to be used at trial, they fail to uphold the law. They condone, even encourage, illegality. How can citizens respect our judicial system if the system accepts illegal practices?

- **Deterrence.** Excluding tainted evidence is the only effective way to prevent police abuse of constitutional rights. If illegally obtained evidence may not be introduced in court, police will not resort to illegal searches and seizures.

The rule has applied to *federal* criminal cases since 1914. The Supreme Court did not at first apply the rule to the states. Instead, the court let states decide how to uphold constitutional rights—whether by the exclusionary rule or by other methods. But in 1961, the Supreme Court decided that the exclusionary rule was required to assure that police would obey the Constitution. In *Mapp v. Ohio*, it applied the exclusionary rule to state criminal trials.

Fruit of the Poisonous Tree

If police find evidence during an illegal search, the exclusionary rule bars prosecutors from using this evidence at trial. But what if the illegally obtained evidence leads police to other evidence? For example, police conduct an illegal search of an office building and find cocaine in Dan's office. When Dan comes to work, they read him his *Miranda* rights and question him. He confesses to possessing and selling cocaine. The cocaine cannot be used as evidence at Dan's trial because of the illegal search. But can the confession be used? Police have complied with *Miranda*. But if Dan can show that police never would have had reason to question him except for their illegal search, then the confession would be excluded from the trial under the "fruit of the poisonous tree doctrine." This doctrine holds that if illegally obtained evidence (the poisonous tree), leads police to new evidence (the fruit), this new evidence may not be used in court against the person whose rights have been violated.

Courts have recognized several exceptions to this doctrine, and in recent years the Supreme Court has liberally interpreted these exceptions:

- **Independent source.** If police did not have to rely on the illegal evidence to find the new evidence, then the new evidence could be used at trial. For example, if a witness had told police that Dan dealt drugs, then they would have had reason to question him and the confession would be admitted. (*Silverthorne Lumber Co. v. U.S.*, 1920, *Segura v. U.S.*, 1984, and *Murray v. U.S.*, 1988.)

- **Inevitable discovery.** If police would have found the evidence eventually, then the evidence can be admitted in court. In *Nix v. Williams* (1984), police were searching for a body. They illegally obtained a confession that indicated where the body was. The body could be used as evidence at the trial because the court ruled the police would have found it eventually.

- **Cleansed taint.** If the connection between the illegal action and the new evidence is weak, then the new evidence will be allowed at trial. For example, if Dan's confession had not taken place the day of the search but had been volunteered by him a week later, a court might allow the confession as evidence. (*Wong Sun v. U.S.*, 1963.)

For Discussion

1. What is the fruit of the poisonous tree doctrine? Do you agree with this doctrine? Why or why not?

2. What are the exceptions to the doctrine? Do they make sense? Why or why not?

Mapp v. Ohio (1961)

Dollree Mapp lived with her young daughter in a two-story house in Cleveland. On May 23, 1957, police arrived at her house and demanded entry. Although they gave Mapp no explanation, they later said they were responding to a tip about a recent bombing. After phoning her attorney, Mapp refused to let the officers in without a warrant. They left. Three hours later, they returned, still without a warrant, but with reinforcements. They pounded on the door. When Mapp did not come to the door immediately, the police broke into the house.

When they entered, Mapp was coming down the stairs. She demanded to see a warrant. An officer waved a piece of paper at her, but it was not a warrant. She grabbed it and stuffed it down her blouse. The officers forcibly retrieved it and handcuffed her. Then they dragged her upstairs to her bedroom and searched through her belongings and personal papers.

Meanwhile, Mapp's attorney arrived, but

the officers would not let him in the house. They continued searching through the rest of the house. After searching everywhere, officers found some obscene materials tucked away in a basement trunk. Mapp was arrested, tried, and convicted of possessing these materials.

During Mapp's trial and her subsequent appeals, the state never denied that the search was illegal. Instead, the state argued that the illegal search was irrelevant. Mapp had obscene materials in her basement. She had broken the law and was guilty as charged. Her conviction should not be overturned because of an illegal search.

The Supreme Court disagreed. Ruling that "nothing can destroy a government more quickly than its failure to obey its own laws," the court threw out Mapp's conviction and returned the case to a lower court for further proceedings. In doing so, the court extended the exclusionary rule to all criminal trials in the country—both state and federal.

The court stated that the constitutional right against invasions of privacy by police should not be an empty promise. The court said it could no longer permit this right

> to be revocable at the whim of any police officer who, in the name of law enforcement itself, chooses to suspend its enjoyment. Our decision, founded on reason and truth, gives to the individual no more than that which the Constitution guarantees him, to the police officer no less than that to which honest law enforcement is entitled, and, to the courts, that judicial integrity so necessary in the true administration of justice.

The Exclusionary Rule Since *Mapp*

The *Mapp* decision affected police behavior immediately. Police, who had rarely bothered to get warrants, started applying for them. In New York City, for example, police had requested no search warrants in 1960, the year before the *Mapp* decision. The year after *Mapp*, the police requested more than 800 search warrants. The exclusionary rule, with its threat of suppressing illegal evidence, pushed police into seeking warrants.

But the *Mapp* decision did not end legal debate over the exclusionary rule. The Supreme Court has considered the issue many times. In recent years, the court has carved out several exceptions to the rule:

- If criminal defendants testify in their own defense, evidence illegally seized can be used to challenge the defendants' testimony. (*Harris v. New York*, 1971, *Michigan v. Harvey*, 1990, and *James v. Illinois*, 1990.)

- Evidence gathered by police acting in good faith can be admitted if the police have reasonably relied on a search warrant issued by a judge which turns out to be technically defective or, through a judge's error, turns out not to be based on probable cause. (*U.S. v. Leon*, 1984, and *Arizona v. Evans*, 1995.)

Critics of the exclusionary rule believe it hampers the fight against crime. Some argue that too many criminals escape conviction because the rule excludes evidence at trial. Others simply say the rule makes no sense. Justice Benjamin Cardozo reflected this opinion in 1926 when he asked: "Is it right the criminal is to go free because the constable has blundered?"

Supporters of the rule say that it affects few criminal prosecutions, partly because police today do a good job of following proper procedure. In response to critics who claim the procedures themselves hinder law enforcement, supporters point out that these procedures are required by the Constitution. The exclusionary rule simply helps ensure that the police follow the Constitution.

For Discussion

1. What is the exclusionary rule? Why was it established? What two justifications are given for it?

2. Do you think it is necessary? Why or why not?

3. Why do you think the court created the good-faith exception to the rule? What problems could arise from this exception? Why?

Class Activity: A Second Look at the Exclusionary Rule

Critics of the exclusionary rule have set forth a variety of proposals to change the rule. These proposals include:

- Abolishing the exclusionary rule and allowing all relevant evidence to be used in court.

- Abolishing the exclusionary rule but establishing other civil and criminal remedies for citizens when the police violate their rights (e.g., a person could bring a civil suit against the officer for invasion of privacy in cases of unreasonable searches and seizures).

- Extending the good-faith exception to all situations where police act in good faith and in the reasonable—although mistaken—belief that their actions were legal.

Critics of the exclusionary rule claim it needs to be changed to prevent criminals from avoiding punishment when police make technical violations of the law. Its supporters argue that any change would encourage police lawlessness.

In this activity, students evaluate the pros and cons of the exclusionary rule and proposed changes to it.

1. Form small groups.

2. Each group should:

    a. Discuss the pros and cons of the exclusionary rule.

    b. Discuss the advantages and disadvantages of the proposed changes to the rule listed above.

    c. Discuss whether there are other alternatives that would respect people's Fourth and Fifth Amendment rights but not place too heavy a burden on police.

    d. Decide whether the group favors changing the rule and if so, what change the group supports.

    e. Prepare to discuss its decision and the reasons for it with the class.

3. Have the groups report back. Write any new alternatives to the exclusionary rule on the board.

4. Conclude the activity by having students vote on whether they think the exclusionary rule should be changed. If they vote to change it, have them vote on the alternatives.

CHAPTER 7
The Limits of Police Authority

Racial Profiling

For many years, blacks and other minorities have complained that police often target minority drivers, pulling them over for minor infractions or no reason at all and often subjecting them to humiliating car or body searches. Christopher Darden, an African American and former prosecutor, has been stopped many times by police. He said that "to be pulled over for no good reason is very offensive. But then to be asked for consent to search your vehicle just ratchets things up another notch. And in those situations where you've been forced out at gunpoint or you've been asked to spread out on the street, to lay out on the pavement, makes you boiling with anger."

John Lambeth of Temple University conducted a study to determine whether blacks were being targeted on the New Jersey Turnpike. He found that African Americans made up 13.5 percent of highway users and 15 percent of the speeders, but he found that they represented 35 percent of those stopped by police. They were almost five times more likely to be pulled over as other drivers. Similar results were found in studies conducted in Maryland and Florida.

Other minority community members complain that they too are stopped and questioned by authorities for no good reason. Latinos protest that they are targeted at Border Patrol checkpoints within the United States, and Arab-Americans claim that they are often detained for long periods by airport security, especially after some terrorist scare.

Pulling over a car, or stopping a person, solely on the basis of the driver's race violates the 14th Amendment to the U.S. Constitution, which guarantees equal protection under the law. If proven, it would invalidate an arrest or the use of any evidence seized from the driver. Federal civil rights laws outlaw it and several states have passed laws specifically against this practice.

The more difficult question arises over police officer discretion in deciding who to pull over. In the 1996 case of *Whren v. U.S.*, the U.S. Supreme Court unanimously ruled that police may stop a car for any traffic or equipment violation even if they have a different motivation for making the stop, such as the suspicion of drug trafficking.

Some experts point to "profiling" as the major cause of disproportionate traffic stops on minorities. Profiles are systems used by police to predict criminal behavior. Some use scientific methods and statistics to develop a list of factors that make up a profile of a potential suspect. They might include age, location, type of car, time of day, driving patterns, route of travel, and whether the driver is alone. Profiles can also target white citizens. For example, a police officer might be more likely to pull over a late-model car for a minor traffic violation if it were driven by a white youth at night in an inner-city neighborhood where drug dealing occurs. In this case, the driver might fit a profile of someone who is likely trying to buy drugs.

There are two types of racial profiling—full and partial. A *full* racial profile is when race is the only factor that causes an officer to stop someone. As mentioned above, this practice is unconstitutional, illegal, and universally condemned. Even so, many minorities complain that it happens all the time. Police officials disagree and say the practice is not widespread.

In 1999, Connecticut and North Carolina passed laws requiring police to keep track of the race and ethnicity of everyone they stop. The data will be forwarded to experts to analyze whether and to what extent officers are

targeting people on the basis of race or ethnicity. These laws are widely supported by minority leaders. Walter Wilson, legislative director of the National Association for the Advancement of Colored People, has stated: "The NAACP believes that comprehensive data collection is critical to the process of ending racial profiling. Without data collection, there is no progress on this issue."

Other states and the federal government are considering such laws. But strong opposition to these laws has come from police groups. They argue that stopping people is already hazardous and forcing officers to ask people about their race and ethnicity will needlessly lengthen stops and inflame the situation. They also don't think the statistics will prove anything because people stopped will probably reflect the racial makeup of the community they are stopped in. They believe that instead of collecting data, all allegations of officers targeting minorities should be thoroughly investigated.

Another set of issues concerns *partial* racial profiling, where race or ethnicity is one of several factors. Many people support this type of profiling. They argue that it is an effec-

tive law-enforcement tool. Bernard Parks, chief of the Los Angeles Police Department, has stated: "We have an issue of violent crime against jewelry salespeople. . . . It's a collection of several hundred Colombians who commit this crime. If you see six in a car in front of the Jewelry Mart, and they're waiting and watching people with briefcases, should we play the percentages and follow them? It's common sense." Parks is an African American. He sees nothing wrong with *partial* racial profiling.

Randall Kennedy, a law professor at Harvard, opposes using race as a factor in profiles. He doesn't think that police necessarily use this practice because they have racist motives. He thinks they may believe it is an effective law-enforcement tool, and Kennedy believes they may be right. But Kennedy points out that many innocent people get stopped by police using these profiles. And, he says, they often don't just get stopped once, but many times. This, he says, causes great anger and alienation. "Alienation of that sort gives rise to witnesses who fail to cooperate with the police, citizens who view prosecutors as 'the enemy,' . . . and jurors who yearn to 'get even' with a system that has, in their eyes, consistently mistreated them. For the sake of better law enforcement, we need to be mindful of the deep reservoir of anger toward the police that now exists within many racial minority neighborhoods. Racial profiling is a big part of what keeps this pool of accumulated rage filled to the brim."

For Discussion

1. A bank is robbed and the suspect is described as an Asian woman driving a red sports car. Police start looking for such a suspect. Is this a racial profile? Explain.

2. What is the difference between *partial* and *full* racial profiling?

3. Do you think profiling is an effective law-enforcement tool? If so, are its benefits worth its costs? Explain.

4. Should police ever be allowed to consider race when deciding whether to stop someone?

Class Activity: What Should Be Done About Profiling?

To find out more about racial profiling, some states have passed laws requiring police to collect data on the race and ethnicity of everyone they stop. Other states and the federal government are considering doing the same. Opponents of data collection support other measures such as police videotaping every traffic stop or police distributing their card to everyone they stop so that people can easily file complaints. In this activity, students role play advisers to a state governor who is considering introducing legislation on racial profiling.

1. Divide the class into small groups.

2. Each group should:

   a. Discuss the problem of racial profiling and various proposals for addressing it.

   b. Decide which proposal, if any, to support. (Students may create their own proposal.)

   c. Prepare to report its decision and the reason for it back to the class.

3. Have the groups report back and discuss the various proposals. Conclude the activity by voting as a class on the proposals.

Corruption

Police work provides many opportunities for corruption. A driver pulled over by police may hand an officer $20 along with his license hoping the officer will let him go without a ticket. A restaurant owner may give police free meals in exchange for them providing extra protection for her restaurant. Bookmakers, prostitutes, and drug dealers may offer payoffs for officers who ignore their operations.

Throughout the history of police in America, many officers could not resist some of these temptations. In the early days, police were loosely controlled and corruption flourished. Most got their jobs as political patronage, and many routinely did favors for their political bosses. The Progressive era at the turn of the 20th century did away with much political patronage. But many reformers also called for strict enforcement of prostitution, gambling, and liquor laws, which in turn often led to bribes, protection money, and other corruption. The Prohibition era in the 1920s saw increasing numbers of law-enforcement officers accept payoffs to leave alone the thriving underground liquor industry, which was usually controlled by mobsters.

In our time, the war on drugs has made drug dealing both dangerous and highly lucrative. With so much money at stake, criminals sometimes have lured officers into accepting bribes and helping their criminal enterprises. Some officers have stolen drugs and money discovered in dealers' residences. A few have even dealt drugs themselves. Almost every large city police force has experienced a major drug scandal in recent years.

For Personal Benefit

Corruption can be defined as misusing one's official powers for gain. Often police corruption is for personal benefit. Officers get money, favors, food, sex, goods, or services in return for doing something they shouldn't do.

One of the most widely publicized cases of corruption was revealed by New York detective Frank Serpico in the late 1960s. (His story was made into a feature-length film starring Al Pacino.) Serpico witnessed widespread corruption and payoffs within the department. For years, he repeatedly reported the corruption to higher-ups and even to the mayor's office. Although some officials paid attention, nothing happened until he told his story to the *New York Times*. When officers learned what he had done, they considered him a "rat" and shunned him. The city formed the Knapp Commission in 1969 to investigate. The commission's report gave some insight into how corruption can remain unchecked in any police department. It divided corrupt officers into two groups—the "grass eaters" and the "meat eaters."

Poll of Police Officers on What They Consider Serious Misconduct

Case Scenario— An officer . . .	How serious Is It? (Ranked from 1, least serious, to 8, most serious)	What discipline do you think the officer should receive?	Would you report a fellow officer who did this? (Averaged from 1 = definitely no to 5 = definitely yes)
runs an off-duty security system business	1	None	1.37
gets free meals, discounts on beat	2	Verbal reprimand	1.94
gets holiday gifts from merchants	3	Verbal reprimand	2.36
covers up a DUI accident of a fellow officer	4	Suspend without pay	2.34
gets free drinks to ignore a bar closing late	5	Suspend without pay	3.47
steals contents of a found wallet	6	Dismissal	4.23
takes a bribe from a speeding motorist	7	Dismissal	4.19
steals a watch from a crime scene	8	Dismissal	4.54

Source: "The Measurement of Police Integrity," National Institute of Justice (2000)

Meat eaters actively seek bribes or other favors. They may extort money from people they stop (in exchange for letting them go) and even commit crimes like dealing drugs, burglary, robbery, or murder for hire. They are the ones who, when caught, make the headlines. But they make up a small percentage of corrupt officers.

Grass eaters compose the overwhelming majority of corrupt officers. They do not actively seek bribes or other favors. But if something is offered to them, they will accept it. They seem less dangerous than the meat eaters, but they can cause serious damage. They create an atmosphere in a department that corruption is acceptable. They help build up the "blue wall of silence" that keeps other officers from reporting any corruption, however flagrant.

For Departmental Benefit

Not all corruption is done for personal benefit. It may be done in a misguided attempt to make sure justice is served or the department or unit looks good. An officer may testify, for example, that he saw a gun lying in plain view in the defendant's apartment when, in fact, he found the gun in the defendant's desk drawer. The officer knows that if he tells the truth, the gun will be excluded from evidence. More dangerous, and much less common, are instances of police planting evidence to make sure a suspect is convicted.

A scandal in the Rampart division of the Los Angeles Police Department was, at least in part, an example of this type of corruption. In 1999, an officer was charged with stealing an eight-pound bag of cocaine from a police evidence room. In return for a lighter sentence, he started accusing other members of his elite anti-gang unit of intimidating witnesses, committing perjury, planting evidence, beating suspects, and even shooting people without justification. The scandal has tainted hundreds of cases, which has led to many people being released from prison. In February 2000, the city council learned it might cost up to $125 million to settle lawsuits stemming from the actions of the corrupt officers. LAPD Police Chief Bernard C. Parks blamed the scandal on a lack of supervision and faulty hiring practices.

What Can Be Done?

Various proposals have been suggested for ridding police forces of corruption. Some are more practical than others.

Get rid of victimless crimes. This is a radical solution that has little chance of being adopted—at least in the short term. Most corruption grows out of so-called "victimless crimes"—drugs, prostitution, gambling. These are crimes that all the parties consent to. A segment of the population desires these goods or services. And the criminals who service this segment are more than willing to pay off police—sometimes with huge sums. Get rid of these crimes and much police corruption will disappear.

Monitor police officers better. Another reason corruption takes place is because the badge gives police great authority, which they can exercise at their own discretion. In some departments, supervisors don't know what their officers are doing and don't care as long as they make arrests. One way to ensure this doesn't happen is to hold supervisors accountable for having corrupt officers in their ranks. New York did this following the Knapp Commission. Another corruption scandal (which produced yet another commission) broke out in the 1990s. But it was far less pervasive than the corruption exposed by Serpico and the Knapp Commission.

Make internal review stronger. Almost every department has an internal affairs unit to investigate police. If this unit is strong, corruption will be lower. Some departments have adopted a policy that internal affairs must investigate every complaint by a citizen. If officers know in advance that complaints will be

A police officer displays money recovered during a drug raid.

investigated and taken seriously, fewer will dare to be corrupt.

Break down the blue wall of silence surrounding corruption. Most people go into policing thinking they can help their community. Few officers start off being corrupt. They usually learn it on the job and it comes over time. It progresses from accepting a meal to taking money for not writing a ticket to accepting bribes from gamblers and finally from drug dealers. To break down the wall of silence, departments must teach and continually reinforce that corruption is unacceptable and hurts the department. They must encourage, not discourage, the reporting of misconduct.

For Discussion

1. In your opinion, which type of corrupt officer is more dangerous—a grass eater or a meat eater? Why?

2. Which type of corruption—that for personal benefit or for departmental benefit—do you think is more dangerous? Why?

3. What do you think can be done to prevent police corruption? Explain.

Class Activity: Preventing Corruption

In this activity, students evaluate different proposals for preventing police corruption.

1. Form small groups.

2. Each group should:

    a. Discuss the pros and cons of the proposals for getting rid of police corruption, listed under "What Can Be Done?" on page 102.

    b. Discuss whether there are other policies that would help prevent corruption.

    c. Decide which proposals should be adopted.

    d. Prepare to present its proposals and the reasons for them to the class.

3. Have the groups report back. Write any new proposals for preventing corruption on the board.

4. Conclude the activity by having students vote on the various proposals.

Use of Force

One of the most controversial aspects of police work is the use of force. Controversy does not arise over whether police should be allowed to use force. Police are authorized to use force to enforce the law and make arrests. Questions arise when an officer uses a gun, a baton, or even restraining holds in particular situations. Did the officer need to use force? Was the force the officer used excessive? Did the force amount to brutality?

As a general rule, police may use whatever level of force is reasonable and necessary to make an arrest. For instance, shooting an unarmed person who has stolen an apple from a fruit stand would not be reasonable. Clubbing a suspect with a nightstick when a simple arm hold would suffice is not necessary.

In training programs, police officers learn how much force may be used in specific cases. They practice adjusting the level of force to the circumstances. For each situation—whether it is an arrest, crowd control, or citizen confrontation—they are taught to begin with the lowest level of force possible. They should only escalate the level of force if the situation requires it. For example, if a suspect quietly submits to an arrest, a simple pat-down search and handcuffing is all that is necessary. But if the suspect suddenly throws a punch, a higher level of force is probably required, such as using a physical-restraint technique. All of this works well in theory. On the street, other factors—including fear, anger, darkness, and split-second changes—can make deciding what force is reasonable and necessary much more difficult.

Police use of deadly force, especially firearms, is often highly publicized and controversial. Deadly force is commonly defined as "force that poses a high risk of death or serious injury to its human target, whether or not death or serious injury actually result." State criminal codes spell out laws governing the use of deadly force. Some police agencies and departments have even stricter standards for their officers. The following factors, among others, are used in determining whether deadly force is justified in a particular situation:

- The officer is making an arrest for a felony violation. (In general, deadly force is not justified in apprehending a person suspected of committing a misdemeanor or lesser offense.)

- The officer has made the reason for the arrest known to the suspect.

- The officer believes that deadly force is necessary to prevent death or great bodily injury to the officer or another person.

- The officer believes that the deadly force does not create a substantial risk to innocent persons.

- The criminal used deadly force or probably will use it if arrest is delayed.

In *Tennessee v. Garner* (1985), the Supreme Court ruled the Fourth Amendment puts a constitutional limit on the police's use of deadly force. In that case, police investigating

**When Is It Wrong
for the Police to Use Force?**

Police may use whatever force is reasonable and necessary to make an arrest. Often it is not reasonable or necessary for police to use force. Professor Albert Reiss has listed six examples when an assault by an arresting police officer would be wrong:

- When the officer does not attempt to arrest the person after using force to subdue the person.

- When the person does not resist arrest.

- When the person resisting arrest can be easily restrained by other methods.

- When many other officers are on the scene and can easily control the person.

- When the person is handcuffed and does not try to escape or resist violently.

- When the use of force goes on after the person stops resisting.

a burglary saw an unarmed teenage boy run out of a house. Giving chase and calling for him to halt, they saw the boy start to climb a chain-link fence. Realizing that the boy would escape if he made it over the fence, an officer shot and killed him. The officer had acted in accordance with Tennessee law. The law gave police authority to use *any means necessary* to arrest a fleeing felon.

The Supreme Court ruled the law did not meet the constitutional standards of the Fourth Amendment. The court held it was not reasonable to use deadly force to arrest someone unless that person posed a threat to another person.

For Discussion

1. Why might deciding what force is reasonable and necessary be difficult for a police officer in the field?

2. Do you agree with the Supreme Court's decision in *Tennessee v. Garner*? Why or why not?

3. In *People v. Gilmore* (1988), Gilmore, a private citizen, found a man trying to burglarize his house. The man ran, but Gilmore yelled three times for him to halt and then fired his gun and killed the man. Gilmore was convicted of manslaughter, but a California Court of Appeals reversed his conviction. It stated that *Tennessee v. Garner* only limits what police officers may do, not private citizens, because the Fourth Amendment only applies to government officials. Under California law, any killing "necessarily committed in attempting, by lawful ways and means, to apprehend any person for any felony committed" is justifiable. So the court found the killing justifiable. Do you think private citizens should be able to shoot non-violent fleeing felons? Do you think police should be able to? Who should have more right to use force—police or private citizens? Why?

Class Activity: Split Second

If you were a police officer in a dangerous situation, how do you think you should respond? In this activity, students decide how they would respond as officers in different situations.

1. Break into pairs.

2. Each pair should:

   a. Read the cases below.

   b. Decide how to handle each case and how much force, if any, is reasonable and necessary.

   c. Review the list of factors (page 105) that police officers might take into account when deciding how much force to use. Discuss:

      (1) Which, if any, went into your decision in the previous cases?

      (2) Did any additional factors go into your decision?

   d. Be prepared to discuss the cases and answers with the class.

3. Call on teams to report and discuss their findings. Close the activity with a discussion using the Debriefing Questions on this page.

Cases

#1: Eulia

Eulia, a 39-year-old black woman, had a dispute with a gas company serviceman. The serviceman appeared at Eulia's home to turn off the gas because of an unpaid bill. She attacked the serviceman and struck him several times with a shovel. The serviceman left and called the police.

When two police officers arrived at Eulia's home to arrest her for the aggravated assault, Eulia screamed at them and threw some dishes on the floor. The noise attracted several curious neighbors to her front porch to see what was going on. While the officers talked to Eulia from a corner of the kitchen, she suddenly picked up an 11-inch knife from the counter and prepared to throw it at them.

#2: Tony

Tony, a tall, thin, 17-year-old boy, was speeding and swerving his car back and forth between the lanes on the highway late one night. Two police officers stopped him and asked to see his driver's license. Tony, who had obviously been drinking, became enraged and verbally abusive.

One of the officers, a 20-year veteran of the police force, attempted to handcuff him, but Tony pushed him away, grabbed a crowbar from his back seat, and waved it at the other officer. "I'll kill you if you come near me again," he screamed.

Factors Police Might Consider

1. Suspect's sex
2. Suspect's age
3. Suspect's race
4. Suspect's demeanor
5. Suspect's height
6. Suspect's weight
7. Suspect's mental condition
8. Police's weapon
9. Suspect's weapon
10. Time of day
11. Visibility
12. Location
13. Distance between suspect and police
14. Cover for officers
15. Cover for suspect
16. Possibility of suspect's escape if deadly force is not used
17. Presence of bystanders
18. Availability of backup
19. Number of suspects
20. Number of officers

Debriefing Questions

1. What was the minimum use of force suggested for each case? What was the maximum?

2. After hearing all the team reports, would you modify the approach you suggested? Why or why not?

3. What factors from the list were most commonly used in making a decision? (List them on the board.) Which factors were least commonly used?

4. What factors should affect an officer's decision to use force in a particular situation? Why?

Note: In a study, 50 police officers were asked to respond to hypothetical cases just as you did here. A majority of the officers considered the following factors important:

1. Suspect's weapon
2. Location
3. Number of suspects
4. Cover for officers
5. Presence of bystanders
6. Availability of backup
7. Distance between suspect and officer

From this study, it appeared that most officers focused on location and the suspects' actions, not the suspects themselves. Other factors, such as suspects' race, sex, height, and weight, did not have as much bearing on the officers' decisions.

Policing the Police

But who will guard the guardians?
    —The Roman writer Juvenal (A.D. 50–130)

Who polices the police? This question has repeatedly come up, especially in minority communities, after incidents of alleged police brutality. Among the most notorious incidents are:

- In 1991, a citizen videotaped several Los Angeles police officers beating Rodney King following a high-speed chase. The Los Angeles County district attorney filed charges against four officers. But in April 1992, a jury acquitted them of all charges. This provoked rioting and outrage in Los Angeles and other cities. It also prompted the federal government to bring criminal charges against the four officers for violating King's civil rights. At the federal trial, two of the officers were convicted. In August 1993, they were sentenced to 30 months in prison.

- In 1997, several New York police officers arrested Abner Louima, a Haitian immigrant. They mistakenly thought he had assaulted an officer during a brawl outside a nightclub. Louima charged that police beat him in the patrol car and that two officers in the station house rammed a broomstick up his rectum. Louima sustained serious injuries. Federal authorities took over the investigation. One officer pleaded guilty to violating Louima's civil rights and was sentenced to 30 years. In June 1999, a jury convicted another officer, who faces life imprisonment. In March 2000, the second officer and two others were convicted of conspiracy to obstruct justice for lying to investigators about what happened to Louima. They face up to five years in prison. Louima has filed a multi-million dollar lawsuit.

- In 1999, four plainclothes officers of the New York Police Department's Street Crime saw Amadou Diallo, an African immigrant, standing in the entrance hall to his

PAUL CONRAD

"I have the right to remain silent. Anything I say can be used against me in court. If I cannot afford a lawyer, one will be provided . . ."

apartment. Police thought he was a burglar and yelled at him to freeze. Diallo tried to open his door. When he reached for his wallet, police thought he had a gun. They opened fire, shooting 41 rounds and killing Diallo. Diallo was unarmed and had no criminal record. The four officers were charged with second-degree murder and five lesser offenses. In February 2000, a jury found the four defendants not guilty on all charges. Diallo's family has filed a large lawsuit.

Many members of minority groups have long complained about police brutality and harassment on the street. What can be done about police officers who behave improperly?

In cases of severe misbehavior, officers can be charged with crimes, such as in the cases above. If officers use excessive force, they can face, depending on the circumstances, charges of assault under color of authority, assault with a deadly weapon, or even manslaughter or murder. Except in the most blatant cases, however, it can be very difficult to convict a police officer for using excessive force. Police reform experts point to the following as likely reasons for this difficulty:

Prosecutors may resist bringing charges against police. Prosecutors work with police on a daily basis. They depend on officers to investigate crimes and testify at trials. When an officer is accused of using excessive force, other police officers tend to rally around the accused officer. Because prosecutors have working relationships with police, many avoid prosecuting police except in obvious cases of excessive force.

Proving excessive force can be difficult. Since police are authorized to use force, the prosecutor does not merely have to prove that the officer assaulted the victim. The prosecutor must show that the officer used excessive force. Many of these incidents happen at night with few witnesses other than the victim and the police. And as with all criminal trials, the prosecution must convince all 12 jurors that no reasonable doubt exists that the officer used excessive force.

Many jurors tend to identify with the police. Like most Americans, jurors worry about crime. They see the police as the thin blue line between them and the criminal element. Knowing how hazardous police work is, they are thankful for the protection police offer them. Since police work is so important and so dangerous, most jurors tend to give the police the benefit of the doubt at trial.

Advocates for the police see the matter in quite a different light. They believe that criminal prosecutions for excessive force are normally inappropriate. They argue that police work is highly regulated and that incidents of abuse are extremely rare. In addition, they claim that criminal laws and departmental rules regulating excessive force are difficult to apply in the field, where officers sometimes work under life-and-death circumstances. Finally, they argue that police are expected to protect citizens, be tough on criminals, and deal with the most dangerous elements in society, often with inadequate resources and little public support.

What about civil lawsuits? Are they more effective at policing the police? The number of lawsuits against police officers has risen steadi-ly over the last 30 years. Some cities pay out millions of dollars annually to plaintiffs alleging police brutality. Because of their high cost, these suits must have some effect on encouraging cities to root out problem officers.

But for an individual with a complaint against the police, filing a lawsuit is seldom an option. Since few people can afford to pay lawyer fees, those choosing to sue must find a lawyer who will take the case on a contingency fee. This means the lawyer will not charge the client unless the client wins. Since lawyers want to get paid, they will only take cases that they have a reasonable expectation of winning. Lawyers know these cases must be very strong. For although civil suits do not share all the obstacles of a criminal trial, they do share one—jurors, most of whom are concerned about crime, may tend to see the case from the police's point of view. This means that civil suits, like criminal cases, are likely to succeed in dealing with only the most outrageous mis-behavior by the police.

So what can individuals with complaints against the police do? One option is to file complaints against the officers. Most police departments have a set procedure for taking citizen complaints. But methods for handling these complaints vary.

In some cities, the police department itself handles complaints against police officers. Other police officers or the chief of police investigate the charges. In larger police departments, an internal-affairs section staffed by

Ask an Expert

Does your police department have a written policy regarding the use of deadly force? If so, ask for a copy and see how it does or does not incorporate the basic requirements as outlined above.

If your police department does not have a written policy, interview officers and find out what, if any, formal or informal guidelines they follow in the use of deadly force.

Also, for most people firearms come to mind when they hear the phrase "deadly force." Find out if other forms of deadly force are used by police in your area.

Rate of Police Use of Force Incidents in One Year	
Type of force	**Rate per 1,000 sworn officers**
Handcuff/leg restraint	490.4
Bodily force (arm, foot, or leg)	272.2
Come-alongs	226.8
Unholstering weapon	129.9
Swarm	126.7
Twist locks/wrist locks	80.9
Firm grip	57.7
Chemical agents (Mace or Cap-Stun)	36.2
Batons	36.0
Flashlights	21.7
Dog attacks or bites	6.5
Electrical devices (TASER)	5.4
Civilians shot at but not hit	3.0
Other impact devices	2.4
Neck restraints/unconsciousness-rendering holds	1.4
Vehicle rammings	1.0
Civilians shot and killed	0.9
Civilians shot and wounded but not killed	0.2

Reported incidents of police use of force per 1,000 sworn officers during 1991 in city departments.

Source: *National Data Collection on Police Use of Force,* Bureau of Justice Statistics (1996)

special officers investigates certain citizen complaints and disciplines police officers who violate the law or police department regulations. These are the ways the police "police" themselves.

In recent years, the number of citizen complaints against the police has increased. Complaints range from relatively minor matters, such as failing to investigate a crime properly, to more serious cases involving police corruption or police brutality. Some complaints charge the police with mistreating people in custody.

Many people have seen a need to give citizens more control over police behavior. Some cities have used **citizen review boards** for this purpose. Composed of community members, these boards investigate reports of police misconduct and recommend what action should

be taken. Citizen review boards may or may not have the power to carry out their recommendations.

Controversy, however, surrounds these boards. Police often oppose creating these boards. They feel that their job is dangerous and not easily understood by the public. They admit that misconduct sometimes occurs and citizen complaints must be treated seriously. But they usually insist that justice is more likely to be obtained if an accused officer is investigated by other officers who know what police work is really like. Furthermore, many police officers believe citizen controls may hamper police work and that outsiders may be hostile to the police.

On the other hand, many citizens argue that in our society civilians must exercise direct control over police behavior. Without effective civilian control, the police may apply their own standards, and abuse may be more acceptable. If this occurs, citizens will lose respect for the police and for the law that the police are expected to enforce.

For Discussion

1. There are several ways of disciplining problem officers—criminal prosecutions, civil lawsuits, departmental action, and citizen review boards. What are the strengths and weaknesses of each?

2. Who should police the police? How should it be done? Explain your answer.

Class Activity: A Board of Rights

In this activity, students simulate a review board on police misconduct and decide hypothetical cases.

1. Break into groups of four members each. Each group will function as a Police Board of Rights whose purpose is to decide about possible disciplinary action against officers receiving complaints from citizens.

2. Each board will deal with the same two cases. In each case, the board must:

a. Determine the guilt or innocence of the officers.

b. If guilty, decide the punishment the officer should receive.

These cases have been thoroughly investigated by the police department's Internal Affairs Division, and the accused officers are fully aware of the charges against them. You and the other Board of Rights members are all high-ranking police officers. You have already heard the evidence for and against the accused officers and you have discussed the contents of each officer's personnel file. (A summary of the events of each case and the evidence before you is given below.)

The board must evaluate the evidence and decide on the guilt or innocence of the officers accused in the two cases.

3. Each group should:

a. Select a chairperson.

b. Read the materials on the two cases to be presented to the board on pages 109–111. Review each case thoroughly with all the members of the group.

c. Using the questions listed under "Recommendations," discuss each case, vote on the guilt or innocence of the accused officer, and decide on an appropriate penalty, if necessary. The chairperson should record the answers to the questions and the recommendations of the group. Minority opinions should also be noted by the chairperson.

d. If the board determines that an accused officer is innocent, recommend that the complaint be dropped. If the board finds an officer guilty, decide on one of the following penalties:

(1) Reprimand (warning to be placed in the officer's file)

(2) Suspension up to six months with loss of pay

(3) Removal from the force

e. After deciding, prepare a brief report discussing the reasons for the decision and be prepared to discuss them with the class.

4. All the boards should report their decisions and reasons to the class. Conclude the activity by holding a discussion using the Debriefing Questions on page 111.

Case #1: Officers Mark Thomas and Stephen Campbell

Description of Events:

Mark Thomas has been on the force for six years and Stephen Campbell for five years. They are good friends. Recently, they met in a cocktail lounge at about 1 a.m. Both were just off duty and still in uniform. They had five or six beers, and Officer Campbell bought several drinks for one of the off-duty waitresses.

The two officers had a running joke about Officer Thomas wanting to buy Officer Campbell's gun. Campbell had brought the gun that evening to sell it to Thomas. Thomas kept offering more money than Campbell was willing to accept and the matter became a joke between them as they passed the gun back and forth under the table.

Meanwhile, Officer Thomas and the waitress had some disagreeable words because the waitress felt Thomas had insulted her. Thomas contends he did not mean to insult her and was only joking.

Later, when Officer Thomas left the lounge, he pretended he was going to steal a decorative keg of beer from the cocktail lounge. Thomas claims he was only joking and had no intention of stealing the keg. But the waitress grabbed the keg and took it back to the bar. The waitress was upset, and Officer Campbell was unable to calm her down.

The next day, the waitress complained to the police department that the two officers had been at the bar waving guns around. She stated it was "a regular O.K. Corral without the shots fired." She also accused Officer Thomas of trying to steal the beer keg. In her written complaint, she said both Thomas and Campbell were drunk.

National Poll of Police Officers on the Code of Silence

	Strongly Agree	Agree	Disagree	Strongly Disagree
The code of silence is an essential part of the mutual trust necessary to good policing.	1.2%	15.7%	65.6%	17.5%
Whistle blowing is not worth it.	3.1	21.8	63.5	11.7
An officer who reports another officer's misconduct is likely to be given the cold shoulder by his or her fellow officers.	11.0	56.4	30.9	1.8
It is not unusual for a police officer to turn a blind eye to improper conduct by other officers.	1.8	50.6	43.3	4.4
Police officers always report serious criminal violations involving abuse of authortity by fellow officers	2.8	36.2	58.5	2.5

Source: "Police Attitudes Toward Abuse of Authority: Findings From a National Study," National Institute of Justice (2000)

The waitress and her girlfriend were later interviewed together by Internal Affairs Division investigators, and so neither could be used to corroborate the other's story. The parking lot attendant was not interviewed, nor were other witnesses found who could verify whether the officers were drunk. The bartender claimed the two officers were not drunk, but by law he must not serve intoxicated persons, so he would most likely claim they were sober. The waitress has a record of being under psychiatric care. All evidence indicates, however, that she is completely sincere and truthful.

Three charges currently exist against the two officers. They are listed below. The recommendation of the captain in charge of these officers was 15 days suspension without pay for Thomas, and 10 days for Campbell. Both officers have appealed their case to the Board of Rights contending that the punishment is unjust and the investigation was improperly handled.

Personnel Records:

Officer Mark Thomas has received only one previous complaint. This was from a motorist who objected to the traffic ticket he received and said that Officer Thomas was rude and did not call him "sir" when he spoke to him. Officer Thomas' evaluation from his superiors describes him as energetic, high spir-

ited, and a good marksman.

Officer Campbell has received no previous complaints and has been found an excellent officer by his superiors.

Recommendations:

Based on your review of this information, do you feel that Officer Mark Thomas should be found guilty of any of the following:

(1) exposing a firearm unnecessarily in public;

(2) misappropriation of property (beer keg);

(3) disturbing the peace?

Should any penalty be applied? If so, what? Do you feel that Officer Stephen Campbell should be found guilty of any of the charges listed above? If so, what penalty should be applied in this case?

Case #2: Officers Sam Allen and Mary McCrea

Description of Events:

Officers Allen and McCrea were summoned about 2 a.m. to a wealthy area of town by a resident. The resident complained of a disturbance from a loud party going on next door. The resident also stated that three people wearing black leather motorcycle jackets who apparently were attending the party had come to his door, obviously drunk. One of the three reportedly carried a kitchen knife and asked to borrow a "cup of sugar and maybe some blood."

As the officers approached the caller's house, they saw a young man, about 21, standing by three motorcycles. When the man saw the officers, he joined a young woman and began walking toward the front door of the house. The officers followed them and ordered them to stop.

Officers could hear a stereo playing music seemingly at full volume inside the house. But the two people in front said that nearly everyone had gone home except maybe for "two or three people in the back yard." It was clear to the officers that the two were under the influence of alcohol or narcotics or both.

When asked what had been going on, the two people replied that some people had "just been listening to music" and "having a good time." The officers explained that a neighbor had called about a disturbance and someone using a knife in a threatening manner. The officers overheard the girl say, "I wonder if Dusty was at it again."

Officers Allen and McCrea asked to speak to the owner of the house but were told that he was not at home. Then the officers asked to speak to the host or hostess and were informed that it was an open party and there was no host or hostess. The two did not know who lived at the house. They went inside, leaving the officers on the front lawn.

Just then, three people wearing black leather motorcycle jackets appeared from the side of the house. Officer Allen ordered the group to halt. He and Officer McCrea approached them. The trio was somewhat belligerent and, when questioned about the neighbor's call, said they knew nothing.

Officer Allen asked for their names. One of the group identified himself as Dusty Adams. The officer asked the group to remain until they could be identified by the complaining neighbor. They refused and said they were going to leave. At this point, Officer Allen ordered the three to stand spread-eagle with their hands on the stone wall next to the driveway. All of them began to curse.

While Officer McCrea held her gun,

Officer Allen began to frisk the group. He found a kitchen knife in the boot of one. As he searched the second man, Dusty Adams turned saying, "Hey, man, listen, you don't want any trouble do you?"

"Keep your hands on the wall or we'll shoot," said Officer Allen. Adams took a step away from the wall. Officer McCrea fired, wounding Adams in the shoulder. No weapon was found on his person.

Subsequently, a complaint was filed against Officer McCrea charging that she overreacted and used unreasonable force. Internal Affairs investigated the complaint and referred it to the Board of Rights.

Officers Allen and McCrea contended that under the circumstances they had probable cause to act as they did and probable cause to believe that Dusty Adams was reaching for another weapon when he moved suddenly and removed his hands from the stone wall. Furthermore, the officers stated that the suspects had been warned, and that under the circumstances the officers had not acted unreasonably. The captain has recommended that no disciplinary action be taken against officers Allen and McCrea.

Personnel Records:

Officers Allen and McCrea have been on the force for three and two years respectively. Both are highly regarded by their superiors. Neither has received any previous complaints.

Recommendations:

In your opinion should Officer Sam Allen or Officer Mary McCrea be found guilty of using unreasonable force? If so, what should the penalty be?

Debriefing Questions

1. What was the most difficult part of deciding these cases? Why?

2. What factors might make the job of a police rights board difficult and controversial? Why?

3. What if your group had been made up only of citizens concerned about police behavior? Would you have decided any of these cases differently?

You and the Police

At some time, you may have a difficult contact with the police. They may want to question you. You may be subject to arrest. It might be because of your conduct or just because you happen to be in the wrong place at the wrong time.

It is important to remember that the police work for you as a citizen of your community, whatever your age, race, or job. The police are required to respect your rights. You, in turn, should respect their authority and understand the difficulties of their job. Mutual respect can go a long way toward easing tension in a difficult situation.

The following is some general advice on what to do if the police stop you. In any particular situation, you should always rely on your best judgment and, when possible, the advice of a lawyer.

If You Are Stopped by a Police Officer

1. Be courteous and cooperative. Avoid hostility, profanity, or aggressive movements. Do nothing to cause an officer to believe you are a threat.

2. Give your name and address, or show an I.D. if requested.

3. The police can search you for concealed weapons by patting your clothing. Do not physically resist, but you have the right to tell the officer that you do not agree to any search of yourself, your car, or your surroundings. By making it clear that you do not consent to any search, you can protect your right against unlawful searches. The police may search you or your surroundings anyway. Do not try to stop them physically. You can question the legality of the search in court. If the police say that they have a warrant, ask to see it.

4. If you believe the police have violated your rights, you have the right to file a complaint.

If You Are Arrested or Held

1. Never run away, strike an officer, or physically resist, whether you are innocent or guilty. If you resist or try to escape, the police can use whatever force is reasonable and necessary to stop you.

2. You are entitled to your *Miranda* rights, which include the right to remain silent. You are required to tell the police nothing except your name and address. Giving explanations or stories or trying to excuse your conduct will rarely benefit you unless your lawyer advises you to do so.

3. Ask to see a lawyer immediately. If you cannot pay for a lawyer, you have the right to request the police to get you a lawyer before you talk to officials.

4. After arrest, use your right to make a telephone call to a relative, trusted friend, or lawyer for assistance. If you are under age 18, you may not be permitted to make telephone calls. Ask to see a lawyer. You generally have the right to go into court the next court day after your arrest and you can ask to be released on bail, although the law may differ for minors.

5. Do not make any decisions in your case until you have talked to a lawyer and understand what your choices are.

For Discussion

1. How can you best assure mutual respect between you and the police?

2. Do you think mutual respect between you and the police is important? Why or why not?

3. Why is it important not to resist police?

Unit 3:
The Criminal Case

On July 6, shots ring out in a quiet residential community. A human life is taken and a suspect arrested . . . .

So begins the criminal case of *People v. Carter*. Although fictional, it is like real-life events that take place each day in cities and towns throughout the United States. There is only one important difference.

This time, you and your class will be on the scene from beginning to end—and not just as observers. You will step into the roles of lawyers, judges, and jurors in a criminal case. You will study the police report, meet the defendant and hear his side of the story, help the prosecutors prepare their case, rule on motions, and select a jury. Eventually, you will see the trial itself unfold and participate in finding the truth about the events on that hot July evening. Ultimately, your actions and decisions will take the case to a final verdict. When you are finished, you will have taken a behind-the-scenes look at how the criminal justice system handles a criminal case and at the philosophies and procedures that shape the system.

CHAPTER 8
Courts and the Case Process

The Two Systems of Criminal Courts

In the United States, the criminal courts belong to two separate systems—the state and federal. The state courts try defendants charged with state crimes and the federal system deals with those charged with federal crimes. Far more criminal trials take place in state courts, because states have traditionally handled most criminal offenses. In recent years, however, the federal government has created more federal crimes and, as a consequence, has increased the workload of the federal criminal courts.

The Federal Courts

The federal court system consists of three basic levels. On the lowest level are more than 90 district courthouses. These handle trials in the federal system.

A single judge presides over a criminal trial. The Sixth Amendment to the U.S. Constitution gives every criminal defendant the right to a trial by jury. For many criminal trials, defendants choose to have a jury, but often they waive this right and let the judge hear the case alone. In jury trials, the jury listens to testimony by witnesses and views other evidence presented. The judge rules on the law—ruling what evidence can be admitted, ruling on different motions from defense and prosecution, and instructing the jury on the law in the case.

If a defendant is convicted in a federal trial court, the defendant may appeal to the next level of courts—the circuit courts of appeals. There are 13 of these courts, each having jurisdiction over a particular part of the United States. Each circuit court has from six to 30 justices. The courts normally hear appeals in panels of three justices.

Appeals courts, also known as **appellate courts**, do not try cases. They review what the trial court has done and rule on matters of law. They rely on the record of evidence presented in the trial court and usually receive written legal arguments, known as briefs, from attorneys for the prosecution and defense. In cases that concern important legal issues, an appeals court might also receive *amicus curiae* (friend of the court) briefs from groups interested in the outcome. The appeals court hears oral arguments from both sides. Then the justices retire and discuss the case among themselves. They vote, and one justice is assigned to write the **opinion of the court**, which states the facts of the case, the issue, the court's decision (known as the **holding**), and the reasons for the holding. If a justice disagrees with the holding, he or she may

Criminal Court Systems	
STATE	**FEDERAL**
State Supreme Court	U.S. Supreme Court
Intermediate Court of Appeal	Circuit Court of Appeals
State Trial Court	District Court

The federal judicial system, and most state systems, have three levels of courts.

write a **dissenting opinion**. Sometimes justices may also write **concurring opinions** when they agree with the holding but disagree with the court's reasoning or want to add something that is not in the opinion of the court.

On the highest level is the U.S. Supreme Court. It hears appeals from the prosecution or defense on federal courts of appeals' decisions. It also can hear appeals of state supreme courts' decisions on issues of U.S. constitutional law.

The U.S. Supreme Court has what is known as discretionary jurisdiction. This means that the court does not have to take every appeal. Parties must petition to have their appeals heard by the court. If four of the nine justices agree that the court should hear a case, then the court grants what is called a **writ of certiorari**, and the court will hear the appeal.

In making their decisions, appeals courts and ultimately the Supreme Court interpret what the Constitution and other federal laws mean. Decisions can actually overturn laws if the court believes they conflict with the Constitution. Their written opinions add to the body of law.

The State Systems

Each state has its own criminal court system. Many states have two types of trial courts—courts of limited and courts of unlimited jurisdiction. Courts of limited jurisdiction try only misdemeanors and lesser offenses. But they may hold pretrial felony hearings also. They are often called municipal, magistrate, or police courts. Courts of unlimited jurisdiction commonly hear felony cases. Depending on the state, these courts are usually called superior, district, circuit, or general-sessions courts.

If convicted, defendants may appeal their cases to appellate courts. Most states have two levels of appeals courts—an intermediate level and the state supreme court. But some states have only a state supreme court. Like the U.S. Supreme Court, many state supreme courts have discretionary jurisdiction. They choose which cases they will hear by granting writs of certiorari.

If a state supreme court hears an appeal, it has the last word on interpretations of state law and the state constitution. Defendants cannot appeal further unless they charge violations of the U.S. Constitution. Then they may ask the U.S. Supreme Court to hear their cases.

For Discussion

1. "We don't have two systems of criminal justice. We have 51." Do you agree? Explain.

2. What is discretionary jurisdiction? Why do you think the U.S. Supreme Court and many state supreme courts have this type of jurisdiction?

3. Under what circumstances could the U.S. Supreme Court overrule a state supreme court's interpretation of its state's law? Explain.

Judges and Judicial Independence

When trial judges preside over criminal trials, they make many legal rulings: Should this evidence be admitted? Should this objection be sustained? What law applies to this case? Is the law constitutional? On appeals, appellate court judges review these rulings. All judges—trial and appellate—are supposed to be fair and impartial. When judges interpret and apply the law, they must base their decisions on statutes, Constitutional law, and prior court cases. They must never be swayed by politics or popular opinion. This is what separates courtrooms from lynch mobs. This is what is meant by the rule of law. Our democracy depends on an independent judiciary.

The U.S. Constitution attempts to ensure judicial independence. All federal judges are appointed by the president, confirmed by the U.S. Senate, and serve for life. There is only one way under the Constitution that federal judges can be removed: The U.S. House of Representatives can vote to impeach any federal judge for "treason, bribery or other high crimes or misdemeanors." The judge is then tried by the Senate. To remove the judge, two-thirds of the Senate must vote to convict. Only 13 federal judges in our history have been impeached by the House and just seven convicted by the Senate. All have been convicted for criminal behavior. None has ever been convicted for making unpopular decisions or for holding an unpopular judicial philosophy.

State Judges

Most judges in the United States are not members of the federal judiciary. Most belong to the various state courts, which differ in how they select judges.

About 20 states hold direct elections for judges. This means that judges run for office. This allows voters to elect judges in their district, but it has some drawbacks. Judges must raise money for campaigns, often from lawyers who will appear before them. That can give the appearance that lawyers are paying for favoritism. Judicial campaigns in themselves are problematic. Judges can't make campaign promises that they will rule in a certain way. That would make the judge biased. Bringing judges into the political process can make them seem less neutral in the courtroom.

For these reasons, most states have moved away from direct election of judges. In these states, the governor usually appoints all state appellate court judges and most trial court judges. In some states the governor makes selections from a list prepared by a judicial commission, which searches for the most qualified judicial candidates.

But most of these states still require judges to face voters. Appellate judges usually go on the ballot in the next general election after being appointed. These are called retention elections because voters get to decide whether or not to retain the judges. No one can oppose them. Voters must choose "yes" or "no." If voters retain them, they serve what

From presiding on the highly publicized O.J. Simpson murder trial, Los Angeles Superior Court Judge Lance Ito became one of the most well-known trial judges in America.

remains of their 12-year term of office and then stand for election to a full 12-year term. Trial judges also go before the voters in the next general election after their appointment. But their terms are shorter, typically six years. And in some states, opponents can run against them.

In addition, in many states, voters can recall judges that they believe do not belong on the bench. People opposing a judge must get a certain number of signatures on recall petitions. Then the judge's name is put on the ballot and voters decide whether they want to retain or recall the judge. If a majority votes to recall the judge, then the judge must be replaced—either by election or appointment, depending on the state.

This system has generally shielded judges from politics. It allows judges to serve long terms with a limited degree of accountability to voters. But in recent years, some recall and retention elections have provoked controversy. The late Bernard Witkin, a noted legal scholar, warned:

"What we're seeing is a new way to approach judicial elections, challenging judges' qualifications on the basis of particular decisions that affect particular groups. . . . If we reach the point where . . . we end up telling the court, 'If you don't do as we want, we'll remove you,' then the courts won't be worth saving."

For Discussion

1. What is judicial independence? Why is it important?

2. What are the differences between the way state and federal judges are appointed and removed?

3. What do you think the best system of appointing and removing judges would be? Why?

Class Activity: Retention Election

In this activity, students take the role of voters in a state retention election for several justices of the Supreme Court, the highest appeals court in the state.

1. Break the class into small groups. In each group, students should:

   a. Discuss each of justices described below.

   b. Decide whether to vote "yes" to retain or "no" to remove each justice.

   c. Prepare to report each decision and the reasons for it to the class.

2. After the groups have made their decisions, have them report back and discuss each justice, indicating the reasons for voting to retain or not. Conclude the activity by holding a discussion using the Debriefing Questions.

Justices

All the justices have much experience as both lawyers and judges and have served at least one term of 12 years. The state bar association rates each as "highly qualified," the highest ranking. Each of the justices has drawn some public criticism for the incidents related below.

Justice #1: Joyce Harris. Justice Harris wrote the majority opinion last term overturning the conviction of a defendant accused of child molestation. The court ruled that police had illegally seized evidence. Without this evidence, prosecutors say they will be unable to retry the defendant.

Justice #2: Samuel Grodin. In the last 12 capital punishment appeals before the court, Justice Grodin has voted to overturn the death sentence nine times. Despite Justice Grodin's votes, the court upheld all 12 death sentences.

Justice #3: John Chen. Justice Chen is known as a law-and-order conservative. He rarely votes against death sentences or against overturning any case on the grounds that police did not conduct a proper search or interrogation.

Debriefing Questions

1. Review the reasons people gave for retaining or not. What do you think are valid reasons for voting for and against judges?

2. Did you have enough information to vote? If not, what additional information would you need?

Criminal Lawyers

Lawyers are highly educated professionals. To become a lawyer, students must graduate from a four-year college and complete three years of law school (obtaining a juris doctorate, or J.D., degree). After law school, they must pass a bar examination in the state in which they want to practice law. This is usually a two to three day examination on all aspects of the law. They also must certify that they have no criminal record. (Those with criminal records must be cleared and found fit to practice law by a state bar committee.) Once they pass the bar exam, they may practice law in the state. Members in good standing of a state bar may practice before federal courts as well.

Although members of the bar may practice in all areas of the law, few general practitioners exist today. Most specialize in one area—corporations, labor relations, real estate, wills and trusts, taxation, personal injury, civil litigation, and other fields. Few practice criminal law, probably less than 1 percent of all attorneys. The criminal bar is divided into prosecutors and defense attorneys.

Prosecutors

Prosecutors are government employees. They represent the public and present the government's case against the defendant in criminal cases. At trial, the prosecutor must prove the defendant's guilt beyond a reasonable doubt.

At the federal level, prosecutors work out of about 90 U.S. attorney offices across the country. Each office is headed by a U.S. attorney, appointed by the president and confirmed by the Senate. U.S. attorneys serve under the U.S. attorney general, the cabinet member who heads the Department of Justice.

Since most criminal prosecutions take place in state criminal courts, there are thousands of prosecutor offices for cities, counties, and states. Most are headed by an elected state, district, or city attorney. In rural areas, the prosecutor's office may consist of one lawyer. The nation's 75 largest counties, however, account for more than half of all prosecutions. Los Angeles County has the largest office, with more than 1,000 deputy district attorneys and an annual budget of more than $200 million. Large offices have specialized units for prosecuting cases involving drugs, juveniles, child abuse, homicide, domestic violence, gangs, career criminals, arson, and white-collar crime.

Aside from presenting cases, prosecutors must decide whether to bring charges, what the charges are, and whether to change or drop charges. They are officers of the court with a duty to protect the integrity of the justice system. The American Bar Association (ABA), the leading organization of lawyers, states in its Code of Professional Responsibility that the prosecutors' job is to "seek justice, not merely to convict." This means that they must only prosecute those they believe are guilty. In addition, they must turn over to the defense any evidence that tends to exculpate a defendant.

Defense Attorneys

Defense attorneys prepare and present defendants' cases at pretrial hearings, at trial, and on appeal. The U.S. Supreme Court has also ruled that a criminal defendant has the right to have a lawyer present at any interrogation (*Escobedo v. Illinois*, 1964) and post-indictment lineup (*U.S. v. Wade*, 1967). To present defendants' versions of the facts, defense attorneys try to find supportive witnesses and call them to testify at trial. They raise reasonable doubts about defendants' guilt and may present affirmative defenses.

Defense attorneys can be either private attorneys or public employees. Historically, most defense attorneys were private attorneys who required payment from their clients. If a criminal defendant could not afford a lawyer, then the defendant might have to go to court without one.

A series of Supreme Court decisions changed this and, in the process, changed the defense bar. In 1932 in *Powell v. Alabama*, the Supreme Court ruled that states must supply attorneys for indigent defendants in death-penalty cases. In 1938 in *Johnson v. Zerbst*, the court ruled that the federal government must provide lawyers for indigent defendants in all federal cases. In 1963 in *Gideon v. Wainright*, the court extended the rule to all felony cases in state courts. In 1972 in *Argersinger v. Hamlin*, the court further extended the rule to any misdemeanor that could result in the defendant spending time in jail. The decisions rested on the Sixth Amendment, which states in part that in "all criminal prosecutions, the accused shall enjoy the right . . . to have the assistance of counsel for his defense." The court reasoned, as Justice Hugo Black wrote in *Gideon*, that "any person hauled into court, who is too poor to hire a lawyer, cannot be assured a fair trial unless counsel is provided for him."

Following these decisions, the defense bar changed. It is no longer dominated by attorneys in private practice. States and counties set up three systems to provide counsel to defendants who could not afford private attorneys. One is the **assigned counsel**

"I just found out your lawyer specializes
in real estate."

Whether attorneys are public defenders or in private practice, defending people accused of crime is difficult. Many people in the community don't understand the important role defense attorneys play. Questions often arise, such as, "How can they defend those people?" or "How can they defend someone they know is guilty?" The answer is that everyone—guilty or innocent—is entitled to a fair trial. Our justice system is an adversary system. For it to work, both the state and defense should have able advocates. The state must prove that a person is guilty beyond a reasonable doubt. This may mean that guilty people will go free, but our system is set up on the principle: "Better that 10 guilty persons escape than that one innocent suffer." (William Blackstone, *Commentaries on English Common Law.*) The entire power of the government—the police and prosecutor's office—is lined up against the defendant. The defense attorney protects the rights of the defendant and in so doing protects the rights of everyone.

The ABA states in its Code of Professional Responsibility that "a lawyer should represent a client zealously within the bounds of the law." In short, an attorney should represent all defendants fully and forcefully.

Defense attorneys, like prosecutors, are officers of the court. As the ABA notes, there are limits on what defense lawyers can do. They cannot, for example, advise a client to break the law or put anyone on the stand who the lawyer knows will lie. In 1986 in *Nix v. Whiteside*, the Supreme Court was asked to rule on these limits. A defense attorney told his client that if he took the stand and told a false story, the attorney would have to report him to the court. The defendant took the stand and did not lie. He was convicted, but he appealed claiming that his lawyer had denied him effective counsel by forbidding him to commit perjury. The Supreme Court ruled that the attorney had acted properly.

For Discussion

1. What does it mean that prosecutors and defense attorneys are "officers of the court"?

system, which is often used in rural areas. A judge appoints private counsel from a list. The lawyers are reimbursed by the government. Another system is **contract counsel**. Private firms under contract with the government provide legal services. The third system, the **public defender**, is the most widely used system. Public defenders work full-time for the government. Their job is to defend indigent defendants. They often work under staggering caseloads.

The public defender system has received criticism on several counts. Some say the heavy caseload causes public defenders to dispose of cases quickly instead of working wholeheartedly for defendants. Others claim that by working day-after-day with the same judges and prosecutors, public defenders feel that they are on the same team and don't vigorously battle in court. Still others claim that since public defenders are on the government payroll, they cannot rock the boat too much.

But many praise the work of public defenders as zealous advocates for their clients. They point out that many public defenders have far more experience and knowledge of the criminal courts than private attorneys, who may not even be specialists in criminal law. They also believe that because public defenders know prosecutors and judges well, they know which tactics work best against them.

Ask an Expert

Invite a representative from a local law school to tell about the requirements for law school and the courses offered.

2. Do you think defense attorneys should defend people they know are guilty? Why or why not?

3. Do you think indigent criminal defendants should be provided lawyers? Explain.

4. In 1979 in *Scott v. Illinois*, the Supreme Court refused to overturn the misdemeanor shoplifting conviction of a man who was tried without a defense attorney because he could not afford one. The statute he was convicted under authorized up to a year in jail but the trial judge sentenced him to pay a $50 fine. The Supreme Court ruled 6–3 that since the judge imposed no prison time, the sentence could stand. Do you agree with this decision? Explain.

The Criminal Case Process

Every year, state and federal criminal justice systems handle thousands of criminal cases. Most cases are routine: A crime occurs, and a suspect is identified, arrested, and charged. If the defendant pleads guilty, which most do, a trial does not take place. Aside from realizing that police departments are overworked, courts are overburdened, and prisons are overcrowded, the general public knows little about the daily routine of criminal justice activity.

What does capture public attention is the big case. A sensational murder or a multi-million dollar fraud case can make headlines in our daily newspapers for months. Reporters clamor for interviews with the prosecution and defense teams, TV-news programs detail the day's courtroom events, and the defendant's name becomes a household word.

Although these big cases are not typical, they do give us a dramatic glimpse of the criminal justice process. These cases introduce us to a mind-boggling array of courthouse characters, legal terminology, procedural steps, and legal issues. At any point along the way, we might throw up our hands and mutter, "What's the point of all this? Did he do it or didn't he do it?" Since no one can read a suspect's mind and no one can peer back into the past to find out exactly what happened, we need some system to find the truth.

The Adversary System

Central to truth-finding in our criminal case process is the so-called adversarial process. In it, opposing attorneys introduce evidence to neutral fact finders—the judge or jury. Ultimately, the fact finder must decide the facts of a particular case and come to a verdict.

In this process, the attorneys are advocates and adversaries. They try to present facts in a light most favorable to their side and point out weaknesses in their opponents' case. Through well-planned strategies and legal arguments, they try to convince the court to see "truth" as they do. In a criminal case, the opposing sides are the prosecution and the defense.

The basic goal of the prosecution is to protect society from crime by making sure the guilty are tried, convicted, and punished. By filing charges against a particular defendant, the prosecutor is claiming that the individual has committed a crime. At trial, the prosecutor must prove the claim beyond a reasonable doubt.

The basic goal of the defense is to challenge the prosecutor's case by raising all reasonable doubts about the defendant's guilt. Defense attorneys must also make sure that the defendant gets every right and benefit guaranteed under the law and Constitution.

By pitting these two sides against one another, it is believed that the truth will come out. For example, if the prosecution's robbery case depends on an eyewitness's identification of the defendant, the defense might go to great lengths to question the memory or eyesight of the witness. The defense can be assured of a similar strict examination of any evidence it produces. Under the adversary system, the judge or jury must decide which version is true.

The fact finder must go through this process with all the evidence produced at trial. Before determining whether or not a defendant is guilty, the fact finder must weigh a lot of evidence and establish facts. Are the witnesses believable? Are the lab tests accurate? Are the connections between the various pieces of evidence logical and supportable? What other explanations for the alleged events are possible? Indeed, the quest for truth pervades a criminal trial.

Because the adversarial process involves humans, it is not foolproof. Memories fail, witnesses see the same event in different ways, reasonable people differ about what is true. Sometimes, biases and prejudices arise, lies are told. In extreme cases, truth can get lost when an advocate goes too far in trying to win. An emotional argument can sway a jury in spite of the facts. Important evidence can be concealed.

To protect against these problems, our criminal-case process has developed sophisticated checks and balances. Some protect the process itself, while others protect the defendant. Judges and jurors can be removed for bias or prejudice. Witnesses are sworn to tell the truth and can be punished if they lie. Lawyers are bound by ethical rules against knowingly presenting false testimony. Criminal defendants in serious cases can count on representation by an attorney, a trial by jury, the right to confront accusers, a speedy and public trial, and the right to appeal. They are also protected against having to post an excessive amount for bail or having to testify against themselves. These protections come from the U.S. Constitution and the constitutions and laws of the various states.

Facts, Facts, Facts

Basic to every criminal case are facts. When used to prove a point before a court, they are called **evidence**. Evidence comes from the testimony of witnesses or from physical items related to the crime. Woven together, evidence can tell a story of guilt or innocence.

As you will discover, facts are important at every stage and to every person in the criminal-case process. Consider just a few examples. A police officer must have sufficient facts to show probable cause to arrest a suspect or conduct a search. A judge examines these facts before issuing a warrant. A criminal trial judge may be called upon to decide whether facts offered in evidence are relevant to the case.

The facts in the case of *People v. Carter* will be important throughout this unit. They are found, among other places, in the Police Investigation Report, in the defendant's story, and in the witnesses' statements. Sometimes you will be using facts as attorneys do. For example, in one activity you will take the role of prosecutors and, based on the facts, decide whether to bring a particular charge. In another, you will cross-examine witnesses to establish or refute facts contained in their testimony.

Other times you will take a more impartial attitude toward the facts. For example, as jurors you will decide what the facts are and whether taken together they amount to the defendant's guilt beyond a reasonable doubt.

For Discussion

1. What is the main purpose of the criminal-case process?

2. What is the adversary system? How does it aid truth-finding in a criminal case? What might be some weaknesses in the system?

3. What are some checks and balances found in the criminal-case process?

Class Activity: Just the Facts

In this activity, students analyze the facts of a hypothetical criminal case in which a defendant (D) is charged with assault with a deadly weapon.

1. Each student should:

    a. Read Prosecutor's Facts and Defendant's Facts.

    b. Write a summary of the sequence of events as the prosecution might see them.

    c. Do the same from the defense's point of view.

    d. Write answers to the following questions:

      • To prove a case beyond a reasonable doubt, which facts must the prosecutor cast doubt upon? Why?

      • If the facts described in point b of Defendant's Facts are proved false, could the defense still win? Why or why not?

      • Why would the examination of witnesses under oath be very important to this case?

2. After students turn in their papers, discuss each point.

Prosecutor's Facts

a. D owns a .38 caliber Smith & Wesson handgun registered in his name.

b. D's pistol was found by the investigating officers at the scene of the shooting on August 1.

c. A fingerprint expert testified that D's fingerprints were all over the handgun found at the scene. The gun had no other fingerprints on it.

d. One witness testified that two hours before the assault, he heard D threaten to shoot the victim.

e. The victim's neighbor, who reported the crime, testified that he heard shots fired at 7:35 p.m. on August 1.

Defendant's Facts

a. D testified that his pistol was stolen from his house about July 29. No police report was made because D did not discover it missing until August 2.

b. D's business partner testified that D was having dinner with her between 6:45 and 8:30 p.m. on August 1.

Using This Unit

This unit has four major features:

The Criminal Justice Case Guide

This chart on page 123 will show you each important step in a criminal case. It starts when a crime is committed and continues through the entire criminal case process. Because procedures vary in different jurisdictions, your state's procedures may vary slightly from this guide.

Key Steps

These special sections are found throughout the unit and provide more detailed information about the various steps outlined in the Criminal Justice Case Guide. A typical key step will give a particular procedure's purpose and describe what happens during that procedure.

Case Notes

These reading selections tell you about the Carter murder case. In them, you will meet all the main characters, discover facts, and learn law about the case.

Activities

Each activity focuses on the criminal case—an issue or event—and *you* will be on the firing line. Sometimes you will be asked to take the role of an attorney, sometimes a judge or a juror. By the time the unit is over, you will have argued constitutional questions, evaluated evidence, examined witnesses, made judicial rulings, and come to a verdict in the case of *People v. Carter*.

THE CRIMINAL JUSTICE CASE GUIDE

INVESTIGATION AND ARREST

- Incident
- Warrant
- Arrest

PRETRIAL

- First Court Appearance
- Probable Cause Hearing—Indictment or Information
- Arraignment
- Pretrial Motions

POST TRIAL

- Sentencing Hearing
- Post-trial Motions
- Appeals to Higher Court

TRIAL

- Jury Selection
- Opening Statement
- Presenting Evidence
- Closing Arguments
- Instructions to the Jurors
- Jury Deliberation
- Verdict

CHAPTER 9

Investigation and Arrest

 ## Key Step: Arrest

What It Is:

An arrest is the taking of a criminal suspect into custody to charge the suspect with a crime.

What Is Required:

An arrest must be based on probable cause and must be made:

- with a valid warrant;

    or

- without a warrant under one of the judicially recognized exceptions to the Fourth Amendment warrant requirement.

Who May Arrest:

Depending on the jurisdiction, arrests may be carried out by:

- Law enforcement officials.

- Private citizens. (Many jurisdictions, however, restrict your right as a private citizen to make an arrest. In some jurisdictions, you may only arrest people for certain offenses, for example, felonies and misdemeanors, but not for violating ordinances. In other jurisdictions you may not make a citizen's arrest for a misdemeanor unless the misdemeanor is committed in your presence. In a few jurisdictions, you cannot make a mistake: If it turns out that the suspect did not actually commit the offense, then the arrest is not valid and you can be sued for false arrest. It is important to find out the law in your own state.)

Police Crime Investigation Report

Date of Investigation: July 6-7

Investigating Officer: Lt. Tony Jackson

Crime Description: At approximately 7 p.m. on Tuesday, July 6, Joyce Ann Miller, age 4, was hit in the head and chest by a shotgun blast at a range of about 10 yards. The victim died instantly.

Arrest: At 11:45 p.m. on July 7, I arrested Thomas Wade Carter and booked him for murder in the first degree.

Report of Investigation:

1. On Monday evening, July 5, the arrestee, Thomas Wade Carter, age 18, went to a party at the home of his girlfriend, Gail Duran. Witnesses at the party report that almost everyone there, including the suspect, consumed a lot of beer. A fight broke out at about 3 a.m. Witnesses could not identify everyone who was involved in the fight, but told me that suspect Carter was clubbed over the head with a beer bottle by another guest named Oscar Hanks. Friends took Carter to the hospital for treatment. Five stitches were required to close the wound.

2. On Tuesday, July 6, at about 5 p.m., Carter visited the apartment of a friend, Joel Robertson. Robertson stated that Carter was still angry about being hit during the fight the night before. Robertson also said that Carter remarked, "I'm going to get that guy once and for all. That man is going to pay in a big way." Carter also asked Robertson how to work one of his shotguns. Robertson is a hunter who owns several guns.

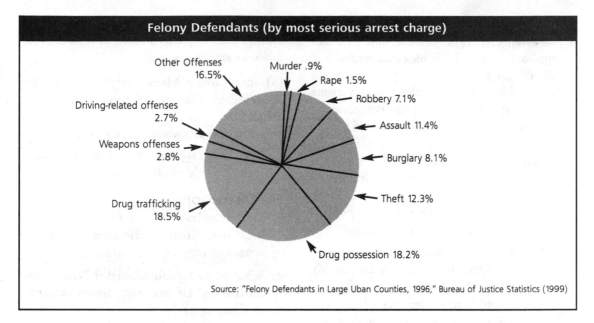

Felony Defendants (by most serious arrest charge)

- Other Offenses 16.5%
- Murder .9%
- Rape 1.5%
- Robbery 7.1%
- Assault 11.4%
- Burglary 8.1%
- Theft 12.3%
- Drug possession 18.2%
- Drug trafficking 18.5%
- Weapons offenses 2.8%
- Driving-related offenses 2.7%

Source: "Felony Defendants in Large Uban Counties, 1996," Bureau of Justice Statistics (1999)

3. At about 6:30 p.m. on July 6, Carter visited the home of Gail Duran. Ms. Duran told me that Carter was still angry about what had happened the night before. She also said that Carter told her he knew who had hit him. Carter invited Duran to go for a ride with him and she agreed. He asked Duran to drive his car while he sat in the back seat giving her directions. Duran stated that Carter directed her to Fourth Street. When he spotted a red Toyota truck parked in front of one of the houses, he told her to slow down. At this point, according to Duran, she noticed for the first time that Carter was handling a shotgun. She said she became very nervous. Suddenly, according to Duran, there was a loud explosion inside the car. Startled, Duran stepped on the gas pedal and quickly drove away. She stopped on a quiet street nearby. Carter then got into the driver's seat and took her home. Duran stated that Carter told her on the drive back to her home that all of a sudden the shotgun had gone off by itself. He also stated that he did not think he had hit anything.

4. The only eyewitness to the shooting of Joyce Ann Miller was her mother, Ms. Karen Miller. At about 7 p.m. on July 6, Ms. Miller told her daughter to close the front gate to the yard. Ms. Miller watched as her daughter went to close the gate. Ms. Miller then noticed a black car driving slowly on the street in front of her house. She also saw a long gun barrel pointing out of its rear window right at her daughter. Before she could say or do anything, Ms. Miller stated, there was a loud blast and Joyce Ann collapsed. Ms. Miller and her neighbors rushed to help Joyce Ann. Paramedics were called, but Joyce Ann was pronounced dead on arrival at Central Receiving Hospital. Ms. Miller stated that she had no idea who killed her daughter and could offer no description of the occupants of the black car except that she thought the driver was a young woman.

5. The Miller residence is located three doors to the east of Oscar Hanks' residence on Fourth Street.

6. That evening at 10:05 p.m., I received an anonymous phone call at the police station. The caller said, "If you want to know who murdered that little girl, you better check out what happened at Gail Duran's party last night." After interviewing a number of witnesses at the party, including Joel Robertson and Gail Duran, I arrested Thomas Wade Carter at 11:45 p.m. on July 7. I read the suspect his Miranda rights and booked him for the first-degree murder of Joyce Ann Miller.

For Discussion

1. To arrest Carter, Lt. Jackson must have had **probable cause**. Probable cause means that the officer has enough evidence to cause a reasonable person to believe that a crime was committed and that the suspect committed it. Murder is often defined as the unlawful killing of a human being with **malice aforethought**. "Malice aforethought" refers to the state of mind of the person doing the killing. Malice aforethought can mean that the killer with no serious provocation from the victim

   - intended to kill;
   - intended to inflict great bodily harm; or
   - intended to do any act where there was an obvious risk that death or great bodily injury might result.

   What evidence did Lt. Jackson have that might give him probable cause to arrest Carter on a charge of murder? *Explain your answer.*

2. According to the information gathered by Lt. Jackson, do we know for sure what happened inside the Pontiac at the moment the shotgun was fired? What else could have happened? What are some other ways the shooting *could* have taken place?

Case Notes: State Criminal Code

In the state where Joyce Ann Miller was killed, the following criminal laws define the various forms of criminal homicide.

Section 274: Degrees of Murder
Any killing committed *with* malice aforethought.

(a) Murder in the First Degree: All killings that are premeditated.

(b) Murder in the Second Degree: All other killings *with* malice aforethought.

Section 298: Manslaughter
Any killing committed *without* malice aforethought.

(a) Voluntary Manslaughter: All *intentional* killings committed as a result of serious *provocation* or *extreme anger*.

(b) Involuntary Manslaughter: All *unintentional* killings that are the direct result of committing:

   1. any *dangerous* and *unlawful* act or
   2. any *lawful act* in an extremely *careless* or negligent manner.

For Discussion

1. Under the laws of Joyce Ann Miller's state, what is the major difference between the crimes of murder and manslaughter?

2. What is malice aforethought? What is premeditation? (If necessary, review materials in Chapter 3.)

3. Reread section 274 of the state code. What is the major difference between first and second-degree murder?

4. Reread section 298 of the state code. What is the major difference between voluntary and involuntary manslaughter?

Class Activity: Is It Murder?

In pairs, read the following descriptions of other killings in Joyce Ann Miller's state. For each one, decide which form of criminal homicide should be charged, based on the elements from the state criminal code.

a. Mr. Jones poisoned his wife's coffee over a period of several weeks, resulting in her death.

b. David, not aiming at anyone, fired his rifle into a passing bus, killing the driver.

c. Mary, furious because Joan hit her with an umbrella, stabbed and killed Joan.

d. Jim threw apples onto the highway from an overpass, causing a car to swerve off the road and crash. The driver died from his injuries. (A state law makes throwing anything off an overpass a misdemeanor.)

e. Donna, a scuba diver, pulled her friend's

Time from Arrest to Adjudication for Felony Defendants	
Most serious arrest charge	**Median number of days**
All offenses	89
Violent offenses	105
Murder	*
Rape	142
Robbery	111
Assault	94
Other violent	95
Property offenses	75
Burglary	70
Theft	76
Other property	82
Drug offenses	90
Trafficking	90
Other drug	90
Public-order offenses	84
Weapons	98
Driving-related	85
Other public order	69

* More than 1 year.

Based on reports from the 75 largest counties in the nation.

Source: "Felony Defendants in Large Urban Counties, 1996," Bureau of Justice Statistics (1999)

mouthpiece regulator out when they were 50 feet underwater as a joke. Her friend drowned.

When everyone finishes, discuss each situation with the whole class.

Case Notes: In the Defense of Thomas Carter

After his arrest, Thomas Carter exercised his *Miranda* rights and remained silent. He called his parents, who hired a private attorney, Susan Jaffee, to represent him. Many defendants cannot afford an attorney and must wait for the court to appoint a public defender or free private attorney to represent them. To qualify for such an appointment, defendants must show that they cannot afford to pay an attorney.

The first thing Carter's attorney did was to go to the police station to interview her client. Jaffee asked Carter to explain what happened. Carter told his side of the story, and she took notes.

Carter's Story

"Last Monday night I went to a party at my girlfriend Gail's house. We drank some beer and had a good time. Then sometime around 3 a.m. a bunch of guys started to fight. I don't even know why it started. All I know is that I got hit on the head with a beer bottle. It split my scalp, and I was all bloody. I had to go to the hospital. It took five stitches to stop the bleeding.

"While we were driving to the hospital I was mad, and I wanted to know who hit me. When one of the guys mentioned that Oscar Hanks could have done it, I knew he was right. Oscar and I got into a fight about a month ago, and he knifed me in the leg.

"The day after Gail's party, I decided to get back at Oscar. I know it was dumb, but I decided to take my Dad's shotgun and blast a bunch of holes in Oscar's truck. He really loves that truck, you know. Well, this is when I got into trouble. I got the shotgun, and even asked Joel Robertson how to work it. He's a hunter and has a couple of his own. Then I went over to Gail's to get her to drive me around Oscar's neighborhood. I spotted his truck and was going to blast it. Before I had a chance, the car swerved or something, and the gun went off. I didn't even think I hit anything. I didn't see anybody. Still, it was real scary! I told Gail to get us out of there fast.

"Look, I know I'm in big trouble. But believe me, I didn't mean to fire the gun or shoot that little girl. I didn't even know she was there! I swear, it was an accident."

How It Looks to Carter's Attorney

Susan Jaffee finished jotting down her notes and then gave Carter an overview of her thoughts on the case.

"Tom, I hope you are telling me the truth. But even if you are, it's still going to be a tough case to defend. For one thing, the shooting death of a 4-year-old girl is going to stir up a lot of emotion in this community. The newspapers have been running stories for weeks on youth violence and gangs, and your case will get a lot of coverage. At this point, the police are talking about first-degree murder, and with all this publicity the prosecutor could stick to those charges. We'll just have to wait until they review the evidence and decide what charges to file. They might decide to charge you with something less serious. Meanwhile, I'll start checking out the witnesses. A lot can happen between now and the trial.

"To begin with, we have to get through your first court appearance. I'll need to ask you some questions. This information might help get you out of here on bail. It will be difficult, but if your family can raise the money, I'll try.

"Next, we have to face a probable cause hearing where the judge will decide whether you have to stand trial on whatever the prosecution charges you with. In the meantime, we have the right to discovery. This means we will find out exactly what evidence the prosecution is relying on. The probable cause hearing will give us a chance to test some of their witnesses.

"If there is a finding of probable cause, you will have to make an appearance at an arraignment. There, depending on what happens, you'll have to plead to the charges, and a trial will be scheduled. At that stage, I might be able to do something about the publicity problem. At the very least, we'll do our best to make sure the jurors are not influenced too much by media reports.

"While we are waiting to hear from the prosecutors, I want you to think about some things. I want you to think over everything you have told me today. If you have forgotten anything, I want to know. If you did not give me the whole story, I want to know. Right now, I'm the best friend you've got. No surprises, OK?"

Back in her office, Jaffee reviewed the information Carter had given her about his background. She knew that another court agency would be compiling a similar report for the judge to consider in deciding on the issue of Carter's pretrial release. A summary of her notes follows.

File: Thomas Carter/Background

Prior Arrests/Convictions

No prior convictions. One arrest for disturbing the peace. The charges were subsequently dropped. At the age of 17, Carter was cited for reckless driving, and his driver's license was suspended for six months.

Employment

Employed full time as an assistant manager of the parts department of a local auto dealership. He has held his present position for nearly six months after having worked there part time during high school. His current income is $26,000 a year.

School Record

Carter was an average student throughout high school. Because of poor attendance, however, he completed some credits for graduation at a continuation high school. He was suspended twice, once for fighting, once for truancy. Recently, he completed a special three-week course offered by Ford Motor Company in parts management before qualifying for his present job.

Residence

Carter's dad died when he was 5. He lives at home with his mother, sister, and younger cousin. He makes monthly contributions for rent, utilities, food, and maintenance.

CHAPTER 10

Pretrial

🔑 Key Step: First Appearance Before a Judge

Purpose:

To ensure that criminal suspects know their rights and are not abused by authorities, most jurisdictions require that the police bring an arrested person (arrestee) before a judge. Some states require that this first appearance take place within a specified period—for example, within 24 or 48 hours after arrest. Other jurisdictions simply say that it must take place without unnecessary delay.

Typical Procedures

The judge:

- **Informs the arrestee of the charges.**

- **Informs the arrestee of the right to counsel.** If the arrestee cannot afford to hire an attorney, the judge will appoint one. (These court-appointed lawyers for criminal defendants are often government employees, known as public defenders. In some cases, the judge appoints private attorneys to represent criminal defendants.)

- **Determines bail.** Generally, state laws or court rules set bail schedules for misdemeanor offenses. Thus, if a person is accused of committing a misdemeanor, the judge simply refers to the predetermined bail list to set bail. In felony cases, the judge must either:

    1. fix the amount of bail (often with reference to state-imposed standards);

    2. release the arrestee without bail (on the arrestee's own recognizance); or

    3. in limited instances, deny bail altogether.

Case Notes: The Question of Bail

As outlined in the Key Step, there are two ways for criminal defendants to be released from jail pending trial. First, a judge might set bail: The judge will require defendants to deposit a certain amount of money with the court as security that they will come back for trial. Some defendants have enough money to pay for bail themselves. Others rely on private bail bond companies to post the necessary amount for a fee—usually between 10 and 20 percent of the amount. If defendants post bail and show up for trial, they get their bail money back. Defendants who fail to appear in court lose all their bail money.

The second method of pretrial release is release on one's own recognizance. This means that a judge releases a criminal suspect after the suspect promises to return for trial. No bail is required. This method is usually available only to persons accused of non-violent and relatively minor crimes. As in bail cases, the judge must be convinced that the defendant will not leave town or try to intimidate witnesses before the trial.

In certain cases, a judge may refuse to release a defendant prior to trial. Many state criminal codes define particular crimes as non-bailable offenses. Typically, these are crimes punishable by death or by life imprisonment without possibility of parole. In some states, defendants who have stalked their victims, who are members of criminal organizations, or who pose a high risk of running away may also be denied bail. These cases present a much greater danger to society or a higher risk of the defendant fleeing to avoid prosecution.

Judicial Criteria for Setting Bail

Under the criminal laws of the state where Joyce Ann Miller was killed, the offense in this particular case is bailable. As for being released on his own recognizance, Carter would have almost no chance in this or any other state. Therefore the criminal court judge must determine an appropriate amount of bail for Thomas Wade Carter.

The criteria that a judge must take into consideration in setting bail include among other things:

- the crime,
- the past record of the accused, and
- the likelihood that the defendant will remain in the state and appear in court.

Class Activity: Bail Hearing

In this activity, students role play the bail hearing in the Carter case. In preparation for this, you might invite a criminal lawyer into the class to take part in the activity and debriefing.

1. Divide the class into three groups. Students in the first group role play prosecuting attorneys, those in the second role play defense attorneys, and those in the third role play judges. Assume that $100,000 is the minimum bail set by law and that the maximum would be $500,000. Each group should meet separately and follow the instructions (below) for its group.

2. After the groups have prepared, form small groups consisting of one prosecutor, one defense attorney, and one judge. The judge in each group should conduct the bail hearing.

3. After both sides have presented their arguments, the judges should write down their decisions on Thomas Carter's bail and their reasoning. Regroup the class and have each judge announce the bail set for Thomas Carter and discuss the facts and arguments that influenced the decision. If a criminal lawyer has taken part in the activity, he or she should be asked to discuss the likely outcome of the bail hearing if this had been a real case.

4. Conclude the activity by holding a discussion using the Debriefing Questions on page 131.

Attorney Instructions

Prosecutors: To make sure Thomas Carter appears for trial, you believe that a high bail is necessary. Work with a partner from within your own group to develop arguments to support your position. Refer to Police Crime Investigation Report on page 124–125. List five or more facts you think are the most important to support your position. Keep in mind the criteria (mentioned above in the Case Notes) that the judge will apply in deciding. Once you have developed your arguments and have listed the facts to back them up, share your ideas with the other members of the prosecution group. What are the three best arguments in favor of a higher bail for the accused in this case? What facts do you have to support your arguments?

Defense attorneys: Follow the instructions in the paragraph above, except that you will be trying to persuade the judge to set as low a bail as possible for your client, Thomas Carter. You believe he will appear for trial and you want to minimize his financial burden. Carter's mom has told you that at most she can raise $15,000. Since a bond requires 10 percent up front, this means the maximum bail the family can meet is $150,000. Work with a partner from within your group to develop arguments in favor of your position. Refer to Thomas Carter's statement on page 127 and Susan Jaffee's file on page 128. List five or more facts you think are the most important to support your position. Keep in mind the criteria (mentioned above in the Case Notes) that the judge will apply in deciding. Once you have developed your arguments and have listed the facts to back them up, share your ideas with the other members of the defense group. What are the three best arguments in favor of a low bail for the accused in this case? What facts do you have to support your arguments?

Judge Instructions

Your job will be to listen to the lawyers' arguments and determine what bail should be set for Thomas Carter. Work with a partner from within your group to develop questions to ask the attorneys. List five or more questions you think are important. Keep in mind the criteria (mentioned above in the Case Notes) that you, the judges, will apply in deciding. Once you have developed your questions, share your ideas with the other members of the judge group.

At the bail hearing, let the attorney for the defendant speak first, then the prosecutor. You may interrupt the attorneys to ask questions. After hearing both sides, make your decision on what Thomas Carter's bail should be. Be sure to base your decision on the criteria. Do not announce your decision to the attorneys. Instead write it on a piece of paper. Be prepared to discuss the facts and arguments that influenced your decision.

Debriefing Questions

1. Do you agree that bail should sometimes be denied and an accused person held in custody? Explain your answer. If you agree, under what circumstances should judges be allowed to deny bail? Why?

2. The American criminal trial system is based on the notion that a person is presumed to be innocent until proved guilty. Do you think that the system of bail runs contrary to this concept? Why or why not?

Case Notes: Prosecutorial Review

After the police make a felony arrest, the prosecutor reviews the case to decide what crimes should be charged and what strategies might be used in handling the case. The prosecutor exercises what is called **prosecutorial discretion** in choosing how to approach the case. Depending on the jurisdiction, the review can be made by an individual prosecutor or by a special team of prosecutors working closely with the police in evaluating cases

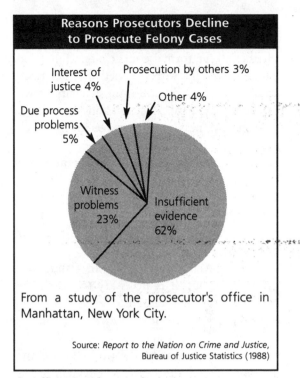

Reasons Prosecutors Decline to Prosecute Felony Cases

Interest of justice 4%
Prosecution by others 3%
Other 4%
Due process problems 5%
Witness problems 23%
Insufficient evidence 62%

From a study of the prosecutor's office in Manhattan, New York City.

Source: *Report to the Nation on Crime and Justice*, Bureau of Justice Statistics (1988)

Insufficient evidence is the main reason prosecutors decline to prosecute felony cases.

after arrest. After the review, the case may be assigned to another prosecutor.

During the initial review, prosecutors must first decide if they have enough evidence to file formal charges against the arrestee. To do this, they must go over the possible charges. Then they must review each element of these crimes and decide whether they have enough evidence to prove it. For example, the crime of larceny usually has the following four elements:

(1) The taking and carrying away
(2) of personal property
(3) that belongs to another person
(4) with intent to *permanently deprive the owner* of possession of the property.

In addition, many states distinguish between the crime of grand larceny (a felony) and petty larceny (a misdemeanor) depending on the value of the property taken. (In many states, for example, taking property valued at $400 or more is a felony; taking property of a lesser value is a misdemeanor.)

Analyzing a Case

Imagine that prosecutors have to decide whether to file formal court charges for grand larceny in a state with the theft laws described above. They have the following evidence drawn from the police investigation and report:

John Witness saw Mary Defendant reach into a car, remove a watch from the dashboard, and walk away with it. John summoned the police. They caught Mary several blocks away while she was trying to sell the watch to a passerby. Other evidence includes a statement by the owner identifying the watch as her property.

Should Mary be charged with grand larceny? To find out, it is necessary to match the evidence with each element of the crime.

In this case, John Witness' testimony establishes a taking and carrying away of the watch. The location of the property (on the dashboard) and the owner's statement establish another person's ownership. The law defines a watch as personal property. The testimony of the police officer and passerby establishes the necessary intent element. (By trying to sell the watch to another, Mary has demonstrated an intent to permanently deprive the owner of the property.)

So far it looks as if the prosecutors have enough evidence to prove a case of larceny beyond a reasonable doubt. But should they file a felony or misdemeanor complaint? The answer to this question depends on the value of the watch. The prosecutor can have an investigator find evidence of the watch's value. If it turns out the watch was worth more than $400, a felony charge can be made. If the evidence does not support such a high value, a charge for the lesser crime of petty larceny can be filed.

As you can see, evaluating a case can be quite complex. Many related issues may come into play. Was all the important evidence legally obtained? Are the witnesses reliable and believable? What evidence might the defense produce which counters the prosecutor's case?

Factors in Exercising Discretion

In general, the prosecutors should prosecute if, after a thorough investigation, they find that:

(1) a crime has been committed,
(2) they can identify the person who committed it, and
(3) they have evidence that supports a guilty verdict.

But as has been mentioned, the prosecutor does have discretion in deciding what charges, if any, to bring. To decide, a prosecutor might consider many factors, for example:

- Is there reasonable doubt that the defendant is guilty?

- Was the harm caused by the offense inconsequential?

- Is the probable punishment out of proportion to the offense or the offender?

- Is the crime itself rarely enforced (to the extent that the community no longer considers it a crime)?

- Is the offender extremely young or old?

- Is the crime not a high priority of the prosecutor's office (e.g., violent crimes tend to have high priority; so-called victimless crimes may not)?

- Is the case too old to find witnesses or physical evidence?

What Should the Charge Be?

In the following scene, three prosecuting attorneys—Martin, Stein, and Kawahara—have been assigned to review the Carter case. They are going over the crimes that they might bring against Carter.

Martin: Let's start with the most serious offense. First-degree murder requires *malice aforethought* and *premeditation*. The decision to kill someone had to have been weighed and reflected upon after the intent to kill was formed. Now, in Carter's case we have evidence that he had more than 12 hours to consider killing Oscar Hanks . . .

Stein: Just one problem—he didn't kill Oscar Hanks.

Kawahara: I don't see any big problem there. If we can show that Carter did form the intent

Prosecutors must carefully evaluate every case to decide what charges to bring.

to kill Hanks, we might be able to invoke the **transferred intent doctrine**. It holds that the elements of first-degree murder can be satisfied even if the killer gets someone other than his intended victim. Also, Carter may have thought that the little girl was Hanks' sister or maybe a relative. Or maybe he formed a whole new intent to kill the little girl and premeditated before pulling the trigger.

Martin: Maybe, but it doesn't seem likely. What about second-degree murder? Remember malice aforethought can be established by an intent to do any act where there is an obvious risk that death or great bodily harm may result. Here we have a guy who stated a desire to get Hanks. He loaded a shotgun, got into a car, and started blasting away. I don't care if he was trying to hit the little girl, the house, or the truck. There were people on the street. He didn't care about their safety, and he should have known that he was endangering them. Also, just firing at the truck is a felony. Any killings that take place while attempting to commit a felony are murder under the **felony murder rule**.

Stein: Let's not be too hasty. What if Carter didn't "start blasting away," as you put it? What if the gun just went off accidentally?

Martin: You would consider a charge of involuntary manslaughter?

Stein: Sure. Such careless handling of a loaded shotgun in a residential area amounts to criminal negligence in my book.

Kawahara: At the very least.

Martin: I suppose voluntary manslaughter is also a possibility.

Stein: Be serious, Martin. After 12 hours? Even if he was seriously provoked by Hanks, he had plenty of time to cool off.

Martin: Maybe so. Anyway, we've got plenty to think about and we've got to decide. The newspapers are showing a lot of interest in this case. The boss told me that she has a personal interest in this case—top priority and all that. We've got to charge Carter with something. But what?

For Discussion

1. In your own words, what is prosecutorial discretion? What are its advantages and disadvantages?

2. Review the factors in exercising prosecutorial discretion on page 132. Which do you think are valid? Which, if any, don't you think should be used? Why?

3. Review "What Should the Charge Be?" on page 132–133. Then answer the following questions:

- What is the doctrine of transferred intent? How does it apply to the Carter case? (Try drawing a diagram on the board using the characters from the case.)

- Why might Prosecutor Stein think that the facts do not support premeditation or transferred intent?

- Why did Prosecutor Stein argue against a charge of voluntary manslaughter? Explain your answer.

- What additional evidence, if any, do the prosecutors need to make a decision?

Class Activity: The Prosecutor Decides

In the following activity, assume that you are a prosecutor working with Martin, Stein, and Kawahara on the Thomas Carter case. Form small groups and exercise your prosecutorial discretion as directed below.

1. Review the following materials:
   a. "Police Crime Investigation Report," pages 124–125.
   b. "State Criminal Code Sections," page 126.
   c. "What Should the Charge Be?" page 132.

   (You may also wish to consult "Murder Most Foul," page 40, for additional background information.)

Ask an Expert

Invite a criminal attorney to your class. Ask how prosecutorial review and discretion work in your area. What factors does the prosecutor use to decide which crimes to charge? Invite the attorney to join you in the activity "The Prosecutor Decides" and lead the debriefing.

2. As a group, answer the following questions about the possible charges. One person should record the group's answers on a sheet of paper. Be prepared to discuss your answers with the class.

Possible Charges:

First-Degree Murder. Is there evidence that...
- Thomas Carter formed an intent to kill Oscar Hanks? Explain.
- Thomas Carter premeditated the crime? Explain.
- Thomas Carter's intent was transferred to the killing of Joyce Ann Miller (using the doctrine of transferred intent)? Explain.

or
- Thomas Carter formed an intent to kill and premeditated the killing of Joyce Ann Miller? Explain.

Second-Degree Murder. Is there evidence that . . .
- Thomas Carter formed an intent to kill Joyce Ann Miller? Explain.

or
- Thomas Carter had the intent to do an act where there was an obvious risk that death or great bodily harm would result? Explain.

Voluntary Manslaughter. Is there evidence that . . .
- Thomas Carter formed an intent to kill Oscar Hanks? Explain.
- Oscar Hanks seriously provoked the actions of Thomas Carter? Explain.
- Thomas Carter did not have sufficient time to calm down after being provoked? Explain.

Involuntary Manslaughter. Is there evidence that . . .
- Thomas Carter committed an act in a criminally negligent manner? Explain.

3. Considering all relevant factors, what crime would you charge Thomas Carter with? (Be prepared to present and discuss your final recommendation with the class.)

Plea Bargaining

This unit takes us completely through the criminal case process. It begins with an arrest and ends with a trial and verdict. Most criminal cases do not go this far. In about 90 percent of all criminal cases, the defendant pleads guilty. Often the defendant does this because of a plea agreement made with the prosecutor. In return for a reduction in charges or a lighter sentence, the defendant agrees to plead guilty. This is known as plea bargaining.

A plea agreement can occur at almost any stage in a criminal case. An agreement is sometimes reached before the preliminary hearing or shortly after. The prosecution and defense can agree to a plea before trial, during trial, and even just before the jury returns with its verdict. In fact, the two sides sometimes carry on plea negotiations throughout all the stages of the case process. The negotiations may not simply cover what charges or sentence each side will accept. Often each side tries to convince the other of what facts can be proven in court. Once they agree to the facts, then they can agree to a plea.

In some jurisdictions, the judge plays an active role in plea bargaining. In most states, however, the judge takes no part in the negotiations. This means that the prosecutor can make no promises about sentencing. The most the prosecutor can offer is to make a sentence recommendation, which judges often accept. But the judge may impose a stiffer sentence than the one the prosecutor recommends. The judge may even refuse to accept the guilty plea if the judge believes the facts do not warrant it (this, however, rarely happens).

Critics have objected to plea bargaining for many different reasons. Some explain that the trial process is carefully designed to protect the defendant's rights, guarantee a fair trial, and ensure that only the guilty get convicted. They argue that plea bargaining subverts all of these. In a plea bargain, a court does not examine whether the defendant's rights were violated, a trial does not take place, and worst of all, they say, an innocent person may go to prison.

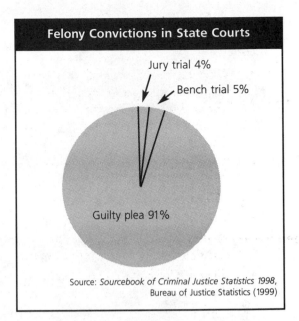

Felony Convictions in State Courts

Jury trial 4%

Bench trial 5%

Guilty plea 91%

Source: *Sourcebook of Criminal Justice Statistics 1998,* Bureau of Justice Statistics (1999)

They point out that a prosecutor with a weak case and a defendant facing a long sentence may not want to gamble with a trial. In this situation, they say, a defendant may plead guilty to get a light sentence even if the defendant is totally innocent.

Some critics emphasize that plea bargaining tarnishes the dignity of the justice system. According to them, it turns the important process of dispensing justice into a game of "let's make a deal." They say it even punishes defendants who refuse to go along with the game and go to trial. These defendants, they say, receive harsher sentences than those who agree to a plea.

Other critics use this last point to complain that plea bargains result in defendants serving less time than they should. Plea bargaining, they say, lets defendants off the hook too often.

Supporters of plea bargaining offer several reasons in favor of it. They point out that the courts couldn't possibly handle the load if every case went to trial. Millions of dollars would have to be spent on new courtrooms, judges, prosecutors, and defense attorneys. Plea bargaining, they say, saves money and time. It gives prosecutors time to pursue more important cases and keeps more police on the streets instead of spending hours in courtrooms. In addition, it saves victims of crimes

James H. Linden, left, discusses his sentencing in 1999, with Franklin County, Idaho, Prosecutor Jay McKenzie, center, and defense attorney John Souza. Linden, accused of a 1986 slaying of a woman, entered into a plea bargain to a lesser felony.

from the emotional trauma of testifying and it gives them the satisfaction of seeing the defendant confess to the crime in court. This admission of guilt, they add, is the first step in rehabilitating a criminal. Moreover, they point out that more criminals go to prison because of plea bargains. They note that anything can happen at trial. A jury may find that the prosecution has not proven guilt beyond a reasonable doubt and set the defendant free. Plea bargaining, they say, gives the prosecution and defense a chance to agree on a fair disposition of the case. It can even help alleviate harsh mandatory sentences that some first-time defendants face.

The Supreme Court has dealt with issues surrounding plea bargaining. The court has upheld plea bargains as long as the defendant has not been coerced and both sides comply with the deal. In 1971 in *Santobello v. New York*, Chief Justice Warren Burger stated that "'plea bargaining' . . . is an essential component of the administration of justice. Properly administered, it is to be encouraged." The previous

year in *North Carolina v. Alford*, the court even refused to overturn a plea agreement when the defendant claimed he did not commit the crime but was just pleading guilty to avoid the death penalty. The court upheld the guilty plea because the record showed strong evidence of the defendant's guilt and the defendant recognized that he would probably be found guilty of first-degree murder at a jury trial.

Some states have attempted to eliminate plea bargains. Alaska did away with them in 1975. The courts did not get overwhelmed with trials. The same percentage of defendants continued to plead guilty. Skeptics think they kept pleading guilty because informal agreements were still made despite the ban. In 1982, California voters approved Proposition 8. Among other things, it banned plea bargains in Superior Courts, which try felony cases. Several years later, a study found that prosecutors and defense attorneys started making their plea agreements earlier in the case process, when felony cases were in pretrial hearings in Municipal Courts.

In recent years, the stakes for plea bargains have risen. Many states have adopted three-strikes laws, which impose harsher penalties and even life sentences on repeat offenders. Some defendants resist pleading to a charge if it will count as a strike, especially a third strike. Therefore many are more willing to opt for a trial, and the process of reaching a plea agreement has become more complex.

For Discussion

1. What are the advantages of plea bargains? What are the disadvantages? Do you think they should be banned? Explain.

2. Assuming that plea bargaining exists, do you think courts should be allowed to take *Alford* pleas? Why or why not?

Class Activity: Plea Bargain

Form pairs. One person in each pair should assume the role of prosecutor and the other of defense attorney. Imagine that the prosecution has charged Thomas Carter with first-degree murder. Spend a few minutes and try to reach a plea agreement that satisfies both of you.

Debriefing Questions

1. How many groups reached an agreement? What did you agree to? Do you think the agreement was fair? Do you think the defendant would accept it?

2. What problems did you have in negotiating? Do you think you had enough time? Enough information? If not, what additional time or information would you need?

3. Defense attorneys sometimes accuse prosecutors of overcharging (charging the defendant with crimes that he or she could never be convicted of) to help them in plea bargaining. Do you think this might be a danger? Do you think your agreement would have been different if the prosecution had started with second-degree murder instead of first-degree?

🔑 Key Step: Probable Cause Hearing

Purpose

Before a felony case can go to trial, a court must find that there is *probable cause* to believe that a crime was committed and the arrestee committed it. The purpose of the probable cause hearing is to keep charges with insufficient evidence from being brought to trial. The hearing thus protects both the accused and the state from spending time and money unnecessarily.

Types of Hearings

Preliminary Hearings. Some states use preliminary hearings or examinations to determine if the arrestee should be brought to trial. Other states use them to determine if the accused should be bound over for a grand jury hearing. At the preliminary hearing, the prosecution presents evidence to a judge to prove that there is probable cause. The defense may cross-examine the prosecutor's witnesses. In many states, however, crime victims do not have to testify in person. Their statements can be read to the court, so the defense cannot cross-examine them.

If the judge finds that there is probable cause, the prosecution is authorized to file a document called an **information** with the court, and preparations for the trial begin.

Grand Jury. In some states and in all federal felony cases, grand juries determine probable cause. A grand jury is made up of citizens—usually 23 people—from the county where the crime occurred. It meets in closed session, and the prosecutor calls witnesses. The defense attorney does not get to cross-examine these witnesses or participate in the hearing. After the prosecution presents its case, the grand jury votes on whether probable cause exists. If a certain number of the 23 grand jurors—often 12 or 14—find probable cause, then an indictment is issued. Like an information, an **indictment** is a document accusing the defendant of committing a crime. Following an indictment, preparation for trial begins.

In most states, the prosecutor has the option of using a grand jury or a preliminary hearing. Since the accused has no right to counsel or to cross-examine the state's witnesses in grand jury hearings, a prosecutor might be more likely to seek a grand jury indictment when cross-examination would be traumatic to a witness (e.g., for sex crimes or for very young or frail witnesses). Most felony cases, however, use a preliminary hearing and information.

Complaint—for misdemeanors only. In misdemeanor cases, there is no separate hearing to establish probable cause after the accused has been arrested. A written complaint against the arrestee serves as the formal accusation to get the prosecution of misdemeanor cases underway. (The defendant can ask for a copy of the complaint with copies of the police report attached.)

Case Notes: Carter's Probable Cause Hearing

When Tom Carter heard Susan Jaffee's voice on the phone, he felt nervous. What she said did not calm him down.

"I've got some news for you, Tom. The prosecutor decided to take your case to the grand jury instead of holding a preliminary hearing."

Tom remembered her saying that the next step would be the probable cause hearing. He asked, "Is it worse to have a grand jury instead of a preliminary hearing?"

"It's worse in that I won't get to cross-examine any of the witnesses. But sometimes prosecutors take their weaker cases to grand juries, because the prosecutors are more in control at grand jury hearings than preliminary hearings. So maybe it's not such bad news."

"So what do we do now?" asked Tom.

"We wait. You might be called to testify before the grand jury. If you are, I cannot go in with you. But you will just refuse to testify. You will take the Fifth Amendment."

Tom heard nothing about the grand jury for two weeks. Finally, Susan Jaffee called. "The grand jury returned an indictment today—second-degree murder."

The words stunned Tom. "Murder?" he stammered.

"Second degree."

"How did the grand jury decide that?" Tom asked.

"I don't know, Tom. We'll get a copy of the grand jury's transcript. We'll read what the witnesses had to say. Then we'll be ready for our next step—your arraignment."

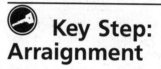 # Key Step: Arraignment

Purpose

After an information, indictment, or complaint has been filed, the defendant is called into court to **plead to the charges**. This court appearance is known as the arraignment. (In most misdemeanor cases, this step takes place at the defendant's first and only pretrial hearing.) Aside from various insanity pleas, the defendant has three basic choices of pleas:

- **Not guilty.**
- **Guilty.**
- **Nolo Contendere.** (No contest. This has the same effect as a guilty plea, except it does not serve as an admission of guilt if the defendant is sued in a civil case.)

Typical Proceedings

The judge:
- Informs the defendant of various constitutional rights.
- Reads the information or indictment and usually gives the defendant a copy.
- Asks the defendant to plead to the charges.
- Asks whether the defendant wants a jury trial or a court trial (decided by the judge without a jury).

The defendant may make pretrial motions (e.g., to suppress illegally obtained evidence or to transfer the case to a different judge).

Juries are supposed to base their verdict solely on the evidence presented at trial. In highly publicized cases, issues of outside influence often arise.

Case Notes: An Issue at the Arraignment

Joyce Ann Miller's death shocked the residents of the community. Many citizens and community leaders condemned what they called "this latest example of youth violence." Newspapers covered the case extensively. Neighbors of the Miller family told TV reporters that they wanted the death penalty for Carter. A police officer was quoted in a local newspaper as saying that he thought Joyce Ann's death must have been a "joy killing." A representative of the district attorney's office announced at a press conference that he believed "drugs were involved." One newspaper headline read, "Child Killer Says It Was 'An Accident!'" Thomas Carter's attorney, Susan Jaffee, also received several anonymous phone calls threatening to harm her if she did not drop out of the case.

A Problem for the Defense

All of this deeply concerned Jaffee. She feared that the publicity would hurt her client's chances of getting a fair trial. Finding jurors who had not already formed an opinion about the case would be difficult. Even if such jurors were found, they could still be influenced by publicity and public opinion during the trial itself.

After the grand jury found that Carter would have to stand trial, his attorney decided to act. At the arraignment, he would plead not guilty and ask for a jury trial. Then she would make a motion for a gag order.

Motion for a Gag Order

Judges may issue **gag orders** to ensure that criminal defendants receive a fair trial. These orders prohibit trial participants and government officials from making statements to the press. By preventing these statements, gag orders make it less likely that pretrial publicity will influence the fact finder—the judge or jury.

It is crucial that the judge or jury be impartial. When judges act as the fact finder, it is assumed they will be able to ignore outside influences and decide the facts solely from the trial evidence. Jurors, who have little or no experience with the law, might be more easily swayed by outside influences, including opinions of friends, statements by public officials, and newspaper or TV accounts of the crime. For example, what might happen if a juror were to read about a piece of evidence legally excluded from consideration at trial that pointed to the defendant's guilt? Knowing this fact might influence that juror's opinion and if he or she shared it with other jurors, it could sway the whole jury. Gag orders are designed to prevent such interference. Those who disobey gag orders can be held in contempt of court and punished.

At the close of her argument for her motion, Ms. Jaffee made the following statement:

"Public reaction to the death of Joyce Ann Miller has almost reached hysteria. Public officials, including the police and representatives of the district attorney's office, have made prejudicial and unfounded statements about the case. The news media is behaving irresponsibly by suggesting that Thomas Carter is already guilty. If these incidents continue, it will be impossible to conduct a fair trial, if indeed it is even possible now. Under these circumstances, a gag order is essential, your honor."

In opposition, the prosecutor argued against issuing a gag order. He reminded the judge that public attention to such a case was natural. Under the First Amendment of the U.S. Constitution, the news media has a right to keep the public informed. If denied access to participants in the trial, various reporters might print or broadcast misinformation. Furthermore, he argued that a gag order should only be used in exceptional circumstances and that normal procedures such as cautioning the jury not to discuss or read about the case would probably be sufficient in this case.

The judge thanked the attorneys and said that she would consider the matter and announce her decision the next day.

Class Activity: Ruling on the Motion

Imagine that you are the judge who must rule on the defense's motion for a gag order in this case. To prepare your ruling, complete the following steps:

1. Review "An Issue at the Arraignment," pages 139–140.

2. In coming to a decision, consider these questions:

   • What is the purpose of a gag order?

   • What are some arguments in favor of issuing a gag order in this case?

   • What are some arguments against issuing a gag order? What rights and interests would be affected?

   • Are the alternatives to a gag order mentioned by the prosecutor sufficient to preserve a fair trial in this case?

   • Should a gag order be issued in the Carter case? Why or why not?

3. Write a one-page decision stating your reasons for it. Be prepared to present it to the rest of the class for discussion.

CHAPTER 11
Trial

◉ Key Step: Trial Procedures

Strict rules ensure that each side in a trial will have an equal chance to present its case. A judge must make sure that each side follows these rules closely. The major procedures observed in a criminal court trial are outlined below.

1. Jury Selection

In all criminal jury trials, the first step is to impanel, or select, a jury. Prosecution and defense attorneys pose questions to prospective jurors. The judge may also take an active role in the process.

2. Opening Statements

After calling the court to order, the judge will ask for the trial to begin with opening statements from the prosecution and defense. The opening statements outline the evidence each side intends to present during the trial. The prosecution delivers its opening statement first. The defense attorney usually follows immediately with a statement, but may delay it until after the prosecution presents all its evidence.

3. Presenting Evidence

The prosecution presents its side of the case first. This is called the prosecution's **case-in-chief**. It usually consists of introducing material objects called exhibits (e.g., a gun), as well as questioning prosecution witnesses. After the prosecution has finished presenting its side, the defense may introduce its exhibits and witnesses. Both exhibits and witnesses' testimony are trial evidence. Strict rules of evidence must be followed, however, before either is allowed into the trial.

Attorneys conduct **direct examination** when they question their own witnesses. After direct examination, opposing attorneys **cross-examine** the witnesses. Lawyers conduct cross-examination to test and find weaknesses in the testimony of their opponents' witnesses. They may also try to put doubts into the minds of the jurors about the believability of these witnesses.

4. Closing Arguments

After each side has presented all its evidence, each side makes a closing statement to the jury. In these closing arguments, attorneys summarize what has been established or not established during the trial. The closing argument presents attorneys with their last chance to persuade the jury. The defense delivers the first closing argument to the jury. The closing argument of the prosecution ends the evidence phase of the trial.

5. Instructions to the Jurors

Following the closing arguments, the judge gives instructions to the jury. These instructions state the law that applies to the case. The judge reminds the jurors to base their verdict solely on the evidence admitted during the trial. Since the prosecution has the burden of proof, the judge instructs the jurors to find a verdict of guilty only if the state has proved its case beyond a reasonable doubt.

6. Jury Deliberations

After hearing the judge's instructions, the jury leaves the courtroom and meets in a jury room to decide on a verdict. Jury members first select a foreperson who will lead their discussions. The jury then reviews the evidence and votes on a verdict. Although the U.S. Supreme Court has ruled that unanimous verdicts of guilty or not guilty are not mandatory in all criminal cases, almost every state still requires them.

Several votes may be necessary before the jurors arrive at a unanimous verdict. If after a reasonable time, the jurors cannot reach a unanimous verdict, they become a "hung jury." The foreperson will report this fact to the judge. If the judge believes that further jury deliberations are futile, the judge will declare a mistrial. The prosecutor will then have to either request another trial with a new jury or drop the charges against the defendant. If the jury returns a unanimous verdict of not guilty, the defendant goes free. When the jury unanimously finds the defendant guilty, the judge will set a date for a sentencing hearing.

Case Notes: Cast of Characters

A criminal courtroom in session is filled with people. Some are spectators. Some are friends and family of the victim or accused. Others take an active part in the trial itself. The following descriptions will give you an idea about the major participants. (Some you have already met, but review them again carefully.) As the trial of Thomas Carter progresses, you will be asked at times to take on their roles.

The **judge** presides over the trial. He or she rules on all motions made by the attorneys, on the admissibility of testimony or items in evidence, and on the procedures to be followed during the trial. At the end of the trial, the judge instructs the jury about the applicable rules of law. In a criminal trial, if the jury reaches a verdict of guilty, the judge then determines the sentence to be given the convicted person. (In almost all states, the jury determines the punishment in death penalty cases.) If the jury reaches a verdict of not guilty, the judge discharges the defendant.

The **bailiff** is usually a deputy sheriff, marshal, or some other law enforcement officer. The bailiff:

- keeps order in the courtroom.
- protects the jury from outside influence.

The Courtroom Setting

As with all dramas, there is a setting for a criminal trial. It is the courtroom. In it the judge presides, the jury is impaneled, witnesses are sworn in and examined, and a verdict is rendered. On this stage, the fates of individuals are debated and decided and the aims of justice are pursued. Some courtrooms are ornately carved in dark woods and rich furnishings. Others are designed with an eye towards efficiency and practicality. Some are old and threadbare. Others are new and starkly modern. All serve the same purpose.

On the opposite page is a diagram of a typical courtroom. When conducting the activities in the trial of Thomas Carter, arrange your classroom similarly.

For Discussion
1. In most courtrooms, the judge's bench is on a raised platform. Why do you think this is so?

2. In all courtrooms, the witness stand is on the side of the judge's bench closest to the jury box. Why do you think this is so?

3. The partition between the spectators and the active courtroom participants has traditionally been called the bar. Why do you think it is there? Who may pass the bar?

- assists the court clerk in ceremonial duties such as asking all to rise when the judge enters the court.

The **court clerk** is the main administrative assistant to the judge. The clerk:

- keeps track of courtroom proceedings.
- catalogs and takes custody of exhibits and other items of evidence.
- prepares all written orders of the court (summons and warrants, for example) as directed by the judge.
- administers oaths to witnesses.
- calls the jurors for selection.

The **court reporter** records by machine or shorthand everything said in the trial. The

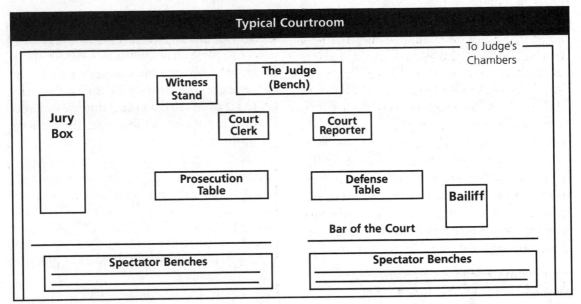

Typical Courtroom

court reporter prepares a typewritten transcript of these records.

The **prosecution lawyers** are members of the district attorney's office, city attorney's office, or state and federal attorney general's office. They represent either the people of the state or the U.S. government. They must prove that the accused is guilty of a particular crime beyond a reasonable doubt.

The **defense lawyers** are private attorneys or members of publicly supported organizations, such as the public defender's office. They must defend the accused by showing that the government does not have enough evidence to convict the defendant. All lawyers—both prosecution and defense—are officers of the court. They must therefore observe all rules of law and ethics so that a fair trial will take place.

The **defendant** is the person accused of a crime. The defendant assists the defense lawyers in presenting the case and accepts or appeals the results of the trial.

Police officers investigate crimes and arrest suspects when they uncover enough facts to establish probable cause. The rest of the criminal case process tests these facts. Their job does not end with arrest, however. They also help prosecutors prepare for trial and frequently testify as witnesses.

Witnesses are persons asked to tell under oath what they know about the case. Most may only testify about what they actually saw and heard. But **expert witnesses** may testify about their knowledge and give opinions. They are persons with special knowledge, such as doctors, psychologists, and scientists.

The **jury** is a panel of adult citizens (usually 12) from the community. It must decide questions of fact from the evidence presented in the courtroom and reach a verdict based on those facts.

For Discussion

1. What are the main functions of the defense and prosecuting attorneys?

2. At trial, whose role is it to decide issues of law? Whose role is charged with deciding issues about facts?

Activity: In the Halls of Justice

There is perhaps no better way to understand the criminal court process than to observe it in person. To do this, you must visit a courthouse.

As a class or in small groups, make arrangements to visit a criminal courthouse. Many courthouses have tour programs or will accommodate groups. Contact the court's clerk of services or the clerk of the criminal docket for information. The clerk can suggest an appropriate time for the visit and help you plan an itinerary. Try to include a visit to (1) a preliminary hearing, (2) an arraignment, (3) a jury selection, and (4) a criminal trial.

When you arrive at the courthouse, observe appropriate decorum. Be especially quiet when entering or leaving courtrooms. Use the following information guide and questions to help arrange your visit and for reporting your experience to the class.

Information You Will Need: (1) name of the courthouse, (2) its address, (3) the telephone number, (4) the reporting time, (5) the contact person (if any).

Questions for Field Experience Report

1. Describe the general environment of the courthouse. Are the court facilities crowded and noisy, or calm and businesslike?

2. Describe the security arrangements in the court building and in the courtrooms.

3. In the arraignment court, *describe what is going on.*

4. In a preliminary hearing, *describe what is going on.*

5. At a criminal jury trial:

   - What is the case about?
   - Is it a felony or misdemeanor prosecution?
   - Who is the prosecutor—a deputy district attorney, deputy city attorney, a federal prosecutor?
   - *What do you observe* the prosecutor doing during the trial?
   - Who is the defense attorney—a deputy public defender or a private attorney?
   - *What do you observe* the defense attorney doing during the trial?
   - *What do you observe* the judge doing during the trial?
   - *Describe* the questioning of one witness in the trial.
   - Do the jurors seem to be attentive? Describe them.

   - What is your overall impression of the courthouse visit? Were you confused by anything you saw or heard?

6. If the opportunity arises or can be arranged, interview an officer of the court (e.g., court clerk, judge, attorney). Select questions from the following list or make up your own.

   - Does the court have a large backlog of cases? If so, why?
   - Does plea bargaining take place? How? What is your opinion of it?
   - What percentage of the cases before the court are disposed of by plea bargaining?
   - How long does it take a criminal case to come to trial in this court? A civil case?
   - What percentage of defendants at trial are represented by public defenders?
   - In what percentage of trials is the defendant found guilty?
   - What percentage of those convicted by the court are locked up in a correctional institution? Put on probation?
   - What percentage of accused persons remain in jail awaiting their trials?

Case Notes: The Trial of Thomas Carter

Thomas Carter felt mixed feelings of dread and relief as he climbed the wide steps leading to the massive courthouse door. In the weeks since the shooting, he had thought of little else. His mind played the events over and over again. Often, he hoped for the trial to start—only when it was over could his life begin again. There had been delays. Motions were made and extensions of time granted. Though he had complete trust in his lawyer, he wished she could move things along faster. Now at last his trial would begin. Today was the day.

Inside the main lobby of the courthouse,

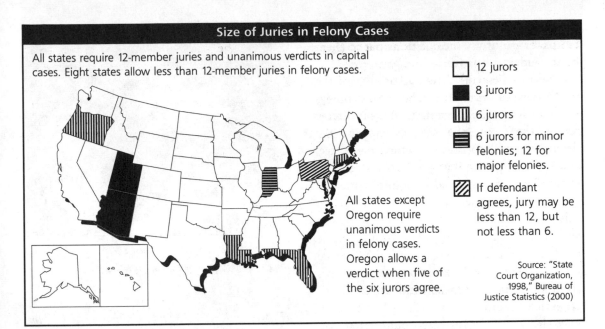

Size of Juries in Felony Cases

All states require 12-member juries and unanimous verdicts in capital cases. Eight states allow less than 12-member juries in felony cases.

☐ 12 jurors

■ 8 jurors

▥ 6 jurors

≡ 6 jurors for minor felonies; 12 for major felonies.

▨ If defendant agrees, jury may be less than 12, but not less than 6.

All states except Oregon require unanimous verdicts in felony cases. Oregon allows a verdict when five of the six jurors agree.

Source: "State Court Organization, 1998," Bureau of Justice Statistics (2000)

Tom looked at a blur of moving figures. The footsteps of people going about court business echoed off the cold marble walls. The drone of a hundred conversations filled his ears, yet he and his parents barely spoke at all. They were too occupied with trying to find the right courtroom by the appointed hour, 9 a.m.

At last they found it, Department D, Criminal Trials Division. Tom breathed a sigh of relief when he saw Ms. Jaffee leaning against the court rail. She smiled as he approached and directed his parents to seats in the spectator gallery directly behind the defense table.

Although she had already prepared Tom for what would take place at his trial, she briefly explained it all again. He listened carefully, vaguely comforted by the confidence in her voice, until she repeated what the charge would be: "Second-degree murder." No matter how she said it, it sent a chill through his body. Ms. Jaffee reached across and patted his arm. "It's a serious thing, Tom," she smiled, "but they haven't proved anything yet."

Just then the clerk stood up and said in a loud voice: "All rise and come to order. The Superior Court is now open and in session. The Honorable Judge Coghlan presiding."

Tom looked up just in time to see a black-robed figure enter from a door behind the bench and sit down. She softly tapped her gavel several times and said, "The case of *People v. Carter*. Is the state ready?"

The prosecutor said, "The state is ready to proceed, your honor."

Turning to Ms. Jaffee, the judge repeated the question, "Is the defendant ready?"

Ms. Jaffee spoke in a loud firm voice, "Yes, your honor."

The trial of Thomas Carter had begun.

For Discussion

1. What is the charge in the Thomas Carter case? What are its elements?

2. Review the "Key Step: Trial Procedures" on page 141. What will happen next in Thomas Carter's trial?

🔦 Key Step: Jury Selection

Selected at random, people on juries come from the defendant's community. Their names may be gathered from voter registration lists or drivers' license lists, depending on the state. These citizens are then called to jury duty. Before a trial starts, a group of up to 40 from the jury pool go to the courtroom where the trial will take place. The court clerk draws the names of 12 of them—called prospective jurors—and asks them to sit in the jury box.

Prospective jurors then take an oath promising to answer truthfully the questions put to them by the judge and lawyers.

Next comes **voir dire**—questioning of the prospective jurors by the judge and attorneys for both sides. The judge starts the voir dire by telling the jurors the charge(s) against the defendant and by asking them their name, age, address, occupation, and previous jury experience. The judge might also inquire if there is any reason why they should not be jurors in this particular case. (For example, a person who had been a victim of a similar crime might not be able to be a truly impartial juror.) The judge will excuse prospective jurors from a case if their answers indicate a bias or prejudice toward one side. Prospective jurors may also be excused if they would suffer economically due to the length of the trial. The excused jurors, however, may have to serve in another case.

If the judge finds no reason to excuse a prospective juror, the attorneys for both sides normally get an opportunity to question them in greater depth. In most states, the attorneys themselves question the jurors. In others, the attorneys submit questions to the judge, who conducts the questioning. Based on the answers jurors give, attorneys can raise challenges to jurors and thus have them excused from a case. There are two types of challenges. A **challenge for cause** occurs when a lawyer claims the prospective juror does not meet the government's legal requirements or is biased and could probably not reach an impartial verdict. After the attorney explains the reasons for challenging for cause, the judge must decide whether to excuse or accept the prospective juror. Usually there is no limit on challenges for cause.

A **peremptory challenge** needs no explanation from the attorney. When a lawyer makes a peremptory challenge, the prospective juror being questioned is automatically excused. Each side, however, has only a limited number of these challenges. According to U.S. Supreme Court rulings, neither the prosecution nor defense may make a peremptory challenge on the basis of a juror's race or gender

All jurors take an oath to base their verdict entirely on the evidence presented in court.

(*Batson v. Kentucky*, 1986, *Georgia v. McCollum*, 1992, and *J.E.B. v. Alabama ex rel. T.B.*, 1994).

The voir dire continues until 12 jurors and alternates have been chosen, usually two or four. (Some jurisdictions allow juries of six, seven, or eight persons.) In some cases, especially those that have been highly publicized, lawyers challenge many prospective jurors before a full jury is selected. This process may take anywhere from a few hours to many days to complete. Once the jury has been chosen, jurors take another oath. They swear that they will try to reach a fair and impartial verdict based solely on the evidence presented during the trial.

For Discussion

1. Why is there no limit on the number of challenges for cause and a limit on peremptory challenges?

2. Should the Supreme Court ban peremptory challenges based on religion or disability? Why or why not?

3. The goals of the judge, prosecution, and defense in criminal trials are often quite different. What differences might they have about jury selection?

Class Activity: Choosing a Jury

In this activity, students simulate the jury selection for the Thomas Wade Carter trial. In advance, you might invite an attorney to attend your simulation and play the role of the judge.

1. Assign the class members the following roles: 2-4 prosecuting attorneys; 2-4 defense attorneys; 14 prospective jurors; 1 court clerk; observers (remainder of class).

2. Students should read their appropriate role descriptions below. In addition, observers and lawyers should read the materials on "How to Ask Effective Questions" and "Sample Questions for Lawyers in a Criminal Case."

3. The court clerk should:
   - swear in the prospective jurors before the voir dire begins, and
   - call the first prospective juror (by name) to the jury box.

4. The judge should tell all of the prospective jurors the charge against Thomas Carter and then ask the first prospective juror some introductory questions.

5. Prosecutors, and then defense attorneys, question the first prospective juror and either accept or challenge the juror. If a challenge for cause is raised, the judge should rule on it. Each side is allowed only one peremptory challenge.

6. Repeat steps 4, 5, and 6 above until all prospective jurors have been questioned. Observers should watch the proceedings carefully and then complete the Observer Evaluation Form.

Lawyers for Both Sides

Lawyers will question each prospective juror searching for persons to accept or to challenge for cause. Before the simulation begins, lawyers should prepare a list of questions to ask prospective jurors.

How to Ask Effective Questions

The following list should be used by the attorney role players in preparing effective questions. In addition, observers should use this list for evaluating the questions asked by the attorney role players.

1. Plan most of your questions ahead of time. Make sure that they are precisely worded.

2. Begin with basic questions about the juror's background. Then ask more advanced questions on the juror's feelings about the case.

3. Always keep the question's purpose in mind when you are formulating it.

4. Individualize your questions. Reword any long or complex question if an individual juror does not understand it.

5. Develop questions that call for short responses. Don't include too many things in one question.

6. Avoid questions that require a single "yes" or "no" answer. You do not want to limit jurors' responses. Prepare questions that allow jurors to express their feelings in their own words. For example, the question, "Do you have any prejudices against insurance companies?" might be changed to "What is your opinion of insurance companies?"

7. Explore incomplete answers. If a juror claims not to know an answer, you should ask questions to find out why.

8. Unless it is crucial to your case, try to avoid questions already addressed to a juror by another attorney. You usually do not need to go over the same ground twice.

Sample Questions for Lawyers: Criminal Case

1. Are you married? Do you have any children? If so, what are their ages?

2. What type of work do you do?

3. Do you belong to any union?

4. What is your educational background?

5. Have you ever had any jury experience before?

6. Would any of the criminal cases you heard in previous jury duty limit your ability to sit on future cases?

7. Was there anything about your previous jury experience that would lead you to feel that you may have some prejudices either for or against the prosecution? For or against the defendant?

8. Do you have an opinion on this case?

9. Is there anything about what you have seen since you came for jury duty that would lead you to feel that you have an opinion on this case?

10. Was there anything in the news media, television, or radio that leads you to believe the defendant is guilty or not guilty?

11. Do you believe that the defendant is innocent until proven guilty?

12. Would you tend to believe the police officers in their testimony more readily than you would a person who was not a police officer?

13. Were you ever connected with any type of police force?

14. Do you have any relatives who would have any interest in seeing the jury reach a verdict either for or against the defendant in this case?

15. If you are chosen as a juror, will you stand on your own individual analysis of the evidence and not be swayed by the emotions of other jurors?

Court Clerk

Before voir dire begins, the court clerk will ask all prospective jurors to raise their right hands and state: "I solemnly swear I will answer all questions truthfully and to the best of my ability." The court clerk will call each prospective juror, in turn, to the witness stand for voir-dire questioning.

Prospective Jurors

Each student should assume the role of one of the prospective jurors described in the biographies below and answer the judge's and attorneys' questions accordingly.

1. **Michael:** Anglo, 38 years old, junior high school education. He is a third cousin to Tom Carter, but has never met him. He is a mechanic, married with five children and is a non-drinker. He has no prior jury duty.

2. **Ralph:** Latino, 61 years old, married with two children, college education. Ralph is a union leader and an officer in his United Auto Workers local. He has no prior jury duty.

3. **Judy:** Of Greek descent, 22 years old, and single. She attends law school and wants to become a criminal defense lawyer. She lives with her parents, does not work, and has no prior jury duty.

4. **Bob:** Anglo, 69 years old, single. High school graduate. Bob is a retired construction worker and has no prior jury duty.

5. **Richard:** Anglo, 38 years old. He is married with six children and is an attorney at law. He has no prior jury duty.

6. **Rosa:** Latina, 62 years old, married with two children and three grandchildren. She finished high school, has been married for 30 years, and is a supervisor at the post office. Her niece was once wounded in a drive-by shooting by a youth gang. She has served on one prior jury, which heard a criminal prosecution for being drunk in a public place. She voted to convict.

7. **Bernice:** African American, 39 years old, married with one child. College graduate with a B.A. in English. Bernice is a counselor at Freedom High School, where she has worked for the past 13 years. She has no prior jury duty.

8. **Russell:** Anglo, 57 years old, college graduate. He has been a vice president in charge of a large business corporation for 10 years. He is married with two children and is a former alcoholic. No prior jury duty.

9. **Carol:** African American, 32 years old, divorced three years ago, with one child. Protestant. She is a marketing analyst, but is currently unemployed and is receiving unemployment benefits. She is active in the feminist movement and the Black

Copy this form on a sheet of paper.

1. Put a (+) next to the most realistic role players. Put a (-) next to the least realistic groups.
   • Prospective jurors
   • Lawyers
   • Judge

2. The jurors who most realistically portrayed their roles were:

3. Based on the jury that was finally selected, who do you think will win this case? Why?

4. An effective question asked by the defense attorney was:

5. An effective question asked by the prosecuting attorney was:

6. A good question not asked of the prospective jurors is:

Community Action Council. She has no prior jury duty.

10. **James:** Of Irish descent, 58 years old, high school education. James is a produce manager in a supermarket, is married, and has one child. As a young man, he was once convicted for a misdemeanor—disturbing the peace. No prior jury duty.

11. **Mary:** African American, 54 years old, widow with three children who live with her. Mary has worked as an insurance agent for over 35 years. She has managed to pay off the mortgage on her modest home and send her oldest child to college. She has no prior jury duty.

12. **Larry:** African American, 38 years old, married with four children. He is a computer programmer. No prior jury duty.

13. **Priscilla:** Asian, 62 years old, widow, ex-college professor. She derives her income from her pension. She has had two prior jury duties. Both cases involved grand theft auto, and she voted to acquit both times.

14. **Janis:** Anglo, 70 years old, single. She works as a secretary for a small accounting firm. She has no prior jury duty.

Observers

As part of the courtroom audience, you can observe all the role players. Your job is to evaluate the simulation. The observer evaluation form should help you focus on the key issues. Copy the form onto a sheet of paper leaving enough room for you to answer the questions. You will present and discuss your impressions with the entire group at the end of the simulation.

Debriefing Questions

1. Have the observers read their evaluations to the class. Discuss the answers.

2. Ask your visiting attorney:
   • How did this simulation compare with real voir dire in your local courts?
   • How fair and effective is voir dire?

Case Notes: Trial Strategy

In his trial, Thomas Carter faces two charges—second-degree murder and manslaughter. Before a trial begins, attorneys for both sides must analyze the case and prepare

Chart for Trial Strategy in *People v. Carter*	
Section 274—Second-Degree Murder. A killing with malice aforethought. **Witness:**	
Supporting Facts for the Prosecution	Supporting Facts for the Defense
element of crime—"a killing"	
element of crime—"with malice aforethought"	

their trial strategies, beginning with a careful review of the charges. To properly defend or prosecute a case, attorneys must understand all potential arguments, both for and against their interests. By completing this analysis *before* the trial begins, every decision and presentation the attorneys make will be informed and will support the outcome they seek.

One way to analyze a case thoroughly is to use a chart identifying all of the elements of the charges, as well as the corresponding evidence that could be used to prove or disprove each of those elements. Above is the outline for a chart based on the charge of second-degree murder. It lists the two elements for second-degree murder—(1) a killing and (2) with malice aforethought. An attorney would fill out a chart for each witness in order to better understand what needs to be proved or disproved at trial.

Class Activity: Preparing for Trial

In this activity, students complete charts that will help prepare trial strategy.
1. Divide the class into two groups of lawyers—one representing the prosecution and one representing the defense. Within

the groups, break into six attorney teams (pairs or triads).

2. Assign one witness statement to each team. (The witness statements are on pages 159–161.)

3. Each team should review the statutory language of second-degree murder. (The charges are on pages 164–165.)

4. Then the team should carefully read the assigned statements and identify supporting facts for **both** the prosecution and defense cases. This information should be recorded onto a chart.

5. The team should make a second chart for involuntary manslaughter by repeating steps 3 and 4.

6. After students complete the charts, regroup the teams with all the members of their law offices and have them present their findings.

7. Students should make copies of the charts so they have a complete view of the what the prosecution and defense need to prove. The charts will help them throughout the trial.

Case Notes: Opening Statements

Once the jury has been impaneled, the attorneys for both sides deliver an **opening statement** about the case to the jury. Opening statements outline the facts that the attorneys expect to prove during the trial. An opening statement should present the jury with an orderly and easy-to-understand version of the case from the attorney's perspective. It should be persuasive but without emotion.

In criminal trials, the prosecuting attorney goes first. Usually, the defense gives its opening statement immediately afterwards. The defense, however, may choose to wait until the prosecution has called all its witnesses and the defense is ready to present its case-in-chief.

Writing an Opening Statement

To prepare an opening statement, attorneys must organize and outline the entire case they intend to prove at trial. A good opening statement should:

- Explain what the attorney plans to prove and how they will do it.
- Present the events of the case in a clear, orderly sequence.
- Suggest a motive or emphasize a lack of motive for the crime.

Attorneys usually begin their statement with a formal introduction:

"Your honor, ladies and gentlemen of the jury, opposing counsel, my name is [full name], representing [the state or the defendant] in this action."

The attorneys then turn to the jury and begin their statements.

Opening statements often include such phrases as:

- The evidence will show that . . .
- The facts will prove that . . .
- Witness [name] will be called to testify that . . .
- The defendant will explain . . .

Class Activity: Writing an Opening Statement

In this activity, each student will take the role of defense attorney or prosecutor and write an opening statement for the Thomas Carter trial. They may find it useful to use the charts they prepared in "Class Activity: Preparing for Trial."

1. Divide the class in half: one half to take the role of lawyers for the state, the other for the defense.

2. At home, list the most important facts of the Thomas Carter case *from your assigned point of view* (prosecution or defense).

3. Write a one- or two-page opening statement from your assigned point of view.

4. In class, have students meet in groups of four, deliver their opening statements to each other, and choose the best one. Then the groups should join together to form new groups of eight, and the two students chosen should deliver their statements. The group should again decide which is best. Have the finalists from each group stand and deliver their opening statements to the whole class.

5. As a class, select the best opening statement given for each side on the basis of: (a) use of facts, (b) clarity, and (c) presentation.

Case Notes: Direct and Circumstantial Evidence

Evidence proves or disproves facts in a trial. The trier of fact—judge or jury—must base its verdict solely on the evidence admitted at the trial. Documents, testimony of witnesses, drawings, and physical objects such as weapons, drugs, clothing, and other items are all forms of evidence that the fact finder considers and weighs in reaching a verdict.

There are two basic kinds of evidence: direct and circumstantial. In a criminal case, **direct evidence** is evidence of one or more of the elements of a given crime. For example:

- Will sees Maria point a gun at Marsha and pull the trigger. In a trial for murder or manslaughter, Will's testimony about what he saw Maria do would be *direct evidence* against her.

- Miguel hears Warren scream at his neighbor, "I'm going to take this bat and kill you, old man!" In a trial for assault, Miguel's and the old man's testimony would be *direct evidence* against Warren.

Circumstantial evidence in criminal cases *indirectly* supports one or more elements of a crime. Circumstantial evidence requires the fact finder to make an inference that something happened. For example:

- Will sees Maria with a smoking gun in her hand standing over Marsha's dead body. In a trial for murder or manslaughter, this would be *circumstantial evidence* that she shot Marsha.

- Miguel sees Warren running away from the old man's house with a bat in his hand. In a trial for assault, this would be *circumstantial* evidence.

It is possible for the same evidence to be both direct and circumstantial. It all depends on how it is used. Imagine that Brad's fingerprints are found on a murder weapon. The fingerprints are direct evidence that Brad had possession of the weapon. It is circumstantial evidence that Brad had used it in a murder.

The distinction between direct and circumstantial evidence may make little difference. Both are important if the fact finder believes them to be convincing or credible in a particular case. In fact, many criminal suspects are tried and convicted only with compelling circumstantial evidence.

Class Activity: Direct or Circumstantial

In this activity, students analyze samples of evidence to determine whether they are direct or circumstantial evidence.

Each student should:
1. Write the letters "a" through "e" down the side of a sheet of paper.

2. Read the items below. For each one write on your paper whether the evidence described is *direct* or *circumstantial*. Explain your answers.

   a. Suzanne is charged with resisting arrest. Officer Monroe testifies that the defendant hit him with her briefcase after he had stopped her on the highway for speeding.

   b. Charles is on trial for vandalism. An expert testifies that the color and composition of the paint found on the school building is identical to that of a can of paint found in Charles' book bag.

   c. Jennifer is on trial for the burglary of a local record shop. Mrs. Ramirez testifies that she saw Jennifer's car parked outside the record shop at the time the burglary is believed to have taken place.

d. Jeff is charged with the sale of marijuana. An undercover narcotics agent testifies that Jeff handed him a large bag of marijuana and took $2,000 in cash from him.

e. Danny is on trial for kidnaping a 2-year-old girl. Ms. Joseph, Danny's landlady, testifies that she saw Danny loading an unusually large bundle covered with a sheet into his car just minutes after the crime was reported by the victim's parents.

Case Notes: Rules of Evidence

Many rules dictate when and how evidence may be presented in court. Known as rules of evidence, they help ensure that trials will be fair, orderly, and more likely to discover the truth. They do this, for example, by excluding from court any evidence that is unreliable or unreasonably prejudicial or inflammatory. Also, in some instances, the rules require that attorneys in a trial take certain steps before they can introduce evidence.

Sometimes judges make their own objections to an attorney's questions or a witness's answer. But in most situations, all evidence will be admitted into a trial unless an attorney objects that it violates one of the rules of evidence. So lawyers must know the rules of evidence well. Such knowledge helps them prove their case, because they can present evidence important to their case and keep out an opponent's improper evidence, which could hurt their case.

The rules of evidence in state and federal courts are complex and often differ. On the next few pages, you will find an explanation of some basic rules of evidence followed in all American courts.

1. Relevance

First and foremost, evidence must be **rele-**vant to an issue in the case. It must help prove the defendant's guilt or innocence. This rule prevents the fact finder from confusing essential facts of the case with extraneous details.

Suppose that a prosecutor is trying to prove that Bob robbed a bank. Evidence offered to prove that Bob speaks several languages is probably not relevant. The defendant's skills in foreign languages are not at issue.

But what if a witness has testified that the robber spoke French? Evidence offered to prove that Bob speaks French would, in this case, be relevant.

But what is relevant to prove that fact? Evidence that Bob owns a French poodle would not be relevant, because it has no value in proving he speaks French. But evidence that Bob has a master's degree in French would be relevant.

Even relevant evidence may not be admissible if its value in deciding an issue—its **probative value**—is *outweighed* by other considerations. Thus a judge may disallow relevant evidence if it is unfairly prejudicial, confusing to the jury, or a waste of time.

How to Object:
- "Objection, your honor. This evidence is not relevant to the issues of this trial."

- "Objection, your honor. Counsel's question calls for irrelevant testimony."

- If the objection is made *after* the witness answers: "Objection, your honor. The testimony is not relevant to the facts of this case. I ask that it be stricken from the record."

If the judge thinks an objection is invalid, the judge will say, "Objection overruled." But if the judge agrees with the objection, the judge will say, "Objection sustained."

2. Foundation

To establish the relevance of evidence, attorneys may need to **lay a proper foundation**. Laying a foundation means that, before a witness can testify to certain facts, it must be shown that the witness was in a position to know about these facts. For example, if a prosecutor asks a witness if he saw Bob leave the scene of the bank robbery, the defense attorney may object for a lack of foundation.

After the court sustains—or upholds—this objection, the prosecutor would have to ask the witness if he was near the bank on the day of the robbery. This lays the foundation that the witness is legally competent to testify to the underlying fact.

Sometimes when an attorney is laying a foundation, the opposing attorney may object that the testimony is irrelevant. The questioning attorney then has to explain how the testimony relates to the case.

How to Object:
- "Objection, your honor. There is a lack of foundation."

3. Personal Knowledge

Witnesses in a trial must have personal knowledge of what they testify about. Jessica could not, for example, testify that Isaac is a bad driver if she had never seen Isaac drive.

How to Object:
- "Objection, your honor. The witness has no personal knowledge to answer the question."

- If the objection is made *after the witness answers*: "Objection, your honor. I ask that the witness's testimony be stricken from the record because the witness has no personal knowledge of the matter."

4. Hearsay

In general, witnesses must have personal knowledge of the facts they testify about. Evidence is more trustworthy if a witness observed something directly ("I saw Bill steal the wallet") rather than heard something secondhand ("Mary told me Bill stole the wallet"). Second-hand statements are normally hearsay evidence.

Consider some examples:
- Sam, a witness in Marty's murder trial, tells the court that he overheard a friend of Marty's say, "Marty killed Joe because he had to."

- The prosecution attempts to introduce a

letter written by Marty's sister, which states: "Marty needed the money so he killed him."

Both of these are examples of hearsay evidence. Neither of them would probably be admissible as evidence in a trial. **Hearsay evidence is any out-of-court statement—oral or written—offered to prove the truth of that statement.** (Think about the word "hearsay." It is something "heard" out of court and "said" in court to prove that what was asserted is true.)

Consider another example from Marty's trial:
- Sam testifies, "I heard Joe yell to Marty, 'Get out of the way.'"

Is this hearsay? It's an out-of-court statement. But it's not offered to prove the truth of the statement. Instead, it is being introduced to show that Joe had warned Marty by shouting. So it is not hearsay, and a court would admit this testimony into evidence. Hearsay is a tricky subject.

It grows even more complicated because there are various exceptions to the rule that hearsay is not admissible. Below are a few of the most common exceptions:

a. Admissions against interest. When parties to a case make statements that go against their legal interest, these statements are admissible evidence. If, for example, Sam testified, "Marty told me that he wanted to kill Joe," this statement would be admissible because it was made by Marty (the defendant and thus a party to the case) and it goes against his legal interest (i.e., it hurts his case).

b. Excited utterance. Any statement made by a person in an excited state is admissible.

c. State of mind. Any statement that shows the speaker's state of mind is admissible. For example, if before the murder Joe told Sam, "I'm really scared." This statement would be admissible in testimony by Sam.

d. Official records and writings by public employees.

e. Records made in the regular course of doing business.

How to Object:
- "Objection, your honor. Counsel's question calls for hearsay."

- If the objection is raised *after the witness answers:* "Objection, your honor. This testimony is hearsay. I ask that it be stricken from the record."

5. Opinion Testimony

With a few limited exceptions, only experts with special knowledge and qualifications can give their opinions in a trial. An attorney who calls an expert to testify, must first qualify the individual as an expert. In other words, an attorney must lay a foundation that the person qualifies as an expert. The attorney does this by asking a series of questions about the person's professional training and experience in a particular field. The attorney then asks the court to acknowledge the witness's specific expertise.

All witnesses, even non-experts, may give their opinions about things like color, size, weight, drunkenness, speed of a moving object—anything within the realm of a person's ordinary, everyday experience or perception.

How to Object:
- "Objection, your honor. Counsel is asking the witness to give an opinion."

- If the objection is made *after the witness answers:* "Objection, your honor. This witness was not qualified as an expert. I ask that the witness's opinion be stricken from the record."

6. Argumentative Questions

Witnesses may ordinarily only be asked questions to get facts from them. Questions that challenge witnesses to reconcile differing parts of their testimony may be objected to as being argumentative. For example, an attorney asks, "How can you expect the court to believe that you were at Main Street that day when you previously testified you were out of town?" This question may be objected to as argumentative.

How to Object:
- "Objection, your honor. Counsel is being argumentative."

- "Objection, your honor. Counsel is badgering the witness."

7. Special Rules for Direct Examination of Witnesses

Direct examination takes place when lawyers call their own witnesses to the stand and ask them questions.

a. Form of Questions

Generally, attorneys must ask questions that evoke a short narrative answer from the witness, but not an answer too long or rambling. In direct examination, attorneys usually may not ask leading questions. A leading question is one that suggests the desired answer. It usually elicits a "yes" or "no" answer. Often, leading questions are really statements with something like, "isn't that right?", "isn't that so?", or "didn't you?" tacked on the end.

For example, this question would be proper on direct examination (assuming that the fact was in issue): "Mr. Stevens, when did you and your wife adopt Charles?"

This one would be improper: "You and your wife adopted Charles two years ago, is that correct, Mr. Stevens?"

How to Object:
- "Objection, your honor. Counsel is leading the witness."

b. Character

Unless a person's character is at issue in a case, witnesses generally cannot testify about a person's character. But a witness's honesty is one aspect of character always at issue. In addition, the defense may introduce evidence of the defendant's good character and, if relevant, show the bad character of an important prosecution witness. Once the defense introduces character evidence, however, the prosecution can try to refute it.

Consider these examples:

- The prosecutor calls the owner of the defendant's apartment to testify. She testifies that the defendant often stumbled in drunk at all hours of the night. This character evidence would *not* be admissible unless the defendant had already introduced evidence of good character. Even then, a judge might disallow it because its prejudicial nature would probably outweigh its probative value.

- The defendant's minister testifies that the defendant attends church every week and has a reputation in the community as a law-abiding person. This would be admissible.

How to Object:

- "Objection, your honor. The witness's character is not at issue in this case."

- "Objection, your honor. The question calls for inadmissible character evidence."

c. Refreshing Recollections

Imagine that you are a witness of a hit-and-run accident. Two years later, the driver of the car comes to trial. The prosecutor calls you to the stand and asks you to describe what you saw. You give as many details as you can, but when the attorney asks you what the license plate number was on the car, you draw a blank. "I know I saw it, and I know I told you when you talked to me after the accident," you answer, "but it's been so long—I just can't remember the number."

Since cases often take time before coming to trial, witnesses often may have a hard time recalling specific details of events occurring months or years earlier. In addition, witnesses may be so nervous that their memories fail them. The rules of evidence deal with this problem by allowing attorneys to help their

witnesses remember. This is called "refreshing the witness's recollection." In the example above, the attorney could take a typed copy of a statement you made near the time of the accident, mark it as an "exhibit," have you read it, and then take the statement away. She could then ask you the question about the license plate number again. *"Now* I remember," you answer. "The number was XOJ 489."

8. Special Rules for Cross-Examination of Witnesses

After direct examination, the lawyer for the opposing side cross-examines each witness. Cross-examination has two purposes. It is designed to:

(1) clarify the witness's testimony from the other side's point of view, and

(2) give the opposing side an opportunity to **impeach** the witness—that is, to attack the witness's credibility.

a. Form of Questions

While leading questions (e.g., "You drank like a fish that night, didn't you, Mr. Saski?") are usually not permitted during direct examination, they are allowed during cross-examination.

b. Scope of Cross-Examination

Cross-examination questions are limited to matters that were brought out on direct examination. In other words, cross-examination may not go beyond the scope of the direct examination. Most judges, however, broadly interpret this rule.

How to Object:

- "Objection, your honor. Counsel's question is going beyond the scope of direct examination."

c. Impeachment

Impeaching a witness on cross-examination is designed to reduce the importance that the fact finder gives a witness's story. An attorney can impeach a witness by asking about:

- **Bias or prejudice** the witness has toward the issues or parties in the case.

- The **accuracy** of what the witness saw, heard, smelled, etc.

- **Prior statements** that the witness made that are **inconsistent** with the witness's testimony in court.

- **Prior criminal convictions** of the witness, but only if they relate directly to truth-telling ability.

- **Prior acts of misconduct,** but only if they relate directly to the witness's ability to tell the truth. (Such questions may only be asked if the attorney conducting the cross-examination has information showing that the bad conduct actually happened. The attorney may not base the question on some rumor or just ask the question to make the witness look bad.)

If the witness's credibility is attacked on cross-examination, the attorney whose witness has been impeached may ask more questions to try to limit the damage done and restore the witness's credibility. This is done on **redirect examination** by the lawyer who put the witness on the stand in the first place.

For Discussion

1. Why is eyewitness testimony ("I saw Bill steal the wallet") more trustworthy than something heard secondhand ("Mary told me she saw Bill steal the wallet")? How can the first statement be tested in court? How can the second statement?

2. When are leading questions permitted and prohibited? Why do you think this difference exists?

3. Can you think of examples of relevant testimony that would not be allowed in evidence?

Class Activity: Objection

In this activity, students decide whether to make objections in trial situations based on the Thomas Wade Carter case.

Each student should write the letters "a" through "l" down the side of a sheet of paper. Each should (1) next to each letter write "yes" or "no" to indicate whether an objection should be made in each situation and (2) give a reason for each answer.

a. Ms. Karen Miller testifies: "I am convinced my little girl was intentionally killed by the Carter boy."

b. Joel Robertson testifies: "A friend of mine said he saw Oscar hit Tom over the head with a beer bottle."

c. The prosecutor asks Gail Duran: "What kind of potato chips did you serve at your party?"

d. Ms. Karen Miller testifies: "I told the police officer that I thought whoever shot Joyce was on drugs."

e. On cross-examination, the attorney asks Gail Duran: "You didn't stop the car when you heard the explosion behind you, did you?"

f. Ms. Karen Miller testifies: "Joyce was shot with a 12-gauge shotgun."

g. Joel Robertson testifies: "Oscar Hanks always parks his truck across the street from his house. It must have been there that day when Joyce Miller was shot."

h. Lt. Tony Jackson of the police department testifies: "We know that Tom Carter had connections with drug dealers in the area."

i. One of the guests from Gail Duran's party testifies: "Tom Carter told me after the fight that he was going to fix Oscar Hanks once and for all."

j. A neighbor of Ms. Miller states that a car with a gun sticking out of the back window drove by at about 15 miles per hour.

k. On direct examination, Carter's attorney asks him: "You never intended to shoot anyone, did you?"

l. Joel Robertson testifies: "If you ask me, a shotgun is effective up to about 20 yards."

Class Activity: Cross Fire

Now that you've had a chance to test your understanding of some basic rules of evidence, take the role of attorneys and prepare to examine witnesses in the case of Thomas Carter.

It is recommended that you invite a lawyer or law student into class to work with the attorney groups and act as judge during the direct and cross-examination of witnesses. (If none is available, the teacher should take the role of judge.)

1. Organize the class into the following groups: Six teams of prosecutors (numbered 1–6) consisting of 2–3 students each; six teams of defense attorneys (numbered 1–6) consisting of 2–3 students each; and six witnesses.

2. Students should prepare by following the instructions for their appropriate group (witnesses or attorneys) described below.

3. After all of the teams have developed their questions, role play the examination of the witnesses. The team assigned to cross-examine a particular witness should be primarily responsible for raising objections to the direct examination, although *all* students on the opposing team may do so. Likewise, a team assigned to direct examination of a particular witness should be primarily responsible for raising objections to the

cross-examination of its witness. The visiting attorney or law student should rule on the objections and help debrief the activity.

4. After all witnesses have been examined and cross-examined, discuss the Debriefing Questions on page 161.

Witness Instructions

Select one of the six witness descriptions on pages 159–161 and study it carefully. For this activity, try to become the character described. Be prepared to answer questions that both the prosecuting and defense attorneys might ask you. When you are on the stand, it will be your job to recall the events leading up to Joyce Miller's killing. Do not add anything to the facts contained in your witness statement.

Attorney Instructions

Assign one of the six prosecution teams to each of these tasks:

1. Direct examination of Joel Robertson

2. Direct examination of Gail Duran

3. Direct examination of Lt. Tony Jackson

4. Direct examination of Karen Miller

5. Cross-examination of Thomas Carter

6. Cross-examination of Lillian Sweet

Assign one of the six defense teams to each of these tasks:

1. Direct examination of Thomas Carter

2. Direct examination of Lillian Sweet

3. Cross-examination of Joel Robertson

4. Cross-examination of Gail Duran

5. Cross-examination of Lt. Tony Jackson

6. Cross-examination of Karen Miller

To prepare to examine witnesses, carefully review:

1. "Rules of Evidence," pages 153–157, so that you can raise or counter objections.

2. The statement of the witness you are assigned, pages 159–161.

Your team should **develop questions** for the witness you are assigned to. Keep in mind the rules of evidence and your team's overall strategy for the case.

The prosecution must prove Thomas Carter guilty of murder beyond a reasonable doubt. It must bring up evidence in its favor and anticipate and attempt to dilute the impact of evidence against it. The defense must raise every reasonable doubt it can about Carter's guilt.

In most states, a defendant charged with murder could be found guilty of manslaughter instead. Since Carter has no alibi and doesn't deny being in the car with the shotgun in his hand, the case will boil down to the issue of Carter's *intent*. The prosecution will try to prove that Carter knew exactly what he was doing and that he intended to shoot the gun. The defense, on the other hand, will try to show that Carter didn't really mean to hurt anyone and that the gun went off accidentally.

Since you can only cross-examine witnesses about what they testified about on direct examination, cross-examination questions can be difficult to write in advance. But the witnesses' statements should give you an idea of what witnesses are likely to be asked on direct, and you can write cross-examination questions accordingly. You should then be alert during direct examination so you can get rid of any inappropriate cross questions you have developed.

Also, be prepared to object to any statements you believe violate the rules of evidence.

Statement of Karen Miller

My name is Karen Miller. I am 25 years old and divorced.

I was home on the evening of July 6. Around 7 p.m., Joyce was playing in the front yard. I asked her to close the front gate and come inside the house, since it was her bath time. As I watched her go to the gate, a black car slowly drove down the block. I think it was a late model Pontiac, but I'm not really sure. Suddenly, the barrel of a rifle or shotgun was pointing from the car window right at Joyce. Before I could say or do anything, there was an explosion, and the car took off quickly.

At that instant, I looked at Joyce and saw her fall to the ground. Horrified, I ran to her and saw blood all over her face and body.

I can't describe the occupants of the black Pontiac. Still, I think the driver was a young woman.

A red Toyota truck was parked in front of my house that evening. I believe it belonged to a teenager named Oscar who lives across the street.

Statement of Joel Robertson

I am Joel Robertson and I am 21 years old. I have known Tom for a few years, but we're not close friends.

On the evening of July 5, I attended a party at Gail Duran's house. I and most of the others at the party drank beer for several hours. Around 3:30 a.m., a fight broke out. I was not involved in the fight, but I saw Tom Carter get hit over the head with a beer bottle. I did not know who did it. I and some of the others at the party took Tom Carter to the hospital for emergency treatment. On the way to the hospital, Carter kept asking who hit him with the bottle. He was really angry. The people in the car suggested several names, including Oscar Hanks.

The next day about 5 p.m., Tom Carter came over to my apartment. Carter was still very angry about what had happened the night before. I know from past experience that Carter is the type of guy to carry a grudge. He's a real hothead. He was always getting into fights with guys at school and in our neighborhood. Carter told me that he thought he knew the guy who split open his scalp. He said he thought the guy was Oscar Hanks. Carter told me, "I'm going to put a scare into that guy that he won't forget."

We watched a video for a while and had a soft drink. Carter was really nervous. A little later, Carter started asking me about my gun collection. I am a hunter and collect rifles and shotguns. Carter was especially interested in one of my shotguns. He asked me to show him how to work it. He also asked me how far a shotgun would shoot. I responded that a shotgun would be effective up to about 20 yards. About 6 p.m., Carter left my apartment.

Statement of Gail Duran

My name is Gail Duran. I am 17. I have been dating Tom Carter for about a year.

On the evening of July 5, I had a party for about 50 of my friends while my parents were on vacation. During the party a lot of people got drunk on beer. Sometime around 3 a.m., a fight broke out among about a dozen guys. Tom was hit on the head with a beer bottle.

There was blood all over the place. I asked Joel Robertson and some others to take Tom to the hospital while I tried to get everybody out of the house before the police came.

The next day Tom called me to say he was all right and would be over to see me later on. Around 6:30 p.m., Tom arrived at my place. He was very upset about getting hit the night before. He said he thought he knew who had hit him with the bottle. He said it was Oscar Hanks. Tom then asked me to go for a ride with him. I agreed to go with him.

Tom asked me to drive his car while he sat in the back. Tom owns a Pontiac Firebird. He told me he wanted to look for Oscar Hanks. He gave me directions to drive to Fourth Street. While driving down Fourth Street, Tom said, "Hey, that's his truck. Slow down, Gail." As I slowed down, I noticed for the first time that Tom had a shotgun in the back of the car with him.

At this point, I really got scared and began to swerve down the street. I had never seen Tom act this way before. Then there was a loud bang, and Tom yelled to me, "Get us out of here, fast!" I managed to drive out of the neighborhood. I stopped on a quiet street. Tom got into the driver's seat and took me home.

On the way home, Tom told me that the shotgun just went off by itself, but he did not think he had hit anything. I did not actually see the shotgun discharge, but I believe that the swerving motion of the car must have caused Tom to accidentally pull the trigger. Tom would never intentionally shoot anyone. He's always been a sensitive and gentle guy. Sure, he had a few fist fights when we were in high school, but he didn't mean anything by it. He's basically a great guy.

Statement of Thomas Wade Carter

My name is Thomas Wade Carter, age 18. I have recently graduated from high school. I work at an auto parts store.

I was totally shocked when I was arrested for shooting a little girl. I have never been in serious trouble before. I was suspended from high school once or twice because of problems with other guys, but they always started the fights, not me.

Gail Duran is my girlfriend. She and I have been going together for about a year. I went to her party on July 5 and had a good time drinking beer with my friends until I got in a fight with a dozen other guys around 3 a.m. During the fight, I was struck in the back of the head with a beer bottle. Joel Robertson and some others at the party took me to the hospital. It took five stitches to close the wound on my scalp.

The next day (July 6), I called Gail and told her I was all right and that I would be dropping by later in the day.

I was angry at Oscar and wanted to pay him back some way. So I decided to take my father's shotgun and scare him a little.

After picking up the shotgun, I stopped by Joel Robertson's apartment around 5 p.m. I knew he was a hunter. I got him to tell me how to work a shotgun so I could make Oscar think I was serious. But I never knew the gun was loaded, and I never meant to hurt him. I just wanted to teach him a lesson.

From Joel's place, I went over to see Gail. I asked her to go with me for a drive. I had her drive my car while I sat in the back seat looking for Oscar's house. I knew he lived somewhere on Fourth Street. I also knew he drove a red Toyota truck. Finally, I spotted his truck parked along the street. But the car suddenly lurched, and the next thing I knew, the shotgun went off accidentally. I panicked. I didn't know it was loaded! I told Gail to get out of the neighborhood fast. I did not see anybody in the yard where Joyce Ann Miller was killed and certainly did not aim the shotgun at her. It was an accident.

Statement of Lillian Sweet

My name is Lillian Sweet. I am a retired school principal. I have a Ph.D. in educational administration from the University of Illinois. I was a history teacher and a school guidance counselor before I became a principal.

I have known Tom Carter since he was a little boy. I've lived down the street from the Carters for almost 20 years, and I was the principal of the high school that Tom attended.

I did have to suspend him for brawling with other boys once or twice. But kids will be kids. I think Tom was just following the lead of his friends in those days. As a principal, I was not very seriously concerned about Tom's behavior. I knew he'd grow up to be the fine young man he is today.

Tom has always been a joy to have in the neighborhood. He is kind to old people and children. He helps his mother with grocery shopping. Sometimes he even drives me to my doctor appointments if the weather is bad or he has a free afternoon.

In my opinion, Tom could never have done what he is accused of doing. He's a very stable and responsible young man. He's just not capable of murder.

Statement of Lt. Tony Jackson

NOTE: For Lt. Jackson's statement see the Police Crime Investigation Report on pages 124–125.

Debriefing Questions

1. Which witnesses were most important to the prosecution and defense? Why?

2. Which questions were most effective during the direct examinations? During the cross-examinations?

3. Which objections were raised most often? Why do you think this happened?

4. What characteristics do you think tend to make a witness seem believable? What characteristics detract from a witness's credibility?

5. What qualities would a person need to be a successful trial lawyer? Explain.

Case Notes: Closing Statements

After the defense's case-in-chief, the opposing counsels make closing arguments. These arguments give the attorneys a chance to summarize their cases, review the testimony of witnesses, and make a last appeal to the judge or jury.

Guidelines for an Effective Closing Statement

An effective closing statement should:
1. Be emotionally charged and strongly appealing (unlike the calm, rational opening statement).

2. Only refer to evidence that was admitted during the trial.

3. Emphasize the facts that support the claims of your side.

4. Note weaknesses or inconsistencies in the opposing side's case.

5. Summarize the favorable testimony.

6. Attempt to reconcile inconsistencies that might hurt your side.

7. Be presented so that notes are barely necessary.

8. Be well-organized (starting and ending with your strongest point helps to structure the presentation and give you a good introduction and conclusion).

9. Focus on reasonable doubt. The prosecution should emphasize that the state has proved the elements of the crime beyond a reasonable doubt. The defense should raise questions suggesting that reasonable doubt exists.

Proper phrasing includes:
> "The evidence has clearly shown that . . ."
>
> "Based on this testimony, there can be no doubt that . . ."
>
> "The prosecution has failed to prove that . . ."
>
> "The defense would have you believe that . . ."

10. Conclude with an appeal to convict or acquit the defendant.

Class Activity: The Defense Rests . . .

In this activity, students take the role of attorneys developing closing arguments in the case of *People v. Carter*.
1. Each student should:
   - Choose to represent either the prosecution or defense.
   - Review the witness statements on pages 159–161 and consider the main points brought out in witnesses' testimony in the previous activity.
   - Develop a three-minute closing argument for presentation to the class. (Be sure to follow the above "Guidelines for an Effective Closing Statement.")

2. Select 12 members of the class to act as a jury. They will judge the quality of the presentations. To do this, each must take a blank piece of paper and make a rating sheet as follows:
   > Write each presenter's name and role (prosecutor or defense attorney). Under each presenter's name, write

the numbers one through nine in a column. Each of the numbers corresponds to one of the "Guidelines for an Effective Closing Statement." After each presentation, place a check mark next to the item if the presenter's statement met the criterion.

3. Call on three prosecutors and then three defense attorneys to make closing arguments. (Alternate defense attorneys and prosecutors with the defense going first.) After all have presented, poll the jury to find out which prosecutor and defense attorney made the best presentation. Jurors should explain their choices based on the listed criteria.

Case Notes: Instructing the Jury

After closing arguments in a criminal trial, the judge gives the jury instructions it must consider when arriving at a verdict. This process is sometimes called **charging the jury**. The primary purposes of these instructions are to explain the law, point out the elements of a crime that must be proved, and show the relationship of the evidence to the issues at trial. In many states, judges base their instructions on models adopted by the legislature. In other states, judges may develop their own. Still, a judge must be careful. Inaccurate or misleading instructions to the jury are the most common reason for verdicts being overturned on appeal.

Imagine you are in the jury box just as the court clerk in the case of *People v. Carter* rises and announces: "The court will now charge the jury. No one may leave or enter the room during the charge." Judge Coghlan then gives the following instructions:

Ladies and gentlemen of the jury:
It is my duty to instruct you in the law that applies to this case. You must follow the law as I state it to you.

1. **Duties of the Judge and Jury**

In determining whether the defendant is guilty or not guilty, you—as jurors—must base your decision entirely on the evidence presented during this trial and on the law as explained by me. You must not be governed by sympathy, guesswork, emotion, prejudice, or public opinion. You must not be influenced by the mere fact that the defendant has been arrested, charged, and brought to trial.

2. **Evidence**

If the evidence equally supports two reasonable versions of the truth, one of which points to the defendant's guilt and the other to the defendant's innocence, it is your duty to adopt the version pointing to the defendant's innocence.

3. **Credibility of Witnesses**

Every person who testifies under oath is a witness. You are the sole judges of the credibility of the witnesses who have testified in this case.

Discrepancies or differences that occur in a witness's testimony, or between one witness and another, do not necessarily mean that a witness is lying. Failure to recollect facts is a common human experience. In addition, two persons witnessing the same incident will often see or hear it differently. You may simply have to decide which version of the facts is more believable.

4. **Statements of Counsel and Evidence Stricken from the Record**

Any testimony or other evidence rejected or stricken from the record is to be treated as if you had never heard it.

Also, if an objection to a question was sustained, you must disregard the question. This means that you

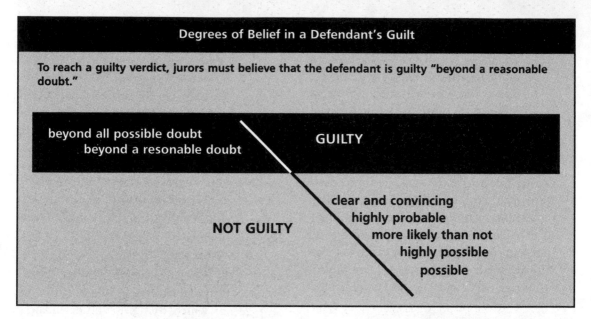

Degrees of Belief in a Defendant's Guilt

To reach a guilty verdict, jurors must believe that the defendant is guilty "beyond a reasonable doubt."

beyond all possible doubt
beyond a resonable doubt

GUILTY

NOT GUILTY

clear and convincing
highly probable
more likely than not
highly possible
possible

must not speculate about what witnesses might have said if they had been allowed to answer. Neither may you speculate about why an objection was made to a question.

5. **Presumption of Innocence—Reasonable Doubt—Burden of Proof**

A defendant in a criminal action is presumed to be innocent until proved guilty. This presumption places upon the prosecution the burden of proving the defendant guilty beyond a reasonable doubt. This does not mean that no possible doubt must exist, because doubt will always exist. Beyond a reasonable doubt means that after hearing all the evidence, a juror is still convinced to a moral certainty that the defendant is guilty.

6. **The Charges in this Case:**

Thomas Wade Carter has been charged with two crimes: Second-degree murder and involuntary manslaughter.

Second-Degree Murder

Second-degree murder is the unlawful killing of a human being with malice aforethought.

Malice aforethought may be either express or implied. It is express when a person intends unlawfully to kill a human being. It is implied when the killing results from an intentional act that:

(1) is dangerous to human life, *and*

(2) was deliberately performed with knowledge of the danger and with conscious disregard for human life.

Malice does not necessarily require any ill will or hatred of the person killed.

Aforethought does not imply deliberation or the lapse of considerable time. It only means that the required mental state must come before rather than follow the act.

If you find beyond a reasonable doubt by the evidence presented in this trial that Thomas Wade Carter intended to kill Joyce Ann Miller, then you shall return a verdict of second-degree murder.

OR

If you find beyond a reasonable doubt by the evidence presented in this trial that Thomas Wade Carter intended to fire the shotgun that killed Joyce Ann Miller, and that the act involved a high degree of probability that death would result, and that it was done with conscious disregard for human life, you shall return a verdict of second-degree murder.

Lesser Charge: Involuntary Manslaughter

Involuntary manslaughter is the unlawful killing of a human being without malice aforethought and without intent to kill. If you are satisfied beyond a reasonable doubt that the killing was unintentional and the direct result of a very dangerous or unlawful act, you shall return a verdict of involuntary manslaughter.

7. **Doubt Whether Murder or Manslaughter**

If you are satisfied beyond a reasonable doubt that the killing was unlawful, but you have a reasonable doubt whether the crime is murder or manslaughter, you must give the defendant the benefit of this doubt and find it to be manslaughter rather than murder.

8. **Unanimous Agreement as to Offense: Second-Degree Murder or Manslaughter**

Before you may return a verdict in this case, you must agree unanimously. If you return a verdict of not guilty, it must be agreed on unanimously. If you return a guilty verdict, you must unanimously find him guilty of manslaughter or of murder in the second degree.

9. **Each Juror Must Make an Independent Decision**

Each of you must decide the case for yourself, but you should also do so only after discussing the evidence and these instructions with the other jurors.

You should not hesitate to change your opinion if you are convinced it is wrong. You should not, however, be influenced one way or the other because the majority of jurors favor a certain verdict.

10. **Concluding Instructions**

You shall now retire and select one of your number to act as foreperson. The foreperson will preside over your deliberations. To reach a verdict, all jurors must agree to the decision. As soon as all of you have agreed upon a verdict, you shall have it dated and signed by your foreperson, and then you shall return to announce it to the court.

For Discussion

1. What things *should* be considered and discussed by the jurors? What things *should not* enter into the jury's deliberations?

2. Review the definition of "beyond a reasonable doubt" in instruction #5. According to this definition, which one of the following statements would be true?

   a. A juror should vote to convict *only* if 100 percent sure that the defendant is guilty.

   b. A juror should vote to acquit if the juror believes there is any possible chance that the defendant is not guilty.

   c. A juror should vote to convict if the juror believes that a very high degree of probability exists that the defendant is guilty.

3. Review the second-degree murder charge against Thomas Wade Carter in instruction #6. According to the prosecution, how was Joyce Ann Miller killed? According to the defense, how was Joyce Ann Miller killed?

Class Activity: We, the Jury

In this activity, students take the role of jury members charged with rendering a final verdict in the case of *People v. Carter*. To complete this activity, follow these procedures:

1. Form two or three juries of 12 students each. (Remaining students may form a smaller jury.)

2. Each jury should appoint a foreperson who will help lead discussions, collect signatures on the verdict, date it, and deliver it to the court.

3. You should refer to the judge's instructions on pages 163–165 during your deliberations.

4. During the deliberations, the foreperson may wish to take one or more polls to determine if the jury has reached a consensus. Remember, your verdict must be unanimous.

5. First determine your verdict on the charge of second-degree murder. If the jury finds Carter not guilty or it deadlocks on this issue, then determine the verdict for involuntary manslaughter.

6. After about 15 minutes, the teacher, acting as judge, will ask if you have reached a verdict.

   • A jury not reaching a unanimous verdict will be considered a hung jury.

   • The forepersons of juries reaching a unanimous verdict will deliver it to the court along with the 12 signatures attesting to it.

7. In either case, the judge may poll individual jurors and ask each to explain the reasons for their decisions. (In a real case, a judge polling individual jurors may not ask for the reasons for their decision.)

Debriefing Questions

1. Sometimes juries are unable to reach a verdict and become what is known as hung juries. How is it possible for people who have heard the same evidence to reach different conclusions?

2. How does this jury activity compare to what you know about real jury deliberations? For example, were some students unable to be objective after having taken the role of the defense or prosecution? Did the jurors know too much about the case?

3. Which witnesses did you find most believable? Least credible? What makes a witness credible?

4. Which roles were the most difficult to play? Why?

5. What did you learn about the job of the judge, attorneys, witnesses, and jurors?

Class Activity: Verdict

As a concluding activity, write an essay explaining your personal verdict in the Thomas Wade Carter case.

Unit 4:
Corrections

Jay is 19 years old. Today, he will appear before a judge to be sentenced. He stole a car. He is about to enter **corrections**—the part of our criminal justice system that deals with convicted offenders. Though Jay has never been in trouble with the law before, he has a lot to worry about. Will the judge send him to prison? Or, because he has no prior record, will he be given some alternative to prison—probation or some kind of community service?

If you asked Jay's victim, you might hear a demand that he go to prison. If you asked someone familiar with the prison system, however, you might get a different opinion. Some might even argue that Jay should be given a second chance. Many experts believe that contact with hardened criminals only locks someone into a life of crime.

In many parts of the country, Jay could be sentenced to a special program in a group home, where he would work under the supervision of a staff of trained specialists. In that setting, he could receive psychological counseling and job training. Or he could be sent to a boot camp program that tries to instill self-discipline in young offenders.

This chapter explores how sentencing decisions are made and what the alternatives are—prison, probation, community service, and several innovative programs, which may be promising alternatives to existing programs. We will also explore how prisons developed, the problems they currently face, and some experimental corrections programs that are under way. Finally, you will take a look at what is perhaps the most hotly debated of all corrections issues—the death penalty.

CHAPTER 12
Corrections and Society

The Purpose of Punishment

All societies have maintained the right to punish people who break their rules. But what is the purpose of punishment? What is it supposed to accomplish? This is a difficult question to answer. Experts and lay people alike often disagree. Over the years, different theories have been advanced. Some of these theories involve very different ways of handling wrongdoers—from ducking stools to imprisonment to psychotherapy.

People advocating one approach have often condemned all others as brutal, or unjust, or ineffective. Recently, scholars have tried to bring some order to the debate by developing an inclusive theory of punishment. This theory holds that one approach might work best in one situation while another would be better in a different situation.

The following are brief descriptions of each of the major reasons for punishing a lawbreaker:

Rehabilitation seeks to treat and reform the lawbreaker. Advocates of this theory believe that prison or release programs should try to turn the wrongdoer into a productive member of society. To implement this theory, the prison system has to provide job training, psychological counseling, and educational programs. And these programs should be tailored to the best interests of the individual prisoner. Critics of the rehabilitation theory admit that it may be a noble idea, but they argue that it just doesn't work in practice.

Restitution seeks repayment. The offender repays the victim or community in money or services. Critics say money and services cannot repay for the harm caused by violent crimes.

A state trooper walks in the shadow of a fence surrounding a prison.

Incapacitation seeks to isolate a criminal from society to protect ordinary citizens. Confinement in a secure prison makes it impossible for a criminal to commit further crimes in the surrounding society. Critics of this theory point out that most criminals have fixed prison terms, and they will be released sooner or later. If nothing is done to reform them, the protection is only temporary.

Deterrence seeks to prevent further crimes. This can operate in two ways. One way, called *specific* deterrence, targets the criminal in question, hoping that the memory of harsh punishment will deter that criminal from any further crime. *General* **deterrence** targets other potential criminals. Others will see the harsh punishment and be discouraged from committing the same crime. Critics argue that few criminals expect to be caught, and deterrence is only powerful when criminals fear they will be caught and punished.

Retribution seeks revenge. This is perhaps the oldest theory of punishment, based on the idea that society has to retaliate against a person who commits a crime. This idea dates back to the ancient "eye for an eye" philosophies of Mesopotamian and Judeo-Christian traditions. Advocates say that by imposing punishment we in some way get even with criminals. Some critics of retribution say it is too cruel for a modern society, and others claim that it does nothing to address serious issues like reforming criminals or protecting the innocent.

For Discussion

1. Which of the five reasons for punishment do you agree with? Disagree with? Why?

2. If someone broke into your house and stole your television, what do you think would be an appropriate punishment? Which of the reasons for punishment did you base the punishment on?

Class Activity: The Student Court

In this activity, students act as members of a student court, assigning penalties to those who break school rules. Wrongdoers may be sentenced to detention, hours of school service, loss of student body privileges, or other penalties the court thinks appropriate.

1. Divide the class into student courts of five students each.

2. Each court should:

   a. Appoint a chief judge to lead the discussion and to assign one of the cases below to each student. Each student is responsible for taking notes and reporting the penalty in that case to the whole class.

   b. Review the cases below, which have come before the court. After discussion, the court should set an appropriate and specific penalty for each wrongdoer.

3. Reconvene the whole class. Make headings on the board using the names of the five rule breakers. Have the appropriate member of each court report its recommended penalty and write it under the appropriate heading.

4. For each sentence described, discuss and decide whether it best meets the purposes of (a) rehabilitation, (b) restitution, (c) incapacitation, (d) deterrence, (e) retribution, or (f) some combination. Conclude with a class discussion using the Debriefing Questions.

Cases

1. **Chris Hodges** was caught smoking in the restroom. This is his second offense.

2. **Terry Rodriguez** was cited for littering the campus quad area during lunch period.

3. **Kelly Janus**, a candidate for student body treasurer, was caught tearing down other candidates' campaign posters.

4. **Linden Sommerville** started a food fight in the cafeteria by smashing an overripe banana in her friend's hair.

5. **Jan Turner** defaced several library books.

Debriefing Questions

1. Which of the sentences recommended by the student courts do you think are fair? Which are not fair? Why?

2. Which of the five theories of punishment comes closest to your idea of what is just? Why?

A Brief History of Punishment in the United States

In the last 30 years, most states have cracked down on crime and sent many criminals to prison. America today has about 2 million people behind bars, almost seven times the number of people in prison and jail in 1970. America has a far higher percentage of its citizens in prison than almost every other country in the world.

This drastic change is not unique. America's attitudes on crime and punishment have changed dramatically many times in its history. Looking back on this history, we can gain some insight into the problems we face today.

In colonial times, a ducking stool was often used to punish offenders.

Punishment in Colonial America

Before the American Revolution, all the colonies punished even minor offenses harshly. They would mete out public humiliation for petty offenses. A lawbreaker might have to stand in a public square, hands locked up in a device called a pillory, or sit with feet locked in stocks. In many towns, offenders were tied to ducking stools and dunked into the icy water of a river or pond. Some lawbreakers were forced to wear a symbol of their crime, such as the large red "A" for adultery that was sewn to the dress of the character Hester Prynne in Nathaniel Hawthorne's *The Scarlet Letter*.

More serious lawbreakers might receive lashings at a public whipping post. Others, particularly runaway slaves in the Southern colonies, might be branded with a hot iron or mutilated by cutting off their toes. In Northern colonies, thieves might have their ears cut off or the letter "T" branded on their necks or faces. This was not only a punishment, but a warning to other thieves. For many serious crimes, the penalty was death by public hanging.

Some colonies had jails to house the accused while they awaited trial. Jailkeepers often ran these institutions for profit, and inmates had to pay for their own food and blankets. Some poor inmates starved to death before their trials began. Many inmates were hired out to work as laborers building roads and working farms, and the profits went to the jailkeepers. One observer noted seeing inmates weighed down by "iron collars and chains, to which bombshells were attached, to be dragged along while they performed their degrading service."

Regret and Remorse: The Penitentiary

After the American Revolution, concerned citizens of the new American republic objected to the brutal treatment of criminals. In Pennsylvania, the Quakers, an influential religious group opposed to war and violence, worked for reform. They introduced the idea of changing criminals' behavior by locking them up behind high thick walls. This reform movement led to the first prisons as we know them today. In 1790, Philadelphia built a block of cells, each one six by eight feet in size and nine feet high. The Quakers hoped that solitary confinement would give criminals the opportunity to think about their deeds and become penitent, or sorry, for what they had done. Early prisons, therefore, came to be called penitentiaries. The Quakers also sponsored other reforms, including separating prisoners by sex, keeping children out of adult jails, and providing food and clothing to inmates at government expense.

The Pennsylvania System, as these reforms were called, represented a change in the philosophy of how to deal with criminals. Its purpose was not just to punish, but also to *correct* the behavior of lawbreakers. This new idea of correcting, or reforming, criminal behavior soon spread throughout the United States and Europe.

Unfortunately, the system of corrections sponsored by the Quakers seldom accomplished its purpose. Prisoners locked up in solitary confinement frequently became sick, went insane, or died. In 1842, Charles Dickens, the famous English novelist and social reformer, visited the Pennsylvania penitentiaries and reported:

> I believe it, in its effects, to be cruel and wrong. In its intention, I am well convinced that it is kind, humane, and meant for reformation, but I am persuaded that those who devised this system of prison discipline . . . do not know what it is they are doing. I believe that very few men are capable of estimating the immense amount of torture and agony which this dreadful punishment . . . inflicts upon the sufferers . . . . I hold this slow and daily tampering with the mysteries of the brain to be immensely worse than any torture of the body.

Leading a Useful Life: The Work System

The failure of solitary confinement led prison officials to try a new system that emphasized work instead of isolation. Under this system, prisoners were locked up in cells at night. But during the day, they worked together in prison shops and ate in a common dining area. At first, rules banned talking among prisoners. Later reforms allowed conversation.

The work system became widely used, and it still influences prison philosophy today. In many prisons, inmates learned to operate simple machines to manufacture items such as furniture for government offices. In some places, prisoners performed services such as growing food or cleaning laundry.

Treating Criminal Behavior: Rehabilitation

Following the Civil War, a new group of prison reformers questioned the work system. These reformers argued that criminal behavior was like a disease and that prisons should try to cure the disease with some form of treatment. Prisoners should be **rehabilitated** and ready to take up a normal life in society when they were released.

A rehabilitation program was first tried in 1877 in a youth reformatory at Elmira, New York. Elmira offered its young offenders school classes, vocational training, health care, and counseling. When inmates demonstrated that they were ready for release, they could leave. Many other youth reformatories soon took up this new system.

Adult prisons also adopted parts of the Elmira system. By 1918, doctors, psychologists, and social workers were being brought into the prison to help rehabilitate prisoners. In addition, many states set up separate prison facilities for dangerous prisoners, low-risk prisoners, women, drug addicts, and the criminally insane. Rehabilitation became the model for American prisons.

As crime rates soared in the 1960s and 1970s, however, many began to question whether rehabilitation worked. They pointed to high **recidivism** rates—the rate that those released from prison go on to commit further crimes. About half of those released from prison were arrested again within three years. As the crime rate grew, the public supported more "get tough on crime measures." Officials turned away from the model of rehabilitation to one of incapacitation, getting criminals off the street so they cannot harm anyone. This has resulted in the staggering number of people behind bars in America today. But the debate over how to treat criminals hasn't stopped. Every generation of

Americans has carried on this debate. It continues today.

For Discussion

1. Why did prisons develop?

2. Discuss this statement: "The history of corrections has been one of good intentions and bad results." What does it mean? Do you agree with it? Why or why not?

Class Activity: Pros and Cons of Punishment

In this activity, students evaluate different types of punishment.

1. Break into small groups.

2. Each group should:

   a. List the advantages and disadvantages of the following kinds of punishment:

      (1) Solitary confinement

      (2) Hard physical labor

      (3) Public humiliation

      (4) Physical punishment

      (5) Therapy

      (6) Fines

   b. Discuss the following questions:

      (1) Which kind of punishment is still in use today?

      (2) Where is it in use?

      (3) What types of criminals or crimes might each punishment fit? Why?

      (4) What other types of punishment can you think of? What are their advantages and disadvantages?

   c. Assign one person in each group to report back to the class on one or two kinds of punishment.

3. Have each group report back.

Sentencing

- William Smith, a banker, has been convicted of fraud. He secretly altered his bank's computer system to steal one dollar a year from every customer. He has no previous record, and no one was badly hurt by the crime.

- Jennie Blaine has been found guilty of manslaughter. She hit and killed an 8-year-old girl while driving drunk. Blaine is the sole support for her own three children and she just lost her job. She has no previous record.

- Andy Travers, a heroin addict, has been found guilty of beating an 80-year-old woman to death during a burglary. He has several previous drug convictions.

Should they all go to prison? Would it be better for society if some criminals are given fines, or probation, or community service, or other alternatives?

These decisions are made at sentencing hearings held shortly after the defendant is found guilty. Most jurisdictions provide that a sentence must be imposed "without unreasonable delay." Many provide an actual time limit such as 14 or 21 days after conviction.

Typically, only juries make sentencing recommendations in death penalty cases. Judges normally make all other sentencing decisions. It's a heavy responsibility. Defendants may be losing years of their freedom. Every defendant is entitled to careful consideration. And, of course, judges must consider the innocent citizens in the community. One dangerous criminal turned loose can harm many people. Judges must try to be fair, objective, and impartial—all of this while burdened by heavy caseloads and busy schedules.

Before the hearing, the judge is usually provided with a pre-sentencing report, usually prepared by the probation department. It includes information about the defendant's family background, previous convictions, character, and attitudes. This report helps the judge understand the defendant and decide

Corrections Population

About 6.3 million adults in the United States were under correctional supervision in 1999.

in prison	1,254,600
in jail	606,000
on probation	3,773,600
on parole	713,000

Source: *Corrections Statistics*, Bureau of Justice Statistics (2000)

whether efforts at rehabilitation might be effective. Many jurisdictions also require a pre-sentencing court conference with the offender and sometimes a psychological examination.

The U.S. Supreme Court has ruled that the defendant is entitled to have an attorney participate at the sentencing hearing (*Mempa v. Rhay*, 1967). The prosecution and defense may present information to the court and make sentencing recommendations. In many states, the crime victim and victim's family may make a statement about how the crime has impacted their lives. The defendant, in most states, also has the right to **allocute**, to make a statement to the court before sentence is passed.

Unless restricted by law, the judge may consider many **factors in sentencing**, such as:
- **The crime.** Was the harm caused by the crime great or small?

- **The offender's actions.** Were the offender's actions brutal, dangerous, and callous, or were they unintentional and restrained?

- **The victim.** Was the victim an aggressor or was the victim particularly vulnerable due to age or reduced mental or physical capacity?

- **Weapon.** Did the offender use a dangerous weapon or was the offender unarmed?

- **Offender's participation.** Did the offender plan and promote the crime or simply aid and follow others?

- **Criminal record.** Has the offender committed previous crimes? How serious were they?

- **Psychological state.** Was the offender deliberate and calculating? Or was the offender provoked or under some sort of stress?

- **Age.** Is the offender either very young and inexperienced or old and infirm?

- **Offender's attitude.** Is the offender hostile and defiant? Or does the offender admit guilt and show remorse?

- **Public's attitude.** How will the public and law enforcement react to the sentence?

- **Other factors.** These might include: What are the offender's reputation, position in the community, general character, and prior contributions to society?

In sentencing, the judge must follow the state penal code, which sets out the punishments for crimes. Misdemeanors are generally punished in increments of days or months—up to *one year*—in a county or city jail. Felonies are generally punished in increments of years in state prison. Sentencing structures vary, depending on the state, and include indeterminate sentences, determinate sentences, mandatory sentences, sentencing guidelines, or some combination.

Indeterminate Sentences. As prison reformers at the turn of the 20th century focused on rehabilitation, they felt that flexible sentencing could better meet the needs of individual convicts. A criminal who reformed sooner could be released sooner, and one who did not reform could be kept a longer time. As long as the corrections system stressed rehabilitation, flexible sentences were the norm. These flexible prison terms became known as

indeterminate sentences, because there was no pre-determined time to serve. Usually, the sentence was stated as a range of years. For example, forgery might carry a penalty of one to five years in prison; burglary, five to 10 years; manslaughter, five to 20. The judge decided the range of the sentence. How much time the prisoner actually served was left to the state **parole board**, which determined when a prisoner should be released.

States with indeterminate sentencing vary on how much discretion they give judges. Many states give judges the power to suspend or give alternative sentences. In some states, the judge decides on both the maximum and the minimum sentences within statutory limits. In other states, the judge sets only the maximum. In still others, the statutes spell out the limits, and the judge has no choice but to apply them.

In recent years, indeterminate sentencing has come under attack from several directions. Some critics say that flexibility has allowed lenient parole boards to let dangerous criminals out too soon. Other critics claim that indeterminate sentencing produces arbitrary and unjust prison terms. One car thief might serve two years in prison, another five, and another seven.

Determinate Sentencing. Since the 1970s, many states have introduced **determinate**, or **fixed-term**, sentencing, which actually was the norm during the 19th century. In this system, parole boards do not decide when to release prisoners. Instead, judges sentence defendants to a specific time of imprisonment, based on the severity of the crime. For example, a robbery might be punished by a year in prison, but an armed robbery could bring a five-year sentence. Prisoners would know at the time of sentencing when their prison terms would end. In most parts of the country, there is a trend back to fixed-term sentencing.

In states with determinate sentencing, judges often have discretion to give alternate sentences. These alternatives include suspended sentences, time in a local jail, time served on weekends, community service, working to pay restitution to a victim, time in halfway houses, or being released under the supervision of a probation officer. But if judges choose to give a prison term, statutes set the term.

Mandatory sentencing laws. These take away the option of alternative sentences. They require judges to sentence offenders to prison terms. Almost every state has passed mandatory sentencing laws for certain situations, such as use-a-gun, go-to-jail laws and repeat-offender laws like three strike laws. Usually, a judge has no option but to impose the mandatory sentence and cannot shorten it, suspend it, or give an alternative sentence. The federal Anti-Drug-Abuse Act of 1986 sets many mandatory-minimum sentences for drug offenses. It allows no exceptions for first offenses or other factors.

Sentencing guidelines. These are a more elaborate attempt to curtail discretion in sentencing. They provide formulas for judges to use in all sentencing decisions. For example, in 1980 Minnesota enacted a grid formula, which reflects two sentencing factors—the crime's severity and the offender's criminal history. The judge does little more than work out where a particular criminal falls on the grid, and the sentence is automatically defined. If the judge wishes to modify the grid sentence, reasons for any variance must be given in writing. On the next page is a simplified version of Minnesota's grid. More than half the states and the federal government have enacted sentencing guidelines.

For Discussion

1. Review the list of sentencing factors on page 173. Which do you think are the most important? Least important? Explain.

2. Are there any additional factors you think judges should consider? What factors should they not consider? Explain.

3. What is the difference between fixed and indeterminate sentencing? What are some arguments for fixed sentences? What are some arguments for indeterminate sentences? Which do you think is more just? Why?

SENTENCING GUIDELINES GRID
Presumptive Sentence Lengths in Months

Italicized numbers within the grid denote the range within which a judge may sentence without the sentence being deemed a departure. Offenders with nonimprisonment felony sentences are subject to jail time according to law.

SEVERITY LEVEL OF CONVICTION OFFENSE (Common offenses)		CRIMINAL HISTORY SCORE						
		0	1	2	3	4	5	6 or more
Murder, 2nd Degree	X	306 *299–313*	326 *319–333*	346 *339–353*	366 *359–373*	386 *379–393*	406 *399–413*	426 *419–433*
Murder, 3rd Degree	IX	150 *144–156*	165 *159–171*	180 *174–186*	195 *189–201*	210 *204–216*	225 *219–231*	240 *234–246*
Rape	VIII	86 *81–91*	98 *93–103*	110 *105–115*	122 *117–127*	134 *129–139*	146 *141–151*	158 *153–163*
Involuntary Manslaughter	VII	48 *44–52*	58 *54–62*	68 *64–72*	78 *74–82*	88 *84–92*	98 *94–102*	108 *104–112*
Burglary	VI	21	27	33	39 *37–41*	45 *43–47*	51 *49–53*	57 *55–59*
Perjury	V	18	23	28	33 *31–35*	38 *36–40*	43 *41–45*	48 *46–50*
Receiving Stolen Property	IV	12	15	18	21	24 *23–25*	27 *26–28*	30 *29–31*
Theft Crimes (Over $2,500)	III	12	13	15	17	19 *18–20*	21 *20–22*	23 *22–24*
Theft Crimes ($2,500 or less)	II	12	12	13	15	17	19	21 *20–22*
Tampering with a Fire Alarm	I	12	12	12	13	15	17	19 *18–20*

Presumptive commitment to state imprisonment. First–degree murder is excluded from the guidelines by law and continues to have a mandatory life sentence.

Presumptive stayed sentence; at the discretion of the judge, up to a year in jail and/or other non–jail sanctions can be imposed as conditions of probation.

Source: Adapted from *Minnesota Sentencing Guidelines & Commentary* (1999)

4. What are mandatory sentences? What do you think are the pluses and minuses of these sentences? Do you think they are a good idea? Explain.

5. What role do you think each of the following groups should have in sentencing: judges, juries, parole boards, and legislatures? Explain.

Class Activity: The Sentencing of Thomas Carter

In this activity, students sentence Thomas Wade Carter, the defendant in the previous unit. If a jury had found Carter guilty, it could have convicted him of one of two crimes—second-degree murder or involuntary manslaughter. For this activity, half of the groups will assume that Carter was convicted of involuntary manslaughter and the other half, second-degree murder. Students will role play judges imposing an appropriate sentence based on three different statutes (Determinate-Sentencing Statute, Indeterminate-Sentencing Statute, and Sentencing-Guideline Statute).

1. As a class, review and briefly discuss each of the three statutes below.

2. Break into pairs, each pair acting as judges. Designate each pair either A or B. Assign A pairs a second-degree murder verdict for Carter. Assign B pairs an involuntary-manslaughter verdict.

3. Each statute—determinate, indeterminate, and sentencing guideline—allows judges to choose within a range of sentences. As a pair, review each of the sentencing factors on page 173 and discuss how these factors affect the Carter case. Refer to information contained in the Pre-Sentencing Report on page 178. In your pair, discuss the following questions:

   a. Which circumstances in Carter's situation point to a harsh sentence? Make a list.

   b. Which circumstances in Carter's situation point to leniency and the probability of his reform? Make a list.

4. As a pair, decide on three sentences, based on the three sentencing statutes:

   a. For the determinate statute, specify the exact number of years.

   b. For the indeterminate statute, specify both a minimum *and* a maximum number of years.

   c. For the sentencing guideline statute, specify the exact number of months. Then figure out the term in years and months for reporting to the class.

5. Assume that your jurisdiction allows you to suspend the sentence under the sentencing statute and to impose an alternative sentence. Discuss and decide whether Carter should serve the statutory prison term or should have his sentence suspended.

Prepare a brief written statement justifying your choice. A suspended sentence would take the following form:

> Tom Carter's prison sentence is hereby suspended. Carter will serve one year in a county jail. For a *certain number* of years following county jail, he will be closely supervised by a probation officer and have to meet *certain probation conditions*. Should Carter violate any terms of probation, he will be returned to prison to serve his prison term.

If you choose to suspend the sentence, decide how long his probation should last and the probation conditions. For a list of possible probation conditions, see page 192.

6. Have a representative from each pair report to the class on the sentences imposed. Write the sentences reported by each pair on the board.

7. After discussing the sentences submitted, take a class vote on the choices recorded on the board.

8. Debrief the activity with the questions on page 177.

§575. Determinate-Sentencing Statute

For all determinate sentences, there are three prison terms listed—a lesser term, a standard term, and a greater term. The standard term is the second one listed. It should be imposed unless the judge decides that aggravating factors or mitigating factors dictate the greater or the lesser sentence.

(a) Involuntary manslaughter is punishable by imprisonment in the state prison for two, three, or four years.

(b) Second-degree murder is punishable by imprisonment in the state prison for 10, 20, or 30 years.

§606. Indeterminate-Sentencing Statute

The court shall impose both a minimum term and a maximum term as follows:

(a) Minimum term of sentence. The minimum term of an indeterminate sentence shall be at least one year and the term shall be fixed as follows:

(1) For involuntary manslaughter, the minimum term shall be fixed by the court and shall not be less than one year nor more than five years.

(2) For second-degree murder, the minimum term shall be fixed by the court and shall not be less than 15 years nor more than 25 years.

(b) Maximum term of sentence. The maximum term of an indeterminate sentence shall be at least three years and the term shall be fixed as follows:

(1) For involuntary manslaughter, the term shall be fixed by the court and shall not exceed 15 years.

(2) For second-degree murder, the term shall be fixed by the court and shall not exceed 50 years.

§898. Sentencing-Guideline Statute

A. All convicted persons shall be sentenced according to the sentencing guideline grid (on page 175).

B. If a judge wants to depart from the sentencing guideline, the reason must be compelling and the judge must explain the sentence in writing.

C. Instructions for using the sentencing guideline grid:

1. Determine the severity level of the crime.

2. Calculate the criminal history score. Juvenile convictions score zero points except for felony convictions, which count one point each. Adult convictions score one point for each misdemeanor and two points for each felony.

3. Find the box where the severity level of the crime and the criminal history score intersect. This box tells the sentence in months.

(a) If the box is shaded, the judge should suspend the sentence and put the offender on probation. At the discretion of the judge, up to a year in jail and other non-jail sanctions can be imposed as conditions of probation.

(b) If the box is not shaded, then the judge should impose a sentence within the range given.

Debriefing Questions

1. Which group of statutes—determinate, indeterminate, sentencing guideline—had the greatest range of sentences? The smallest range? Why?

2. Which sentences seemed the fairest? The most unfair? Why?

3. Which type of sentencing statute would you support in your state? Why?

4. Would you favor judges having the discretion to give alternative sentences instead of prison terms? Why or why not?

5. In most states, mandatory sentencing laws would force a prison term on Tom Carter because he used a gun. Do you think mandatory sentences are a good idea? Why or why not?

6. There is a great difference in punishment between second-degree murder and involuntary manslaughter. Do you think a jury should be told of the difference before it decides a verdict of guilty or not guilty? Why or why not?

Ask an Expert

Invite a criminal attorney or criminal court judge to take part in and help debrief the activity "The Sentencing of Thomas Carter."

Pre-Sentencing Report

Below is a pre-sentencing report submitted by the probation department:

Background Report on Thomas Wade Carter

Age: 18

Social background: Thomas Wade Carter is the oldest of five children. As the oldest child, he was pressured to excel in sports and school as his father had done. Around age 12, Carter began rebelling against his parents and school. He ran away from home two times. At school, he received failing grades and got into numerous fistfights. He was suspended from middle school once for fighting and from high school once for carrying a knife. His teachers and friends report that Carter had a quick temper and would carry a grudge for a long time. At age 17, Carter was transferred to a continuation high school because of poor attendance and lack of credits at his regular high school. He attended the continuation school and earned enough credits to get a high school diploma. Carter worked for short periods of time as a fast food cook, gas station attendant, and car wash worker.

Prior Record: Carter, Thomas Wade

Age	Arrest Record	Action by Juvenile Authorities
10	Runaway	Counseled and released to parents by police
12	Runaway	Counseled and released to parents by police
13	Curfew	Counseled and released to parents by police
17	Reckless Driving (misdemeanor)	Formal probation (six months)

Age	Arrest Record	Action by Adult Authorities
18	Disturbing the peace (bar fighting) (misdemeanor)	Conviction; $50 fine

Current Background: Carter now lives in his mother's home with his sister and younger cousin. His parents were divorced when he was 16. He contributes $500 per month out of his salary to household expenses. Carter is currently employed as an assistant parts department manager at a local auto dealer. His income is $26,000 per year. His immediate supervisor, Hans Spencer, reports that Carter has performed well in his current position and is effective in dealing with customers. Neighbors report that except for some loud parties and squealing tires, Tom seems to have settled down since high school. A number of his neighbors and friends have offered to vouch for his character.

Police informants indicate that Carter and Oscar Hanks have had a long-standing feud going back to high school. One month before Carter was arrested for the Joyce Ann Miller shooting, he and Oscar Hanks were arrested for disturbing the peace at a local bar. According to some witnesses, Hanks knifed Carter in the leg during the fight at the bar. Carter, however, refused to cooperate with the district attorney in the prosecution of Hanks for assault with a deadly weapon.

CHAPTER 13
Current Debates

Are Too Many People Behind Bars?

As crime rates started rapidly rising in the 1960s and 1970s, the public demanded that officials do something about crime. Politicians started promising to "get tough on crime." They adopted new policies designed to put more criminals behind bars.

For most of the 20th century, our nation's prison and jail population had remained stable—at or below 300,000 prisoners. Beginning in the 1970s, the states and federal government started locking up more prisoners. By 1990, they had put 1 million prisoners behind bars. One decade later, the total had almost reached 2 million prisoners. An additional 4 million convicts are currently on probation and parole. The rate of incarceration in America is second only to that of Russia. The rate is six to 10 times higher than most other industrialized countries. (See chart on page 204.)

The Bureau of Justice Statistics estimates that it costs about $20,000 per year to house each prisoner. With 2 million in prison or jail, it costs taxpayers $40 billion each year to house the prisoners. Is it worth it?

Supporters of get-tough measures, such as the American Legislative Exchange Council (ALEC), think so. ALEC is a non-profit bipartisan membership organization for conservative state legislators. In the foreword to its 1994 Report Card on Crime and Punishment, former U.S. Attorney General William P. Barr emphasized that *getting tough works.* He said that "increasing prison capacity is the single most effective strategy for controlling crime."

The ALEC report documents that the violent crime rate in 1992 was almost five times higher than that of 1960. The report blames this increase on the failure of states to lock up greater numbers of violent criminals. It notes that until 1975, despite increasing violent crime, the actual number of inmates in state prisons fell. The report says that, responding to public demands, state legislatures in the 1970s started adopting mandatory sentencing laws. These laws required judges to sentence certain offenders to prison. By 1975, the number of prisoners started climbing and has been climbing steadily ever since.

Because of this new trend in incarceration, said the report, some progress had been made in reducing violent crime. The report attributed the falls in violent crime in the early 1980s and 1990s to the rise in incarceration. In the words of former Attorney General Barr, "the eighties worked and the sixties didn't. It doesn't take a rocket scientist to decide which path to follow." Following this report, the incarceration rate continued to climb, and the crime rate started dropping.

Supporters of get-tough policies give two reasons why increased incarceration works. First, it deters others from committing violent acts. When people realize that they will go to prison for a long time, they think twice about committing a violent crime. But even staunch advocates of get-tough policies admit that deterrence is difficult to document. So most cite the second reason: Locking criminals up keeps them from committing crimes. This is known as incapacitation. By some estimates, the average violent street offender commits 12 crimes a year. If the offender is in prison, this saves the public from 12 violent crimes. Moreover, studies indicate that a small percentage of offenders commit many crimes. (See "Studies Show That a Few Criminals Account for Much Crime" on page 180.) If these habitual offenders were imprisoned, the nation would experience a significant drop in serious crime.

Studies Show That a Few Criminals Account for Much Crime

A long-term study by criminologist Marvin Wolfgang followed the arrest records of all males born in the years 1945 and 1958 in Philadelphia. A mere 7 percent of the males was responsible for more than half the crime stemming from the group. Those in the 7-percent group had been arrested at least five times each by age 18. They committed two-thirds of all the violent crime and about three-fourths of all rapes, robberies, and murders.

A study by the RAND Corporation found that each year the most active robbers averaged almost 90 crimes and the most active burglars averaged more than 200 offenses. A review of habitual offender studies by criminologist Alfred Blumstein showed that the most active 10 percent of criminals committed about 100 crimes in a year.

Get-Tough Policies

Supporters of getting tough have advocated policies that send more convicted felons to prison and make them serve longer sentences. There are three main policies that they have relied on:

Mandatory sentencing. Mandatory sentencing laws require judges to sentence offenders to prison terms. Since the 1980s, almost every state has passed mandatory sentencing laws for certain situations, such as repeat-offender laws and use-a-gun, go-to-jail laws. Usually, a judge has no option but to impose the mandatory sentence and cannot shorten it, suspend it, or give an alternative sentence. In 1973, New York passed harsh mandatory minimum sentences for drug offenses. In the 1980s, the federal government and many other states followed New York's lead. Soon a quarter of all prison inmates were offenders who only committed low-level, non-violent drug offenses.

Three strikes and you're out. This is a more recent form of mandatory sentence for repeat offenders. It mandates a lengthy, or even a life prison term, for certain third felony convictions. The federal government and many states have adopted versions of the three-strikes law. The three-strikes provision in federal law requires that the three convictions must be for violent felonies. In some states, like California, only the first two convictions must be for violent or other specified felonies. The third can be for any felony.

Truth in Sentencing. These laws attempt to reduce or eliminate parole. Before the end of a sentence, most convicts are released into the community on parole under the supervision of a parole officer. In some cases, they are put on parole after serving less than half their sentence. Some prisoners are released by state parole boards. Others are released early because they have earned credits, called **good time**, against their full term. They can earn good-time credits by behaving well and participating in special programs. Some jurisdictions allow prisoners to earn as much as one day of good time for every two days served. Prison authorities say they need good-time programs to keep order. Truth in sentencing laws, however, force convicts to serve close to their full sentences. Since 1987, the federal government has adopted truth in sentencing. All federal convicts must serve at least 85 percent of their sentence. The 1994 and 1995 federal crime bills offered prison construction aid to states that adopt truth-in-sentencing laws similar to the federal law. Most states have already passed such laws.

Pros and Cons

Some critics of massive incarceration doubt that it affects crime rates. They cite the strong economy, better policing, the end of the crack epidemic, and other factors as causing the drop in crime rates in the 1990s. They point out that incarceration rates have been climbing since 1975 and during much of that time, crime rates increased. Supporters of increased incarceration counter that crime would have been much worse during that period without the increased incarceration. A Bureau of Justice Statistics study in 1991 supported that view. But a study published in *Crime and Delinquency* in 1992 comparing two states with far different incarceration rates found that these rates didn't affect the rates of violent crime.

Some critics of massive incarceration believe it may reduce crime. But they say it is an incredibly inefficient way to do it. They claim the get-tough policies result in **collective incapacitation**—long sentences given to all felons. This means that non-dangerous prisoners serve along with the dangerous and that prisoners serve time long after they reach an age where they pose no danger. These critics advocate **selective incapacitation**—targeting the small percentage of career criminals who commit most crimes and targeting other offenders during their most crime-prone years (usually between the ages 15 and 24). This, they say, would reduce crime without requiring so many in prison. The only practical way to do this, however, would be to allow judges and parole boards more discretion in sentencing. Those who favor getting tough on crime oppose this, because they believe judges and parole boards are frequently too lenient on criminals.

Other critics of massive incarceration cite its cost. With states and the federal government paying about $40 billion each year to house prisoners, critics argue that corrections budgets are crowding out other worthwhile items. California, for example, for the first time now spends more on its prison system than on its University of California system. Critics say crime prevention programs and even police are feeling the squeeze. A 1999 study by the Rockefeller Institute of Government reported that in 1983 police received 52 percent of all U.S. criminal justice spending compared to 28 percent for prisons. By 1995, prisons' share had climbed to 37 percent and the police's had dropped to 43 percent.

But the question is whether incarceration is worth its price. In 1987, Edwin Zedlewski, an economist for the National Institute of Justice, did a cost-benefit analysis of incarceration. He figured the annual cost of housing an inmate

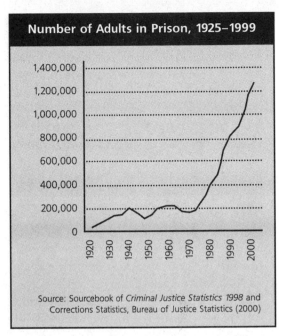

Number of Adults in Prison, 1925–1999

Source: Sourcebook of *Criminal Justice Statistics 1998* and Corrections Statistics, Bureau of Justice Statistics (2000)

as $25,000. He estimated that each criminal committed an average of 187 crimes each year and that the average cost of each crime was $2,300. Based on these figures, he calculated that the benefits outweighed the costs by 17 to 1. Critics pointed out that only the most active criminals would commit so many crimes. Zedlewski stood by his estimates, but limited them to the prison population remaining in the 300,000 to 600,000 range (which is now far surpassed). Above that range, the law of diminishing returns may set in, as most high-rate offenders may already be in prison.

But still experts differ. Criminologist John DiIulio strongly supports three-strike laws as highly effective at targeting high-rate offenders. Critics of three strikes cite a study by the RAND Corporation. It found that less than $1 billion of crime-prevention spending would have the same impact on crime as California's three-strikes law, which costs an estimated $5.5 billion a year.

Both DiIulio and another RAND study agree that mandatory minimums for drug offenses should be repealed because they are not cost effective. Jay Apperson, a federal prosecutor, disagrees. He thinks they are necessary to convict high-level drug dealers. He states: "Our experience is that without tough mandatory minimum sentences, defendants facing a

What About Rehabilitation?

Massive incarceration has caused the nation's correctional systems to turn away from rehabilitating prisoners. With so many inmates in custody, the best that most prison systems can do is warehouse them. Supporters of massive incarceration say that rehabilitation never worked and incapacitation does work. They point to a review of more than 200 studies of correctional programs by criminologist Robert Martinson in 1974. The review found that no program reduced the rate of recidivism (the rate of those released from prison who go on to commit other crimes). Since "nothing works," it's pointless and wasteful, they argue, to try to rehabilitate prisoners.

But critics disagree that "nothing works." Although several studies have supported Martinson's findings, a few have found programs that do work, particularly drug treatment programs and programs outside of prison settings. Critics further point out that more than 500,000 convicts are released into society every year and that some effort should be made to make sure they don't return to crime.

few years time are generally willing to serve it, rather than finger violent suppliers and big-time traffickers."

America continues on the course of incarcerating more people. One critic of massive incarceration has warned that it would be difficult to change course. He claims that a "prison-industrial complex" has developed, consisting of prison guard unions, politicians using the fear of crime to win votes, rural areas whose economies depend on nearby prisons, and private companies who look on the large prison budgets as opportunities for profit. But this "complex" is not invincible. In recent years, as the crime rate has gone down, voters in some states have turned down bond issues for new prisons.

For Discussion

1. What are "truth in sentencing" laws? Do you think they are a good idea? Explain.

2. The United States has the second highest rate of incarceration of any country in the world. What dangers might too many people in prison pose to a democratic society? What dangers might come from having too few in prison? Do you think it is a good idea to have so many people locked up? Why or why not?

Class Activity: Three Strikes

In this activity, students role play advisers to a state legislator who is considering introducing three-strikes legislation.

1. Form small groups. Each is a group of advisers to a state legislator who is considering introducing three-strikes legislation.

2. Each group should:

   a. Make a list of the pros and cons of three strikes.

   b. Consider whether any felony or only violent felonies should count as strikes.

   c. Decide whether or not to recommend three-strikes legislation.

   d. Prepare to report back its recommendation and the reasons for it.

3. Have the groups report back and hold a discussion. Conclude the activity by taking a voting on two different three-strikes proposals—one with all felonies counting as strike and one with only violent felonies counting.

Activity: Prison Sentences

Write a brief essay, either supporting or opposing the following proposition: *America should continue to put more people convicted of crimes behind bars.*

Do Some Mandatory-Minimum Sentences Violate the Eighth Amendment?

MICHAEL RAMIREZ

Excessive bail shall not be required, nor excessive fines imposed, nor cruel and unusual punishments inflicted.

—Eighth Amendment to the U.S. Constitution

Does the Eighth Amendment prohibit excessive or inappropriate punishment? For example, would a prison sentence of 25 years to life for stealing a slice of pizza be thrown out as a violation of the Eighth Amendment? More specifically, would it matter that the sentence was part of a repeat-offender law?

In 1983, the U.S. Supreme Court did rule that an overly harsh sentence was unconstitutional. A South Dakota court had sentenced a man to life in prison for passing a $100 bad check. The sentence followed a state repeat-offender law that allowed a life sentence for anyone convicted of a fourth felony. A 5–4 majority of the Supreme Court in *Solem v. Helm* (1983) struck down the life sentence. It ruled "as a matter of principle, that a criminal sentence must be proportionate to the crime for which the defendant has been convicted."

The court pointed out three objective factors to decide whether a sentence is proportionate to the crime. These include comparing (1) the seriousness of the crime to the severity of the penalty, (2) the kinds of sentences other criminals were given for the same crime, and (3) the kinds of sentences given in other jurisdictions.

In 1991 in *Harmelin v. Michigan*, however, the Supreme Court seemed to back away from its ruling in *Solem*. Harmelin, an Air Force veteran with no prior record, was convicted of possessing 672 grams of cocaine. Under a Michigan mandatory-sentencing law, he received a sentence of life in prison with no possibility of parole. This is the same sentence that a person convicted of first-degree murder would receive in Michigan. In neighboring Ohio, Harmelin would have received a sentence of from five to 15 years. A 5–4 majority of the court upheld the sentence. Three of the justices in the majority ruled that the sentence was not "grossly disproportionate" to the crime. Two justices, Scalia and Rehnquist, declared that *Solem* was "simply wrong" and that the Eighth Amendment to the Constitution does not require felony sentences to be proportionate to the crime except in death penalty cases. They argued that a "proportionality principle" would be simply an invitation for the court to impose its subjective opinion over that of a legislative body.

The four dissenters believed the sentence failed to pass the proportionality test stated in *Solem*. They rejected Justices Rehnquist and Scalia's argument that the Eighth Amendment only required proportionality in capital cases. They argued it was required in all punishments.

For Discussion

1. Are the decisions in *Solem* and *Harmelin* compatible? Explain.

2. Do you think the Eighth Amendment requires sentences be proportional to the crime? Why or why not?

Class Activity: Cruel and Unusual?

In this activity, students take part in a role play of court decision on the constitutionality of a sentence under a three-strikes law.

1. Ask students to imagine that a three-strikes law exists in their state that mandates a sentence of 25 years to life on conviction of a third felony. Under this law, any felony counts as a strike.

2. Inform them that a man a has been convicted of breaking into a restaurant and stealing four cookies. Since this was his third burglary conviction, he was sentenced to 25 years to life. The convicted man has appealed his sentence to the U.S. Supreme Court.

3. Divide the class into groups of three. Assign every student in each triad one of these three roles: prosecutor, defense attorney, or justice of the Supreme Court.

4. Have all the prosecutors, defense attorneys, and justices meet separately to prepare for the role play. Attorneys should think up their best arguments and the justices should think of questions to ask each side.

5. Regroup into triads and begin the role play. The justice should let the defense attorney speak first and then have the prosecutor speak. The justice should ask questions of both. After both sides present, have the justices move to the front of the room, discuss the case, and vote. Each justice should individually state the reasons for his or her decision.

6. Debrief by asking what were the strongest arguments on each side.

Are Federal Drug-Sentencing Laws Unfair to Blacks?

In 1980, federal prisons held only 24,000 people. By 1996, the federal prison population had soared to more than 100,000. This increase was due mainly to the war on drugs. In 1980, drug offenders accounted for only a quarter of all federal prisoners. By 1996, more than 60 percent were drug offenders.

Many of the drug offenders put in federal prison were African Americans. Blacks make up about 12 percent of the general population and about the same percentage of drug users. Yet the percentage of African Americans, mostly drug offenders, in federal prisons jumped from 30 percent in 1987 to more than 40 percent in 1996. The reason for the increase was a change in federal sentencing laws.

In the 1980s, crack cocaine hit the streets. Crack is made by cooking a mixture of water, baking soda, and powder cocaine. When the concoction dries, it becomes hard. "Rocks" can be broken off and sold in small amounts to users. Unlike powder cocaine, which is usually snorted, crack is smoked and quickly produces an intense high. (Powder cocaine can do the same if it is injected.)

Offering a cheap high, crack quickly grew popular in inner-city neighborhoods where it was sold on the streets. Soon rival gangs started fighting over who controlled the crack trade on different streets. Neighborhoods became terrorized by these turf wars. The media filled with stories of drive-by shootings and "crack babies" born addicted to cocaine. The 1986 drug-related death of University of Maryland star basketball player Len Bias drew further national attention to the cocaine problem.

Congress responded by passing the Anti-Drug Abuse Acts of 1986 and 1988. The acts created the Office of National Drug Control Policy. Its director, commonly called the "drug czar," plans the nation's strategy in the drug war.

Among other things, the acts also set harsh penalties for dealers in cocaine. The law

required a mandatory minimum 10-year sentence without parole for those dealing 5,000 grams or more of powder cocaine (about 10 pounds). Those dealing 500 grams or more (about one pound) receive a mandatory 5-year minimum.

Congress also set a similar two-tiered structure for crack sentences. But Congress believed crack cocaine to be more addictive, more linked to violent crime, and more likely to be dealt in small quantities than powder cocaine. It therefore set the minimum amounts of crack drastically lower than powder cocaine. A person dealing 50 grams (about two ounces) of crack receives the same 10-year-minimum sentence as a person with 5,000 grams of powder cocaine. A person with 5 grams (about two-tenths of an ounce) of crack gets the same 5-year-minimum sentence as a person with 500 grams of powder cocaine. In other words, Congress set a 100:1 ratio between powder and crack cocaine. (Most state drug laws also set a ratio between the two drugs, but none as large as 100:1.)

When Congress passed these laws, no one objected that they would affect blacks more than other groups. Because of its price, crack was favored by inner-city, predominantly black, drug users and dealers. Police concentrated on inner-city neighborhoods where crack was dealt on the street or in "crack houses" known to neighbors and police. It was more difficult to track down white crack and powder-cocaine dealers who usually met indoors in various neighborhoods. As a result, more African-American dealers were arrested and more than 80 percent of the crack dealers sentenced in federal courts were black. In the early 1980s, the sentences and time served in federal prison for blacks and whites averaged about the same length. By 1995, blacks were serving federal sentences 40 percent longer than whites.

Pros and Cons

This disparity has provoked debate over the fairness of the sentencing laws. Critics have questioned the wisdom of punishing crack and powder cocaine differently. They point out that both are cocaine and that powder cocaine can quite easily be made into crack. Criminologist Jerome Skolnick stated: "The law is equivalent, if eggs were illegal, to punishing the possession of omelets 100 times more severely than the possession of raw eggs."

Critics also argue that the law makes small-time crack dealers suffer the same punishment as higher-level cocaine dealers. Five hundred grams of powder cocaine produces 2,500 to 5,000 doses and has a street value of from $32,500 to $50,000. This compares to 5 grams of crack, which produces 10 to 50 doses and is worth between $225 and $750.

Critics further question the association of crack and violence. Crack users, they argue, are no more prone to violence than powder cocaine users. The violence associated with crack, they explain, comes from the drug trade. Violence of this sort, they argue, could be linked to any illegal drug. They point out that Miami in the 1980s had the nation's worst rate of violence, and it was linked to trafficking powder cocaine.

Finally, some critics think the laws are racist. Whites commit the most drug crimes. Yet blacks get the most punishment.

Supporters of the laws believe they make sense. Crack, they argue, devastated inner-city neighborhoods. Because it was sold openly, it threatened these areas. Drive-by shootings and gang wars erupted over control of the crack business. Unlike crack, cocaine was usually sold behind closed doors and therefore did much less harm to communities.

Prisoner Profile

Location
90% in state prisons
10% in federal prisons

Gender
93%   male
7%   female

Race
49%   black
48%   white
3%   other

Hispanic origin
15.8%   Hispanic
84.2%   Non-Hispanic

Most Serious Offense

State inmates

Violent	47%
Property	23%
Drug	23%
Public-order	7%

Federal inmates

Violent	13%
Property	9%
Drug	60%
Public-order	19%

Detail may not add to 100% due to rounding.

Source: "Correctional Populations in the United States, 1996,"
Bureau of Justice Statistics (1999)

that "there's a difference between something being mistaken and counterproductive and something being racist. . . . [T]he war on drugs may very well be counterproductive, but no, I don't think it's racist."

Court Challenges

Defendants have challenged the 100:1 ratio in federal appeals courts, but the courts have refused to overturn the sentencing laws. The Supreme Court has declined to hear any of these cases. The challenges have been mainly based on three legal grounds.

The first is that the 100:1 ratio, in practice, discriminates against African Americans and denies them equal protection of the law. (The 14th Amendment prevents states from denying anyone equal protection. The courts have held that the Fifth Amendment's due process clause requires the same of the federal government.) The courts have found, however, that neither the laws nor lawmakers had a discriminatory purpose. Therefore the courts have held that the laws must simply pass a "rational basis" test. Courts have ruled that the laws pass this test, because Congress had a legitimate purpose in protecting the public against a cheap, addictive drug and it believed that the 100:1 ratio would help do this.

One state court struck down its sentencing law as violating the state's guarantee of equal protection. Minnesota law had a 100:30 powder-to-crack ratio. The court noted that the ratio affected mainly African American drug users and therefore violated the state's guarantee of equal protection (*State v. Russell*, 1991). The Minnesota legislature rewrote the law and made sentencing the same for 30 grams of cocaine as it was for 30 grams of crack.

The second legal argument is that the laws violate due process because there are different punishments for the same drug—crack and powder cocaine. Some courts have rejected this argument stating that the two drugs are different. Other courts have stated that even if they are the same drug, they differ in usage and effect on the user.

The final legal argument is that the laws violate the Eighth Amendment's ban on cruel

Supporters also argue that crack is far more addictive than powder cocaine (as the two drugs are usually administered). Crack addicts, they say, pose special problems. Many commit crimes to support their habits. Pregnant addicts give birth to "crack babies," born addicted and damaged. Supporters say that crack's relatively low cost and greater addictiveness makes it more likely to spread and a greater threat to society than powder cocaine.

Further, even some who think the laws are misguided do not think they are racist. Randall Kennedy, a black Harvard law professor, believes they are not racist because they weren't passed with racist intent. He has stated

and unusual punishment. The Supreme Court in *Solem v. Helm* ruled that criminal punishments cannot be disproportionate to the crime. The Third Circuit in *U.S. v. Frazier*, however, found that:

"There are reasonable grounds for imposing a greater punishment for offenses involving a particular weight of [crack] than for comparable offenses involving the same weight of cocaine. These grounds include differences in . . . the method of use, the effect on the user, and the collateral social effects of the traffic in the drug."

The Supreme Court has never heard a case on the constitutionality of the 100:1 ratio. But it has decided a case that charged prosecutors of singling out African Americans for prosecution under federal crack laws. Four defendants moved to have their case dismissed because all 24 crack cases prosecuted in 1991 by one office had black defendants. The trial judge ordered prosecutors to provide a list of all crack cases and the race of the defendants for the previous three years. Prosecutors refused and appealed all the way to the Supreme Court. In 1996 in *U.S. v. Armstrong*, the court in an 8–1 decision reversed the trial judge's order. The court ruled that to prove a selective prosecution case, defendants must show that prosecutors are refusing to prosecute other cases involving white defendants. The statistics shown by the defendants in this case, said the court, proved nothing, because "people of *all* races" do not "commit *all* types of crimes." The court pointed out that statistics showed that more than 90 percent of all convicted LSD dealers, prostitutes, and pornographers were white.

Congressional Action

In 1995, the U.S. Sentencing Commission recommended that the 100:1 ratio be equalized to 1:1. The commission is an independent, permanent agency set up by Congress. It develops sentencing guidelines for federal crimes. Congress rejected the recommendation. Two years later, the commission again recommended a change, but this time suggested a 5:1 ratio reached by increasing the amount of crack cocaine and lowering the amount of powder cocaine. The Clinton administration advocated a 10:1 ratio. Senator Spencer Abraham (R-MI) introduced legislation for a 20:1 ratio that keeps the five gram level for crack cocaine but lowers the amount of powder cocaine to 100 grams. Congress has not acted on any of these proposals.

For Discussion

1. What is the 100:1 ratio?

2. If Congress were to equalize the crack-powder ratio at 1:1, what might be some reasons for and against either lowering the amount of powder, raising the amount of crack, or moving both? Explain.

3. Do you think the federal sentencing laws on crack cocaine discriminate against African Americans? Explain.

Class Activity: The Ratio

In this activity, students role play a congressional committee deciding whether to recommend changing the 100:1 ratio.

1. Form small groups. Each is a congressional committee considering changing the 100:1 ratio.

2. Each group should:

   a. Make a list of the pros and cons of the 100:1 ratio.

   b. Decide whether or not to recommend changing the ratio.

   c. If the group decides to change the ratio, decide what the new ratio should be and whether to lower the amount of powder, raise the amount of crack, or move both.

   d. Prepare to report back its recommendations and the reasons for them.

3. Have the groups report back and hold a discussion. Conclude the activity by taking a vote on whether or not to change the ratio.

CHAPTER 14
Alternatives to Prison

The Need for Alternatives

Since the 1970s, the public has grown increasingly impatient with America's crime problem. This has led to an increased demand for strict punishment, tough sentencing, and long prison terms. More and more offenders are imprisoned each year. Prisons and jails have filled and suffer severe overcrowding. Because of the overcrowding, each year federal and state governments spend billions of dollars building and staffing prisons. During the 1990s, space for about 1 million new prisoners was built. Yet prisons and jails remain overcrowded, and more are slated to be built.

Costs of housing prisoners have become so staggering that many legislators are looking at less costly, but effective, sentencing alternatives. Many corrections specialists insist that community-based correctional alternatives, which are far cheaper, can be more effective than prison sentences. These alternatives may be better at helping a criminal learn how to function effectively in society. Some common alternatives are fines, probation, community-service programs, and supervision in a halfway house.

Fines

Imposed in about three-fourths of all cases, fines are the most common punishment inflicted on convicted offenders. They can be imposed along with other punishments, such as probation or prison, or as the sole punishment. If a fine is the only punishment, the offender can continue living at home without supervision and the government will get some additional money. As such, fines offer clear cost savings over imprisonment.

But judges seldom impose fines as the sole punishment for serious offenders, because the offenders would remain in the community with no one keeping tabs on them. So usually only low-risk offenses, such as traffic infractions, many misdemeanors, and some non-violent felonies, are punished by fines alone.

Fines raise two problems. The first is purely a practical problem. Since most criminals are poor, does it make sense to punish them with fines? A fine might push an offender into committing new crimes simply to pay for the old one.

The second problem is one of fairness. If two criminals, one rich and the other poor, are fined $500 for the same offense, have they received equal punishment? A $500 fine could create hardship on the poor criminal, but mean little to the rich one.

To balance the equation, some jurisdictions are experimenting with **day fines**, which are calculated on how much a person earns each day. The penalty for drunk driving, for example, might be 30 day fines. This would mean that a person earning $300 per day would pay 30 times $300, or $9,000. A person earning $40 per day would pay 30 times $40, or $1,200. But this method also raises questions of fairness: Why should two people who commit the same act be fined such different amounts?

The Supreme Court has made one important ruling on the fairness of fines. Judges commonly used to issue alternative sentences, such as 30 days in jail or $300 in fines. In the 1971 case of *Tate v. Short*, a unanimous Supreme Court ruled these alternative sentences unconstitutional. The court stated these sentences violated the equal protection clause of the 14th Amendment, because they forced the poor into jail while permitting the rich to pay their way out.

Prison Spending		

States spent about $22 billion on prisons in fiscal year 1996.
The average annual operating expenditure per inmate was $20,100.

Operating expenditures	**$20.7 billion**	**94%**
Salaries and wages	10.8	49
Employee benefits	3.0	14
Other	6.9	31
Capital expenditures	**$1.3 billion**	**6%**
Construction	0.8	4
Equipment	0.3	1
Land	0.2	1
Total	**$22.0 billion**	**100%**

Source: "State Prison Expenditures, 1996," Bureau of Justice Statistics (1999)

For Discussion

1. In what circumstances do you think fines are appropriate punishment? When would they be inappropriate? Explain.

2. Do you think fines could substitute for imprisonment in some cases? Why or why not?

3. What are day fines? What problem do they address? Do you think they are a good idea? Why or why not?

4. Do you agree with the Supreme Court's decision in *Tate v. Short*? Why or why not?

Class Activity: One Fine Day

Some criminal justice experts recommend using day fines for most non-violent offenses. In this activity, students role play advisers to a governor considering instituting a comprehensive day-fine program.

1. Form small groups. Each is a group of advisers to the governor who is considering introducing legislation making day fines the only punishment for first and second offenses of non-violent crimes.

2. Each group should:

a. Make a list of the pros and cons of such a proposal.

b. Decide whether or not to recommend the proposal.

c. Prepare to report back its recommendation and the reasons for it.

3. Have the groups report back and hold a discussion. Conclude the activity by taking a vote on whether or not the class favors the proposal.

Probation

Probation is from the Latin word *to prove*. An offender sentenced to probation is allowed to return to the community, but must regularly prove that he or she meets certain conditions set by the court. The court retains the authority to cancel probation and imprison the offender if the conditions are violated.

Probation was developed in the mid-1800s as a humanitarian measure to keep petty offenders away from the corrupting influence of prisons. By 1925, every state offered probation for juveniles, but it was 1956 before every state offered it for adults.

Probation only works well if it is combined with effective supervision. Offenders must report on a regular basis to a probation officer to make sure they meet all the conditions set by the court. Originally the probation officer was a judge or a citizen volunteer. Early in the 20th century, however, supervising probation became a career in itself.

Individuals interested in becoming probation officers often take college degrees in social work, with special classes in criminology and corrections. Some probation officers also take classes in psychology and therapy to help offenders with their emotional problems.

Recent probation theory emphasizes the need to establish strong links between the offender and the community. Family, school, business, and church connections help an offender feel part of a community. These ties make a return to criminal behavior much less likely. Unfortunately, many probation departments, like other government agencies, lack sufficient resources and personnel. As a result, many probation officers must handle high caseloads, making adequate supervision difficult.

High-Tech House Arrest

In recent years, courts have begun to experiment with house arrest for non-violent criminals. Offenders are required to wear small radio transmitters to monitor their activities and location, usually to make sure they remain at home when they are not at work. So far, this has only been imposed on a voluntary basis, as an alternative to imprisonment.

The offender must wear the transmitter on an ankle or wrist strap. In some systems, the device broadcasts continuously to a second unit on the telephone, and this unit tells the probation department immediately if the offender leaves home. In other systems, the offender is telephoned at random times and must verify being home with a tone from the device.

Electronic house arrest costs less than $10 per day to monitor each device, compared to about $100 a day for jail time. In addition, the offender is usually required to pay between $10 and $20 a day. Some advantages for the prisoner are obvious—staying at home, being able to continue in a job, and avoiding the humiliations and dangers of jail. This form of monitoring can also be combined with community service or other forms of community-based corrections. Some experimental programs also use the tracking device to monitor those awaiting trial for minor crimes.

A few critics have objected because electronic monitoring is usually reserved for middle-class offenders, at least in part because the poor cannot afford to pay the daily charge for the transmitter. Some of the experimental programs address this problem by offering the device for free to those who cannot pay. Most states now have experimental programs of high-tech house arrest for their non-violent criminals. Because it is cheaper than jail time and relieves jail crowding, it seems likely that this practice will become more common in the future.

Who Should Be Placed on Probation?

There is general agreement about the criteria that should be used in deciding whether an offender should be placed on probation. The following is a list of factors that might be used by a judge to help identify likely candidates for probation:

a. The defendant did not cause or threaten serious harm.

b. The defendant did not intend to cause or threaten serious harm.

c. The defendant acted under a strong provocation.

d. Some factors tend to excuse or justify the criminal conduct.

e. The victim contributed in some way to the commission of the crime.

f. The defendant has agreed to compensate the victim.

g. The defendant has no recent history of prior delinquency or criminal activity.

h. The criminal conduct was the result of circumstances unlikely to occur again.

i. The defendant's character and attitudes show that he or she is unlikely to commit another crime.

j. The defendant is likely to benefit from probationary treatment.

k. The imprisonment of the defendant would cause excessive hardship to the defendant or his or her dependents.

For Discussion

1. What are some advantages in granting probation to an offender? What are some possible disadvantages?

2. What are some qualities that it would be helpful for a probation officer to have?

3. Do you think high-tech house arrest should be used more commonly? Why or why not? If you agree that it should be used, for what crimes is it best suited?

4. Which of the factors for identifying likely candidates for probation do you think are most important? Least important? Why?

Class Activity: Who Gets Probation?

In this activity, students decide whether convicted offenders should be placed on probation.

1. Break into small groups.

2. Each group should:

    a. Review the list of factors for identifying likely candidates for probation.

    b. Assign two or three of the factors to each person.

    c. Discuss the cases below, one by one. For each case, have each person in the group say whether his or her assigned factors apply to that case. Then discuss whether the factors apply or not.

    d. For each case, decide if the offender should be placed on probation and why

3. Reassemble the class and have groups report their answers and the reasons for them. Students should compare their decisions with those from other groups.

Ask an Expert

Interview a probation officer in your community. To find one, consult the governmental listings in your phone book or contact your local court. Find out about your jurisdiction's probation procedures and administration. For example, you might ask:

- How are probation services organized in your jurisdiction?

- What is the average caseload of a probation officer?

- What percentage of offenders successfully complete their probation? How does this compare to other jurisdictions?

- What is the typical day of a probation officer like?

- What conditions are most important for successful probation?

- What are the biggest challenges to successful probation?

Cases

A. Art Lewis, while setting off fireworks in a wilderness area, started a fire which burned down a U.S. Forest Service utility shed and destroyed a bulldozer. He has no prior criminal record.

B. Barbara Keane was convicted of pickpocketing. She has one prior conviction for prostitution. She has paid back the money she took and has become actively involved in church charitable work.

C. Carol Doepel was convicted of the attempted murder of a co-worker. Though she has no prior criminal record, she has been fired from three jobs for assaulting employees. She is currently undergoing therapy.

D. David Perkins was convicted of embezzling $20,000 from his employer. Twenty years ago, he served one year in prison for forgery. Since that time, he has raised a family and has been active in community-service work.

Revoking Probation

The probation officer is an agent of the court who monitors the activities of **probationers**— offenders on probation. For probation to be effective, probation officers must carefully supervise offenders. Unfortunately, budget constraints often require probation officers to take on heavy caseloads. Officers usually require probationers to report regularly and they sometimes make surprise spot checks of probationers' condition, activities, and whereabouts.

If a probationer violates the terms set by the court, the probation officer has two choices. The officer may issue a warning, or if the violation is serious enough, the officer may order the probationer back to court for a probation revocation hearing.

At a revocation hearing, the judge decides whether to continue probation or revoke it. If probation is revoked, the probationer is usually fined or imprisoned. Sometimes, a judge will continue probation but add new, stricter conditions.

Conditions of Probation

When an offender is convicted and placed on probation, the judge almost always sets a number of conditions of probation. These conditions limit the offender's behavior, and they are often related to the offender's crime or criminal inclination. Below, you will find a list of the kinds of conditions of probation a criminal court judge might set depending on the crime.

1. Spend a short time in the county jail before probation begins.
2. Pay a specified fine, plus a penalty assessment.
3. Make restitution of a specified amount to the victim through the probation officer.
4. Do not drink alcoholic beverages and stay out of bars.
5. Do not use or possess narcotics or associated paraphernalia, and stay away from places where drug users congregate.
6. Do not associate with persons known by the defendant to be drug users or sellers.

7. Submit to periodic drug testing.
8. Possess no blank checks, write no checks, and have no checking account.
9. Do not gamble, engage in bookmaking, or possess gambling paraphernalia, and do not be present in places where gambling or bookmaking goes on.
10. Do not associate with certain named persons.
11. Cooperate with the probation officer in a defined plan of behavior.
12. Support dependents.
13. Seek and enroll in schooling or job training as approved by the probation officer.
14. Maintain a steady job.
15. Stay at a residence approved by the probation officer.
16. Perform a certain amount of community service each month.
17. Submit to a 10 p.m. curfew.
18. Surrender any driver's license to the court clerk to be returned to the Department of Motor Vehicles.
19. Do not drive a motor vehicle unless lawfully licensed and insured.
20. Do not own, use, or possess any dangerous weapon.
21. Submit to search at any time of day or night by any law enforcement officer with or without a warrant.
22. Obey all laws, orders, rules, and regulations of the Probation Department and of the court.

Class Activity: Probation Revocation Hearing

In this activity, members of the class role play a probation revocation hearing. At the conclusion of the role play, the class will decide whether probation should be revoked in the case presented.

1. If possible, invite a probation officer, criminal lawyer, or judge to help you conduct and debrief this activity. Ask the guest to compare the procedures in this activity with those followed in your jurisdiction.

2. Divide the class into groups of four.

3. Each group should:

   a. Assign students the following roles: judge, probationer (named Lee Miller), probation officer, and public defender. Assign any remaining students as additional probation officers.

   b. Read and study the probation report on pages 194–195 and the description of the roles. (As a option, students can prepare for their role by meeting with those in other groups who are playing the same role.)

   c. When ready, conduct the probation revocation hearing with members of the group, using the Procedures for Revocation Hearing, below.

4. When you are finished with the simulation, reassemble the entire class. Judges from each group should announce their decisions and the reasoning behind them. Ask any guests how these simulated decisions compare to actual decisions. Debrief the activity with the questions on page 195.

Procedures for Revocation Hearing

1. The judge opens the hearing and asks if all parties are present and ready.

2. The judge asks the public defender to present the probationer's case.

3. The public defender may cross-examine the probation officer.

4. The public defender may call Lee Miller to testify. If this happens, the judge may also ask questions.

5. The judge may ask the probation officer questions at any time.

6. The public defender should close by summarizing the arguments against revoking Lee Miller's probation.

7. The judge should then ask the probation officer to summarize the arguments in favor of revoking probation. If there is more than one probation officer, both should participate.

8. Finally, the judge decides whether to revoke Lee Miller's probation. Refer to the alternatives listed in the judge's role description in the next section.

Role Descriptions

Probationer Lee Miller. You feel that circumstances forced you to violate the conditions of your probation. Consequently, you feel your probation should not be revoked. Talk with the public defender who is representing you and discuss the strategy you should follow at your hearing. Decide with the public defender whether you should take the witness stand and testify on your own behalf, but remember that this will subject you to cross-examination by the judge. You have the right to remain silent if you wish.

Public Defender. You represent Lee Miller at the probation revocation hearing. Discuss with your client the strategy to follow in attempting to convince the judge not to revoke probation. Decide whether to call the probation officer to the witness stand in order to cross-examine the officer's recommendations about revoking probation. Also, decide whether your client should take the witness stand to testify. Your client has the right to remain silent, but if the client does testify, the judge may also ask questions.

Probation Officer. You are Lee Miller's probation officer. You have written the probation report on pages 194–195. This will be the focus of this hearing. If you are called to

PROBATION REPORT

Name of Probationer: **Lee Miller**
Age: **38**
Marital Status: **Divorced**
Occupation: **Assembly line worker**
Employer: **United Radio Company**

Current Conviction

1. Probationer Lee Miller was convicted two months ago of manslaughter. Probationer Miller, while driving an automobile under the influence of alcohol, struck and killed a 5-year-old girl.
2. Sentence: One year in county jail (suspended), $1,000 fine, placed on two-year formal probation.
3. Conditions of probation:
    a. Probationer must pay the fine within six months.
    b. Probationer must not drink any alcoholic beverages and must stay out of places where they are the chief items of sale.
    c. Probationer must cooperate with the probation officer in a plan for commuting without the use of a motor vehicle.
    d. Probationer must provide $300 per month toward the support of the dependent daughter Maria, now residing with the grandmother.
    e. Probationer must maintain employment with United Radio Company.
    f. Probationer must maintain residence at current address, as directed by the probation officer.
    g. Probationer must surrender driver's license to the clerk of the court to be returned to the Department of Motor Vehicles.
    h. Probationer must obey all laws, orders, rules, and regulations of the probation department and of the court.
    i. **Special condition:** Probationer is not to drive any motor vehicle during the period of probation.

Probation Violation Report

1. Two weeks ago at 7:55 a.m., probationer Miller was stopped for speeding and driving erratically by a highway patrol officer. The officer administered several field tests for drunk driving and concluded that probationer Miller may have been driving under the influence of alcohol. Probationer Miller was arrested and taken to a local highway patrol station where a chemical test for alcohol consumption was administered. The result of this test showed no indication of alcohol. Probationer Miller was cited for speeding and driving without a license, then released. Probationer reported the violation and admitted that he had a couple of beers the night before with a friend.

2. Probation Violations:
    a. Probationer Miller drank an alcoholic beverage.
    b. Probationer Miller drove an automobile without a license, and violated the speed law.
    c. **Special condition:** Probationer Miller drove a motor vehicle during the period of probation.

(Continued on next page.)

(Probation Report continued. . .)

Statement of Probationer

I admit that I drove an automobile and was speeding in violation of my probation. But I reported these violations myself to my probation officer within 24 hours of the incident.

I admit that I had a couple of beers the night before, but only in my own apartment. A friend had come over to spend the evening, and brought some beer. But I was asleep by midnight.

I overslept the next morning and had to get to work in half an hour. I have been taking the bus to work, but this takes an hour. I decided to ask a neighbor if I could borrow his car so that I could get to work on time. He said it was okay to take the car.

I already had been late to work two times this month. So I was speeding and moving in and out of lanes to get to work on time. I was afraid that if I lost my job I would not be able to make support payments for my daughter and pay off my fine to the court. Both are conditions of my probation.

As it turned out, I was half a day late for work, but my boss listened to my story and decided to give me one more chance. I believe that I have learned my lesson from this, and promise to strictly follow my conditions of probation in the future.

Recommendations of Probation Officer

Probationer Miller seems to mean well but also appears weak-willed. I recommend that the probation be revoked and the suspended one-year county jail sentence be imposed.

— END —

testify, you should defend your recommendation that Miller's probation be revoked and that the one-year suspended jail sentence be imposed.

Judge. You were the trial judge at Lee Miller's trial. After the conviction, you sentenced Miller to a one-year county jail term. Then you suspended the sentence and placed Miller on probation. Today, you must decide what to do in view of the probation violations. Your alternatives are as follows:

1. Continue the probation under the existing conditions.

2. Continue probation with additional conditions that you will impose.

3. Revoke probation and impose the one-year sentence.

Debriefing Questions

1. Did some judges decide differently from others? If so, how do you account for these differences?

2. Assume that there was a great deal of publicity surrounding Lee Miller's original manslaughter trial and that many people in the community were angry because Miller was placed on probation rather than being sent to jail. Do you think the judge's decision should be affected by community feelings of this sort? Why or why not?

3. How is the probation revocation hearing different from a trial? How is it similar?

4. In your opinion, is the probation revocation hearing a fair way to decide whether probation should be revoked? Why or why not?

In May 2000, former Olympic figure skater Tonya Harding used a weed trimmer as she performed community service work at the Camas Cemetery in Washington. This was part of her punishment for a disorderly conduct charge.

Community Service

Probation is only one possible alternative to imprisonment. Another increasingly common alternative is community service. Community service can benefit both the offender and society as a whole, as demonstrated by the following examples.

Chris Lester, 18, was convicted of destruction of public property after he vandalized his school. Because this was his first offense, the judge did not think that a jail sentence was necessary. Instead, the judge fined him $1,000 and required him to clean graffiti off the walls of public buildings.

Albert and Miriam Johnson, a husband and wife, were convicted of criminal child neglect. Because of their religious beliefs, the couple kept their son away from medical care when he was very ill. As a result, the boy nearly died. The judge sentenced the couple to do volunteer work at a nearby state hospital.

The community-service approach to sentencing is generally limited to people who have committed non-violent crimes. These can include traffic offenses, public drunkenness, drug abuse, and white-collar offenses. Often,

the assigned work, such as cleaning up graffiti, is directly related to the kind of crime committed.

The Los Angeles County System

Los Angeles County has developed a broad system for referring offenders convicted of misdemeanors to community-service agencies. This system, called the **Court Referral Community Service Program**, involves the cooperation of three groups:

1. Municipal court judges who agree to refer some misdemeanor offenders to community service instead of imprisonment or other punishment.

2. Community agencies that need volunteer help. These agencies include hospitals, the YMCA and YWCA, the Red Cross, suicide and rape-crisis centers, teenage hot lines, alcohol and drug-abuse clinics, and many other community-based agencies that depend heavily on volunteers

3. Volunteer Action Centers (VACs). A county-wide system of these centers was in existence before the court referral program. The VACs act as clearinghouses for anyone wishing to do volunteer work. They regularly contact community agencies to create lists of volunteer positions that need to be filled. The courts asked the VACs to begin placing referrals from the court system alongside their regular volunteers. The VACs help find useful jobs in many community agencies for non-violent offenders.

The Case of Cory Baker

Cory Baker, age 40, was speeding in a school zone. He struck a car and injured a child. Just before the accident, Cory had lost his job as a carpenter on a construction project. In municipal court, Cory was convicted of speeding and reckless driving.

Instead of sentencing Cory to jail or requiring him to pay a large fine, the judge instructed him to do 40 hours of work for some community-service agency. The court referred Cory to a nearby volunteer action center for placement with a community agency.

Within a week, Cory had made an appointment for an interview at a local VAC office. He was asked about his skills and interests, and about his willingness to do volunteer work. Cory said that he was happy to become a court-referral volunteer.

The VAC interviewer then showed Cory a list of volunteer jobs near his home. Cory noticed that several agencies needed skilled workers, including carpenters. He chose the George Henry Home for Boys, a private group home for delinquent boys.

Next, Cory scheduled an interview with the George Henry Home. The director of the home was satisfied with Cory and promptly put him to work.

Cory worked at the George Henry Home for about five hours a week for two months. During this time, he got to know many of the boys, and he showed some of them how to do basic carpentry. Cory's work impressed the director and staff at the home. After he had put in his 40 hours of referral volunteer work, Cory was asked to continue at the home as a paid worker. Cory accepted and was hired to set up a carpentry shop for the boys.

Does It Work?

Not all court-referral volunteers are as fortunate as Cory Baker. Nevertheless, most do have a positive experience. As one Los Angeles Municipal Court judge noted:

"Community service . . . can work wonders. That's the beauty of it. Oftentimes, personal stress is the reason the people are here in the first place. If the man gets involved in helping others, he is helping himself as well."

Some critics of this form of sentencing say that it is too soft. They call for stronger punishments such as prison terms. In response to such criticism, a federal judge said, "We have to examine the overall public interest. 'Warehousing' criminals in prison has not been successful. It just spawns more criminals."

For Discussion

1. Do you approve or disapprove of community-service sentencing? Why or why not?

2. Should community-service sentencing be available to convicted adult felons? To juvenile criminal offenders? Why or why not?

3. What might be some problems in expanding community-service sentencing to those convicted of violent crimes?

Community Corrections

Community-service referrals provide one alternative to prison that can help offenders develop roots in their communities rather than pushing them away or locking them out. There are several other programs such as halfway houses and treatment centers that can offer similar benefits. These are often called **community correctional programs**, and they can help offenders such as the following:

Rudy was lonely, bored, and 19. He got talked into something he didn't want to do. At a friend's urging, he helped steal a late-model Mercedes-Benz from a shopping-mall parking lot. Caught only a few blocks away, he is now awaiting sentencing for grand theft auto.

Anna has completed more than two years of a three-year sentence in prison for passing bad checks. This was her second offense. She wants to get out, but she is a little frightened. She wonders what might happen if she can't make it. Without support, will she be tempted to pass bad checks again? She worries whenever she thinks about going out on her own.

Both Rudy and Anna might benefit from a community correctional program. Rudy is not a hardened criminal, and he may only need help learning how to funnel his energies into positive activities. Anna, too, wants to make a go of her life. To make the transition out of prison, she needs to live in a structured environment for a time to give her direction and support.

What is a Community Correctional Program?

Community correctional programs are based in local facilities such as halfway houses, community treatment centers, residential care facilities, and group homes. Local centers offer

A director at a halfway house in Columbia, Missouri, leads a group discussion on making the transition from prison to freedom.

individualized care and supervision for those who would benefit from such a program. This approach can involve the community more directly in dealing with problems of crime.

Most prisons are run by state and federal agencies. And most jails, though they are locally run, are largely intended to hold people who are awaiting trial or have been given fairly short jail terms for misdemeanors. They offer few opportunities for counseling, rehabilitation, or job training. Advocates of community corrections argue that most of our criminal justice system is already locally based—the police, courts, prosecutors, and public defenders—so there should be local responsibility and control in the correctional system as well.

The community-corrections approach began in the early 1970s. Since then, some states have tried to divert a large percentage of state and county prisoners into correctional programs located closer to their home communities. Community facilities can provide a supervised environment for troubled juveniles, non-violent offenders, and some prison inmates who are ready to start taking steps back into society.

Pre-Release Programs

Some of the first programs developed by the community-corrections movement were halfway houses. These serve as way stations in helping prison inmates re-enter society. The Federal Bureau of Prisons and most state correctional systems offer pre-release programs. They are mainly for prisoners, like Anna (from our example above), in the last few months of their term who are judged a low risk of returning to crime.

Some pre-release programs operate businesses, providing both income and work experience for the residents. Others simply provide a home and supervision, and the residents are allowed to leave during work hours to go to jobs in the community. As residents demonstrate more responsibility, they are granted more privileges and independence. Gradually, offenders assume complete responsibility for their everyday activities and are ready to re-enter the community.

Beyond Pre-Release Programs

In 1974, Minnesota put into practice a Community Corrections Act. This act extended the state's community corrections beyond pre-release halfway houses. Minnesota's goal was to divert all but the most serious offenders into programs in their home communities. The state set up an extensive community system that accepts many of its offenders into programs *immediately* after sentencing. Those offenders never see the inside of a prison.

Goals of Community-based Corrections

The overriding goal of any community corrections program is to guide ex-offenders back into the community and help them develop positive, law-abiding lifestyles. This process works best under the supervision of professional counselors who can offer support and guidance.

Many offenders may need family, child, and marriage counseling. Others need legal counseling. Ex-alcohol and drug abusers often face severe temptation and require counseling and supervision. Offenders who want to go back to school can discuss their plans with educational counselors. Some may choose job training. Others simply need a therapist or support group to discuss their problems.

Group support can be very important. Many offenders identify best with people who have similar backgrounds and with people who have themselves overcome criminal attitudes and behavior.

The community facilities often look a lot like ordinary neighborhood homes and apartment buildings. They blend in, rather than stand out. Residents have their own bedrooms. Some have roommates. They share cooking and cleaning responsibilities, much like a large family. Residents are encouraged to develop a closeness that offers emotional support, companionship, and shared responsibility.

Obstacles to Community Corrections

There are obstacles facing community-based correctional programs. These obstacles—many deep-rooted in the community itself—keep state, county, and federal correctional administrators from transferring all eligible prisoners into community programs. They include funding, habitual and violent criminals, and community attitudes.

Funding

Operating the nation's prison system now costs about $40 billion a year, involving tens of thousands of administrators and correctional officers. To divert a large percentage of the nation's prisoners into community correctional programs would require a tremendous restructuring and rechanneling of funds. This would require a fundamental and wrenching reform of a correctional system that is over 100 years old. Many people working in the correctional system would resist such sweeping changes.

Habitual and Violent Criminals

Certain types of criminals pose further problems. Halfway houses require a certain minimum level of cooperation and social behavior. Habitual lawbreakers often cannot meet that standard. They have always lived in a criminal culture, and they commonly reject opportunities to explore and develop new community contacts.

In addition, there is a constant fear that offenders with records of violent behavior will not change. They might harm innocent community members while staying in a halfway house. Some programs simply refuse to admit criminals with histories of violence.

Community Attitudes

When an old home or apartment building is converted into a halfway house, nearby residents often fear a wave of crime will sweep their neighborhood or that property values will decline. Residents predict that homes will be burglarized, women raped, automobiles stolen, and eventually, property values lowered—all because convicts live in the neighborhood and come and go as they please. Fear drastically multiplies if a halfway house resident does in fact commit a crime in the neighborhood. These fears are often reinforced by feelings that halfway houses are soft on criminals and don't punish their residents enough.

These are serious problems. To work properly, community-based corrections need to win the support of the community. And the facilities need to be highly structured, supportive environments with frequent counseling and training and effective supervision. For all their good intentions, community facilities must not endanger their neighborhoods.

For Discussion

1. What are some of the advantages of community-based corrections programs? What are some disadvantages?

2. What types of offenders do you think community-based corrections are appropriate for? Inappropriate for? Why?

Class Activity: Halfway House

If a halfway house were proposed for your neighborhood, would you support it? Would your neighbors? In this activity, students role play a city council hearing determining whether to grant a zoning variance that would allow a halfway house to be placed in a particular residential neighborhood.

1. In this activity, a non-profit group has opened a halfway house that treats drug offenders referred to it by the courts. Neighbors learning of the halfway house objected to its presence and went to a lawyer. The lawyer learned that zoning regulations for the neighborhood allow only five unrelated persons in a single dwelling. The purpose of these regulations is to preserve parts of the city for family homes. The non-profit has requested that the city council grant a zoning variance (an exception to the regulation).

2. Divide the class into three groups—city council (seven members), residents opposing the halfway house (half the remaining students) and people from the non-profit and other parts of the community who favor the halfway house (other half of the students).

3. The three groups should meet separately. Those favoring and opposing the variance should develop arguments supporting their position. They should each pick three people to speak at the city council hearing. The city council should develop questions to ask the opposing sides. It should also select a person to chair the hearing and one member to represent the neighborhood (the other six members represent other parts of the city).

Ask an Expert

Many communities have ex-convict self-help groups. If there is such a group in your community, ask if it would provide speakers to your class. Questions to ask the visitor might include:

- What are conditions like in prison? What was the hardest part of prison life?

- Did your experiences help you adjust to life after you were released? If so, how? If not, why not?

- What was the hardest aspect about your adjustment to freedom once you were released from prison?

- Do you know about pre-release or halfway house programs? Did you participate in one? If so, what were your experiences?

- Do you think that a community corrections program is helpful to the offender or community? Why or why not?

- How do you feel society should deal with the criminal offender?

4. When the hearing begins, the chairperson should state the issue to be decided and call alternately one person in favor and one person opposed to the variance. After all six people have spoken and been questioned by the council, the council should vote.

5. Debrief the activity by asking how realistic students think the fears expressed by the residents in the role play are.

CHAPTER 15
Prisons Today

The vilest deeds like poison weeds
Bloom well in prison air:
It is only what is good in man
That wastes and withers there. . . .

—Oscar Wilde, from *The Ballad of Reading Gaol*
(1898)

Prison in America

Today in the United States, there are about 2 million people behind bars. The more than 1,000 state and federal prisons hold about two-thirds of them. More than 3,000 county and municipal jails hold the other third. Some prisons may be well-designed, progressive institutions, but far too many are overcrowded, filthy, and brutal. Some have become notorious for extortion, violence, homosexual rape, and vicious racial gangs—a virtual hell of fear and savagery.

At their best, our prisons can provide well-planned opportunities for education and vocational training, but at their worst, they offer little more than a few hours a day out of the cell to stand around in a crowded prison yard. More than half of all prison inmates are idle for most of the day. The former head of the Federal Bureau of Prisons has said, "Idleness is the most serious problem in virtually every penal institution."

Security Levels

Prisons typically fall into three security levels. Maximum-security prisons are usually large institutions holding several thousand prisoners. High fences (sometimes electrified), thick walls, and guard towers separate the prisoners from society. Inside, armed guards watch over prisoners, who live in spartan cells. A group of cells make up a cell block, which can be locked down from other cell blocks. In large prisons, several cell blocks make up a prison wing, which also can be shut down separately. The prisoners wear drab uniforms and each is assigned a number. They are given little opportunity to associate with one another. Even tighter security exists for prisoners awaiting capital punishment on death row, a separate cell block of a maximum-security prison. About 40 percent of all prisoners reside in maximum-security prisons.

Medium-security prisons are typically smaller versions of maximum-security prisons. They do, however, allow prisoners a greater degree of freedom. They are permitted, for example, to use the library, exercise yard, and showers with fewer restrictions. At specific times each day, however, they must be in their cell or assigned place for the day's headcount, which can take place up to four times a day. About 40 percent of all prisoners are in medium-security prisons.

Minimum-security prisons can be far different. They usually allow prisoners to roam within the confines of the prison. Some have dormitory rooms and others have private rooms instead of cells. Prisoners usually wear uniforms, but some prisons allow inmates the freedom to choose their own wardrobe.

In the federal prison system, the three levels of prisons carry different names. High-security prisons are U.S. Penitentiaries. Medium-security prisons are known as Federal Correctional Institutions. Minimum-security prisons are called Federal Prison Camps.

Super-Maximum-Security Prisons

To hold the most dangerous prisoners, super-maximum-security prisons have been developed. The practice dates back to 1934, when the federal government started Alcatraz. Known as the Rock, the penitentiary was located on a small island in San Francisco Bay. The treacherous ocean currents made escape all but impossible. A small prison, Alcatraz housed in single cells about 300 of the most hardened federal prisoners. No one is known to have escaped and survived. Of the 14 escape attempts made, prison officials captured all but five inmates, who remain missing and are presumed drowned.

When Alcatraz closed in 1963, a new U.S. Penitentiary opened near Marion, Illinois. At first, prison officials did not use this prison to replace Alcatraz. Within a few years, however, officials started transferring the worst federal prisoners to Marion and turned it into a super-maximum-security facility. Prisoners were kept in individual cells. During the few hours each week that they left their cells, they wore handcuffs and sometimes leg shackles.

In 1994, the federal government opened a new super-maximum-security prison in Florence, Colorado. It holds about 500 prisoners, each in a separate cell and isolated from other prisoners. Every cell has a bed, stool, toilet, sink, and shower. A small black-and-white television in each cell can deliver orders from guards. The only view outside the cell is through a tiny window showing the sky. The plumbing is flood-proof; the bedding, fireproof. The furniture is made of cement and cannot be moved. Prisoners get their meals through a slot in the door. They leave their cells a couple times a week to exercise alone in wire cages. Guards watch the prisoners through almost 200 video cameras and can control 1,400 gates electronically. Escape is almost impossible.

Many states have started building super-maximum-security prisons or adding them as wings to other prisons. California's Pelican Bay State Prison, located near the Oregon border, is an example. One wing holds about 200 minium-security prisoners. Another holds 2,000 in maximum-security. A third wing houses 1,500 prisoners in super-maximum-security. Prisoners in the super-maximum-security wing live alone in windowless cells that they seldom leave.

Because they lock up the most dangerous offenders, super-maximum security prisons enjoy widespread support from the public. But several human rights groups have lodged com-

Located on a small island in San Francisco Bay, Alcatraz was the first super-maximum-security prison.

plaints against them. Jenni Gainsborough, public policy coordinator for the National Prison Project of the ACLU, has stated: "There is tremendous potential for abuse in these places—the isolation, the weapons, the lack of any clear independent oversight. And the mental effect on people, particularly those who come in with mental problems, can be horrifying." In 1994, several prisoners brought a successful class-action suit against the super-maximum-security wing at Pelican Bay. A federal trial judge in *Madrid v. Gomez* upheld several allegations of brutality by guards and ruled the prison could not hold inmates with mental illnesses in isolation.

Poor Prison Conditions

One of the biggest prison problems is overcrowding. California prisons, for example, are operating at almost double their capacity. In fact, the federal prison system and more than half of all state prisons are running over capacity. In some cases as many as 11 prisoners are held in cells designed for four. Overcrowding can lead to discipline problems, unrest, unhealthy conditions, and far too often, violence.

The following prison conditions were described in the 1978 Supreme Court decision of *Hutto v. Finney*:

The ordinary Arkansas convict had to endure . . . "a dark and evil world completely alien to the free world . . . ."

Confinement in punitive isolation was for an indeterminate period of time. An average of four, and sometimes as many as 10 or 11, prisoners were crowded into windowless 8' x 10' cells containing no furniture other than a source of water and a toilet that could only be flushed from outside the cell . . . . At night the prisoners were given mattresses to spread on the floor. Although some prisoners suffered from infectious diseases, such as hepatitis and venereal disease, mattresses were removed and jumbled together each morning, then returned to the cells at random in the evening. Prisoners in isolation received fewer than 1,000 calories a day; their meals consisted primarily of four-inch squares of "grue," a substance created by mashing meat, potatoes, oleo, syrup, vegetables, eggs and seasoning into a paste and baking the mixture in a pan.

Beginning in the late 1970s, the federal judiciary began ordering states to upgrade their prisons and reduce overcrowding. Cases brought by public-interest lawyers charged that inmates in the most dangerous and overcrowded prisons were being subjected to "cruel and unusual punishment" as forbidden by the Eighth Amendment of the U.S. Constitution.

In several cases, the Supreme Court agreed. It held that the Eighth Amendment prohibits penalties that "transgress today's broad and idealistic concepts of dignity, civilized standards, humanity and decency." (*Estelle v. Gamble*, 1976.)

Some federal courts imposed rigid deadlines to end overcrowding. These deadlines had short-term and long-term effects. In Alabama, for instance, some 200 prisoners were released well before the end of their sentences to satisfy a federal court order. Texas was repeatedly forced to halt new prison admissions to satisfy the courts, and a federal judge threatened the state with fines of $800,000 a day until it alleviated overcrowding. Some Texas legislators even proposed holding prisoners on prison barges, unused oil-drilling rigs, and foreclosed buildings.

In most states, the 1980s saw a surge of new prison construction to try to keep pace with the increasing number of prisoners. Building prisons became a $17 billion a year industry. A new prison could cost as much as $70,000 per cell to build, and annual costs rose to about $20,000 to guard and house each prisoner. Some prison authorities were pleased by the court actions since the judicial orders forced reluctant state legislatures to appropriate funds.

In 1981, however, the U.S. Supreme Court seemed to back away from further prison reform. The court decided the case of *Rhodes v. Chapman*, which had raised the issue of whether confining two prisoners in a cell built for one violated the Eighth Amendment. The court ruled that it did not. Voting 8–1, the justices held that overcrowding does not in itself violate the Eighth Amendment, if overall prison conditions meet contemporary standards of decency. Justice O'Connor wrote for the majority that "harsh conditions" are the price of crime and the Constitution does not require comfortable prisons. The court seemed to be saying it had gone about as far as it would go in ordering reform. Federal courts, however, still can demand changes to prisons where overcrowding causes dangerous, unfit conditions.

Private Prisons

Since the 1980s, some states have turned to private industry to help reduce prison overcrowding. Private security firms have gone into the prison business, in some cases contracting to operate existing prisons and jails, and in others, building new prisons for the states. In several cases, private operators have built prisons hoping to get a contract to hold prisoners.

Private prisons now exist in more than 30 states, and hold about 1 percent of the prison population. The three states with the most private prisons are Texas, California, and Florida. Charles W. Thomas, a criminologist at the University of Florida, estimates that up to 10 percent of all prison beds may eventually be in private hands, mostly in minimum-security institutions.

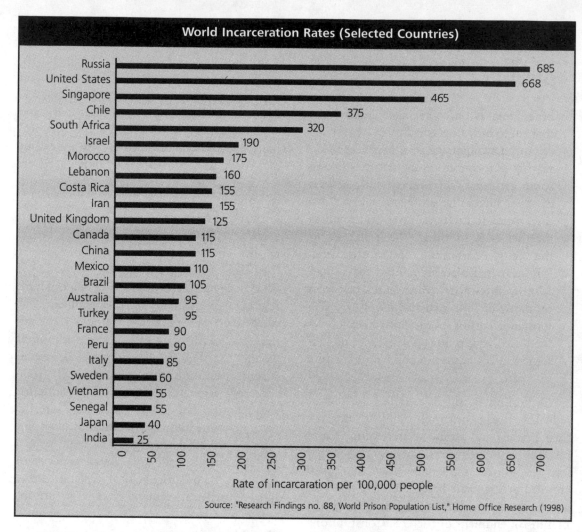

World Incarceration Rates (Selected Countries)

Country	Rate
Russia	685
United States	668
Singapore	465
Chile	375
South Africa	320
Israel	190
Morocco	175
Lebanon	160
Costa Rica	155
Iran	155
United Kingdom	125
Canada	115
China	115
Mexico	110
Brazil	105
Australia	95
Turkey	95
France	90
Peru	90
Italy	85
Sweden	60
Vietnam	55
Senegal	55
Japan	40
India	25

Rate of incarceration per 100,000 people

Source: "Research Findings no. 88, World Prison Population List," Home Office Research (1998)

The idea of privatizing prisons has drawn criticism. Ira P. Robbins, a professor at the American University Law School in Washington, D.C., says, "It's privatization run amok." The American Civil Liberties Union has expressed fears that private companies will be less accountable than the state and may even try to prolong prison sentences to keep earning their per-day fees. Neighbors often wonder if private companies will maintain the same standards for security. Over the long term, some critics also a fear that putting a large number of prison beds in private hands will create a permanent lobby in favor of long prison sentences. They think the drive to increase profits may well hold back the move to community corrections and alternative sentencing.

Supporters of private prisons dismiss these claims. They argue that private prisons are newer, better managed, and less costly than government-run institutions. As for security, they argue that most private prisons take only minimum-security prisoners anyway. Finally, they maintain that it is unlikely private-prison companies would lobby for longer prison terms because there is such an excess of prisoners already.

For Discussion

1. Do you think super-maximum-security prisons are a good idea? Explain.

2. Do you agree with the U.S. Supreme Court decision in *Rhodes v. Chapman*? Why or why not?

3. Do you think privatizing prisons is a good idea? Why or why not?

Class Activity: Should Prison Be Even Tougher?

In some states, there has been a "penal harm" movement. Members of this movement want to make prisons tougher. They favor removing televisions, weights, and college classes from prisons. In this activity, students role play advising the governor on the merits of a proposal to institute "penal harm" in the state.

1. Divide the class into small groups. Each group will role play a group of advisers to the governor. The governor is considering proposing a law that would remove all televisions, weight equipment, and classes from all prisons in the state.

2. Each group should:
   a. Make a list of the positive aspects of this proposal.
   b. Make a list of the negative aspects of this proposal.
   c. Weigh the positive and negative aspects and decide whether to favor, oppose, or modify the proposal.
   d. Be prepared to report back to the class on its decision and the reasons for it.

3. Have each group report back. After they have reported, have the class vote on the proposal. Use the Debriefing Questions below to conclude the activity.

Debriefing Questions

1. What do you think the purpose of incarceration is? Does "penal harm" fit this purpose?

2. Do you think making prisoners suffer more will change their behavior? Explain.

Prison Revolts

In February 2000, the national media reported that guards shot nine prisoners, killing one, during a race riot at California's Pelican Bay Prison. Since the 1950s, at least one major prison riot has erupted each year. The two most famous revolts took place in 1971 and 1980.

In September 1971, more than 1,200 prisoners at New York's Attica State Prison seized Cell Block D and took 38 guards hostage to protest what they called oppressive prison conditions. Influenced by the political movements of the 1960s, particularly radical African-American organizations, the prisoners immediately organized themselves, setting up a sick bay, clean-up details, an elected negotiating committee, and a security force to guard and protect the hostages. One guard who had been seriously injured was sent out to the hospital and 10 other hostages needing medical aid were released. The prisoners' first statement said, "We are men. We are not beasts, and do not intend to be beaten or driven."

The prisoners met with a mediating team that eventually included the New York director of prisons, lawyers, journalists, and local political leaders. Their demands were mostly for humane treatment: better prison conditions, freedom of religion to allow Muslim worship, meaningful job training, the right to hold political meetings, and an amnesty for the takeover. Most of the demands, except the amnesty, were granted. But this omission became crucial when the injured guard died in the hospital. Still, by the third day, most of the mediators felt they were near a deal if Governor Nelson Rockefeller would come to Attica to give any agreement credibility. Rockefeller thought it would be unwise and stayed away.

On Monday, the fourth day of the revolt, guards and state police assaulted Cell Block D with helicopters and nausea gas. More than 500 men firing rifles and shotguns poured into the yard. The gunfire killed 33 inmates and nine hostages and seriously wounded more

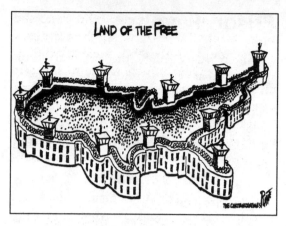

LAND OF THE FREE

than 100 other prisoners. In the aftermath, prisoners were stripped and beaten, and forced to run gantlets of angry guards. Some observers charged that a few of those killed died hours after the prison had been retaken. More than 20 years later, a civil court awarded prisoners millions of dollars in damages for violations of their civil rights after the assault.

Life at Attica

Almost everyone, including the head of New York prisons, agreed that the uprising had been sparked by terrible prison conditions. Every inmate entered Attica in shackles and leg-irons. He was issued gray prison clothes and then placed in an isolation cell where he stayed for two full days. After four to eight weeks of lockup for about 20 hours a day, he was assigned a job and transferred to a cell block.

Each prisoner at Attica had a cell about the size of a walk-in closet, six feet by nine feet. The nearest window was across the corridor. He had a bed, a metal stool, a small table, a two-drawer metal cabinet, an open toilet, a cold-water sink, and one 60-watt bulb. For the rest of his imprisonment, he spent 14 to 16 hours a day alone in this cell.

Five hours a day were for work or school, one hour or so for recreation, and about half an hour for each meal. Each man could shower once a week. During weekdays, the daily routine began at 5:50 a.m. and the men were locked in for the night at 6:30 p.m. They could talk between cells until 8 p.m. Then silence was required. The lights went out at 11 p.m.

Vocational training was mostly work in a huge laundry at 30 cents a day or being assigned with 15 other men to a one-man machine tool in a shop that never dropped below 100 degrees F. Little education was available, the meals were often inedible, and there were hundreds of prison rules. Prison officials read all mail. In addition, more than 75 percent of the prisoners at Attica were black or Puerto Rican and all 383 guards were white, and charges of racial discrimination were common.

The revolt spurred four separate investigations of conditions at Attica and many of the more serious abuses were eventually corrected.

New Mexico State Prison

The revolt at New Mexico State Prison nine years later could hardly have been more different from the one at Attica. In February 1980, prisoners at the New Mexico prison broke into the control room, seized the guards, and opened all the cells. The political movements of the 1960s had passed, and no one at New Mexico thought of trying to organize or control the revolt. Some prisoners went to the sick bay and started a drug orgy. Others went on a rampage smashing furniture and setting fires. One group broke into an isolation area where prison informers were held. Thirty-three prisoners were hacked to death or tortured to death with blowtorches. Prison officials tried to negotiate, but they found no one in charge to negotiate with.

As the violence died down, most of the prisoners came out one-by-one to surrender peacefully. Those who didn't come out offered no resistance when police and National Guardsmen stormed the prison 36 hours later. At Attica, all the deaths, except the one guard injured in the takeover, had come at the hands of the police. In New Mexico, the inmates themselves had done all the killing.

Despite the differences, post-riot commissions found many of the same abuses in New Mexico. In fact, some conditions were probably worse. In New Mexico, prisoners did not have individual cells, and homosexual rape was widespread. Also, drugs had become much more common by 1980, and many of the prisoners were intoxicated during the riot. The following is one convict's letter, detailing some of his complaints:

> We seldom see any kind of exercise, the heat is turned on high in some of the dorms whether it is a warm day or not, the food is bad, the mail is lost or comes late, the lighting in most dorms is bad, and all around we face harassment by the guards.

Attica and New Mexico by no means represented the worst prisons in the United States. They were just unlucky enough to have the necessary conditions come together to set off riots. Other prisons have even worse reputations. Louisiana's New Orleans Parish Prison, for example, crams six men into each 7-by-14 cell. Ohio State Prison is a gray and gloomy fortress built in 1834. New York's Sing Sing Prison—its proper name is Ossining Correctional Facility—is almost as old as the Ohio prison and houses prisoners in zoo-like cells stacked five high. And all of these conditions have been made worse by the prison population explosion.

Gangs

Some conditions at Attica and New Mexico have improved since the uprisings, but these prisons are still subject to the overcrowding and other problems that plague most of our maximum- and medium-security institutions. Perhaps the biggest new prison problem has been the growth of violent, race- and ethnic-based gangs. Beginning in the 1970s, as dramatized in Edward James Olmos' film *American Me*, these gangs were organized almost exclusively along racial or ethnic lines. They have spread to almost every American prison. The best known are the Black Guerrilla Family for African Americans, two competing families of what is popularly called the Mexican Mafia for Hispanics, and the Aryan White Brotherhood.

These groups demand obedience and provide a sense of protection and community for their members. Because of their racial and ethnic makeup, many of the gangs make heavy use of racist slogans and symbols, and they glory in violent acts against other races and ethnic groups. Conflicts among the gangs grew so intense that in the 1980s some institutions such as San Quentin were forced to segregate the bulk of their prisoners by race, putting them into separate cell blocks. Prison authorities were reluctant to give official sanction to racial separation, but they had little choice if they wanted to protect the lives of the prisoners.

For Discussion

1. How did the revolts at Attica and New Mexico prisons differ? Why? Give several reasons.

2. What, if anything, do you think can be done to prevent future prison revolts? Explain.

3. How might conditions in a maximum-security prison affect a first-time offender?

4. How do you think the racial divisions in the prisons can be resolved?

Class Activity: Prison in the Classroom

In this activity, students simulate living in prison cells.

1. Break the class into three or four groups. Select corners of your classroom and, with masking tape, have the students mark off areas nine feet long by six feet wide.

2. In each area, use the tape to mark off an area large enough for a bunk bed, table, two-drawer cabinet, toilet and sink. Put a chair or stool in the open area of this imaginary cell. Assign two students to share this space. Try to imagine spending 14 to 16 hours each day locked up there.

3. Then assign another pair of students to try it. Continue until all the students have had an imaginary prison experience.

4. Now try the same thing with three students in each imaginary cell, then four students. Discuss what overcrowding feels like and how it might cause conflicts.

5. Ask students to remember some event that happened to them about two years ago and then to imagine spending all the time since that event in a cell. The average prisoner spends about two years in prison.

Debriefing Questions
1. What do you think would be the most difficult part of prison life?
2. What kinds of conditions should be maintained at prisons? Describe.
3. Should non-violent offenders be locked up with violent offenders? Explain.

Parole

Just as probation comes from the Latin word "to prove," the word **parole** comes from the French for "to speak," or "to give your word." Parole is a process of returning prisoners to society if they have displayed good behavior in prison and if they give their word to avoid further crime. Near the end of their prison terms, prisoners come before a parole board where their behavior and attitudes are examined. Those who are judged rehabilitated or ready for release are granted parole. The parolee is then supervised for a specified time after release to make sure the promise is kept. A parole officer sees to it that the conditions of parole are met and that the parolee makes a successful transition to life on the outside.

Some critics believe that the extensive use of parole is a mistake and too lenient on prisoners. They argue that hardened criminals come to think of tricking the parole board as a game. Others take the view that parole offers a stepping stone back into the real world, and the time of release should be tailored to the individual prisoner.

Today the trend is toward fixed sentences and a reduced role for the parole board. But many prisoners serving fixed sentences still can be released on parole by earning good-time credits against their sentences.

In fact, most prisoners are eventually released on parole. Nationwide, there are about two-thirds more people on parole at any time than are locked up in prison. Yet the public hears little about this part of the corrections system. When the public does hear something about parole, it is usually about one of its failures or mistakes.

Parole has many of the same problems as probation. The number of people to be supervised is growing rapidly while the number of supervisors is staying the same or even shrinking. Although county or state officials may oversee probation, a state parole board runs parole in many states. Both systems in most states have suffered badly from limited budgets.

The Parole Process

The parole system is generally defined by state statutes, or in the case of federal prisoners, by federal law. Most states have independent parole boards. The boards function as hearing panels to determine whether prisoners eligible for parole deserve it. Parole board members are often political appointees who have professional staff members and case workers to advise them.

The case workers compile reports on prisoners eligible for parole. They gather information about an individual's behavior while in prison and what awaits the prisoner in the community. They find out about the prisoner's family, opportunities for employment, access to friends, availability of housing, and the general climate that awaits the parolee in the community. An offer of employment is often key to winning parole board approval. A prisoner's success is much more likely if a stable job is available.

If released on parole, offenders must meet regularly with a parole officer and show that they are living up to the conditions of their release. Most often, these conditions forbid the use of alcohol and controlled substances, possession of firearms, or association with other ex-convicts. Offenders must ask permission to change their residence, to travel from one area to another, to marry, or even to buy a car.

The parole officer has two, sometimes conflicting, roles. The first is as a social worker,

Characteristics of Adults on Parole

Gender
12%	Female
88%	Male

Race
55%	White
44%	Black
1%	Other

Hispanic origin
79%	Non-Hispanic
21%	Hispanic

Status of supervision
83%	Active
5%	Inactive
7%	Absconded
5%	Supervised out of state

Adults Entering Parole
42%	Discretionary parole*
50%	Mandatory parole**

Adults leaving parole
43%	Successful completion
42%	Returned to incarceration
	11% With new sentence
	31% Other
10%	Absconder
2%	Other unsuccessful
1%	Transferred
1%	Death
2%	Other

* Discretionary parole means a prisoner was put on parole by a parole board.

**Mandatory parole means a prisoner was released because of good-time credits or a sentencing statute.

Detail may not sum to total because of rounding.

Source: "Probation and Parole in the United States, 1999," Bureau of Justice Statistics (2000)

trying to help the parolee make a successful transition from prison to the community. The second is as a corrections officer, watching for any criminal tendencies. If necessary, the parole officer may have the individual jailed pending an investigation of parole violations or new criminal acts.

Ideal caseloads are considered to be roughly 35 per officer, or as few as 20 for serious offenders. In some jurisdictions, however, budget problems have pushed case loads up as high as 250 parolees per case worker. That's less than 10 minutes per week per case, which is rarely adequate to check up on a parolee, let alone offer help or advice.

Notorious Cases

Notorious cases pose special problems. One problem is whether publicity denies some prisoners equal treatment. The case of **Sirhan Bishara Sirhan** illustrates this problem. In June 1968, Sirhan shot and killed U.S. Senator Robert F. Kennedy, who had just won the presidential primary in California. Convicted of murder, Sirhan was sent to the maximum-security Soledad prison in California. A tentative parole date was set for 1982, but a public debate erupted over whether Sirhan should ever be paroled. Many people thought that the killer of a presidential candidate should never walk free. Nearly 4,000 letters flooded the parole board, as well as a petition bearing over 8,000 signatures—all opposing parole.

Sirhan's attorney claimed that his client had a nearly spotless prison record, that his 13 years in prison were already twice as much time behind bars as most murderers served in California, and that there was no solid evidence that he was any longer a threat to anyone.

The Los Angeles District Attorney presented new evidence that Sirhan was a continuing danger. The D.A. said Sirhan had written two threatening letters in the early 1970s. One corrections department psychiatrist did not feel this was unusual considering the stress that Sirhan had been under. Others were not so sure. The D.A. also cited testimony from fellow prisoners that Sirhan had threatened to kill others. But questions were raised about the accuracy of this testimony.

In its reconsideration of the release date, the board finally denied Sirhan parole. In all subsequent hearings, it has denied him parole. Many people believe the board has based its decisions on the nature of the original crime and worries about Sirhan's continuing danger to others. Some people believe the parole board has yielded to public pressure and will never release Sirhan.

A second problem arises when notorious offenders do get released. Parolees normally must return to the counties they lived in before their conviction. But communities often object to the return of notorious criminals, particularly child molesters and murderers. **Lawrence Singleton** offers an extreme example. In the late 1970s, Singleton picked up a 15-year-old hitchhiker, brutally raped her, chopped off her forearms, and left her in the California desert to die. Somehow she lived. Convicted for the crime, Singleton was sentenced to 12 years in prison, the maximum then possible under California law. A model prisoner, he earned enough good time to be released in 1987 after only eight years. His crime had aroused so much attention that parole authorities did not know where to place him. They tried convincing other states to take him, but none would. They even talked of housing him on prison grounds. Finally, amid much outcry and media coverage, they placed him in his original community in Northern California. But citizen protests proved so intense that Singleton could not remain. Encountering protests wherever he went, he moved from community to community in Northern California. When his parole ended, he moved to Florida. In 1997, he murdered a prostitute and was sentenced to death.

For Discussion

1. How are probation and parole alike? How are they different?

2. What problems do parole officers face?

3. Why do parole boards have less power in states with fixed sentencing laws?

4. Infamous convicts, such as Charles Manson and Mark David Chapman (the murderer of John Lennon), have been repeatedly denied parole. Do you think public opinion or pressure about such cases should influence parole board decisions? Why or why not?

5. Where should notorious offenders be placed if their community does not want them back? Explain your answer.

Class Activity: Parole Board

In this activity, students role play members of a parole board deciding whether to grant parole to convicts.

1. Form groups of three to five students. Each will role play a parole board.

2. Each group should:

   a. Read each of the cases below.

   b. Decide whether to grant or deny parole in each case.

   c. Prepare to present its decisions and reasons for them to the class.

3. Have the groups report on their decisions and reasons for them. Discuss what purpose further imprisonment would serve in each case. (Refer to the purpose of punishment discussed on pages 168–169.)

4. Conclude the activity by holding a class vote on whether to grant or deny parole in each case.

Case 1: Sirhan Bishara Sirhan. See details on this case in the article above.

Case 2: Leonard Smith. Smith is one of the oldest prisoners held in your state. Fifty years ago when he was 18, he took part in a bank robbery. He held a knife to a teller's throat. When she did something that displeased him, he slit her throat. Smith has been a model prisoner, has earned a college degree, and is deeply remorseful for his criminal act. He is serving an indeterminate sentence of one to 75 years.

Case 3: Helen Campbell. Five years ago Campbell was convicted of second-degree murder and sentenced to a fixed term of 15 years. Campbell murdered her husband in his sleep. Campbell testified (and witnesses supported her testimony) that her husband had beaten her for 10 years. Campbell has been a model prisoner. This is her first parole hearing.

Case 4: David Garcia. Garcia was convicted of burglary and sentenced under to an indeterminate term of from two to 10 years. He has served seven years, twice as long as most for his crime. Prison officials consider him dangerous and potentially violent.

Staying Out of Prison

Many ex-convicts have difficulty staying out of trouble—and out of prison—once they are released. Ex-convicts have special needs that the parole program alone often cannot address. Several special programs, however, have been developed to help them. One such program, the 7th Step Foundation, uses ex-offenders as counselors to help juveniles, parolees, and those who are soon to be released.

Case Study of an Ex-Offender

The following case study is based on an interview with a 7th Step counselor.

"One of the inmates who had a life sentence without parole organized a group of the most dangerous criminals in the prison. I joined the group. We got together to help keep juvenile delinquents from turning to crime. Every Saturday these kids would be brought into the prison. We would talk to them and show them around. We showed them death row and the electric chair. It really shook them up. That program helped those kids, and it also helped me get turned around.

"When I left prison I felt totally helpless and frightened. I didn't know how to talk to a lady, how to take a lady out, or how to dress. Fitting into society is a real problem. You have a feeling you want to make up for lost time—and it's hard to sit still even for five minutes.

"As far as adjusting to society, I don't know how long it will take. For me, getting in my car and coming to work is a thrill. To go to the icebox and get a drink is a great feeling for me. I've only been out four months. That's a small amount of time compared to 21 years in an institution. The adjustment period is not over, and I don't have any more chances. Next time I'll be sent away for the rest of my life.

"I've been a thief all my life, and I've been a pretty good thief. For me, it is easy to be bad and it's a struggle to be good. I could go out and get money just like that. It's my profession—the only thing I am good at—so far.

"How do you tell someone you've been in prison for 21 years—how do you tell them? How do you tell them you've been arrested for murder? How do you tell them these things and then expect them to give you a job?"

Class Activity: Staying Out

Imagine that you are just paroled and trying to stay out of prison. Write a journal of your experiences in the first few weeks after release. Include the following incidents and give an account about how you deal with them.

- Finding a place to live.

- Relating to your family and loved ones.

- Searching for a job and going to a job interview.

- Running into an old friend from your criminal days, one you are forbidden to associate with.

- Reflecting on your time in a maximum-security prison.

When everyone finishes, students who want to, should read the journals aloud in class and discuss them.

CHAPTER 16
Capital Punishment

History of the Death Penalty in America

Capital punishment is another expression for the death penalty, or the legal execution of a criminal. The word capital comes from the Latin word for head. In ancient times, capital punishment was often carried out by beheading. This method has never been used in America. But criminals have been put to death by shooting, hanging, electrocution, poison gas, and lethal injection. Today, the most common method is lethal injection, followed by electrocution. Some states, however, allow one of these other methods as an option.

Once a person is sentenced to death in America, most states follow a similar procedure. The sentenced criminal is normally held in a maximum-security prison's special section known as death row. Usually, prisoners on death row have little contact with other prisoners. Each occupies a small cell alone, and each takes meals and exercises alone. This life may continue for years during appeals of the sentence. An appeal hearing for a death sentence is automatic in every state except Arkansas.

In the American colonies legal executions took place as early as 1630. As in England, the death penalty was imposed for many different crimes, even minor ones such as picking pockets or stealing a loaf of bread. During the 1800s in England, for example, 270 different crimes were capital offenses, or crimes punishable by death. Thousands of people sometimes attended public hangings. Gradually, however, England and America reduced the number of capital offenses, until the main focus was on first-degree murder—murders showing deliberation, willfulness, and premeditation. They also moved executions within the walls of prisons to eliminate the spectacle of public executions.

In the 1800s, many people in America and Europe began to oppose the death penalty altogether. Michigan abolished it in 1845 and Wisconsin entered the Union in 1848 without a death penalty in its statutes. The movement against the death penalty grew stronger after World War II, especially in Europe, where many were weary of so much killing during the war. One by one all the Western European nations and Canada did away with capital punishment, until the United States was the last Western democracy that still executed criminals. Twelve American states, mainly clustered in the Midwest and Northeast, have also banned executions. New York, which had banned the death penalty 30 years before, reinstated it in 1995.

Public opinion on the death penalty has varied over time. In the 1930s, opinion polls showed strong support for capital punishment. From that time, support gradually declined. By the mid-1960s, it had fallen to less than 50 percent. But then support started to rise again. By the 1990s, following decades of widespread anxiety over crime and violence, some states such as California were showing almost 80 percent of the population in favor of executing criminals. Other polls showed that 62 percent of the population felt that the death penalty deterred crime, and 51 percent said they would support it even if it did not deter crime.

In 1991, researcher Robert M. Bohm did an analysis of 21 different polls on the death penalty. He found that certain factors—people's religion, age, occupation, or size of the city they lived in—showed little relation to their attitude on capital punishment. But other factors did. Men were more likely to favor it than women. Whites supported it more than blacks. Republicans endorsed it more

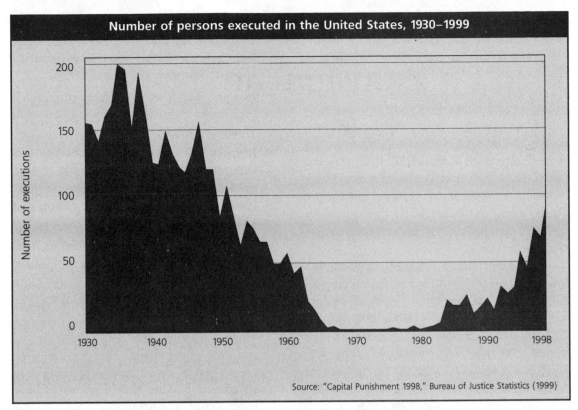

Number of persons executed in the United States, 1930–1999

Number of executions (y-axis): 0, 50, 100, 150, 200

Years (x-axis): 1930, 1940, 1950, 1960, 1970, 1980, 1990, 1998

Source: "Capital Punishment 1998," Bureau of Justice Statistics (1999)

than Democrats. The wealthy approved it more than the poor. People from the South were more likely to oppose the death penalty than people from other regions.

Recent Legal History of the Death Penalty

Following public protest over capital punishment in the 1950s and 1960s, the number of executions in America gradually declined. In 1967, there were only two, and the following year the Supreme Court struck down death-penalty laws for crimes other than murder—crimes such as kidnaping, rape, and federal bank robbery. That year also saw the beginning of an unofficial moratorium on executions. States waited to see how the Supreme Court would rule on the constitutionality of capital punishment. No executions took place in the United States from 1968 through 1976.

In the 1972 case of *Furman v. Georgia*, the Supreme Court declared capital punishment unconstitutional as it was then applied. The court said the death penalty was a violation of the Eighth Amendment prohibition against cruel and unusual punishment because there

did not seem to be any consistency in who was given a death sentence and who was not. The court suggested that new laws might be acceptable, if they provided clear standards for which criminals should be given death sentences.

Between 1972 and 1976, 35 states wrote new capital punishment laws to try to meet the Supreme Court's suggestions. These new laws fell into two broad groups. One group, represented by laws in Georgia, Texas, and Florida, clearly described which capital crimes could be punished by death. These laws also set up a weighing system for deciding when the death penalty should be applied. In a separate penalty trial after a conviction for first-degree murder, a jury would consider **mitigating** circumstances that tended to excuse the crime or the criminal's behavior, and **aggravating** circumstances that made the crime seem worse. The court could only sentence someone to death if the aggravating circumstances outweighed any mitigating circumstances.

A second group of laws, represented by statutes from North Carolina and Louisiana, sought to overcome the Supreme Court's objections in another way. These laws simply made the death penalty mandatory for anyone convicted of a capital crime.

In 1976, the Supreme Court in *Gregg v. Georgia* ruled that the first type of law, based on the act of balancing mitigating and aggravating circumstances, was constitutional. This upheld the Georgia, Texas, and Florida death penalties. The court, however, struck down the second type. It declared unconstitutional North Carolina's and Louisiana's mandatory death sentences. The court said a mandatory sentence was unduly harsh and rigid and made no allowance for the particular circumstances of each case.

Executions began again in 1977, though many states still waited for a ruling on one further major issue: whether the death penalty was being applied equally. From 1977 through 1985, only 50 executions took place, though almost 2,000 prisoners waited on death row.

The test case came with the Georgia case of *McCleskey v. Kemp* (1987). In it, lawyers for the condemned man submitted a careful study of how the death penalty had been applied in Georgia during the 1970s.

The study, by University of Iowa Professor David Baldus, showed that blacks who had killed whites had been sentenced to die seven times more often than whites who had killed blacks. Even after accounting for other variables, such as the viciousness of the crime, blacks had been sentenced to die more than four times as often as whites.

In its decision, the U.S. Supreme Court acknowledged that there seemed to be some *statistical* racial discrimination in Georgia's application of the death penalty. But the justices ruled by a 5–4 vote that a mere statistical variation was not enough to invalidate the death penalty. To do that, the defendant would have to show that the state had somehow encouraged the result or that there was actual discrimination in a particular case. Since the defendant had offered no such proof, which would be difficult to acquire, the court upheld the death penalty.

In a series of decisions since *McCleskey*, the court has tended to support the prosecution and make appeal of a death sentence more dif-

ficult. The justices have ruled that:

- Death-row inmates have no right to free legal assistance after an initial round of appeals. *Murray v. Giarratano* (1989).

- Inmates may lose their right to appeal if they make procedural errors. *Coleman v. Thompson* (1991).

- Inmates can't take advantage of any rule changes or precedents set *after* they have exhausted their appeals. *Teague v. Lane* (1989) and *Butler v. McKellar* (1990), and *Saffle v. Parks* (1990).

- The death penalty can be applied to mentally retarded criminals. *Penry v. Lynaugh* (1989).

- The prosecution may introduce victim-impact statements in penalty hearings. These statements may detail the pain and suffering of the victim. This decision overturned several earlier rulings banning such statements because they tend to inflame juries against convicted murderers. *Payne v. Tennessee* (1991).

- Death-row inmates cannot get a federal hearing on new-found evidence proving their innocence unless that evidence overwhelmingly proves their innocence. *Herrera v. Collins* (1993).

In 1996, Congress passed the Anti-Terrorism and Effective Death Penalty Act. Part of this act limited state prisoners' habeas corpus appeals in federal court. The writ of habeas corpus is guaranteed by the U.S. Constitution. The writ is an order to bring a prisoner before a court to determine if the prisoner is legally held. Many death penalty appeals are petitions of habeas corpus. Supporters of the act say many prisoners are simply buying time by filing frivolous habeas corpus petitions. Opponents of the law argued that capital cases should be carefully reviewed and that the act prevents this. In *Felker v. Turpin* in 1996, the Supreme Court upheld this part of the act.

But in 2000, the Supreme Court overturned two federal court decisions that had rejected state habeas corpus appeals because of

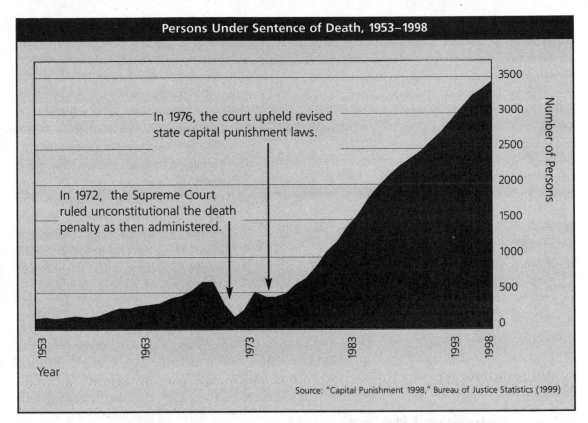

Persons Under Sentence of Death, 1953–1998

In 1976, the court upheld revised state capital punishment laws.

In 1972, the Supreme Court ruled unconstitutional the death penalty as then administered.

Number of Persons

3500
3000
2500
2000
1500
1000
500
0

Year
1953 1963 1973 1983 1993 1998

Source: "Capital Punishment 1998," Bureau of Justice Statistics (1999)

the 1996 act. The Supreme Court said that the 1996 act only banned unreasonable appeals. When "clearly established" constitutional rights have been violated, the federal courts may intervene. The two Virginia cases involved defendants with the same last name, but the defendants were not related.

In *Terry Williams v. Taylor*, the court ruled 6-3 that the defendant had been deprived of his right to effective counsel. The defense attorney failed to mention at the sentencing hearing that the defendant was borderline mentally retarded, he had been fed whiskey as a child, and his parents had been jailed for child abuse and neglect.

In *Michael Wayne Williams v. Taylor*, a unanimous court ruled that the defendant did not receive a fair trial. The jury forewoman failed to disclose that she was the ex-wife of the sheriff and a former client of the prosecutor.

In recent years, about 70 prisoners have been executed each year. More than 3,000 inmates wait on death row in prisons across America. Much of this backlog is caused by appeals. Even though recent rulings have made

it harder to appeal, it still takes an average of nine years for each prisoner to exhaust the appeals process. And it costs a state from $2 to $3 million to process each case.

A study published in 2000 found that most death-row appeals succeed. A Columbia Law School professor surveyed the almost 5,000 capital cases appealed in state and federal courts between 1973 and 1995. His study revealed that appeals courts found errors serious enough to overturn convictions in almost 70 percent of the cases. Three-fourths of those with overturned convictions got a sentence less than death when the case was retried or plea bargained. Seven percent were found not guilty at their new trial. Eighteen percent were again sentenced to death, but many of these defendants had their cases overturned again on appeal.

Opponents of the death penalty argue that these statistics expose a deeply flawed system. Supporters of the death penalty counter that it reveals how carefully the system reviews each case to make sure only those deserving the death penalty receive it.

For Discussion

1. Why do you think prisons separate those sentenced to death from other prisoners?

2. Why do you think the United States is the only Western democracy that executes criminals?

3. What reason did the Supreme Court give in *Furman* for saying that death penalty statutes were unconstitutional? How did states change their statutes to make them constitutional? Do you agree with the court that these statutes are constitutional? Why or why not?

4. What did the court decide in the *McCleskey* case? Do you agree with its decision? Why or why not?

5. Which of the decisions after *McCleskey* do you agree with? Disagree with? Why?

6. Some have argued that executions should be televised. Do you agree? Explain.

Class Activity: Life or Death

In this activity, students role play sentencing juries in capital cases using a capital punishment statute. The defendant in each case has already been convicted of first-degree murder. Each jury must determine the penalty. The only two choices available are life imprisonment or death.

1. Divide the class into four juries. Review the Capital Punishment Statute, below. Assign each jury one of the four cases on pages 216–217.

2. Members of each jury should:

   a. Make a list of the *mitigating circumstances*, those that seem to call for mercy.

   b. Make a list *aggravating circumstances*, those that make the crime seem especially violent or repulsive.

   c. Weigh the *mitigating* and the *aggravating* circumstances against each other. If they feel the case calls for

leniency, they should recommend life imprisonment. If they think the case is particularly barbarous or savage, they should recommend death. The recommendation does not have to be unanimous. Only a majority is required for a sentencing recommendation.

   d. Prepare to report to the class. One student in each group should report the mitigating circumstances the group considered. Another student should report the aggravating circumstances. A third student should report the sentence and the number of students who voted each way.

Capital Punishment Statute. After finding a defendant guilty of murder in the first degree, the jury shall look at the circumstances of the crime and at the character of the individual defendant. If it finds the aggravating circumstances of the crime and the defendant outweigh the mitigating circumstances, it shall return a recommendation of the death penalty. Otherwise, it shall recommend life imprisonment.

Case 1: Luby Waxton
Age: 22
Sex: Male

Luby has been in and out of jail ever since he was a teenager. He was convicted of shoplifting, burglary, and assault with a deadly weapon. He received a light sentence for each, because he has the mental capacity of an 8-year-old.

On June 3 of this year, Waxton began drinking in the morning. He decided to rob a local grocery store to get some money. That afternoon, Waxton bought a small handgun.

When he got to the market, he entered the store, bought some cigarettes, and then announced a holdup.

Waxton went behind the counter and emptied the cash register. He put his gun to the sales clerk's head and pulled the trigger. The clerk, an old woman, died instantly.

Waxton was convicted of armed robbery and murder in the first degree.

Case 2: James Woodson
Age: 24
Sex: Male

Woodson has no prior record of being arrested.

Woodson has been active in the anti-abortion movement. He believes that abortion is murder. After taking part in picketing an abortion clinic, Woodson became frustrated that the clinic remained open. He believed that much stronger action was necessary, but knew his fellow picketers would not go along with him.

So late on the night of July 17, he broke into the clinic. He poured gasoline throughout the first floor and put a match to it. The clinic burned to the ground. Unknown to Woodson, a security guard was on the third floor. The guard died in the fire.

Woodson was convicted of arson and first-degree murder.

Case 3: Phong Tran
Age: 18
Sex: Male

Tran has a series of prior juvenile arrests for petty theft and assault. He has been involved in gang activity for the past five years.

His family immigrated to the United States when he was 7 years old. His father abandoned the family shortly afterward, and his mother could not handle three children by herself. Placed in a foster home at age 13, he ran away and took to the streets.

He found a new family in a local gang, headed by Tony Chin, age 35. Chin provided boys in the gang free housing, meals, movies, and video games. In return, they ran errands, protected Chin's businesses, and helped Chin's criminal enterprises. Tran looked on Chin as his father.

On January 7 of this year, Chin handed Tran a gun and told him that a "customer" needed a new Mercedes. Tran went to a mini-mall and waited in the parking lot. When Sally Kim drove up in a new Mercedes, Tran ran up, pointed a gun at her, and demanded she get out. The car lurched and Tran shot Kim, killing her.

Phong Tran was convicted of first-degree murder.

Case 4: Sonia Williams
Age: 27
Sex: Female

Williams has no prior record.

On September 10 of this year, Williams called the police and reported that she had been raped by a man named Gregg. She was taken down to a hospital where a doctor examined her. He said he could find no evidence of rape.

The police investigated her report and told Williams they could not arrest Gregg. It was dark, they said, and so she could have been mistaken about the identity of the attacker. Besides, they said, Gregg had a perfect alibi for the night in question.

Williams decided to take matters into her own hands. She bought a gun and waited around the corner where he allegedly first attacked her. When Gregg and a friend approached, she told Gregg she had been looking for him and was glad to see him. She invited the two men to go somewhere for a drink. They got into her car and drove to a secluded spot, where she shot and killed both men.

Sonia Williams was convicted of first-degree murder.

Debriefing Questions

1. Do you think different juries would weigh the aggravating and mitigating circumstances differently? If so, is this fair? Why or why not?

2. If you were called to jury duty in a capital case, could you vote for the death penalty if circumstances warranted it? Why or why not?

3 Assume for the moment that you approve of the death penalty. What crimes should it apply to? Why?

Public Opinion on the Death Penalty

The public's attitude toward capital punishment has changed over the years. Polls show that the American public today strongly supports the death penalty. This support has grown much stronger since the 1960s. But polls also show that the strength of this support depends on how you ask the question. Note the differences between the Harris and Gallup polls.

The Harris Poll

"Do you believe in capital punishment, that is, the death penalty, or are you opposed to it?"

	Believe in It	Opposed to It	Not Sure
	%	%	%
1999	71	21	8
1997	75	22	3
1983	68	27	5
1976	67	25	8
1973	59	31	10
1970	47	42	11
1969	48	38	14
1965	38	47	15

The Gallup Poll

"What do you think should be the penalty for murder: the death penalty or life imprisonment with absolutely no possibility of parole?"

	Death Penalty	Life Imprisonment	No Opinon
	%	%	%
2000	52	37	11
1999	56	38	6
1997	61	29	10
1994	50	32	18
1993	59	29	12
1992	50	37	13
1991	53	35	11

For Discussion

1. What do you think accounts for the shift in public opinion favoring capital punishment?

2. What do you think accounts for the difference between the Harris and Gallup polls? Which poll's question do you think is better? Why?

Activity: Death Penalty Poll

In this activity, students conduct a poll on the death penalty.

1. Decide who you are going to poll. It can be the community, the school, or just one grade level.

2. Decide on how to get a random sample of the group you are polling. Determine how large a sample you will take.

3. Divide the class in two. One group should ask the Harris question; the other group, the Gallup question.

4. Tabulate the results.

Debriefing Questions

1. How do your results compare with the official poll results?

2. How do you account for the similarities or differences?

Recent Developments in Capital Punishment

As of 1998, more than 3,000 prisoners were on death row in the United States. California held the most (512), followed by Texas (451), Florida (372), and Pennsylvania (224). Despite these numbers, only about 60 are executed each year. Part of this can be explained by the long appeals process. But there also appears to be a social reluctance to begin executing massive numbers of prisoners. Between 1977 and 2000, fewer than 700 executions took place, most of them in the South. In fact, seven Southern states carried out three-fourths of all executions. The state of Texas by itself accounted for one-third of them.

Most of the executions have provoked little protest within the United States. Overseas, many of the executions have drawn widespread attention and some massive protests. The only recent execution hotly debated in America was that of Karla Faye Tucker, the first woman to be executed in Texas since 1863.

Karla Faye Tucker

Tucker had been a heroin addict since the age of 10. By 13, she was traveling with a rock band. For many years, she worked as a prostitute. In 1983 at age 23, she and her 37-year-old boyfriend broke into a biker's apartment. Intoxicated on drugs and alcohol, they intended to steal money that the biker owed them. Her boyfriend attacked the biker with a hammer as he lay in bed. As the man lay unconscious, he moaned. Tucker later testified she found the moaning annoying and started striking him with a pickax. Her 28 blows killed him. Then she discovered that the biker was not alone in bed. A woman crouched in the corner. Tucker did not have enough energy left to attack her, so her boyfriend killed the woman.

Awaiting trial for the brutal murders, Tucker started reading the Bible. She said she soon realized the enormity of her crime. "At the time, I didn't understand how the Holy Spirit works," she said. "I just remember the whole weight of everything I had done suddenly became a reality. Two precious lives were gone because of me." She agreed to testify against her boyfriend with no promise of leniency. She thought she deserved the death penalty.

Both she and her boyfriend were convicted and sentenced to death. During the 14 years she waited on death row, she became a born-again Christian. In 1993, she married a prison minister. She spent her days acting as a minister and anti-drug counselor to prisoners. She also changed her mind about the death penalty. "I can't take back the lives I took, but I can

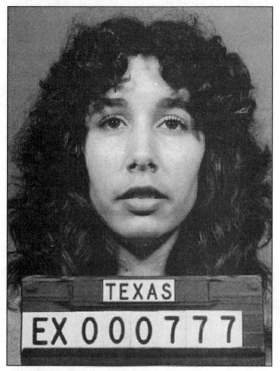

Karla Faye Tucker, shown in a 1984 mugshot, was the first woman executed in Texas since 1863.

help save lives now," said Tucker. "I can be a part of the solution."

She drew supporters from unlikely quarters. The Rev. Jerry Falwell, a strong supporter of the death penalty, argued she should be spared. The detective who arrested her and the prosecutor in the case believed her change was genuine and hoped her sentence would be commuted to life. Even the brother of the woman she killed urged authorities not to execute her. A poll of Texans, who overwhelming support the death penalty, found less than half thought she should undergo it. In the two months before the execution, about 25,000 letters, faxes and phone calls reached the governor's office. They ran about 5 to 1 against killing her.

The governor only had power to commute her sentence to life if state Board of Pardons and Paroles recommended it. The board voted unanimously against her, as it had in 17 straight cases. On February 3, 1998, she was executed.

One reason Tucker's case drew so much attention was that few women are executed. About one of every eight people arrested for murder is a woman. But only one out of 50 people sentenced to death is a woman. One in 70 people on death row is a woman, but only one other woman since 1977 had been executed.

But Tucker's supporters argued that they didn't champion her cause because she was a woman. Another woman was put to death in Florida a few weeks after Tucker with little protest. They wanted Tucker saved because she felt genuine remorse and had changed into a new person.

Some who thought she should be executed did not believe she had really changed. Others, however, did believe her. But they didn't think this should make a difference. She had committed a brutal crime, they argued, and she deserved to pay for it with her life. "She's had her mercy," said Dianne Clements, president of Justice for All, a Houston-based criminal justice reform organization. "She's had 14 years to put herself right by God."

Are We Executing Innocent People?

Tucker never claimed to be innocent. But many on death row do. In fact, according to the Death Penalty Information Center, an anti-capital punishment group, more than 80 prisoners since 1977 have been released from death row because they were innocent. Many were exonerated due to the efforts of the Innocence Project. Led by Cardozo Law School professors Peter Neufeld and Barry C. Scheck, the Innocence Project provides free legal assistance to inmates who want to prove their innocence through DNA tests. The project is run by volunteers, and inmates must pay for the DNA testing themselves. Because of budget constraints, the project can only offer its services to a select number of prisoners. Scheck has argued that all states should authorize DNA testing when the tests could prove a person's innocence. Thus far, only two states—New York and Illinois—provide for such testing.

In Illinois, 12 inmates on death row have been executed since capital punishment resumed in 1977. But 13 have been released because they were innocent. One of the 13 was two days away from being executed before his execution was stayed. In November 1999, the *Chicago Tribune* ran a series of investigative articles analyzing all 285 death penalty cases in Illinois since 1977. The *Tribune* found that 40 percent of these cases had at least one of the following elements:

1. The defendant had an attorney who had been disbarred or suspended, penalties reserved for lawyers who are unethical or incompetent.

2. The prosecution's case relied on a jailhouse informant, who received lenient treatment for naming the defendant. Many consider this type of evidence highly unreliable.

3. The prosecution's case relied on testimony from a crime lab technician who made a visual comparison of hairs. This is an outmoded practice that some states bar from being used in court.

4. The defendant was black and the jury was all white.

In January 2000, Illinois Republican Governor George H. Ryan, a supporter of capital punishment, took the extraordinary step of placing a moratorium on all executions in the state. He said he had "grave concerns about . . . [the] state's shameful record of convicting innocent people and putting them on death row." He called for an investigation of the state's death penalty procedures. Some have criticized Ryan, saying that the state legislature is already investigating the problem. They argue that blocking all executions is wrong because most inmates on death row have been clearly proven to be guilty.

In Congress in 2000, Democratic Senator Patrick Leahy of Vermont introduced the Innocence Protection Act. Among other things, it would allow federal and state prisoners easier access to DNA tests in cases where test results might exonerate them, ban the government from destroying biological evidence used for DNA testing, and issue minimum standards for court-appointed defense attorneys. If states did not comply with the act, they would be denied federal law-enforcement grants.

Opponents of the bill believe that states, like Illinois, with some problems in death penalty cases are already working to fix them. The federal government, they argue, does not need to intervene. They point out that the appeals process already takes many years, and federal involvement would just lengthen it further. They emphasize that no innocent person has been executed in at least 50 years.

Scheck supports Leahy's bill. He says: "The two states that have the most post-conviction exonerations [are] 13 in Illinois and 7 in New York. It's no coincidence." Scheck believes many innocent people are on death row. Although he strongly advocates DNA testing, he says that it cannot solve all the problems in the criminal justice system, because biological evidence is only available in about 60 percent of all violent crimes.

For Discussion

1. Do you think Karla Faye Tucker should have been executed? Explain.

2. Do you think Illinois Governor George H. Ryan was correct in suspending all executions in the state? Why or why not?

3. Do you think the federal Innocence Protection Act is needed? Explain.

Class Activity: Taking a Stand on Capital Punishment

In this activity, students take a stand on the death penalty and reflect on arguments for and against the death penalty. The chart on page 222 summarizes some of these arguments.

1. Have the class form a line based on how each person feels about the death penalty. Make one end of the room mark the spot for those who absolutely favor the death penalty. The other end marks the spot for those who are absolutely opposed to capital punishment. The stronger that people feel one way or the other, the closer they should be to the ends of the line. Those unsure of their opinion belong in the middle.

2. Select the first person from each end of the line. These people are advocates—pro and con—for argument number one on the chart. Have them sit together at a table and silently read and think about argument one. **The advocates' job is to present their assigned argument in their own words.**

3. Select the second person from each end of the line. These people are advocates for argument number two. Have them sit together at a different table and read argument two. Continue through the line until you have tables with pro and con advocates for all eight arguments.

4. Assign the remaining students to sit as arbiters at the tables. **The arbiters' job is to evaluate the advocates' arguments.**

5. Give the advocates 30 seconds each to make their arguments to the arbiters at their table.

6. After hearing the arguments, have the arbiters form a new line showing how they now feel about capital punishment. Like before, one end of the line should mark absolute approval and the other end absolute disapproval of the death penalty.

7. After forming a new line, let each pair of advocates make their arguments in turn to the standing arbiters. After each pair has spoken, let the arbiters move on the line if they are swayed by the argument.

Debriefing Questions

1. Which arguments for and against the death penalty do you find most convincing? Least convincing? Why?

2. Can you think of other arguments for or against the death penalty?

Death Penalty Arguments

Pro

1. Capital cases are carefully reviewed. Mistakes are discovered. It has been more than 50 years since an innocent person has been executed.

2. Capital punishment keeps people from committing serious crimes. It is difficult to find direct evidence of a deterrent effect, but it certainly must deter people who think about their crimes—like hired killers.

3. If a person takes a life, that person should pay by giving a life. "An eye for an eye and a tooth for a tooth." This is in accordance with the *punishment* purpose of the criminal justice system.

4. To receive capital punishment, a person must be convicted of committing a horrible crime. The jury is carefully instructed and appellate courts scrutinize the case. If a defendant has been discriminated against, the appellate court will overturn the conviction. The procedure meets all "due process of law" standards.

5. Some criminals are so dangerous that they must never be allowed to live in society. They cannot be rehabilitated. If allowed to live, they may escape or kill a guard or another prisoner. They should be executed to make sure make sure they never harm anyone again.

6. Capital punishment is specifically allowed by the language of the Bill of Rights. The Fifth Amendment says that no person shall be deprived "of *life*, liberty or property without due process of law." [italics added]

7. The public wants the death penalty. Polls in some states run as high as 80 percent in favor of it.

8. Capital punishment would be less expensive if frivolous appeals were eliminated. But even if it is more expensive, it's worth the cost.

Con

1. Many innocent people have been released from death row. Many undoubtedly remain. Are we willing to risk executing innocent people?

2. There is no evidence that capital punishment has a deterrent effect. In states that have abolished the death penalty, murder rates have declined or remained the same.

3. Killing a criminal is an evil on top of an evil. All the Western democracies have abolished it, many religions oppose it, and it is abhorrent to most civilized people.

4. It is almost impossible to apply capital punishment fairly. Evidence shows that African-Americans and other minorities are sentenced to death far out of proportion to others, especially when a white victim is killed. Chance and arbitrary decision making can affect the sentence in many ways. Chance should not be a factor in a life-or-death decision.

5. Life imprisonment without the possibility of parole is punishment enough, and it keeps criminals off the streets just as well as executing them.

6. Customs and conditions have changed since the Constitution was written. Just as slavery is no longer acceptable, the death penalty should be considered cruel and unusual punishment.

7. Public opinion has gone up and down on the death penalty. No other Western democracy executes criminals. We should join the ranks of these countries.

8. Capital punishment costs more than life imprisonment. At current costs, the appeals and hearings for a single death-penalty case cost the government between $2 and $3 million.

Unit 5:
Juvenile Justice

In 1716, Elizabeth Hickes of Huntington, England, was accused of witchcraft. Her neighbors reported that Hickes used dolls to cast evil spells and that she'd made several of her enemies very sick. After hearing the evidence, a judge found Hickes guilty as charged, and she was burned alive at the stake. Elizabeth Hickes was born in 1705. She was 11 years old.

What if Elizabeth had been an American born in 1900, 1950, or 1990? In the first place, times have changed and practicing witchcraft is no longer a crime. But what if she were accused of a different crime? What would happen to the 11-year-old Elizabeth Hickes today?

For one thing, she wouldn't get a trial. She'd have a hearing. It would take place in a special juvenile court. Her family history, school records, and other personal information would be closely examined. Even if the juvenile court judge decided something was wrong with Elizabeth, she wouldn't be punished. Instead, the court would prescribe a special rehabilitation program designed to help Elizabeth adjust to society.

Why are children treated so differently today? Nineteenth and early 20th century reforms produced two separate systems of justice in America, based on almost opposite philosophies. The adult criminal justice system applies to supposedly mature, responsible persons who have lived, depending on the state, at least 16 or 18 years. All those younger than the specified age fall under the jurisdiction of the juvenile justice system.

This dual system has its critics. Many Americans believe that all persons in trouble with the law, no matter what their age, should have the benefit of the due process protections found in the adult system. Others argue that some juveniles should be processed according to the rules of the adult system not for their protection, but for society's protection. They feel that the juvenile justice system, with its emphasis on rehabilitation, puts too many young, hard-core criminals back on the streets. The fact that these criminals are only 14 or 15 doesn't prevent them from committing crimes and ruining other people's lives. Others have yet another perspective: Whether or not the theory behind our current juvenile system is correct, it just isn't working. Modifications must be made for the benefit of troubled young people and for the good of society.

After exploring the history and philosophy of the juvenile justice system, this unit examines issues raised by its critics and supporters. Who ought to be there? What rights should young people have as protection against the system? Should the system focus on rehabilitation or punishment?

Finally, statistics show that people under 18 are responsible for almost 20 percent of American crime. Many criminals start their life of crime as juveniles. To find solutions to our crime problem, we must examine how the law currently treats juveniles and how that treatment can be improved.

CHAPTER 17
From Criminal to Delinquent

History: Children and the Law

In the Middle Ages, children took part in adult activities as soon as they could walk and talk. They were working by the age of 5 or 6. Most families needed every available pair of hands to grow enough food or weave enough cloth to survive. Shorter life expectancy also forced people into early adulthood. The average life span was only 40 years. No one had time for a leisurely childhood, much less an adolescence.

Children not only were expected to work hard, they were also expected to obey adult laws. Anyone old enough to commit a crime was thought old enough to be punished for it. Painful forms of trial, like ordeal and combat, and harsh punishments, like being hanged or burned at the stake, fell on all criminals, no matter what their ages.

In the 16th and 17th centuries, medieval attitudes began to soften. Though children were still thrust into adulthood at the age of 4 or 5, most of Europe began to think of them as needing adult protection and guidance. In England, the common law reflected this change in attitude. The king or queen became the *parens patriae*—the parent of the country. Representing the monarch, English courts acted as *parens patriae* to manage orphans' estates, protect children's property from wasteful parents, and provide for abandoned young people.

The Age of Reason

About this same time, another important concept worked its way into English common law: the idea of intent. To commit a crime, a person not only had to perform a forbidden action, the person also had to intend to commit that act.

The concept of intent changed how children were treated under English common law. Society now believed that children were naive and innocent. Though they might accidentally cause harm, children did not know enough about right and wrong, or about the effects of their actions, to form criminal intent. Since they couldn't form intent, children couldn't commit crimes.

At what age could they form the intent necessary for committing crimes? The 18th century's answer to this question was based on traditional Christian beliefs, which held that 7 was the "age of reason." After age 7, according to the church, children knew the difference between right and wrong and became responsible for their actions and moral decisions.

By the late 18th century, English common law had taken this rationale one step further. English judges usually dismissed cases against defendants under age 7. In recognition of society's changing view about the length of childhood, they also dismissed cases against persons aged 7 to 14 unless the prosecution could prove that the child was capable of forming criminal intent.

The English criminal justice system treated everyone over 14 years old—and everyone between 7 and 14 proven capable of forming criminal intent—exactly alike. Officially, all were tried in the same courts by the same rules. If convicted, all were locked up in the same jails and subject to the same harsh penalties. In actual practice, however, the system showed children and adolescents some leniency. For example, although English courts sentenced 103 persons age 8 and under to death between 1801 and 1836, not one of these executions actually took place. Even so, the law allowed people of a very young age to be executed or imprisoned.

On the lower east side of New York City around 1900, children often took to the streets to escape their cramped living quarters

Colonists transplanted the English common law, complete with the concepts of *parens patriae*, criminal intent, and the age of reason, to North American soil. The religious beliefs of many of these settlers emphasized training children for obedient, religious, and productive adult lives.

Save the Children

By the 19th century, America was rapidly changing. Factories sprang up across the Northeast, and the nation's urban population was growing faster than its rural population. In 1820, 7 percent of America's people lived in cities. That proportion had risen to 15 percent by 1850 and 35 percent by 1890.

Many of the new city residents were immigrants. Others were country people looking for greater opportunity and a path out of the exhausting routines of rural life. Survival in the city, however, was a full-time occupation. Crowded into small rooms with their struggling family, urban children often escaped to the streets. Other children were abandoned by their parents and turned to picking pockets, shoplifting, begging, and looting for survival.

Often, young people banded together. As early as 1791, children's gangs were noted on the streets of Philadelphia scaring horses with firecrackers. During the 19th century, gangs turned from pranks to serious crime. By the Civil War, youth gangs took part in arson and mob violence, and regularly fought battles with the police.

Though citizens' groups in every American city expressed concern about these wayward youngsters, people were unsure of what to do about them. If caught in a crime, children over 7 and under 14 faced prosecution in the adult criminal justice system and often ended up in adult prisons. Many people questioned the wisdom of this result. Through contact with older criminals, children learned to perfect their skills at robbery, mayhem, and murder. Also, then as now, adults in prison regularly abused younger and weaker inmates.

House of Refuge

Early in the 19th century, American cities began to provide alternatives to adult prisons for children. In 1824, using *parens patriae* as its rationale, the New York City government established the New York House of Refuge for abandoned, deprived, and criminal children. Other state and local governments soon followed suit. These institutions, which came to be known as reform schools, opened in almost every large urban center.

The reform schools tried to break youngsters' bad habits by a combination of religion, education, and hard work. Run by private organizations, many schools, however, began to operate not for reform, but for profit. They glossed over moral and practical education. As headmasters pressed for greater productivity, children spent more time in workshops and less in classrooms.

As living conditions deteriorated, many young people rebelled. In 1859, 15-year-old Dan Crean set fire to the Massachusetts Reform School. Two years later, in another part of the state, angry girls burned their school to the ground. Reform schools, like prisons before them, came to be known as "universities of crime."

Stuck in the System

Once in these schools, students could not easily get out. In 1838, for example, a court committed Mary Ann Crouse to the Philadelphia House of Refuge because her mother complained about her behavior. By the time her father found out, Mary Ann was already locked up. When the House of Refuge refused to release her to his custody, Mr. Crouse began a legal battle to get his daughter back.

His battle eventually took him to the Supreme Court of Pennsylvania. He argued that the House of Refuge had violated his daughter's constitutional rights. Mary Ann had been locked up without a jury trial, a right guaranteed to all Americans.

After lengthy deliberation, the court ruled in favor of the House of Refuge. The court stated that the right to a trial by jury did not apply to juveniles taken to the House of Refuge. It only applied to people accused of crimes. Since Mary Ann was not accused of any crime, she had no right to a jury trial.

According to the court, Mary Ann was institutionalized not because of criminal guilt, but because her mother no longer wanted to take responsibility for her upbringing. Citing the doctrine of *parens patriae*, the court declared that the state, in this instance represented by the House of Refuge, had every right to assume the parental role. As the court concluded, Mary Ann "had been snatched from a course which must have ended in confirmed depravity, and not only is the restraint of her person lawful, but it would be an act of cruelty to release her from it." (*Ex Parte Crouse*, 1838.)

For Discussion

1. What is the doctrine of parens patriae? Do you think it has validity today? Why or why not?

2. At what age do you think children should be held criminally responsible for their actions?

3. What were the negative effects of placing juveniles in the adult criminal system?

4. What arguments can you think of against keeping Mary Ann in the House of Refuge?

From Criminal to Delinquent: A Time for Reform

American cities didn't rely entirely on reform schools to cope with young people in trouble. During the latter half of the 19th century, other innovative ideas developed as well.

Because contact between juveniles and adult criminals was seen as a major problem, many states began setting aside special times for juvenile trials, keeping juvenile records separate from adults, and sentencing juveniles to age-segregated prisons.

Massachusetts began experimenting with probation as an alternative to imprisonment. But probation presented problems when applied to young urban criminals. Sending them back to their communities usually meant returning them to an environment that was the root of their problems. If a juvenile's family couldn't provide a good home, the courts sometimes tried to identify a relative or family friend to take responsibility for the child's probation.

This led to the development of another innovation: the foster family. Recognizing that reform schools or problem families could cause more harm than good, government officials compiled lists of trustworthy families and individuals who could provide temporary care for children in trouble. Abandoned or neglected children were also placed in foster homes.

Though each of the experiments in juvenile reform was successful to some degree, by the 1890s, it became obvious that more inventive methods were needed.

The situation in Chicago was especially bad. Vice and crime plagued the Chicago Reform School. Judges preferred to send all but the most hardened juvenile offenders to the adult jail. They felt the jail was safer. The school's reputation was so bad that when it burned down in 1871, the government refused to provide money to rebuild it. This left Chicago, one of the nation's largest cities,

At New York's Randall Island Reformatory about 1900, young men work in a shoe workshop.

with no system for handling neglected or criminal young people.

The Chicago Women's Club stepped in to fill the gap. It set up a school for young people serving time in the city's jails. It opened a city police station for women and children arrestees so they wouldn't have to mingle with hardened male criminals.

Working with juveniles made club members come to some radical conclusions. Members felt that placing juveniles in the adult criminal justice system made matters worse. Why not start over and build a separate justice system, just for juveniles, based on principles related to the needs and problems of children?

In the first place, club members believed that no rational adult could hold children responsible for their actions. Wayward, disobedient, and criminal behaviors, they believed, were diseases caused by poverty and neglect, circumstances over which a child had no control. One might as logically blame children for catching the measles as blame them for running away from troubles at home or following bad examples set by friends.

Secondly, the concept of crime—specific prohibited acts—was too limited to help children. Certainly, young people must be prevented from robbing, raping, and murdering. But they also must be protected from other, less well-defined actions, like associating with immoral people, staying out too late at night, or disobeying authority. These actions greatly damaged young people by encouraging bad habits and leading to more destructive behavior.

Furthermore, it was unfair to label children as criminals. A new word for wrongdoers was needed. The word "delinquent" seemed much more appropriate. The Women's Club also decided that children convicted of crimes should not be punished. Instead, young persons who committed delinquent acts should be re-educated and rehabilitated so they would not repeat their offenses.

Moreover, young persons should not necessarily undergo the same rehabilitation programs. Some children would best benefit from the harsh life of reform school. Others would do better in the gentler care of foster parents. Still others could be returned to their families on probation. Each child should receive **individualized treatment**.

Finally, since no one was being punished, there was no need for the carefully regulated trial process of the adult courtroom. That process tended to intimidate children and might hinder rather than help, the Women's Club reasoned. To consider each child's best interests and deliver the personalized justice demanded by this new system, a judge needed more freedom than adult procedures permitted. Judges hearing juvenile cases should work in informal rooms, more like counseling offices than courtrooms. Questioning and decision making should also be flexible and informal. Only in such a non-adversarial atmosphere could judges determine appropriate ways to help young people in trouble.

When the Women's Club first raised these ideas in 1892, its own lawyers argued that the system was unconstitutional. Not only did it reverse or suspend the basic principles of American justice, it stripped the accused young persons of their rights. Club members retorted that children needed help, not rights.

In spite of the initial negative response, the Women's Club proposal was widely discussed. In 1898, the Illinois State Board of Charities asked the Chicago Bar Association to draft legislation based on the club's plan. After hearings, the Illinois legislature passed the Juvenile Court Act. The nation's first juvenile court officially opened its doors on July 1, 1899.

Other states responded enthusiastically to this new system. Within 25 years, all but Maine and Wyoming had passed laws based on the Illinois model. Over the years, court decisions and administrative policies have slightly modified the juvenile justice system. But the current juvenile justice systems throughout the United States owe their roots to that first Chicago experiment.

For Discussion

1. Do you agree with the reasoning advanced by reformers in the Chicago Women's Club? Why or why not?

2. Are young people incapable of forming criminal intent? Should they be treated rather than punished when they harm others?

3. Should young people who commit crimes be treated differently from adults? Explain.

Class Activity: Same or Different?

Should juveniles be treated the same as adults? In this activity, students evaluate situations to determine whether the juvenile and adult in each case should be treated the same or differently.

1. Divide into small groups.

2. Each group should:

   a. Examine each of the four pairs of cases listed below. In each, after considering the individuals' intent and responsibility, decide whether the juvenile and adult should receive the same treatment or punishment.

   b. Be prepared to explain the reasons for each decision.

3. After the groups decide all the cases, they should present their findings to the class and compare their decisions with those made by other groups. Conclude the activity with a discussion using the Debriefing Questions, below.

Case 1

- Jerry, 27, lives in an adult apartment complex. One of his neighbors regularly holds loud parties lasting long into the night. After a frustrating confrontation late one evening, Jerry picks up a rock and throws it through his neighbor's window.

- A neighbor chases Harold, 10, and his friends from her yard and warns them not to play baseball on her property. In retaliation, Harold throws a rock through her window.

Case 2

- Cynthia, 35, finds out that her husband is leaving her. At the height of an argument, she kills him.

- Mike, 8, is furious with his 4-year-old sister for ruining his favorite toy. He picks up his father's shotgun and kills her.

Case 3

- When the store clerk's back is turned, Connie, 23, slides an expensive scarf into her purse and walks out of the store. Apprehended by store detectives on the sidewalk, she complains that she was tired of paying exorbitant prices for everything.

- Nancy, 14, steals a digital watch from a department store display. Her only excuse, when she's caught, is that her friends dared her to do it.

Case 4

- Jim, 39, makes obscene phone calls to women in his neighborhood. He enjoys their confused and helpless reaction and likes to give them a good scare.

- Andy, 15, makes an obscene phone call to one of his teachers. He wants to see how she will react.

Debriefing Questions

1. Which cases were the most difficult to decide? Why?

2. Do you think the criminal justice system should treat children differently from adults? If so, at what age should they be treated the same as adults?

Different Worlds

Under current law, the treatment of juveniles differs greatly from that of adults. Though the specifics of treatment vary from state to state, the chart notes many common differences in the juvenile and adult systems.

Adult System	Juvenile System
Persons can be legally **arrested** if they are suspected of committing a **crime**.	Juveniles can be **taken into custody** if they are suspected of committing a **delinquent act**.
The state files formal criminal charges in the form of an **indictment, information,** or **complaint**.	The state files a **petition** with the juvenile court.
Persons may be released on **bail** or **on their own recognizance** or **may be held in jail** until trial.	Juveniles may be released into the **custody of their parents, held in custody** until an official hearing, or placed on **probation** without an official hearing.
Decisions are made by **judges** and **juries**.	Decisions are made by **hearing officers, commissioners,** and **juvenile court judges**.
A **trial** determines whether or not an accused person is guilty beyond reasonable doubt of a specific crime.	An **adjudicatory hearing** determines the truth or falsity of the petition beyond a reasonable doubt.
After a **verdict of guilty**, a **sentencing hearing** is held to determine the sentence.	After a **finding of delinquency**, a **dispositional hearing** determines if the juvenile is in need of state supervision or care.
A convicted person may be placed on **probation, fined,** or sentenced to a specified length of confinement in a **jail** or **prison**.	Juveniles judged in need of care are made **wards of the court**. They may be placed on **probation**, placed in a group or individual **foster home, fined**, or committed to an unspecified length of confinement in a **reform school, state institution,** or **camp**.
Before the end of a prison term, a prisoner may be released and put on **parole**.	After release from confinement, juveniles may be supervised in a program of **aftercare**.
Proceedings and records are **public**.	Proceedings and records are kept **private**.
The main goal is **punishment**.	The main goal is **rehabilitation**.

For Discussion

1. Which differences seem to be merely words? If some differences are just words, does it make any sense to use different words? Why or why not?

2. What are the major differences between the two systems? Try to explain some of these important differences in light of the early 20th-century reforms. In your opinion are these differences justified? Explain.

CHAPTER 18
The Problem of Delinquency

What Is Delinquency?

The definition of delinquency varies greatly from state to state. Specific acts and behaviors are often classified as delinquent for two general reasons. Such actions either:

1. would be termed criminal if committed by an adult, or

2. are thought harmful to young people because they might be dangerous or lead to criminal behavior. (These are often called **status offenses** because they only apply to those who have the status of juveniles.)

Status offenses cover a wide variety of behaviors—running away from home, drinking alcohol, skipping school, disobeying parents, violating curfews, etc. Some states classify youth who exhibit these behaviors as "wayward" or "incorrigible." Others term status offenders as CHINS, PINS, or MINS—children, persons, or minors in need of supervision. Other states simply lump all the behaviors together as delinquent.

Since states must define status offenses, the laws can be quite broad and even vague. California's old section 601 of its Welfare and Institutions Code was a good example:

Any person under the age of 18 years who persistently or habitually refuses to obey the reasonable and proper orders or directions of his parents . . . or school authorities, . . . or who is habitually truant . . . or *who . . . is in danger of leading an idle, dissolute, lewd, or immoral life*, is within the jurisdiction of the juvenile court which may adjudge such person to be a ward of the court. (Emphasis added.)

California's code no longer contains the emphasized words.

An officer takes a young driver into custody.

For Discussion

1. What is delinquency?

2. What are status offenses? Do you think they should be classified as delinquent behavior?

3. Why do you think California removed the words *"who . . . is in danger of leading an idle, dissolute, lewd, or immoral life"* from its code?

Class Activity: Are You Now or Have You Ever Been?

What is delinquency? Which juveniles should be processed through the juvenile justice system? In this activity, students clarify their opinions about these issues.

1. Form small groups.

2. As a group, carefully read the list "Should It Be Classified as an Act of Delinquency?" In many states, the actions described in this list will justify a finding of delinquency when committed by persons under 18. Discuss the items using these questions:

   • Which are actually crimes?

   • Of the remainder, which do you think are harmful to young people? Why?

   • Which of the actions on the list should not, in your opinion, be classified as delinquent?

3. Have the groups report back their answers.

Should It Be Classified as an Act of Delinquency?

a. Taking a car without the owner's permission

b. Disobeying your parents

c. Cutting school

d. Going into a building you aren't supposed to be in

e. Running away from home

f. Taking something from a store without paying for it

g. Driving recklessly

h. Buying or drinking alcoholic beverages

i. Using or selling marijuana or drugs

j. Smoking cigarettes at school or in public

k. Hitting a teacher

l. Having sexual relations

m. Deliberately damaging school property

n. Getting in a fight

o. Taking something that does not belong to you

p. Staying out past midnight

Debriefing Questions

1. Which of these behaviors did most groups think were criminal? Delinquent? Neither?

2. How would you define a juvenile delinquent?

A Tour of the System

Recent statistics indicate that more than 1 million American youth pass through the juvenile justice system each year. The statistics overlook the many juveniles who never enter the system, but who are referred to social welfare agencies because of abuse, neglect, or status offenses. Although the system still takes status offenders in extreme cases, it handles at least seven times as many delinquency cases. The chart on page 233 shows what happens to those brought into the system for delinquency.

Police bring most juveniles into the system. But 14 percent are brought in by parents, school officials, and social welfare agencies.

Slightly more than one-fifth of those brought in are accused of violent crimes—murder, rape, robbery, or assault. Over half are detained for property crimes—vandalism, theft, and burglary. Almost another one-fifth are taken into custody for public-order offenses, such as obstruction of justice, disorderly conduct, weapons charges, and public intoxication. The remaining juveniles—about 10 percent—are accused of drug offenses.

At the juvenile court, an intake worker, usually a probation officer or a social worker, must decide what to do with these juveniles. The worker typically looks at the offense, the strength of the case, and the juvenile's history and needs. After consulting with a prosecutor, the worker may choose to file a petition against the juvenile. This will lead to a hearing in juvenile court.

But more than 40 percent of the juveniles are not petitioned. Of these juveniles, most are simply let go. The remainder agree to be

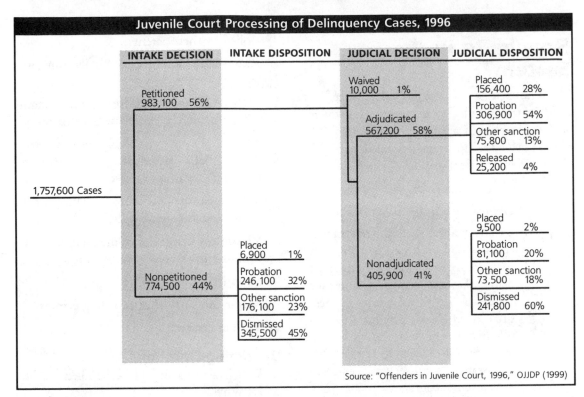

Juvenile Court Processing of Delinquency Cases, 1996

INTAKE DECISION	INTAKE DISPOSITION	JUDICIAL DECISION	JUDICIAL DISPOSITION

1,757,600 Cases

Petitioned 983,100 56%

Waived 10,000 1%

Adjudicated 567,200 58%
- Placed 156,400 28%
- Probation 306,900 54%
- Other sanction 75,800 13%
- Released 25,200 4%

Nonpetitioned 774,500 44%
- Placed 6,900 1%
- Probation 246,100 32%
- Other sanction 176,100 23%
- Dismissed 345,500 45%

Nonadjudicated 405,900 41%
- Placed 9,500 2%
- Probation 81,100 20%
- Other sanction 73,500 18%
- Dismissed 241,800 60%

Source: "Offenders in Juvenile Court, 1996," OJJDP (1999)

informally processed in the system, often with the understanding that if they break the agreement, a petition will be filed. About one-third of those not petitioned are put on probation. The remainder pay fines or restitution, or are referred to social agencies.

Those petitioned must appear at initial hearings. At these hearings, juvenile court judges examine the petitions. They decide to hold adjudicatory hearings for about 60 percent of the petitions. Of the cases not heard, a tiny percentage are waived to adult court. These cases represent the most serious offenders. Most juveniles not having adjudicatory hearings, however, are released. The rest are handled informally. About one-fifth are put on probation. And most others are referred to social agencies.

Finally, what happens to those having adjudicatory hearings? A very small percentage are released or referred to social agencies. Most receive probation. Fewer than one-third are placed out of their homes into foster homes, group homes, or secure facilities.

As you can see on the chart, many juveniles are put outside the system, or diverted, at each stage. Of the original juveniles taken into custody, fewer than 10 percent wind up placed outside their homes. The juvenile court system relies on decision makers at each stage to act "in the best interests of the child." Each of these decision makers—from the police officer to the intake worker to the juvenile court judge—is given wide discretion in resolving delinquency problems. The system encourages these decision makers to resolve the problems informally, if possible, instead of sending a juvenile deeper into the system.

For Discussion

1. How do police officers, intake workers, and juvenile court judges exercise discretion in the juvenile justice system? Give some examples. What are some advantages and disadvantages of this discretion? Explain.

2. Why do you think juvenile justice officials prefer to resolve delinquency problems informally? What are the advantages and disadvantages?

3. Look at the chart. At what stage do juveniles have the best chance of getting their cases dismissed? At what stage do they have the worst chance? How do you account for this?

Class Activity: Who Should Be in the System?

Who belongs in the juvenile justice system? In this activity, students evaluate which, if any, government agency should be responsible for juveniles in different situations.

1. Break into pairs.

2. Each pair should:

   a. Discuss each of the situations below.

   b. Decide which, if any, government agency should be responsible for *juveniles* in the situations described below. (Do *not* answer what agency should deal with the adults in these situations.) Decide whether the juvenile in each situation should be sent to:

      - state or local service agencies,
      - juvenile courts,
      - adult criminal courts, **or**
      - no government institution (the matter should be handled privately).

   c. Write the conclusions on a sheet of paper.

3. Regroup the class and have students compare their answers. Debrief the activity using the questions below.

Situations

a. **Abuse or neglect.** Children are poorly fed or clothed, beaten, sexually molested, or denied vital medical treatment by their parents.

b. **Criminal influence.** Children are exposed to or taught illegal behavior (e.g., drug abuse, criminal acts) by their parents.

c. **Economic hardship.** Children have parents who cannot afford to take care of them.

d. **Unconventional homes.** Children have parents who live according to moral standards different from those of the general community (e.g., unmarried or homosexual parents, those with unusual religious beliefs).

e. **Ungovernability.** Children cannot be controlled by their parents.

f. **Runaways.** Children habitually run away from home.

g. **Status offenses.** Children commit status offenses, such as curfew violations or truancy.

h. **Abuse of intoxicating substances.** Children use drugs or alcohol.

i. **Misdemeanors.** Children loiter, joy-ride, make obscene phone calls, etc.

j. **Victimless crimes.** Children commit victimless crimes such as prostitution.

k. **Shoplifting.**

l. **Major theft or other property crimes.**

m. **Violent crimes.**

Debriefing Questions

1. Which actions should be handled privately? Why?

2. Which actions deserve court involvement? Why? How do you determine whether juvenile or adult criminal courts should handle the matters?

3. Which actions should be handled by social service agencies? Why?

4. Which situations do most people agree about? Which cause the most disagreement? Why?

Initial Detention of Juveniles

When first taken into custody, juveniles go to a detention center, often called juvenile hall. Unlike adults, juveniles may be held in custody until their hearings without any chance of bail. At the option of a probation officer, they may be released into their parents' custody before the hearing. If the probation officer decides to keep a juvenile in custody, a judge reviews this decision, usually within 48 hours.

In some jurisdictions, most juveniles spend at least one day in custody. From 1986 to

NAME OF MINOR _____ PFN _____ ADMIT DATE _____
                                                        ADMIT TIME _____
MOST SERIOUS INSTANT OFFENSE_____ ARREST TIME_____

INSTRUCTIONS: Score minor for each factor below and enter the appropriate score in spaces provided in the right hand column.

FACTOR   *SCORE*

1. MOST SERIOUS INSTANT OFFENSE (Score one charge only)
   Serious Violent Offenses
      WIC 707(b) offenses 10
      Other listed violent offenses 7
   Narcotics/Weapons Offenses
      Possession of firearms 10
      Sale of narcotics/drugs 7
      Possession of narcotics/drugs for sale 6
      Felony possession of narcotics/drugs 5
      Misdemeanor possession of narcotics/drugs 3
   Property Offenses
      Felonies 5
      Misdemeanors...3
   All Other Crimes or Probation Violations 0   _____

2. NUMBER OF PRIOR ARRESTS, LAST 12 MONTHS
   Prior felony arrest within the last 7 days 5
   6 or more total arrests, last 12 months 3
   4 to 5 total arrests, last 12 months 2
   1 to 3 total arrests, last 12 months 1
   No arrests within the last 12 months 0   _____

3. PROBATION/PETITION STATUS
   Active cases (select only one score)
      With petition now pending 6
      With last adjudication within 90 days 4
      With last adjudication more than 90 days ago.........................2
   Not an active case..0   _____

4. SPECIAL DETENTION CASES (Check whichever applies)
   Escapee_____ Failed placement_____ Transfer In _____
   Arrest Warr_____ Bench Warr_____ Court Order _____
   Other (describe) _____10
   Not Applicable..0

DETAINED RELEASE DECISION SCALE
Score 0–9 = RELEASE Score 10+ = DETAIN   *TOTAL SCORE_____*

1990, surveys were taken of pre-hearing detention in three California counties—San Francisco, Los Angeles, and Santa Clara. The surveys revealed that three-fourths of all juveniles were held more than 24 hours regardless of offense.

Aside from worsening overcrowding, such detention creates several other problems. First

of all, it's expensive. San Francisco estimated it cost more than $100 to house one juvenile per night, which amounted to more than $40,000 per year.

Second, it crowds together juveniles who shouldn't be together. In Los Angeles, juvenile hall held those awaiting their hearings. It also held juveniles who had already had their hearings and either were waiting to be placed elsewhere or were serving their time in juvenile hall itself. Serious offenders stayed alongside lesser ones.

Finally, pre-hearing detention creates risks to inmate safety. Not only do violent offenders present a threat to others, but troubled youth in detention pose a high risk of suicide.

Santa Clara, San Francisco, and Los Angeles counties decided to do something about pre-hearing detention. Obviously, they could not just release all the juveniles. Some posed a threat to the community. Others might not show up for their hearings. The counties had to find a solution that would satisfy the need for public safety. They needed a way to identify youth in custody who could be safely released.

They came up with a screening checklist for each juvenile. A copy of San Francisco's is on page 235. Probation officers score each juvenile according to this checklist. Those scoring 10 points or more are detained. Those scoring under 10 go home. But the probation officers have the right to override the score. So whether a juvenile scores over or under 10 points, a probation officer still makes the final decision on whether to detain or release the juvenile.

The checklist has thus far proved successful. A 1990 study in San Francisco showed that 94 percent of the juveniles released were not rearrested before their hearings and 100 percent showed up for the hearings. Plus the city reaped savings. In 1989, the juvenile hall averaged 123 juveniles per day. By 1990, the average had dropped to 90.

Class Activity: Detain or Release

In this activity, students role play juvenile probation officers in charge of intake at a juvenile facility in a large city.

1. Break into pairs. Each pair will determine whether juveniles remain in detention or are released to their parents.

2. Each pair should:

    • Use the "San Francisco Juvenile Detention Screening Criteria" on page 235 to help make the decisions. But regardless of the score, you make the final decision to release or detain the juvenile.

    • Review the "Six Sample Cases" on pages 237–238.

    • Score each case on a sheet of paper.

    • Make a recommendation to release or detain. If your recommendation goes against the Screening Criteria's recommendation, write an explanation for your decision. If the two of you cannot agree on a case, write down both your decisions.

3. Go over the cases with the whole class. Have students explain their decisions. Debrief the activity using the questions below.

Debriefing Questions

1. On which cases did most people agree with the screening criteria recommendation? Were there some cases that most people disagreed with its recommendation? Why?

2. Are there other criteria that you believe should be added? Some that should be changed? Why?

3. What sorts of juveniles, if any, should be held in custody before their hearings? Why?

WIC 707(b) Offenses for Screening Criteria

Murder

Arson of an inhabited building

Armed robbery

Rape

Kidnaping

Assault with a deadly weapon

Aggravated assault

Discharging a firearm in an inhabited building

Six Sample Cases

Case 1: Tom Sugino
Age: 16
Charge: Motor vehicle theft (felony)

Circumstances: Late one Thursday night, Sugino and a 19-year-old friend hot-wired an expensive sports car parked in the garage of an apartment complex where both worked as maintenance workers. They drove the car 120 miles to an ocean-side resort. The theft was discovered approximately 48 hours later when the two young men were arrested for disorderly conduct.

Previous Record: Three recorded detentions by police, all within the last 12 months, two for curfew violations, one for underage drinking. Released on summary probation, without formal adjudication, in all three instances.

Personal Background: Junior in high school—an average student with an average attendance record. Only child, father deceased, lives with mother who works nights as a waitress and his elderly grandmother. Part-time work since age 14, fired from current job because of this incident. One psychologist's report indicates normal profile. Another suggests serious emotional disturbance as a result of father's death.

Case 2: Linda Dubrensky
Age: 15
Charge: Selling narcotics (felony)

Circumstances: Dubrensky's arrest came from police undercover work at a local community college where Dubrensky, a high school junior, was not enrolled. After selling small amounts of heroin to police agents posing as students, Dubrensky volunteered to set up a major purchase for agents. In the middle of this $100,000 transaction, both Dubrensky and her 35-year-old supplier were arrested.

Previous Record: Two recorded police contacts (one for curfew violation) in the last year. One prior juvenile adjudication for possession of heroin about eight months ago. Served one month in the County Home for Girls; six months participation in a diversion program for drug abusers.

Personal Background: School records indicate a moderate rate of truancy, a bright student who does not work up to potential. No work record. Medical report indicates that Dubrensky is addicted to heroin. Family of two children, mother, stepfather. Mother works as a tax accountant, stepfather is a currently unemployed aerospace engineer; both are members of Alcoholics Anonymous.

Case 3: Martin Robinson
Age: 16
Charge: Armed robbery, first-degree murder (felonies)

Circumstances: Robinson and three other juveniles, two armed with handguns, robbed a local market. The owner, a 66-year-old woman, pulled a gun and in the following shootout, was killed. Robinson was not armed and did not shoot the woman, but he did most of the talking during the robbery. Robinson and two others, both 14, were apprehended shortly after the incident. The fourth suspect, a 15-year-old, is still at large.

Previous Record: None

Personal Background: School records indicate a high rate of truancy. Minimal work record, no steady job at time of arrest. Psychiatric report indicates severe emotional disturbance. Family of three children, mother, grandmother. The mother works as a store clerk.

Case 4: Patricia Ann Warner
Age: 15
Charge: Breaking and entering, burglary (felony)

Circumstances: Warner and her 20-year-old boyfriend broke through the back windows of a local electronics shop after neutralizing the alarm. Police on patrol detected the crime in progress. Warner was apprehended carrying two video cassette recorders to the car. Her boyfriend was picked up several blocks away attempting to escape. In the car, police found a home computer, portable stereo players, and other equipment with an estimated total value of more than $9,000.

Previous Record: Two prior detentions for questioning by police. One resulted when Warner and a 32-year-old female companion were picked up for selling dinnerware from the back of a van. Neither female had a bill of sale for the merchandise. Because of her youth, Warner was released without charge. Her companion was cited for peddling without a license, a misdemeanor. One juvenile adjudication for marijuana possession about nine months ago. Spent 10 weeks enrolled in a diversion program.

Personal Background: School records indicate a high rate of truancy; poor scholastic achievement probably caused by a minor learning disability. No work record. Psychological reports indicate emotional instability and suggest the possibility of child abuse in the Warner home. She is the oldest of four children; both parents presently are employed at blue collar jobs.

Case 5: Tom Kennedy
Age: 16
Charge: Possession of a concealed weapon (misdemeanor)

Circumstances: Kennedy, not a gang member, has to contend with two rival neighborhood gangs. Although he knows members of both and has been approached to join, he has resisted. Three days ago, a rumor circulated around the school that one gang was out to "smoke" him. Fearing for his life, Tom took his father's unloaded revolver to school the next day. He let word out through his friends that he had a gun and that "nobody had better mess with me." Hearing about Tom's threat, a security guard stopped Tom, frisked him, and called the police.

Previous Record: None.

Personal Background: School records indicate a poor student, but teachers consider him bright. No work record. Family of four children, three younger sisters. Both parents present in home. Father unemployed and has drinking problem. Mother supports family as a cashier in a supermarket.

Case 6: Roger Duncan
Age: 16
Charge: Arson (felony)

Circumstances: Roger and a 20-year-old friend set fire to an apartment building under construction in their neighborhood. Roger's mother had been served with an eviction notice earlier in the week. The landlord also owned the burned building. A neighbor saw the two boys fleeing the scene. They were taken into custody the following day.

Previous Record: Three prior detentions in the last year. One month ago was put on probation for shoplifting.

Personal Background: School records indicate a moderate rate of truancy and low scholastic achievement. No work record. Family of five children, two of whom are in jail. Mother present in home. Father's whereabouts unknown.

CHAPTER 19
Children and the Constitution

The Rights of Juveniles

*P*arens patriae, "individualized treatment," and "the best interests of the child" are the cornerstones of the juvenile justice system. Children are delinquents not criminals; they are not imprisoned; they are detained. This special treatment is often necessary and beneficial. It can also raise serious constitutional questions. What provisions of the Constitution and Bill of Rights apply to juveniles? Which do not? The Supreme Court has faced these problems many times. Consider the following landmark case.

Sorry, Wrong Number

On the evening of June 8, 1964, Mr. and Mrs. Gault of Maricopa County, Arizona, returned from work and couldn't find their 15-year-old son, Gerry. He wasn't at school. He wasn't with any of his friends. After a frantic search, they finally found out police had taken their son to the Children's Detention Home. Gerry had been arrested that afternoon for allegedly making an obscene phone call to a neighbor.

The Gaults rushed to get their son, but the Detention Home would not release him. Instead, the family was told there would be a hearing about Gerry's case the next day. On June 9, an Arizona probation officer filed a petition with the juvenile court. It stated that Gerry was a delinquent minor, but it contained no details about his alleged crime. Gerry and his parents were not told he could consult an attorney or refuse to answer questions. The offended neighbor wasn't even present at the hearing. After it was over, Gerry was sent back to the Detention Home.

When Gerry was released a few days later, his mother received a notice of another hearing on June 15. Again, the neighbor was absent.

Again, no records were kept. When it was over, the juvenile court judge committed Gerald Gault, a juvenile delinquent, to the Arizona State Industrial School until he reached age 21. In other words, Gerry received a six-year sentence. The maximum adult punishment for his alleged crime was a $50 fine and two months in jail.

The Gaults immediately filed a petition of habeas corpus on Gerry's behalf, arguing that their son had been denied his due process rights. The Arizona state courts, however, denied the petition. Because the adult and juvenile systems had different aims, explained the Arizona Supreme Court, they required different definitions of due process. If the state applied strict adult regulations to juvenile cases, it could not provide the individualized justice that was the heart of the juvenile system. Though Gerry's treatment did not meet adult due process requirements, the boy had not been treated differently from other juveniles. Arizona agencies had followed their normal procedures, and the decision to confine the boy was therefore upheld.

Unconvinced, the Gaults appealed to the U.S. Supreme Court. In 1967, the high court responded, shaking the foundation of the American juvenile justice system. A majority of five justices reversed the Arizona ruling and granted the Gaults' habeas corpus petition.

In Re Gault (1967)

Prior to *Gault*, U.S. courts had upheld the idea that young people had a right "not to liberty, but to custody." In other words, their right to protection outweighed their right to independence. In the *Gault* decision, the Supreme Court held that juveniles, just like adults, have a vested interest in not getting locked up. It makes no difference whether the jail is called a reform school, a detention home, or a prison. Any juvenile proceeding

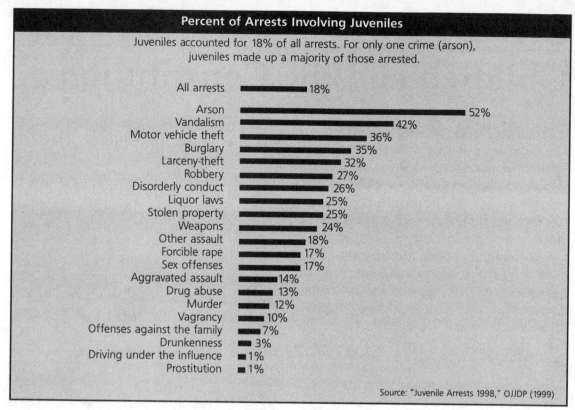

Percent of Arrests Involving Juveniles

Juveniles accounted for 18% of all arrests. For only one crime (arson), juveniles made up a majority of those arrested.

All arrests	18%
Arson	52%
Vandalism	42%
Motor vehicle theft	36%
Burglary	35%
Larceny-theft	32%
Robbery	27%
Disorderly conduct	26%
Liquor laws	25%
Stolen property	25%
Weapons	24%
Other assault	18%
Forcible rape	17%
Sex offenses	17%
Aggravated assault	14%
Drug abuse	13%
Murder	12%
Vagrancy	10%
Offenses against the family	7%
Drunkenness	3%
Driving under the influence	1%
Prostitution	1%

Source: "Juvenile Arrests 1998," OJJDP (1999)

that could lead to confinement must follow minimum standards of fairness and due process.

The majority opinion explicitly stated what some of these standards were.

1. Defendants must be informed of the charges against them. Notice of the charges is an essential element of a fair trial. Until he found himself in a hearing room, neither Gerry nor his parents knew the charges against him. The official petition, which the Gaults did not see prior to the hearing, said only that Gerry was "in need of protection of this Honorable Court." The Supreme Court was not satisfied with this general charge. Detained juveniles and their parents must be told specifically what conduct is under question and why a hearing is being held. Moreover, this information must be provided well in advance of the hearing so the accused can prepare a response.

2. All young people subject to confinement have a right to an attorney and must be informed of this right. The state must provide attorneys for those too poor to afford

legal fees. In theory, the hearing and probation officers were supposed to be looking out for the young people's best interest. But since confinement is so much like punishment, the court decided that young people needed legal counsel. Attorneys would also help young people better understand what was happening to them in the juvenile justice process.

3. Before questioning at hearings, juvenile court judges must inform young persons of their right to remain silent. In addition, if a young person refuses to answer questions, that refusal cannot be used as an indication of guilt. Under oath during the habeas corpus proceedings, Gerry's hearing officer testified that at both hearings the boy had confessed to making the offensive phone call. Also under oath, Gerry's mother, who was present at both hearings, denied this claim. She asserted that her son only confessed to dialing the phone, but that another boy had done all the talking. The Supreme Court announced that the conflicting testimony was irrelevant because neither Gerry nor his family had been informed of the boy's right to remain silent. The

Constitution protected juveniles as well as adults from self-incrimination.

4. Juveniles have the right to cross-examine their accusers. The neighbor who accused Gerry Gault never appeared at a hearing to confirm her accusation or explain why she blamed Gerry for the phone call. The Supreme Court decided that was not fair. Confronting and questioning witnesses is an important part of determining the validity of evidence.

Though it marked the first big step in asserting juveniles' rights, the *Gault* decision was also significant because of the rights it did not guarantee. The court refused to apply its due process requirements to cases where the detained juvenile was sent to a foster home or in other ways "set free." Nor did it insist that juveniles receive all the constitutional protections available to adults. *Gault* left questions about whether other constitutional issues, such as the exclusionary rule, *Miranda* warnings, and the rights to speedy, public, and jury trials, applied to juveniles.

In a series of cases in the 1970s, the Supreme Court ruled on some of these constitutional issues. But in 1984 in *Schall v. Martin*, a more conservative Supreme Court reaffirmed the basic principle of the juvenile justice system—*parens patriae*. In that case, New York authorities had charged Gregory Martin with robbery, assault, and possession of a weapon. They held him in custody until his adjudicatory hearing under the New York Family Court Act. The act allowed detaining juveniles who might commit further crimes before their hearing. In upholding this act, the court recognized that juveniles have an interest in liberty. "But," stated the court, "that interest must be qualified by the recognition that juveniles, unlike adults, are always in some form of custody. . . . They are assumed to be subject to the control of their parents, and if parental control falters, the State must play its part as *parens patriae*." In this role, the state was not punishing Martin by locking him up prior to his hearing, but, according to the court, merely acting to protect him from further wrongdoing.

For Discussion

1. Why do you think Gerry Gault's hearing officer decided that the 15-year-old was delinquent and in need of the state's protection? Do you think Gerry could be defined as delinquent? Why or why not?

2. What rights did the Supreme Court guarantee juveniles in the *Gault* decision? What rights were not guaranteed?

3. It has been said that *In Re Gault* "shook the American juvenile justice system to its foundations." How did it contradict the philosophy behind our juvenile justice system?

4. Do you agree with the court in *Schall* that locking Martin up before his hearing was not meant as punishment? Why or why not?

Class Activity: The Court Decides

In the years since Gerry Gault's release, the Supreme Court has been asked to answer some of the questions raised by the *Gault* decision. The facts and arguments of four of these important cases are noted below. In this activity, students role play Supreme Court justices and decide these cases.

1. Form courts consisting of an odd number of students (three or five is preferable).

2. Appoint one member of each court chief justice to lead the discussions.

3. Assign each court one of the Four Important Juvenile Justice Cases (pages 242–245), making sure that each case is heard by at least one court.

   Each court should:

   a. Read and discuss the facts and arguments of its case.

   b. Have the chief justice poll the justices one at a time to express an opinion on the issues of the case (majority wins).

   c. Have one representative report its decision and the reason behind it to

the class as a whole. If some members of the group disagree with the decision, have a second representative report the minority opinion.

4. Debrief the activity using the questions below.

Debriefing Questions

1. What decision did each student court reach? Compare your decisions with those made by the U.S. Supreme Court, noted in the teacher's guide.

2. What are some of the advantages of applying the reasonable-doubt standard of proof in juvenile cases? What are some of the disadvantages?

3. How might making juvenile hearings public help society? Help accused individuals? Why might this be harmful to society?

4. If you were accused of an unlawful act, would you prefer a jury trial or a delinquency hearing? Why? Would you want proceedings at your trial made public?

5. If juveniles were given jury trials, who should serve on the jury? The juvenile's peers? Adults? A mixture of both groups? Why?

6. Why should double jeopardy protection attach to juvenile hearings? Why should it not?

Four Important Juvenile Justice Cases

Case #1: A Standard of Proof
In Re Winship (1970)

Adults can be convicted of crimes only if their guilt is proved beyond a reasonable doubt. In non-criminal cases, the standard of proof is different. To win a civil suit, parties normally only have to have the greater amount of evidence—the "preponderance of evidence," as it is known. Since New York considered juvenile proceedings to be civil, its legislature passed a law stating that delinquency did not have to be proved beyond a reasonable doubt. Juvenile courts could declare a young person delinquent based on a preponderance of the evidence.

Samuel Winship was 12 years old when brought before a New York juvenile court for allegedly stealing $112 from a woman's purse. Based on a preponderance of the evidence, the judge found Samuel delinquent and committed him to a training school until he reached age 18. After state courts upheld the commitment, Samuel appealed his case to the Supreme Court.

On appeal, Samuel's attorneys argued that:

- Winship's commitment was, in effect, punishment for stealing the $112.

- Winship was being punished unfairly because his guilt had not been proved beyond a reasonable doubt.

- The reasonable-doubt standard is an integral part of due process guaranteed by the 14th Amendment.

Attorneys for the state on appeal claimed that:
- Winship's commitment was not punishment. The court made no determination about his guilt. Juvenile courts do not determine guilt because it does not fit the purpose of the juvenile justice system.

- If forced to apply the stricter reasonable-doubt standard, juvenile courts would lose their informality and personalized justice, which are why these courts exist.

- The reasonable-doubt standard comes from English common law. It is not expressly required by the Constitution or the 14th Amendment.

- Each state legislature has the right to determine the standard of proof most appropriate to its own citizens.

Issue for Decision:

Does due process as guaranteed by the Constitution and its 14th Amendment require that juvenile courts apply the reasonable-doubt standard?

Case #2: Trial By Jury
In Re Burrus (1971)

Barbara Burrus and several of her friends, ranging in age from 11 to 15, strongly disagreed with decisions made by their principal and school board in Hyde County, North Carolina. After organizing a series of demonstrations, they were arrested and turned over to juvenile authorities. If the offenders had been adults, their activities would, at most, have resulted in misdemeanor charges.

Attorneys for the young people requested that:
(1) their juvenile hearings be opened to the general public, and

(2) they be given jury trials.

The hearing officer denied the request for trial by jury and excluded the general public from the hearings. After the hearings, he declared the young people juvenile delinquents and committed them to an institution until they reached the age of majority. He then suspended all these commitments and placed all the offenders on probation.

An appeal to the North Carolina Supreme Court successfully reversed the commitments, but that court upheld the delinquency findings and ruled that a juvenile was not guaranteed trial by jury under the Constitution. Lawyers for Burrus and her friends appealed the case to the U.S. Supreme Court.

On appeal, Burrus' attorneys argued that:

- The findings of delinquency were, in effect, convictions.

- The Sixth Amendment guarantees Americans a public trial by jury prior to conviction of a criminal offense.

- Barbara and her friends experienced precisely the kind of treatment the Sixth Amendment guarantee of a public jury trial was meant to prohibit. The young people were convicted and sentenced for activities that were at heart political. Had the case been heard in public before a jury, this abuse of judicial power probably would not have occurred.

Opposing attorneys on appeal argued that:
- The findings of delinquency were not convictions and that the young people were never accused of crimes. Such accusations do not fit the spirit of juvenile justice.

- The Sixth Amendment mandates a jury trial only in criminal prosecutions. Trial by jury therefore was not required by the Constitution.

- Requiring that states give juveniles jury trials would turn such proceedings into an adversary process. This would result in delays and formalities which contradict the juvenile system's idealistic goals.

- Privacy in juvenile proceedings protect the reputations of the young people involved.

- The issue of whether to give people public or jury trials should be decided by the individual states.

Issue for Decision:

Under the Sixth Amendment of the Constitution, are juveniles entitled to a public, jury trial in juvenile court?

Case #3: Trial By Jury
McKeiver v. Pennsylvania (1971)

McKeiver, 15, had never been in trouble before. He joined a group of about 25 young friends as they chased three younger teenagers down the street. When the group caught up with their victims, they threatened the youngsters and took 25 cents from one boy. McKeiver and a 16-year-old friend were caught and charged with theft and assault. Both boys requested to have their cases tried by a jury, and in each instance, the request was denied. At their juvenile hearings, both teenagers were found to be delinquent. McKeiver was put on probation. His friend was committed to an institution. Ultimately, the case was appealed to the Supreme Court.

On appeal, McKeiver's attorneys claimed that:

- The State of Pennsylvania had interfered with both defendants' rights under the Sixth and 14th amendments by denying them trials by jury.

- Juvenile court proceedings are so similar to criminal trials that defendants' due process rights must be protected.

- Trial by jury is one of the most fundamental of all American due process rights.

- If accused of McKeiver's alleged offense, an adult would have been given a jury trial. It was unfair to discriminate against McKeiver and his friend merely on the basis of their ages.

Attorneys for the state of Pennsylvania on appeal argued that:

- The Constitution only mandates trials by jury in criminal cases.

- No matter how many similar features the two processes share, a juvenile proceeding is not a criminal prosecution. A juvenile hearing differs both in philosophy and in practice from a criminal prosecution.

- A judge or hearing officer is just as competent to determine facts as a jury would be.

- Giving juveniles jury trials would destroy the system's design as a protective mechanism for handling young people in trouble. Government studies have recommended against using jury trials for juveniles.

- Each state should be allowed to decide whether it wishes to extend the right to a jury trial to young people in its own jurisdiction.

Issue for Decision:

Under the Sixth and 14th amendments to the Constitution, are juveniles entitled to a jury trial in juvenile court?

Case #4: Protection Against Double Jeopardy
Breed v. Jones (1975)

The Fifth Amendment states that no person shall "be subject for the same offense to be twice put in jeopardy . . . ." Simply put, this means that no person can be tried twice for the same crime.

But there are instances where defendants are put on trial twice, which are not considered double jeopardy. Consider the following examples:

- A jury is unable to reach a verdict in George's murder trial. The judge declares a mistrial. George may be tried again.

- George is found guilty of murder. On appeal, an appellate court overturns his conviction because the prosecution introduced illegally obtained evidence at the trial. George may be retried without the illegal evidence.

But the following are clear examples of double jeopardy:

- State X tries George for murder. A jury finds him not guilty. State X may not try George again for the same murder.

- State X tries George for murder. A jury finds him guilty and sentences him to 20 years in prison. State X may not try George again for the same murder when he gets out of prison.

Jones, 17, allegedly committed an armed robbery. Taken to Los Angeles County Juvenile Court, he was detained until a petition against him was heard. At the adjudicatory hearing, two prosecution witnesses testified and Jones testified in his own defense. The juvenile court judge found him delinquent. At the dispositional hearing two weeks later, the juvenile court judge found that Jones did not belong in the juvenile system. The judge ruled that Jones should be tried as an adult. Over objections by Jones' attorney that Jones had already been

tried, Jones was transferred for trial. In adult court, he was tried, convicted, and sentenced for armed robbery.

On appeal, Jones' attorneys claimed that:

- Because Jones had already been tried in juvenile court for armed robbery, his trial in adult court violated his right against double jeopardy guaranteed by the Fifth Amendment.

- Juvenile court hearings are essentially criminal hearings. They determine whether the juvenile committed an offense and they may take away the juvenile's liberty.

- Applying double jeopardy protection to juvenile court proceedings will help adjudicatory hearings. Juveniles will be more cooperative if they know what they say will not be held against them in adult court.

- If juveniles are to be transferred to adult court, this must be done before any adjudication in juvenile court.

Attorneys for the state of California on appeal argued that:

- The Constitution only protects against double jeopardy in criminal prosecutions.

- Juvenile court hearings are not criminal proceedings. The juvenile system tries to rehabilitate delinquents. All the court did was determine that Jones did not belong in the juvenile system.

- Even if double jeopardy applies to juvenile proceedings, the adult court proceedings were merely part of the same process as the juvenile court proceedings. Jones was only going to be punished once for his offense. Therefore his trial in adult court did not amount to double jeopardy.

- Juvenile court proceedings are informal and need to be flexible to best treat juveniles' interests.

Issue for Decision:

Under the Fifth and 14th amendments to the Constitution, does an adjudicatory hearing in juvenile court and a subsequent trial in adult court for the same offense amount to double jeopardy?

School Searches

Does the Fourth Amendment Protect High School Students From Searches by School Officials?

Since its *Gault* decision, the Supreme Court has ruled several times on the rights of juveniles. It has held that the Fourth Amendment applies to juveniles as well as adults. But does it apply to students in school? Does it restrict searches by school officials? Or are these officials merely filling a parental role and, acting as parents, can they conduct searches without restrictions from the Fourth Amendment? In *New Jersey v. T.L.O.* (1985), the court decided how the Fourth Amendment applied to high school students.

In this case, a high school teacher caught T.L.O. smoking in the girl's bathroom. (The court used the student's initials in accordance with New Jersey's practice for juveniles.) When taken to the vice principal, T.L.O. denied smoking. The vice principal took T.L.O.'s purse and searched it. Finding cigarettes and rolling paper, he kept searching. He found marijuana, plastic bags, a roll of dollar bills, and a customer list. So he called the police.

Charged with possession of marijuana with intent to sell, T.L.O. was found delinquent by a juvenile court. T.L.O. appealed the finding, arguing that the search of her purse violated her Fourth Amendment rights. The case ultimately went to the U.S. Supreme Court.

The state of New Jersey argued that the Fourth Amendment only applied to police searches, not to searches by school officials. The Supreme Court rejected this argument. The amendment covered searches by all government officials.

The court similarly rejected New Jersey's claim that because school officials must closely supervise students, students have no reasonable expectation of privacy "in articles of personal property 'unnecessarily' carried into a school." The court stated that students routinely bring legitimate personal items to school—keys, money, pictures, diaries—and there is no reason to deny students an expectation of privacy in these items.

But the court also recognized that schools need to maintain discipline. To determine whether the search was reasonable and constitutional, the court balanced the student's expectation of privacy against the school's need for discipline. In doing so, it made two important decisions about school searches:

- **School officials do not need warrants.** Requiring warrants would disrupt the informal discipline procedures necessary to run a school. All the members of the court agreed with this conclusion.

- **School officials do not need probable cause.** All searches, whether with or without a warrant, traditionally require probable cause. Probable cause means that the facts leading up to the search must be strong enough that an independent, cautious person would have good reason to believe that the person committed a crime (or school infraction). Again, because of the school setting, the court felt school officials needed a lesser standard. The court settled on "reasonableness" as the new standard for school searches. Two justices dissented from the court's decision to abandon the traditional, well-defined probable cause standard.

Since T.L.O. had denied the teacher's accusation of smoking, the court found it reasonable for the vice principal to search her purse for cigarettes. Once he found the rolling paper, the court believed it was reasonable for him to continue searching the purse. So the court found the search constitutional. The dissenters believed that the principal had probable cause to search the purse for cigarettes, but once finding them, had no probable cause to continue rummaging through her purse.

For Discussion

1. Do you think school officials should have probable cause to conduct a search? Or do you think the new reasonableness standard is better suited for schools? Explain.

2. What effects might this decision have on schools and students?

CHAPTER 20

Juvenile Corrections

Options for Placing Juvenile Offenders

After finding juveniles delinquent, juvenile court judges must decide what to do with the young offenders. This is called making a disposition. As with adult court judges, they have a number of options. Judges try to choose the option that has the best chance of rehabilitating the particular delinquent youth. Depending on the jurisdiction, judges must choose among:

- **Juvenile detention centers.** These are facilities where juveniles are first brought. Many await their hearing here. Others await placement following disposition. But juveniles may also be confined in these centers, usually for short terms, following a finding of delinquency.

- **Training schools.** Often located in rural settings, these large, state-run institutions typically hold from 100 to 1,000 juveniles. They are meant for the most serious offenders.

- **Small, secure residential facilities.** Holding only 10 to 15 juveniles and an equal number of staff, these facilities confine serious, violent offenders. They may be run by the state, but often small non-profit groups operate them.

- **Camps and ranches.** Located in rural areas, these secure facilities normally accommodate about 100 juveniles. They emphasize discipline and school work. Most offer counseling.

- **Boot camps.** Run like Army basic training, these camps subject juveniles to shaven heads, physical training, and strict discipline. Known as shock incarceration, boot camps take juveniles for short terms and try to shock them into changing their behavior.

- **Wilderness programs.** In rigorous outdoor settings, these programs try to build self-esteem and teamwork in troubled youth.

- **Group homes.** Often called halfway houses, these facilities typically house about 20 young people. Juveniles living in these homes often attend school, hold jobs, and move about the community. But they must obey house rules. Most group homes also provide counseling.

- **Substance-abuse treatment centers.** These residences focus on treating drug and alcohol abuse. Like halfway houses, they normally hold about 20 juveniles. But these facilities often limit residents' contact with the community during treatment.

- **Foster homes.** Screened by the state, families take juveniles into their homes. States set standards about food, clothing, and other treatment, and they limit the number of children a foster family may care for. In return, foster families receive a certain amount of money for each child's upkeep.

- **In-home placement.** Under this disposition, juveniles return to their homes.

When judges choose in-home placement or foster homes, they may have several more options to choose from:

- **Diversion to day treatment programs.** These programs differ greatly. Some are all day, every day. Others meet after school or on weekends. Some replace school. Others teach about the legal system or the effects of substance abuse. Others provide supervised recreational activities. Juveniles diverted to these programs must attend for a specific length of time.

- **Intensive or highly intensive probation.** Working with few juveniles, probation officers meet often with them. In intensive probation, they meet every day. In highly

Offense Profile of Juveniles in Residential Placements (by most serious offense)

Person 33%

Property 30%

Public Order 21%

Drug 9%

Status 7%

Person offenses include murder, rape, robbery, assault, etc.

Property offenses include burglary, theft, arson, etc.

Drug offenses include trafficking and possession.

Public order offenses include weapon, alcohol, and other offenses.

Status offenses include running away, truancy, curfew, underage drinking, etc.

Source: *Juvenile Offenders and Victims: 1999, National Report,* OJJDP (1999)

intensive probation, they meet several times a day.

- **Probation.** Juveniles are released under fairly strict conditions. They may, for example, be required to:

  - report often to a probation officer,
  - stop associating with certain friends,
  - submit to home or body searches on request, and
  - take a weekly urine test (if they have been detained on a drug charge).

Juveniles who break the terms of their probation can be returned to court for an alternative disposition.

- **Summary probation.** After assuring the authorities that they will not misbehave, juveniles are released under parental or adult supervision. If they break their promise, the juveniles return to court for stricter treatment and supervision.

Which Options Do Judges Choose?

In most jurisdictions, judges do not have this vast array of choices. Thus they frequently either place juveniles on probation or send them to secure facilities, usually juvenile detention centers or training schools. Community placements and intensive probation are often not available.

Their unavailability is ironic. The juvenile justice system has always encouraged community-based treatments for young people in trouble. Such programs can often more easily adapt to the needs of individual juveniles than institutional programs. But in the late 1970s, a public backlash against community programs arose after juvenile court judges began assigning violent offenders to programs designed for non-violent offenders. Today, many communities have mixed attitudes about both the safety and the effectiveness of rehabilitating delinquents in non-institutional settings.

This backlash arose at the same time that the rate of juvenile violent crime started declining. From 1980 to 1986 the rate of violent victimizations per 100,000 juveniles fell from about 3,200 to 2,500. The relative number of juveniles in society declined during this same period. But the victimization rate starting rising again dramatically. It soared to about 4,200 in 1993. Then it started dropping sharply. By 1997, it had almost reached 2,500 again even though the number of juveniles was increasing. It had started increasing in the 1990s and is projected to continue rising. By 2007, the number of 15-, 16-, and 17-year-olds will reach the same level as in the mid-1970s. This is the age group accounting for two-thirds of all juvenile arrests. Many had predicted the volume of juvenile crime would climb sharply. Thus far it hasn't occurred.

States have reacted with different programs to treat juvenile offenders. The urge to get tough on young lawbreakers has taken control in many states. Responding to public demand, legislators have written statutes curbing judges' discretion in sentencing and mandating long periods of detention. They have turned away from the traditional model of rehabilitation to one of punishment. Other states, keeping rehabilitation as a model, have tried to institute more community programs. The states of California and Massachusetts illustrate two diametrically opposed approaches.

Locking Them Up in California

California has 10 percent of the juvenile population in the United States. Yet it houses about 20 percent of all the juveniles in custody in the United States. This high percentage reflects California's get-tough-on-crime policy of the 1980s and 1990s. The state built more prisons, sentenced prisoners to longer sentences, and limited criminal defendants' rights. This policy also resulted in more juveniles in secure facilities for longer periods.

The California Youth Authority takes charge of the most serious youth offenders in California. It runs 11 large institutions, which average 600 beds each, but which are alarmingly overcrowded. These institutions serve as the places of last resort for serious juvenile offenders. Once locked up by the Youth Authority, offenders often serve far more time than adults convicted of similar offenses in California.

The Youth Authority's institutions share the problems of all large training schools. Violence threatens juveniles and officials alike. Gang culture predominates. Drugs somehow make their way in. Suicides occur. The most that can be said of them is that they keep offenders off the streets. Although almost all training schools make efforts at rehabilitation, these efforts usually fail in such an atmosphere. In fact, 70 percent of the juveniles released from the California Youth Authority are rearrested within one year; 85 percent are rearrested within five years.

Putting Them in the Community in Massachusetts

Jerome Miller became director of Massachusetts' Department of Youth Services in 1970. At first, he tried to reform the large training schools that held most of Massachusetts' juvenile detainees. He wanted the schools to become centers of rehabilitation. He soon gave up. In 1972, he instituted

one of the most radical reforms in the history of juvenile corrections: He closed down all the training schools in the state.

Taking the money saved from closing the expensive-to-run training schools, he invested it in small, secure units for the most dangerous offenders. These sites sheltered no more than 15 juveniles each. While costing even more to run per juvenile than the training schools, they cost less overall because they housed fewer individuals. The remaining juveniles, he sent into community-based programs, run by non-profit agencies.

Today, long after Miller's departure, his department still operates without training schools. It assigns a caseworker for each juvenile put in its care. The caseworker develops a treatment plan for each juvenile and oversees its implementation. Massachusetts' out-of-home placements consist of:

- 13 small secure units (for the most serious offenders)
- 16 small detention centers (for juveniles awaiting hearings)
- 30 groups homes
- 1 forestry camp
- 7 foster care agencies

The remaining juveniles under the department's supervision are at home. They either attend day treatment centers or are supervised by probation officers. Only the most serious offenders, about 10 percent of the juveniles, remain in the system for long. Placed in secure units for about a year, they move to group homes and then to highly supervised probation. If they fail at any step, they return to secure units.

Which Works Better?

Differences in geography, size, and populations make it difficult to compare California's and Massachusetts' juvenile corrections. Critics of the California Youth Authority point to its failure to isolate hard-core, violent offenders from mere repeat offenders. They claim these training schools are training grounds for crime, and its students are an overwhelmingly minority

Rates of Juveniles in Custody	
Custody rate (per 100,000 juveniles)	
National average	**368**
10 Highest States	
Louisiana	582
South Dakota	556
California	549
Wyoming	511
Connecticut	508
Georgia	480
Nevada	460
South Carolina	427
Alaska	418
Rhode Island	412
10 Lowest States	
Mississippi	218
West Virginia	200
Arkansas	198
Oklahoma	196
North Carolina	196
Massachusetts	194
New Hampshire	154
Idaho	145
Hawaii	106
Vermont	70

Source: *Juvenile Offenders and Victims: 1999 National Report,*
OJJDP (1999)

For Discussion

1. What are the benefits and costs of Massachusetts' approach to juvenile offenders? What are the benefits and costs of California's? Which do you think is most effective?

2. Which of the placement options described above sounds least effective for juvenile offenders? Why?

3. Are any of the options better suited to particular problems? Explain.

population. Critics of Massachusetts' Youth Services claim that the state is releasing dangerous juveniles back into the community where they commit more crimes.

An early study by Harvard's Center for Criminal Justice came to the startling conclusion that Massachusetts had fewer repeat offenders *before* Miller's reforms. It found programs in some parts of the state were not structured to meet the needs of the juveniles. It reported far fewer repeat offenses in other parts of the state where the programs were offering more options to juveniles.

More recent studies by the National Council on Crime and Delinquency found repeat offenses far lower since the reforms. Two studies even tried to compare California's and Massachusetts' rate of repeat offenses. They both found serious offenders passing through Massachusetts' system had a lower rate of repeat offenses than those passing through the California Youth Authority. This was true even though the average length of confinement was far shorter in Massachusetts.

Problems With Locking Up Juveniles

In May 1982, Christopher Peterman, 17, found himself in the juvenile section of the Ada County Jail in Boise, Idaho. He had been picked up because he had failed to pay $73 in traffic tickets. Instead of sending him to the juvenile detention center, authorities sent him to the jail to teach him a lesson. Housed with him were other juveniles sent over from the center because they were too violent or difficult to handle. Five of these juveniles attacked Christopher in his cell. For four-and-one-half hours, they took turns burning, gouging, and kicking him. Christopher died from his injuries.

Christopher's case is a horror story about what can happen when violent and non-violent juveniles are locked up together. Not surprisingly, the results of incarcerating non-violent juveniles with violent adults can be equally as tragic. Rape is a common occurrence. The suicide rate of young people in adult jail is *seven times* greater than those incarcerated with other juveniles. In adult institutions, young people can receive the same rough treatment meted out to adult inmates. Even if the juveniles survive physically, they are likely to carry psychological scars.

In the mid-1970s, almost 500,000 juveniles were locked up in adult jails. In 1974, Congress passed the Juvenile Justice and Delinquency Prevention Act. This law declared that no state could receive federal grants unless it separated adults from juveniles in jails. Congress amended the act in 1980 mandating that adults and juveniles be kept in completely separate facilities.

By 1997, fewer than 10,000 remained in adult jails. Almost all of them were allowed to be held under exceptions created by federal regulations to the act. Regulations permit jail confinement of juveniles convicted or awaiting trials as adult offenders. More than three-fourths of the 10,000 fit this category. The remainder fell under regulations allowing adult jails to hold alleged delinquents for six hours before and after initial court appearances until other arrangements can be made.

The 1974 act also ordered states to remove status offenders from locked facilities. In 1975, status offenders made up about 40 percent of those held in secure juvenile facilities. By 1996, fewer than 10 percent remained. Regulations to the act allow accused status offenders to be locked up for a maximum of 24 hours following their first contact with police or juvenile court. Most of the status offenders locked up probably fall under this exception.

For Discussion

1. What does the 1974 Juvenile Justice and Delinquency Prevention Act compel states to do? How is the act enforced?

2. Do you agree with the purposes of the act? Why or why not?

3. The reading mentions three regulations to the act. What are they? Do you agree with them? Explain.

At Home Plus

Sending juvenile offenders back home has serious risks. The juveniles will likely act as they always have. Why should they change? Nothing in their environment has changed. Many juveniles got in trouble in the first place because of problems with family, friends, or school. Sending them back to these problems risks further problems. Yet sending juveniles back to their homes can help juveniles deal with their problems head on. But the young people are going to need help. The following are descriptions of three innovative programs designed for young offenders at home or in foster homes.

Day Treatment Program: Associated Marine Institutes, Inc.

Based in Florida, this privately operated organization runs 48 programs in seven states. The programs focus on improving juveniles' self-esteem and respect for others by building teamwork and academic skills. Attending classes in a marine environment, juveniles learn about boating, scuba diving, and sailing. Each student receives an individual education plan and takes academic classes. Students earn points, which allow them greater privileges and advancement in the programs. Limited to fewer than 50 juveniles at any time, programs last 150 to 170 days. Students return home each night. With one staff member for every seven juveniles, staff can give individuals a lot of attention. The juveniles in the programs range in age from 14 to 18 and include moderate to serious offenders. Most have eight to 12 offenses. Most students are far below grade level in school on entering the programs. A remarkably low 21 percent of those completing the programs commit offenses again. Compared to residential care programs, these programs cost very little.

Highly Intensive Probation: KEY Outreach and Tracking Program

Begun in 1972 after Massachusetts closed its training schools, KEY contracts with the state to provide close supervision of juveniles released to their homes or to foster homes. KEY may serve as the final step in a juvenile's treatment program or it may be the only step. To start a KEY case, a caseworker meets with the juvenile and the juvenile's family, and together they draw up a behavior contract. Each caseworker only has eight juveniles to supervise and meets with each juvenile several times a day. The contacts range from mere checkups to counseling to finding jobs and community services for the juvenile. The program normally lasts 90 days. KEY costs very little compared to secure facilities.

Juvenile Alternative Work Service

At dispositional hearings, Los Angeles County judges sentence juveniles who have broken probation to short juvenile-hall time, normally about 20 days. But this disposition may be put on hold if a juvenile agrees to take part in JAWS, a county-run program. Instead of spending the 20 days in juvenile hall, the juvenile works for 20 Saturdays or Sundays on JAWS work crews. Los Angeles sends out about 25 of these crews each weekend. With about 10 to 12 members each, the crews do manual, outdoor labor, usually painting and cleaning. If the juvenile forgets to show up or acts up on the job, then the court imposes the original sentence in juvenile hall. But most are happy to take care of their sentences outside juvenile hall. And the county is pleased because it receives money from cities and school districts that contract to have the work done. The money pays for over half the cost of the program, which makes it far cheaper than sending juveniles to juvenile hall.

For Discussion

1. What are the main benefits of all these programs?

2. Which program do you think would be most effective in preventing juveniles from committing another offense? Least effective? Why? Does the program you consider least effective have any value?

Class Activity: Individual Treatment Plan

In this activity, students prepare individual treatment plans for juvenile offenders.

1. Divide the class into groups of three.

2. Members of each group role play case workers. They are assigned six cases to provide individual treatment plans (the "Six Sample Cases" on page 237–238). Each case has been found delinquent.

3. Members of each group should:

   a. Divide the cases equally among the group. (If the group has three mem-bers, then each member is responsible for two cases.)

   b. Write a treatment plan for each case using what they have learned about various dispositional options for juveniles. The treatment plan should include various placements, the length of stay in each, and what behavior would allow the juvenile to progress from one placement to another.

   c. When finished with the plans, discuss the cases with the other members and explain the reasoning behind your decisions.

4. Go over each case and compare the different approaches that members of the class proposed. Debrief the activity using the questions below.

Debriefing Questions

1. Which cases were the easiest to decide? The most difficult? Why?

2. Did you choose relatively costly or inexpensive treatment plans?

3. Which of the options you chose are available for juveniles in your area?

The Question of Waiver

- John S., 15, has been charged with murder while attempting to rob a gas station.

- Mary B., 16, has been charged with prostitution, her fifth arrest on this charge. Living by herself on and off since she was 14, she has run away from two foster homes and one halfway house.

What do these two offenders have in common? Both may be subject to waiver—transfer to the adult criminal courts. In certain cases, a motion may be filed in juvenile court asking that it waive its jurisdiction and transfer the matter to a regular adult court. If this motion is granted, the juvenile is then treated just as an adult offender would be. The issue of waiving juvenile jurisdiction with certain types of

Characteristics of Juveniles Tried as Adults	
Characteristic	Percent of all juveniles who are tried as adults
Age	
14 or younger	8
15	24
16	27
17	40
Sex	
Male	92
Female	8
Race	
White	31
Black	67
Other race	2
Offense	
Murder	11
Rape	3
Robbery	34
Assault	15
Burglary	6
Theft	8
Drug	14
Public order	3

Detail in each characteristic may not total 100% because of rounding.

Source: *Juvenile Offenders and Victims: 1999 National Report*, OJJDP (1999)

young offenders has been hotly debated in recent years.

Legal Standards for Waiver

In 1966, a year before *Gault*, the U.S. Supreme Court in *Kent v. U.S.* made a significant ruling on waiving jurisdiction to adult courts. In this case, a juvenile had confessed to serious crimes. His attorney, fearing the juvenile would be transferred to adult court, filed a motion requesting a hearing on this issue. The juvenile court judge did not rule on the motion, but simply waived jurisdiction to adult court, stating he had made a "full investigation" of the case. The Supreme Court ruled that this did not meet due process standards. The court held that juvenile courts waiving jurisdiction must hold a special hearing—often called a fitness hearing. At that hearing, the accused juvenile must be represented by an attorney who has access to all relevant court

files. In addition, the hearing officer must state the reasons for the decision in writing so that the decision can be reviewed.

The Supreme Court also issued guidelines for making waiver decisions. Before sending a young person through the adult courts, a hearing officer should consider:

1. How serious was the crime? Does the community need to be protected from the offender?

2. Was the crime committed in a violent or aggressive manner? Was it premeditated?

3. Was it a crime against persons or against property?

4. Will the adult court prosecute the case?

5. Are the co-defendants, if any, adult? If so, should all the defendants be tried together?

6. How sophisticated and mature is the juvenile? (This is to be determined by examining the youth's home life, emotional stability, and lifestyle.)

7. What is the juvenile's prior court record and history of contact with law enforcement?

8. Can the juvenile be rehabilitated through normal juvenile procedures? If so, can the public be protected during the juvenile's treatment?

Every state now has a method for treating minors as adults in certain cases. In fact, states may have a combination of methods, depending on the crime charged and the age of the juvenile. The methods fall into three categories:

Judicial Waiver. The judge, at a fitness hearing, decides whether the juvenile should be tried in adult court. For example, Alabama and Florida allow judges to waive juveniles to adult court for any offense at age 14. California sets the age at 16 for most offenses and at 14 for murder and some other serious crimes. Under judicial waiver, the judge must comply with the standards set forth in *Kent* and appeals courts may review the decision. Almost every state uses judicial waiver for certain crimes.

Prosecutorial Discretion or **Direct File.** The prosecutor decides whether to file the case in juvenile or adult court. For example, Vermont allows prosecutors to file cases in adult court for any offense at age 16. Florida allows it at age 16 for some crimes and at age 14 for murder and a few other serious crimes. Unlike judicial waiver, the prosecutor has complete discretion and the decision cannot be overturned on appeal. More than a dozen states allow prosecutorial discretion in some cases.

Legislative Exclusion. In more than half the states, the legislature mandates that certain crimes be prosecuted in adult court. For example, Arizona excludes juveniles over 15 from being tried in juvenile court if they are charged with murder, specified felonies, or any felony if they have previously been charged with a felony.

Vermont and Kansas allow juveniles to be tried as adults at the youngest age—10. More than 20 states set no minimum age. Sixteen states set the minimum age at 14. Moreover, most states have adopted the rule of "once an adult, always an adult." This means that if convicted as an adult, a juvenile will be tried as an adult for any subsequent offense.

Those who favor treating more juveniles as adults believe that juveniles who commit horrible crimes must pay for them. They also think the policy serves two other purposes—incapacitation and deterrence. The young people, they point out, will be locked up far longer in adult prisons than in juvenile facilities. (The California Youth Authority, for example, may only hold juvenile offenders until age 25.) They emphasize that those locked up will not be committing crimes. Furthermore, they believe that getting tough will deter other juveniles from committing crimes.

Many juvenile justice experts doubt that treating more juveniles as adults will reduce the crime problem. They think that putting juveniles in adult prisons means we are giving up on them. They explain that adult prisons have abandoned rehabilitation. When these inmates get out, they argue, they will be hardened criminals. Others point out that we are not just sending away violent predators. Many waiver provisions allow non-violent offenders as well as violent offenders to be tried as adults.

For Discussion

1. Do you think waiving jurisdiction of some juvenile offenders is a good idea? Why or why not?

2. If you think waiver is a good idea, what offenders should be transferred to adult courts? Should it be done through judicial waiver, prosecutorial discretion, or legislative exclusion? Explain.

3. Would you add any additional guidelines for determining judicial waiver? Describe them.

Class Activity: A Waiver Hearing

In this activity, students role play juvenile judges in a waiver hearing. Divide the class into groups of three. Each group should:

1. Take the role of a juvenile court judge in a state allowing waiver of jurisdiction when the juvenile is over 14 and accused of a felony.

2. Apply the eight general guidelines on page 253 to the "Six Sample Cases" beginning on page 237. Discuss each case.

3. Decide which (if any) of the young people should be tried as juveniles and which (if any) should be tried as adults.

4. In accordance with the Supreme Court ruling, write a statement of the reasons for your decisions.

Debriefing Questions

1. Compare your decisions with those of your classmates. Is there a general agreement about the reasons for these decisions?

2. Based on their alleged crimes, which juveniles represent the clearest threat to the community? Which are least harmful?

3. Based on prior records and personal backgrounds, which juveniles are most potentially harmful?

4. Of these two factors, crime and background, which was most important to your decisions?

5. Which of these juveniles do you think should be punished? Which could be rehabilitated? Which seem most, and least, likely to be rehabilitated by the juvenile justice system?

6. In adult court, these cases will be tried by juries unless the defendants waive their rights to a jury trial. Do you think any of these juveniles would benefit by a jury trial? Why or why not?

7. What do you think should be the youngest age that juveniles should be waived from juvenile court jurisdiction? Why?

8. Are there any circumstances under which juvenile courts should not be allowed to waive jurisdiction?

Wayne Thompson and the Death Penalty

The sixth of eight children, Wayne Thompson grew up in Chickasha, Oklahoma, a small town about 30 miles southwest of Oklahoma City. He also grew up in the shadow of his brother-in-law Charles Keene's violent rages. He saw his sister Vicky beaten by Keene. Sniffing paint, Keene often grew violent and spared no one. He beat Wayne repeatedly. He struck Wayne's mother, other sisters, and even his older brothers. Keene once even carried his infant son to the top of his trailer and threatened to drop him off.

When Vicky finally divorced Keene, the family thought their long nightmare was over. But Keene kept returning, threatening and abusing Vicky. Finally, Wayne decided to put a stop to Keene's abuse once and for all. Together with his adult, older brother Tony and two of Tony's adult friends, 15-year-old Wayne Thompson set out to kill Keene. Before dawn on January 23, 1983, they found Keene at his home in Amber, Oklahoma. They kidnaped him, beat him, cut open his stomach, chest, and throat, and shot him twice. Before heaving his body in a river, they chained it to a cement block.

Twenty-six days later, it surfaced. At the fitness hearing shortly after his arrest, Wayne was certified to stand trial as an adult. Charged with first-degree murder, he was found guilty. During the trial, the prosecution had introduced three color pictures of Keene's body. The prosecution introduced the same pictures at the sentencing hearing. The jury found the murder to have the aggravating circumstance of being "especially heinous, atrocious, or cruel." It returned a sentence of death for Wayne.

On appeal, Wayne's attorney argued that the pictures should not have been allowed into evidence at trial or at the sentencing hearing. Further, he argued that sentencing a 15-year-old boy to death violated the Eighth Amendment's ban against cruel and unusual punishment.

The Oklahoma Court of Criminal Appeals upheld the conviction. It did, however, agree with the defense on one point: The pictures should not have been allowed in evidence at the trial. But the court said this error was not sufficient to overturn Wayne's conviction because of the overwhelming evidence of his guilt.

Otherwise the court sided with the prosecution. The sentencing judge did not err in admitting the pictures because they helped prove the aggravating circumstance of the murder. The sentence did not violate the Eighth Amendment. Wayne had been certified to be tried as an adult, so he should be sentenced as an adult. Wayne's lawyer appealed to the Supreme Court.

Wayne waited on death row in a cell next to his brother. In separate trials, all three adults had also been found guilty of first-degree murder and sentenced to death. One of the men was killed in a jail-yard fight shortly after his trial. Another's conviction was reversed on appeal because of trial court error, and at his second trial, he was found not guilty.

For Discussion

1. Since the pictures could have proved several relevant facts at Wayne's trial (e.g., that Keene was dead, how he died, etc.), why do you think the appeals court ruled they should not have been allowed in evidence?

2. When a trial court's error is not important enough to overturn a conviction, it is known as "harmless error." Do you think introducing the pictures at the trial was a harmless error? Do you think the doctrine of harmless error should apply to murder trials? Explain.

3. At the time of Wayne's sentence, 13 states did not allow the death penalty. Of the remaining 37 states, 18 states set the minimum age for execution at 16. The other 19 states had not set a minimum age. Are these statistics relevant in determining whether the death penalty for juveniles under 16 is cruel and unusual punishment?

Why or why not? Is it relevant that only a few nations in the world allow such punishment?

4. Do you think that executing juveniles under 16 is cruel and unusual punishment? Explain.

Thompson v. Oklahoma (1988)

In its *Thompson v. Oklahoma* decision, the Supreme Court voted 5 to 3 to throw out Wayne's death sentence. Four of the justices in the majority thought that executing juveniles under 16 violated the Eighth Amendment. But the fifth justice in the majority, Sandra Day O'Connor, did not agree. She stated in a concurring opinion that there probably was a national consensus against executing juveniles under 16. But she voted with the majority only because Oklahoma's death penalty statute had no minimum age. Because Oklahoma may have enacted its death penalty without considering whether juveniles under 16 should be executed, she sided with the majority.

Although five justices voted to stop the execution, only four justices agreed with the opinion of the court. This made *Thompson* a "plurality opinion," which holds less weight than an opinion joined by five or more justices.

The following year, the Supreme Court considered whether juveniles under 18 could be executed. Two similar cases presented themselves to the court. One involved a 17-year-old (*Stanford v. Kentucky*) and the other a 16-year-old (*Wilkins v. Missouri*). Both had brutally murdered victims of their crimes because they wanted to leave no witnesses.

This time the Supreme Court upheld both convictions in 5-to-4 votes. The majority, including Justice O'Connor, argued that the nation had not reached a consensus against executing 16- or 17-year-olds. So executing them did not constitute cruel and unusual punishment. In a separate concurring opinion, O'Connor stated this lack of a national consensus made it irrelevant that Missouri did not have a minimum age for executions.

The four dissenting justices in an opinion by Justice Brennan made two basic arguments. First, a majority of states and the federal government banned executions of those under 18 and most juries refuse to sentence those under 18 to death. This should add up to a national consensus against executing those under 18. Second, the death penalty is too severe for juveniles—it serves neither retribution nor deterrence.

For Discussion

1. Do you agree with the Supreme Court's decision in Wayne Thompson's case? Why or why not?

2. Do you agree with its decisions in *Wilkins* and *Stanford*? Why or why not?

3. Justice O'Connor cast the crucial swing vote in all three cases. What do you think of her reasoning in these cases?

4. Wayne Thompson was not set free by the Supreme Court's decision. He will now probably serve a life sentence in prison. Many argue that a life sentence is worse than the death penalty. Do you agree? Do you think courts should be allowed to send juveniles to prison for life? Explain.

Class Activity: Should Juveniles Convicted of Murder Be Executed?

In this activity, students literally take a stand on the execution of juveniles and discuss their stand with others.

1. Have students form a single line in the room according to how they feel about this question: Should juveniles convicted of murder be executed? Make one end of the room mark the spot for those who believe the death penalty is absolutely right for juveniles convicted of murder. The other end marks the spot for those who believe the death penalty is absolutely wrong for juveniles. The stronger that people feel one way or the other, the closer they should be to the ends of the line. Those unsure of their opinion belong in the middle. In a class of 26 students, for example, the line could look like this:

absolutely wrong   absolutely right
ABCDEFGHIJKLMNOPQRSTUVWXYZ

2. While they are standing in line, ask students to pair up with a person next to them in line and share three reasons for their opinions.

3. As indicated by the diagram below, divide the line in half and move students on one half of the line so that they face students on the other half of the line. In this manner, students with strong positions (A B C, X Y Z) should be facing students with moderate positions (K L M, N O P).

A B C D E F G H I J K L M
N O P Q R S T U V W X Y Z

4. With the lines parallel, each student now faces a partner with a vastly different opinion, e.g., A-N. Partners are to exchange opinions with each other. One partner starts speaking. When the first one finishes, the other partner must paraphrase what the speaker said. If the paraphrase is not right, then the speaker should explain again until the partner gets it right. Then the other partner may speak. The partners can go back and forth, but each time they must correctly paraphrase what the other said before they respond.

Debriefing Questions

1. Did you find it difficult to paraphrase the other person's opinions? Why or why not?

2. Which reasons did you find most persuasive? Least persuasive? Why?

International Challenges to the Death Penalty

Half the states currently allow capital punishment for murderers who kill at age 16 or 17. Since 1985, nine juvenile offenders have been executed in the United States. Although all nine were 17 years old at the time of their offenses, they were well into adulthood by the time they were executed.

The nine executions account for more than half of all juvenile executions worldwide. Only six countries in the world carry out such sentences: Iran, Nigeria, Pakistan, Saudi Arabia, the United States, and Yemen. The U.N. Convention on the Rights of the Child bars both capital punishment and life imprisonment without the possibility of release for crimes committed by juveniles under 18 years of age.

Only two members of the United Nations have failed to ratify this international treaty—Somalia and the United States. Many nations are urging the United States to ratify this and other treaties against capital punishment. If the U.S. government ratified any treaty banning capital punishment, it would bind every state. Article VI of the U.S. Constitution says that all ratified treaties "shall be the supreme Law of the Land; and the judges in every state shall be bound thereby, any Thing in the Constitution or Laws of any State to the contrary Notwithstanding."

Supporters of the death penalty strongly oppose any treaty that forbids capital punishment. They view this penalty as a fitting one for murder and a sensible response to the still-high (though declining) murder rate in the United States. They see these treaties as threats to the democratic right of any state to impose capital punishment.

International Trend Against Capital Punishment

America's strong support of the death penalty contrasts with international trends. The use of the death penalty is declining around the world. In 1981, 27 countries banned

In January 2000, an Italian group protests the death penalty. In the background is the Colosseum in Rome. It is illuminated with golden light for 48 hours whenever someone in the world is spared from execution.

the death penalty. By 2000, this number had risen to 73. More than 35 other nations have severely restricted capital punishment: They either limit it to wartime crimes or have not used it for 10 years or more. The United States and 87 other countries currently still use it.

In 1998, governments in 40 countries executed slightly more than 2,000 prisoners, according to Amnesty International, an international human rights organization. More than 80 percent of these executions took place in only four countries: 1,067 in China , 66 in Iran, more than 100 in Democratic Republic of Congo, and 68 in the United States. It is believed that Iraq executed hundreds of political prisoners, but these are unconfirmed.

In May 1998, the British House of Commons voted to adopt the European Convention for the Protection of Human Rights and Fundamental Freedoms. Along with other things, this human rights declaration requires those who sign it to abolish the death penalty for all civilian crimes. Among the major European nations today, only Russia refuses to abolish its death penalty, mainly because of a severe crime problem that began after the breakup of the Soviet Union.

Regional and international declarations against the death penalty obligate nations who agree to them. Thirty-two nations have signed and ratified one of these documents—the International Covenant on Civil and Political Rights. The covenant protects fundamental rights and specifically forbids the death penalty for juvenile offenders. In 1992, the U.S. Senate ratified this covenant, but only after reserving the right to execute juvenile offenders.

Criticism of the U.S.

The United States has long championed human rights. But in 1998, the U.N. Commission on Human Rights issued a stinging report. It criticized the United States for its recent increase in death sentences and executions. It especially condemned the execution of women, mentally impaired persons, and juvenile offenders. The report denounced the United States for signing the International Covenant on Civil and Political Rights and reserving the right to execute juvenile offenders. This reservation, it stated, violated the purpose of the treaty. Also, according to the report, capital punishment in the United States is applied unfairly to disproportionate numbers of minorities and the poor who often fail to receive adequate legal representation.

U.S. officials quickly called the U.N. report inaccurate and unfair because it "fails to recognize properly our extensive safeguards and strict adherence to due process." They argued that the Commission on Human Rights should spend more of its efforts investigating countries like China, which commonly violates basic due process of law and gives those sentenced to death little, if any, time to appeal.

Capital punishment for those who commit horrible crimes as juveniles provokes strong opposing opinions. Miriam Shehane, president of Victims of Crime and Leniency, argues, "If someone does an adult crime, they are acting as adults, and they have to take responsibility." On the other side of the debate, the National Coalition to Abolish the Death Penalty contends, "When we as a society sentence a child to death . . . we surrender to the misguided notion that some children are beyond redemption."

For Discussion

1. Do you think international opinion on the death penalty should affect U.S. policy on it? Explain.

2. Why did the U.N. Commission on Human Rights denounce the United States for signing the International Covenant on Civil and Political Rights and reserving the right to execute juvenile offenders? Do you agree with its criticism? Explain.

3. The appeals process in death penalty cases averages about eight years in the United States. China sometimes executes prisoners the day after they are sentenced. Which system comes closest to your view of how death-penalty appeals should be handled? Why?

Class Activity: Senate Hearing

The United States has signed, but the U.S. Senate has never ratified, the U.N. Convention on the Rights of the Child. The treaty contains this language: "Neither capital punishment nor life imprisonment without possibility of release shall be imposed for offenses committed by persons below eighteen years of age . . . ."

In this activity, students role play a hearing of the Senate Foreign Relations Committee on ratification of the convention.

1. Divide the class into the five role groups listed below.

2. Each group should read its role and use the reading and other sources to prepare for the simulated hearing. Groups will testify before the committee and they should prepare arguments in favor of their position.

3. When ready, the chairperson should call the hearing to order and invite the individual groups to testify. The members of the committee should ask questions.

Minimum Death Penalty Ages (by American Jurisdiction)

Age 18		Age 17	Age 16	
California*	New Mexico*	Georgia*	Alabama*	Montana**
Colorado*	New York*	New Hampshire*	Arizona**	Nevada*
Connecticut*	Ohio*	North Carolina*	Arkansas**	Oklahoma*
Illinois*	Oregon*	Texas*	Delaware**	Pennsylvania**
Kansas*	Tennessee*		Florida**	South Carolina**
Maryland*	Washington*		Idaho**	
Nebraska*	Federal*		Indiana*	South Dakota**
New Jersey*			Kentucky*	Utah**
			Louisiana*	Virginia**
			Mississippi**	Wyoming*
			Missouri*	

* Express minimum age in statute

**Minimum age required by U.S. Constitution per U.S. Supreme Court in *Thompson v. Oklahoma* (1988)

Source: "Juveniles, Capital Punishment, and Sentencing," Coordinating Council on Juvenile Justice and Delinquency Prevention (1999)

4. After the testimony, the committee should discuss the arguments and then vote whether to recommend ratification by the full Senate. If ratified, the convention would become the law throughout the United States.

5. After the vote, each member should explain his or her vote.

6. Debrief the activity using the questions on this page.

Group Roles

U.N. Commission on Human Rights: The convention should be ratified, thus enabling the United States to comply with international law, which condemns sentencing juveniles to death or life in prison without possibility of release.

State of Texas: The convention should not be ratified since each state and its people should democratically decide whether or not to have capital punishment.

National Coalition to Abolish the Death Penalty: The convention should be ratified since juvenile offenders are not as responsible as adults for their criminal acts.

Victims of Crimes and Leniency: The convention should not be ratified because some juvenile offenders are so dangerous and lacking in remorse that they should be treated as adults.

Senate Foreign Relations Committee: Members should prepare questions to ask the groups appearing before them. They should also select a chairperson to run the hearing.

Debriefing Questions

1. What were the best arguments? What were the weakest?

2. Do you think the U.S. Senate should ratify this treaty? Why or why not?

Current Trends and Controversies

Over the years, reformers have focused on different issues in the juvenile justice system. During the 1960s and early 1970s, advocates pushed for due-process rights for juveniles. The U.S. Supreme Court responded with its *Gault* decision, which declared juveniles did have these rights. Subsequent court decisions and much state legislation have further defined juveniles' rights.

Beginning in the mid-1970s, reformers turned their focus on detention issues, particularly on restricting who could be in secure lockups. The Juvenile Justice and Delinquency Act of 1974 and its subsequent amendments achieved two major reforms of detention. It outlawed placing status offenders in secure detention, and it mandated separate facilities for adults and juveniles.

From the late 1970s to the present, the public in many states has called for getting tough on juvenile offenders. Some jurisdictions have resisted. Many states, however, have locked up juveniles in record numbers. Even in periods when the juvenile arrest rate for violent crimes dropped, the incarceration rate climbed. In the wake of highly publicized, violent juvenile crimes, many have called for even harsher sentences on juveniles. Princeton Professor John DiIluio once warned of a "rising wave of superpredators," caused by the growing teen population. Shay Bilchik, former head of the Office of Juvenile Justice and Delinquency Prevention, dismissed the idea of a growing number of superpredators. "For starters, only about one-half of 1 percent of juveniles ages 10 to 17 were arrested for a violent crime last year, and of all juvenile offenders, just 6 to 8 percent are serious, violent, or chronic offenders. So to talk of a generation of superpredators is not only false but unfair." Bilchik and others believe that getting tough has not and will not prevent violent crimes. They urge a return to the traditional model of rehabilitation for juvenile offenders.

The high detention rates have given rise to another controversy. Today, the overwhelming majority of juveniles in detention are minorities. Although African-Americans constitute only 15 percent of juveniles aged 10–17, they make up about 40 percent of the juveniles in custody. Only 37 percent of those in custody are white. Blacks do not commit more crimes than whites. The number of whites arrested far surpasses the number of blacks arrested. But as they make their way through the juvenile justice system, blacks tend to stay in the system and end up in custody. Whites tend to get out of the system and not be placed in custody. In fact, minority youth make up almost 70 percent of those in secure detention.

So the controversy arises: Does the juvenile justice system unfairly discriminate against minorities, particularly African-American youths?

Many experts believe that racial discrimination does not cause black youth to remain longer in the system. They point to two separate studies which have shown that black judges are more likely than white judges to keep a black juvenile in custody. They believe that social class rather than race explains why blacks stay in the system. Most of the blacks caught in the system come from poor inner-city neighborhoods. Most of the whites come from a middle-class background. If a middle-class white juvenile gets into trouble, the parents may get a lawyer and a psychologist to help. They will come to court with a plan of action. On the other hand, an inner-city juvenile may only have an overworked public defender, who probably will meet the juvenile just before the hearing. This juvenile has limited access to social services, community agencies, or psychologists. And the juvenile's neighborhood may be filled with gangs and drug traffickers. What is the best interest of each child? Given each juvenile's resources, a judge might find it better to let the middle-class juvenile stay at home and better to send the inner-city offender to a detention facility that offers some social services. So social class rather than race may explain the different treatment of whites and blacks.

Other experts disagree. They say that while class may account for some of the disparity, racism also plays a role. The juvenile justice system allows decision makers wide discretion at every stage of the juvenile justice process. Racism, they argue, can easily creep into such a system.

The Office of Juvenile Justice and Delinquency Prevention commissioned a project to examine all the existing research about race in the juvenile justice system. In 1992, the project issued a report concluding that "there is substantial support for the statement that there are race effects in operation within the

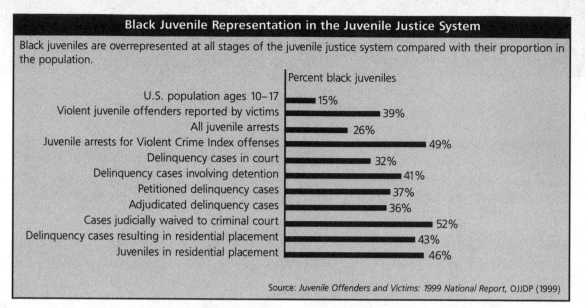

Black Juvenile Representation in the Juvenile Justice System

Black juveniles are overrepresented at all stages of the juvenile justice system compared with their proportion in the population.

Percent black juveniles

U.S. population ages 10–17	15%
Violent juvenile offenders reported by victims	39%
All juvenile arrests	26%
Juvenile arrests for Violent Crime Index offenses	49%
Delinquency cases in court	32%
Delinquency cases involving detention	41%
Petitioned delinquency cases	37%
Adjudicated delinquency cases	36%
Cases judicially waived to criminal court	52%
Delinquency cases resulting in residential placement	43%
Juveniles in residential placement	46%

Source: *Juvenile Offenders and Victims: 1999 National Report,* OJJDP (1999)

juvenile justice system, both direct and indirect in nature." By "race effects," the project meant that race explains why blacks remain in the system.

In 1989, Congress amended the Juvenile Justice and Delinquency Act. It required states to examine why so many minorities were in their lockups. States must justify any over-representation of minorities at every stage of their juvenile justice systems. In 1992, Congress further amended the act tying funding to compliance. Since then, about 40 states have started intervention and prevention programs aimed at helping youth who are at risk of engaging in crime.

One final controversy should be mentioned. It's one that has plagued the system from its beginning: What should be done with status offenders? Although status offenders have been removed from locked facilities, some still pass through the juvenile justice system along with more serious offenders. Current debate arises over whether status offenders belong in the juvenile justice system at all. Many experts believe status offenders should be treated as cases of abuse or neglect—not as offenders. They argue that the court should turn its control of status offenders over to welfare agencies, private charities, and counseling centers.

For Discussion

1. Do you think the juvenile justice system should focus on rehabilitation or punishment? Why?

2. How do you account for the great number of minority youth in detention? What do you think can be done about it? Explain.

3. Should status offenders be treated as offenders or as cases of abuse and neglect? Why?

Class Activity: What Should Be Done?

Write a brief essay either supporting or opposing the following statement: *Instead of trying to rehabilitate serious offenders, the juvenile justice system should impose longer sentences to keep them off the streets.*

Unit Six:
Solutions

Crime affects all of us. Even if we aren't touched directly, we pay extra for insurance, we worry about the safety of our family and friends, and we worry about where we can walk safely. Americans regularly list crime as one of their top concerns. Billions of dollars are lost every year to criminals, and billions more are spent in the fight against crime.

One major problem in finding solutions to crime comes from basic disagreements over its causes. Sociologists, criminologists, politicians, and ordinary citizens often debate the issue. We begin this unit with an examination of some of the debates about the causes of crime.

We then turn to an examination of the role government plays in combating crime. You have already seen examples of the direct role played by the police, prosecutors, courts, and correctional systems in dealing with criminals. We will examine our government's crucial role in determining policies to reduce crime. We will take a look at the executive, legislative, and judicial branches throughout our federal system. In our examination, we will discuss the debate over whether our criminal justice system, in its battle against crime, discriminates against minority groups.

Finally, we will address the role ordinary citizens can play in fighting crime. We will explore both negative and positive actions citizens have taken to guard their communities—from vigilante action to neighborhood watch groups. Then you will get a chance to form a citizen task force and make practical proposals for reducing crime.

The problem of crime is complex. Every theory and every proposed solution raises fundamental ethical, political, and economic questions. These questions must be squarely faced if America is to make any progress in its battle against crime.

CHAPTER 21
The Causes of Crime

Theories and Approaches

America has a serious crime problem. The rate of property crimes, such as theft and burglary, are actually on levels similar to or even below other countries. But the rate of violent crime is another matter. Statistics show that the U.S.'s rate of violent crime far surpasses that of any Western democracy. The city of New York during the 1990s cut its number of murders in half. But the city, with a population about 9 million, still had half as many murders each year as the entire nation of Italy, population 58 million. Homicide is the second leading cause of death for Americans age 15 to 30 and the leading cause of death for African Americans in that age bracket.

Looking at these statistics, doctors at the U.S. Centers for Disease Control have called violent crime an epidemic in the United States. Along with many others, they seek measures to deal with this problem. By examining the causes of crime and violence, they believe individuals, communities, and the nation can take action to stem the tide of violence in our society.

What then are the causes of crime? There is no easy answer. Some people have argued that all crime comes from inborn traits. Others have insisted that it comes from poverty, discrimination, lack of hope, or the breakdown of family values. Still others have contended that crime comes from personalities warped by drugs, disease, or childhood abuse. The list of possible causes can go on and on.

While few people today would argue crime has but one cause, people still emphasize one factor over another. And they debate whether one factor is a cause or effect of another. The diagram below charts some of the most commonly cited causes of crime. For convenience, we have put them into two groups—(1) social and cultural factors and (2) individual and situational factors.

Social and Cultural Factors

Social problems—such as poverty, unemployment, racial discrimination, and child abuse—and cultural influences—such as American values and violence on television—are often mentioned as causes of crime. They do not cause crime in any direct sense. The vast majority of poor people, for example, remain law-abiding all their lives. But these factors may make it more likely that some people turn to crime.

Social & Cultural	Individual & Situational
• POVERTY • UNEMPLOYMENT • RACIAL DISCRIMINATION • CHILD ABUSE • AMERICAN VALUES • VIOLENCE IN THE MEDIA	• BIOLOGY • RATIONAL CHOICE • GUNS • ALCOHOL • DRUGS

THE PROBLEM: UNEMPLOYED, UNSKILLED, UNEDUCATED, UNMOTIVATED.

THE SOLUTION: BUILD MORE PRISONS

...BECAUSE SOONER OR LATER. HE'S GOING TO TURN TO DRUGS.

Poverty, Unemployment, and Racial Discrimination

Many people believe that poverty contributes to the crime rate. Statistics do show much higher rates of crime in poor communities. You only have to drive through a high-poverty area and look at the barred windows and security doors to know that the people who live there worry about crime.

A study using data from Columbus, Ohio, showed that neighborhoods with the most poverty had the highest rates of crime. Neighborhoods with poverty rates above 40 percent had crime rates three times higher than neighborhoods with poverty rates under 20 percent.

Poverty and unemployment is highest in minority communities and particularly among young African-Americans and Latinos. Almost a third of all black and Latino children grow up below the poverty line, compared to 14 percent of white children. Despair and hopelessness gives rise to crime in these communities. Black males between the ages 15 and 19 are nine times more likely to die from homicide than white males the same age. Inner-city residents, mostly minorities, get arrested and jailed at high rates.

One of the great causes of poverty, of course, is lack of jobs. In 1992, the crime rate was high and so was unemployment. Throughout the rest of the 1990s, unemployment dropped rapidly and so did the crime rate. This decline in crime went against expectations because more people in the 15–24 age

group entered the population. This is the most crime-prone age and many experts had predicted rising crime rates. Some experts attribute the fall in crime to the booming economy. They argue that unlike the 1960s when the economy also boomed, this economy provided more jobs for the poor.

Some social scientists have found a direct relationship between joblessness and crime and other social problems. A detailed long-term study by Dr. Harvey Brenner of Johns Hopkins University found that for every 1 percent increase in the unemployment rate, the United States sees:

- 650 extra homicides,
- 3,300 extra state prison admissions,
- 920 extra suicides, and
- 500 extra deaths from alcoholism.

Other studies have been less conclusive. A review of 30 studies on whether joblessness leads to crime found insufficient evidence proving or disproving the connection.

Child Abuse and Neglect

The family is usually the greatest single influence on a person's life. In a family, we learn how to behave, how to treat other people, and how to view ourselves. Children can be very sensitive to cruelty or lack of affection, which can create anti-social habits or serious mental problems. Some problems may not even show up until much later, as the child grows. Many sociologists believe that parents who abuse their children start a cycle of abuse from generation to generation. Abused children often grow up to abuse their children.

In a study reported in *Science* magazine, sociologists found that neglected children were one and one-half more times as likely to commit violent crimes later in life than non-neglected children. Abused children were twice as likely to become violent criminals. Abused children are also six times as likely to abuse their own children. The study concluded that the abusive family was one place where society should try to break the cycle of violence. Neglect and abuse within a family can lay the roots for a life of violent crime.

Almost 1 million children were reported as victims of abuse or neglect in 1996. This represented about a fifth more than in 1990. Some of this increase may have come from renewed attention to the problem and better reporting. But many cases of abuse undoubtedly never get reported.

Juvenile crime statistics show that teenage boys who were abused as children are two to three times more likely to turn to crime than other boys of the same age. Some social scientists insist that almost all career criminals, particularly those involved in crimes of violence, were abused as children.

Values That Make Crime More Acceptable

Many people believe that Americans hold certain values or beliefs that may encourage criminal conduct. One such value might be our **love of material goods**. Judging by our mass media, our society seems to place a high value on owning new things. In fact, the cumulative message of most advertising is that happiness comes from having things. Wealth and material possessions translate into status or position in society. Thus people often want things they cannot afford to buy, and some people may steal and rob for this reason.

Another value or belief that some claim affects America's crime rate is the idea that **violence is acceptable** and even admirable. Part of American folklore is the hero who fights criminals. Our movies and television programs often show sheriffs, police officers, and cowboys using guns and violence to combat the violence of criminals. Similarly, such programs may show people committing violent acts. This does not mean that individual Americans favor the use of violence. Rather, it means that Americans may view violence as a normal part of life. Some people believe that this idea may encourage criminal behavior.

Finally, some people have connected our crime problem to the **decline of traditional family values**. They argue that many of our social problems, including crime, stem from

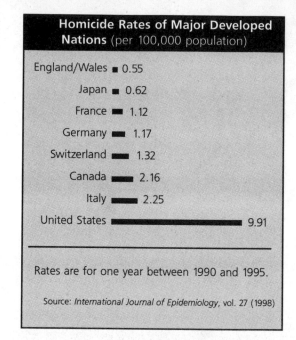

Homicide Rates of Major Developed Nations (per 100,000 population)

England/Wales	▪ 0.55
Japan	▪ 0.62
France	▪ 1.12
Germany	▪ 1.17
Switzerland	▪ 1.32
Canada	▪ 2.16
Italy	▪ 2.25
United States	▪ 9.91

Rates are for one year between 1990 and 1995.

Source: *International Journal of Epidemiology*, vol. 27 (1998)

the rise of **permissiveness** and the **breakdown of religion**. Permissiveness means being tolerant of a wide range of behavior, especially among children, and of avoiding judgment about the acceptability of others' behavior. Some people believe that permissiveness may encourage toleration of any behavior, even criminal behavior.

The Media

The American Psychological Association says that by the seventh grade, the average American will have watched on television 8,000 murders, plus another 100,000 acts of violence. Does watching this much violence make Americans more prone to violence? In 1972, the U.S. surgeon general, the highest medical officer in the federal government, announced that "televised violence, indeed, does have an adverse effect on certain members of our society."

In the years that followed, the National Institute of Mental Health, the Department of Justice, the American Academy of Pediatrics, and numerous scientific studies have backed up the words of the surgeon general. Many social scientists have concluded that televised violence can contribute to antisocial behavior in children. This is particularly true when the children come from violent homes or neighborhoods. It adds to the culture of violence surrounding them. After a five-year study, the American Psychological Association reported in February 1992 that "TV violence can cause aggressive behavior and can cultivate values favoring the use of aggression to resolve conflicts."

Critics complain that violence has crept into all the media—network television, cable television, movies, videos, video games, music lyrics, and the Internet. They believe the media are creating a culture of violence.

But defenders of the media believe that it is far too simple-minded to blame violence on the media. Millions of people, they point out, view violence in the media. Only a few commit acts of violence. According to them, the reasons some people commit violence are complex and rooted in various social problems such as increasing poverty and unemployment. Violence in entertainment, as they see it, is being made a scapegoat for society's problems. They contend that television simply reflects the level of violence in society. It does nothing to cause the violence.

A recent study published in *Pediatrics* lent some support to this viewpoint. The study, by Mark Singer of Case Western Reserve University in Cleveland, examined more than 2,000 third to eighth grade students. It found "disturbingly high" levels of violence among the students. But the study found only a small link between this violence and watching heavy doses of television violence. Instead, the study mainly linked the violence to students witnessing or being a victim of real-life violence at home, in the community, or at school.

The question of violence in the media has become a battleground between those who insist on First Amendment free-speech rights and those who insist the question is really one of corporate responsibility.

For Discussion

1. Which do you think are the most important cultural or social factors that contribute to crime? Which are the least important? Why?

2. Which factors are most difficult to change? Which are the easiest?

3. If all murderers drank milk as children, does this prove drinking milk leads to murder? Explain.

Individual and Situational Factors

Another approach to studying crime is to focus on the individual and on situational factors. Crimes, after all, are committed by particular individuals in particular situations. Are some individuals more likely to commit crimes? Do crimes arise more often in certain situations? Scientists looking at individuals have looked at many possible causes of crime, including such diverse causes as biology and rational choice. Other scientists looking for situational factors in crime have studied guns, alcohol, and drugs.

Biology

Some modern researchers believe that **biological traits** may predispose some people to crime. Professors Richard J. Herrnstein and James Q. Wilson in *Crime and Human Nature* cite various studies. Studies of twins show that identical twins are much more likely than fraternal twins to have the same criminal records. Unlike fraternal twins, identical twins share the same genetic makeup. So these studies seem to indicate biology plays a role in criminality.

Even more startling is a study comparing two groups of adopted boys. The first group contained boys raised by non-criminal adopted parents but whose natural parents were criminals. The second group had boys raised by criminal adopted parents but whose natural parents were not criminals. Most people would think that the boys in the second group—raised by criminal parents—would be more likely to commit crimes. But the studies found otherwise. The boys in the first group were more likely to have criminal records.

Herrnstein and Wilson point out several biological traits that predispose a person to crime. The first is simply being male. In all known societies, young males account for almost all violent crimes. Experiments have shown male sex hormones increase aggression. Young males often have some trouble adjusting to the hormones. Many engage in rowdy behavior. Some commit crimes.

A second biological trait, according to Herrnstein and Wilson, is intelligence. Studies have shown that criminals generally score low on intelligence tests. It isn't really known why low intelligence and crime are related. One theory is that people with low intelligence may get frustrated with school, grow angry and resentful, and start committing delinquent acts.

Another biological trait, according to Herrnstein and Wilson, is temperament. They point out that high-rate offenders typically are impulsive, rebellious thrill-seekers. To some extent, these characteristics may be inherited.

These studies provoke much controversy. Critics cast doubt on the twin and adoption studies. They criticize classifying intelligence and temperament as biological traits. But the critics are far less harsh on Herrnstein and Wilson's prescription for change:

"We know that a very small fraction of all young males commit so large a fraction of serious street crime that we can properly blame these chronic offenders for most such crime. We also know that chronic offenders typically begin their misconduct at an early age. Early family and preschool programs may be far better repositories for the crime-prevention dollar than rehabilitation programs aimed—usually futilely—at the 19-or 20-year--old veteran offender."

Drugs and Alcohol

More than 30 percent of state prison inmates report that they were under the influence of drugs when they committed their crimes. Over half admit to using drugs during the month prior to their offense. But drugs are not the only substance linked to crime. Half of all murders involve people who have been drinking. And 30 percent of all inmates report drinking alcohol every day. This compares with 10 percent of the general population.

The connection between crime and alcohol has long been noted. What to do about it is another question. Reformers at the turn of the 20th century managed to pass the 18th Amendment to the Constitution. Effective in January 1920, it banned the sale and distribution of alcohol. But this amendment and laws supporting it were vastly unpopular. People flaunted the law and continued drinking. Gangsters grew rich smuggling and distributing alcohol. In 1933, the 21st Amendment repealed the ill-fated 18th, and alcohol has remained legal in most of the country ever since.

Guns

In the United States each year, handguns are used in about 35 percent of all robberies and in about half of all homicides. Some criminologists tie the easy access to guns, particularly handguns, to America's high rate of violent crime.

Guns and gun ownership are common in the United States—far more so than in other democracies, which have stricter gun laws. Historically, Americans needed guns to survive on the frontier. In more recent years, incidents of violent crime, especially in urban areas, have caused millions of Americans to believe that they cannot rely on police protection alone. Experts claim 13,500 of every 100,000 Americans own handguns. As a comparison, the rate per 100,000 in Canada is 3,000 and in England, under 500. (In England, even the police do not normally carry guns.)

In 1998, the U.S. Centers for Disease Control conducted a survey of 36 developed countries. It found that the United States had the highest rate of gun-inflicted homicides. The U.S. rate of 12.95 gun homicides per 100,000 contrasted sharply with England's rate of .41 and South Korea's rate of .12. Other studies in the United States have linked the availability of handguns in a community to its rate of gun injury and homicide.

Sixteen Techniques of Situational Crime Prevention			
INCREASE THE EFFORT	**INCREASE THE RISKS**	**REDUCE THE REWARDS**	**REMOVE THE EXCUSES**
Harden targets *steering locks* *anti-robbery screens* *tamper-proof seals*	**Screen entrances and exits** *electronic merchandise tags* *baggage screening* *ticket gates*	**Remove targets** *removable car radios* *women's refuges* *phone cards*	**Set rules** *hotel registration* *customs declaration* *codes of conduct*
Control access *entry phones* *PIN numbers* *fenced yards*	**Formal surveillance** *security cameras* *security guards* *burglar alarms*	**Identify property** *vehicle licensing* *property marking* *car-parts marking*	**Alert conscience** *roadside speedometers* *"idiots drink-and-drive" signs* *"shoplifting is stealing" signs*
Deflect offenders *street closings* *separation of rival fans* *bus stop placement*	**Surveillance by employees** *park attendants* *concierges* *CCTV systems*	**Reduce temptation** *rapid repair of vandalism* *off-street parking* *gender-neutral listings*	**Control disinhibitors** *drinking-age laws* *car ignition breathalyser* *V-chip in TV*
Control facilitators *credit card photos* *caller ID* *gun controls*	**Natural surveillance** *street lighting* *low hedges* *defensible space*	**Deny benefits** *ink merchandise tags* *PIN for car radios* *graffiti cleaning*	**Assist compliance** *litter bins* *public lavatories* *easy library check-out*

Source: Clarke, Ronald. V. (Ed.). *Situational Crime Prevention: Successful Case Studies*, Second Edition. Albany, NY: Harrow & Heston (1997)

Several studies have questioned the link between guns and violent crime. Although many criminals use guns, these studies have found no evidence that decreasing the availability of guns would lower homicide rates.

This debate on the link between guns and violence often arises over the issue of gun control. This is one of the most hotly debated topics in America. One side argues that "guns don't kill people; people kill people." People on this side believe that to stop violent crime, we must focus on criminals, not guns. The other side argues that "people with guns kill people." Those on this side believe violent crime can be lowered by making guns less available in society.

Rational Choice

Many people believe crime involves rational choice on the part of criminals. This theory takes various forms.

In its simplest form, this theory means that people choose to become criminals. People make some sort of cost-benefit analysis before committing crimes. They calculate the benefits—these could be economic gain, the thrill of committing the crime, or any pleasure they could derive from the crime. They weigh the benefits against the costs. These could be the risk of getting caught, the harshness of punishment, pangs of conscience, or any pain they could receive from the criminal act. If the benefits outweigh the costs, then they will commit the crime.

After making a cost-benefit analysis, certain people would be more likely to choose to commit crimes. Poor people would have more to gain than rich people. **Psychopaths**—people without consciences—would feel freer to commit crimes than most people.

Another form of rational-choice theory does not attempt to explain why people become criminals. It simply notes that criminals act rationally in at least one sense: *Most do not want to get caught.* This means that criminals will most often take the easiest path to commit a crime and may be deterred if something stands in their way. Thus car thieves prefer an unlocked car to a locked car, a car without an alarm to one with an alarm, and an empty car to one with a person in it. This logic applies to many crimes. Robbers, for example, seem to prefer lone victims. The risk of being robbed increases tenfold when a person is alone.

According to this theory, the way to cut crime is to make it more difficult, more risky, and less rewarding for the criminal. This can be done in many ways—stronger locks, increased police patrols, fewer people carrying cash, etc. The chart on the previous page lists quite a few techniques.

The question is: Do these techniques reduce crime or do they merely displace it? What happens, for example, if we make cars difficult to steal by equipping them with anti-theft devices? Will car thieves, frustrated with not being able to break into cars, turn to the violent crime of carjacking—stealing cars at gunpoint? Or, will they turn to a different kind of stealing, such as committing daytime burglaries? Or, will they stop committing crimes? Researchers have not conclusively answered these questions.

For Discussion

1. Which do you think are the most important individual or situational factors that contribute to crime? Which are the least important? Why?

2. Which factors are most difficult to change? Which are the easiest?

3. Which of all the theories discussed do you think is most important? Which is least important? Why?

4. What additional factors do you think contribute to crime?

5. White-collar crimes are often committed by employed, well-educated people from good family backgrounds. If they don't need money, why would such people commit fraud or embezzlement?

Class Activity: The Causes of Crime

In this activity, students develop solutions to the problem of crime.
1. Divide the class into groups of four members each. Each group should:

   a. Discuss the various causes of crime and select the one cause it considers most important.

   b. Brainstorm solutions to crime, based on the cause it has chosen.

   c. Discuss the solutions it comes up with and choose its best solution.

   d. Discuss the costs and benefits of this solution.

   e. Prepare a brief presentation for the class on the solution.

2. Reconvene as a class. Have each group make a brief presentation supporting its solution. List the solutions on the board. Hold a debriefing discussion. Conclude by taking a class vote on which solution is best.

Debriefing Questions
1. Which causes seemed easier to find solutions for? Why?

2. Which solutions would be easiest to put into effect? Why?

3. Which solutions do you think would work best? Why?

CHAPTER 22
Crime and the Government

The Role of Government

Americans often look to government to solve problems, and the problem of crime is no exception. Politicians, from presidents to mayors, are elected, evaluated, and replaced on the basis of how well they meet our expectations. Political campaigns often center on promises or proposals for reducing crime, yet the problem remains. What can government do to help solve America's crime problem?

Crime and the Federal Government

The U.S. Constitution divides the power of government into three distinct branches—the executive, legislative, and judicial. The Constitution then lays out the responsibilities and powers of each branch. All three branches have responsibilities in addressing the crime problem.

The Executive Branch

As head of the executive branch, the president is responsible for enforcing federal laws. Article II, Section 3 of the Constitution holds that the president "shall take care that the laws be faithfully executed." One way that the president exercises this power is by supervising executive agencies and departments, particularly the Department of Justice, headed by the attorney general.

Five main agencies handle most federal investigations:
- The Federal Bureau of Investigation
- The Drug Enforcement Administration
- The Secret Service
- The Postal Inspection Service
- The Bureau of Alcohol, Tobacco, and Firearms.

Although states and local governments handle most crime, the federal government plays an important role in addressing the crime problem.

In addition to the big five, many other federal agencies conduct investigations: the Customs Service, Internal Revenue Service, Food and Drug Administration, Immigration and Naturalization Service, and Securities and Exchange Commission. Most of these agencies can investigate lawbreaking, collect evidence, make arrests, and present cases to federal prosecutors.

Federal cases are prosecuted by the Department of Justice and its U.S. attorneys throughout the country. U.S. attorneys are appointed by the president.

The Legislative Branch

The Constitution outlines the powers of the U.S. Congress. In the area of criminal justice, Congress makes laws that define federal crimes and set punishments. Some of these laws were made to meet the specific requirements of Section 8 of the Constitution, which says that Congress must control America's postal services, mints, revenues, and taxes. To carry out these responsibilities, Congress has passed laws against tampering with the mail, counterfeiting coins, or smuggling. Congress has also passed statutes that outlaw spying and espionage against the United States. And Congress has used its powers over commerce to make laws against carrying stolen goods across state lines or kidnaping. These are all federal crimes.

Congress also makes laws for those parts of the country that do not fall under the jurisdiction of a state government. Some of these are the District of Columbia, federal forests, military bases, post offices, federal courts, and ships at sea or airplanes in the air. In most areas, however, the bulk of the criminal laws are made by state and local legislatures, because the framers of the Constitution did not want all lawmaking power centralized.

Whether a specific act falls under federal or state law depends on the act and on where it is committed. For example, if John Deadly shoots and kills a man on a street in Wichita, he has committed murder and would be tried under the Kansas State Penal Code. On the other hand, if John Deadly kills a letter carrier who is out delivering mail in Wichita, he has not only committed a murder, punishable by the state of Kansas, he has also committed the federal crime of assaulting a federal employee. If he's caught, John can be tried under state law for the murder and under federal law for the assault.

But the situation is different if John Deadly shoots and kills the letter carrier *inside* the post office. Even though it is in Kansas, the post office is considered federal territory. If John is caught, he can be tried according to federal murder statutes.

Congress does not merely define crimes. It also passes legislation and creates agencies to study and reduce crime. The Office of Juvenile Justice and Delinquency Prevention (OJJDP) is an example of one such agency. Under congressional mandate to "improve the quality of juvenile justice in the United States," OJJDP allocates federal funds and coordinates programs to reduce juvenile delinquency and exploitation of children.

The Judicial Branch

The Constitution places the power of the judicial branch in the hands of "one Supreme Court and in such inferior courts the Congress may from time to time ordain and establish." Today, the federal court system consists of three basic levels—the district courts, which handle trials; circuit courts of appeals; and the U.S. Supreme Court.

Courts at all levels, state and federal, must interpret the meaning of laws. Even trial courts must construe the meaning of statutes. Consider the following criminal statute, passed by the California State Legislature in 1901:

> Every person who maliciously, forcibly or fraudulently takes or entices away any minor child with intent to detain and conceal such child from its parent, guardian or other person having the lawful charge of such child, is punishable by imprisonment in the state prison not exceeding twenty years.
>
> —California State Penal Code, Section 278

Now imagine that a woman takes her 14-year-old niece on a two-week trip to Hawaii against the wishes of the child's parents. The parents are furious and have the woman arrested for violating this law. But the woman argues at her trial that she didn't fraudulently take or entice the child to go.

A California judge must interpret the law. In this case, the judge might decide that the woman did entice the child. Though she did not drag her niece onto the airplane forcibly, she knew that the idea of the vacation would be too good for the teenager to resist and she was taken fraudulently.

The judge's decision does much more than resolve this one case. It sets a **precedent**—or a general rule to follow. The next time someone is charged with child stealing in the same way, the prosecutor can refer to this judgment and ask that the new case be decided according to the precedent. If the precedent is upheld by higher courts, the judge's decisions can alter the law, just as surely as if the legislature had made a new statute to include psychological as well as physical force.

For Discussion

1. For what part of the American criminal legal process is the legislative branch of the federal government responsible? The executive branch? The judicial branch?

2. Describe two crimes that fall under the jurisdiction of federal rather than state law.

3. How do courts set precedents? How can precedents change the law? Do you think courts should follow precedents? Why or why not?

Federal Policy: Civil Forfeiture

Under state and federal forfeiture statutes, law enforcement officers can seize and confiscate assets used in illegal activity or derived from it. An old procedure adopted from English common law, forfeiture historically played little role in fighting crime in America. But forfeiture has become an important part of our nation's war on drugs. Since drug dealing depends on high profits to survive, forfeiture laws take aim at these profits.

For example, Congress passed the Comprehensive Drug Abuse Prevention and Control Act of 1970. As amended, it now provides for the civil forfeiture of:

(1) illegal drugs.

(2) material and equipment for illegal drug manufacturing.

(3) containers for illegal drugs.

(4) vehicles for transporting illegal drugs.

(5) books and records of illegal drugs.

(6) anything of value exchanged for illegal drugs, including money or anything traceable to the exchange.

(7) all real property used to facilitate a drug offense.

Law enforcement has increasingly turned to statutes such as this in its fight against crime. In 1985, the federal government alone seized $27 million in assets. Each year the amount has increased. Recently, it has averaged nearly $500 million in assets each year. The assets included cash, real estate, motor vehicles, boats, and airplanes. The forfeited assets were then either used by the law enforcement agency itself or sold and the proceeds turned over to the Department of Justice's Asset Forfeiture Fund. The fund is used for law enforcement purposes.

There are two types of forfeiture laws: criminal and civil. **Criminal forfeiture** laws apply to criminals convicted of crimes. As part of the sentence, the judge confiscates the criminal's assets that were used in the crime or that were derived from it. These laws have caused far less controversy than civil forfeiture laws.

Civil forfeiture laws work differently. If law enforcement officers have probable cause to believe that particular assets have been used in a crime, they can seize them under civil forfeiture laws. The laws are written so that the government is taking action against things, not people. Bizarre case names result: *U.S. v. One 56-Foot Motor Yacht Named Tahuna* (1983) or *U.S. v. One Parcel of Land . . . Commonly Known as 4204 Cedarwood, Matteson, IL* (1985) or *U.S. v. $321,470 in U.S. Currency* (1987).

If no one claims the assets, they are forfeited to the government. If someone does claim them, there will be a civil trial over one issue: Are the assets connected to illegal activity? If so, the property is forfeited to the government. Because the action is supposedly against the property and not against persons, many statutes do not allow claimants to argue that they knew nothing of the illegal activity.

Unlike a criminal trial, in civil forfeiture cases the government does not have to prove its case beyond a reasonable doubt. Instead, the person claiming the property must prove by a preponderance of evidence that the assets are not connected with illegal activity. This means that a defendant could be acquitted of a criminal charge but lose seized property in a civil forfeiture trial. (See *U.S. v. One 1977 Lincoln Mark V*, 1988.)

Forfeiture laws have come under harsh attack. Since law enforcement agencies often get to keep the assets they seize, they have sometimes been accused of acting overzealously. In 1992, for example, Los Angeles County Sheriff deputies shot and killed Malibu millionaire Donald Scott in a drug raid on his 200-acre ranch. A federal agent, who had flown over the ranch at 1,000 feet, had thought he observed marijuana plants growing. Deputies obtained a warrant and raided the ranch. A thorough search of the ranch turned up no trace of drugs. The ensuing five-month district attorney investigation concluded that the raid was illegal and that one reason deputies rushed to raid the ranch was because they were anxious to confiscate the high-priced land. In January 2000, Los Angeles County and the federal government agreed to pay Scott's family $5 million to settle a lawsuit.

Civil forfeiture laws also raise major constitutional issues. In a series of cases, the Supreme Court has dealt with challenges based on the Fifth, Eighth, and 14th amendments.

The Eighth Amendment bans the government from imposing "excessive fines." If John smokes a marijuana cigarette at home, can law enforcement confiscate the home? Or would this be an excessive fine? The Supreme Court has dealt with this issue in two major cases.

The first was *Austin v. U.S.*, decided in 1993. In June 1990, an undercover agent entered Austin's automobile body shop in Sioux Falls, South Dakota, and asked for drugs. Austin agreed to sell him some. Austin left his body shop, went to his mobile home, and came back with two grams of cocaine. Convicted of possession of cocaine with intent to distribute, Austin was sentenced to seven years in state prison. Federal agents seized his body shop and mobile home in a civil forfeiture action. Appealing the forfeiture all the way to the U.S. Supreme Court, Austin argued that this seizure amounted to an excessive fine. The government countered that the Eighth Amendment did not apply to civil actions, only criminal actions. A unanimous Supreme Court held that the Eighth Amendment applies to any fine—civil or criminal—and that the forfeiture

amounted to a fine. The court ordered lower courts to decide if Austin's fine was excessive.

The second major case was *U.S. v. Bajakajian*, decided in 1998. This was a criminal, rather than civil, forfeiture case. Bajakajian and his family were in Los Angeles ready to board a plane for Syria, his place of birth. In his suitcase, Bajakajian carried more than $300,000 in cash. He had earned the money legally and intended to use it to repay family and friends who had loaned him money years before. Customs agents approached members of the family and informed them that they must report any amount more than $10,000 being taken out of the country. Bajakajian lied and said he had nothing to report. The agents then searched his luggage and found the cash. Bajakajian pleaded guilty to failing to report the money. The reporting law authorized forfeiture of "any property, real or personal, involved in such offense." The prosecutor asked for this penalty, but the judge limited the forfeiture to $15,000. The prosecution appealed, asking the court to impose a forfeiture of all the money. The U.S. Supreme Court ruled 5–4 that such a forfeiture would amount to an excessive fine in violation of the Eighth Amendment. The court majority stressed that Bajakajian possessed the money legally. His "violation was unrelated to any other illegal activities. . . . [He] does not fit into the class of persons for whom the statute was principally designed: He is not a money launderer, a drug trafficker, or a tax evader." His "crime was solely a reporting offense. . . . Had his crime gone undetected, the government would have been deprived only of the information that $357,144 had left the country." The court held that a forfeiture of this amount "would be grossly disproportional to the gravity of his offense." The dissenters disagreed, arguing that smuggling money was a serious crime and that forfeiting all the money was perfectly proportional to the crime.

The court has also dealt with two other major constitutional issues on forfeiture. One case involved double jeopardy, which is banned by the Fifth Amendment. Double jeopardy means punishing a person twice for the same crime. If the government in a civil forfeiture takes a person's property because it was involved in a crime, can the government then file criminal charges against the person for the same crime? Or would this be double jeopardy?

In 1996 in *U.S. v. Ursery*, the Supreme Court ruled 8-1 that this is not double jeopardy. The court noted that "in a long line of cases, this Court has considered the application of the Double Jeopardy Clause to civil forfeitures, consistently concluding that the Clause does not apply to such actions because they do not impose punishment."

The other case involved both the Fifth and 14th amendments. A Michigan woman and her husband jointly owned a family car. Her husband had taken the car, picked up a prostitute, had sex with her in the car, and got caught by police. The police confiscated the car under a Michigan forfeiture law. The wife appealed the forfeiture because she owned half the car and had known nothing about her husband's actions. Federal statutes allow a so-called "innocent owner" defense. If the owners of property can prove they knew nothing of the illegal activity, they won't lose the property. But Michigan's and many other states' laws do not provide an innocent-owner defense. The wife argued that Michigan's law violated the 14th Amendment's due process clause and the Fifth Amendment's takings clause. The due process clause says that no state shall "deprive any person of . . . property . . . without due process of law . . . ." The tak-

ings clause declares that the government cannot take a person's property "without just compensation."

In 1996 in *Bennis v. Michigan*, the U.S. Supreme Court upheld the Michigan law by a 5-4 vote. The court majority again cited "a long and unbroken line of cases [holding] that an owner's interest in property may be forfeited by reason of the use to which the property is put even though the owner did not know that it was to be put to such use." The court pointed out that forfeiture laws deter illegal uses of property and that they are not unique in this respect. "Michigan also deters dangerous driving by making a motor vehicle owner liable for the negligent operation of the vehicle by a driver who had the owner's consent to use it . . . ." The dissenters believed forfeiture laws must distinguish between three categories of property—(1) contraband (such as illegal drugs), (2) proceeds from criminal activities, and (3) items used by a criminal (car, house, ship, hotel). According to the dissenters, the first two categories of property would not require an innocent-owner defense, because nobody is entitled to this property. But, said the dissenters, due process requires an innocent-owner defense for the third category of property, because people legally own it.

In 2000, Congress passed the Civil Asset Forfeiture Reform Act. It makes federal civil forfeitures more difficult. To seize property, prosecutors must prove that the property was involved in criminal activity by a preponderance of the evidence. The old law required only probable cause, a much easier standard of proof. Prosecutors must also notify property owners of any forfeiture action. If owners claim they knew nothing of the illegal activity, prosecutors must prove this false by a preponderance of the evidence. The new law also makes the government pay for the owners' lawyers if the owners are indigent or if they win the property back.

Civil libertarians say that this new law helps, but is not enough. They want Congress to ban civil forfeitures. The government, they argue, should have to prove a person guilty beyond a reasonable doubt before forfeiting the person's property. As it stands now, prosecutors do not file criminal charges in many civil forfeiture cases. When they do file charges, prosecutors still most often seek civil forfeitures instead of criminal forfeitures.

The government adamantly supports civil forfeitures. Officials believe the new law offers more than adequate safeguards. They point out that no one even contests forfeitures in eight out of 10 cases. Cary Copeland, director of the Justice Department's Office for Asset Forfeiture, argues that in most cases "the circumstances are so incriminating that nobody wants to challenge us. With all that crime out there we don't have time to run around and take property from innocent people."

For Discussion

1. What is the difference between civil and criminal forfeiture?

2. Why do you think prosecutors most often file civil forfeiture actions instead of criminal ones?

3. How are the three branches of government—executive, legislative, and judicial—involved in setting federal civil forfeiture policy?

4. What did the court decide in *Bennis v. Michigan*? Do you agree with this decision? Why or why not?

5. The Supreme Court ruled in *Austin* that the excessive fines clause applies to civil forfeitures. It then sent the *Austin* case back to lower courts to decide whether the forfeiture was, in fact, excessive. Do you think it was? Why or why not?

6. What did the court decide in *U.S. v. Bajakajian*? Do you agree with the court? Explain.

7. What are the benefits of civil forfeiture? The costs?

Class Activity: A Model Forfeiture Statute

Civil asset forfeiture continues to be debated. Some push for its elimination; others for a return to how it was before Congress reformed it in 2000. In this activity, students role play a congressional subcommittee recommending elements of a new civil forfeiture statute, which will also serve as a model for state legislatures to adopt.

1. Divide the class into small groups. Each group will role play a congressional subcommittee.

2. Each group should discuss and decide on the following questions:

   a. What standard of proof should prosecutors have to prove before seizing assets—probable cause, preponderance of the evidence, clear and convincing evidence, or proof beyond a reasonable doubt? Why?

   b. Should there be an innocent-owner defense? If so, who should have the burden of proving that the owner did or did not know about the illegality—the owner or the prosecutor? What should the standard of proof be? Explain all your answers.

   c. Who should get the proceeds from the forfeited property—the police agency that conducted the seizure, the law-enforcement budget, or the whole government's budget? Why?

   d. Should the government have to return property forfeited in a civil action if the property owner is acquitted at a criminal trial? Explain.

3. Each group should report back its answers and the class should hold a discussion.

Debriefing Questions

1. What were the easiest issues to decide? The hardest? Why?

2. Do you think civil forfeiture is a good idea? Why or why not?

Federal Policy: Gun Control

Americans possess more than 200 million firearms. Each year about 640,000 violent crimes, including 16,000 murders are committed with guns, mostly handguns. Some people believe gun-control laws, which restrict gun ownership, can reduce the bloodshed. These laws range from gun registration, to bans on certain types of ammunition, to complete bans on handguns and military-assault weapons.

Can gun-control laws stop this violence? Americans have highly conflicting views on gun control. According to recent opinion polls, about 70 percent favor various gun-control measures. But a similar percent oppose an outright ban on handguns. Other polls indicate that the American public is evenly split on whether stricter gun control will reduce violent crime.

Gun control faces stiff opposition in the United States. Millions of Americans believe that gun ownership is a right and that guns serve a legitimate purpose in society. They argue that guns are not the problem. Rather than penalizing law-abiding gun owners, they favor punishing more harshly those who use guns to commit crimes.

The opposition is led by the National Rifle Association (NRA) and the gun industry. The NRA represents about 3-million hunters and gun enthusiasts. The gun industry, made up of manufacturers and retailers, earns more than $2 billion annually. Together they form a powerful opposition to legislation imposing controls on guns.

Over the years, however, the federal government has enacted five major nationwide gun laws. In 1934, it prohibited the possession of machine guns, sawed-off shotguns, and silencers. The Gun Control Act of 1968 limited the importation and sale of cheap handguns, known as Saturday Night Specials, and prohibited the interstate sale of handguns. The Brady Act, passed in 1993, requires a five-day waiting period for all handgun purchases. The 1994 crime bill banned the import and manufacture of certain military assault weapons. A 1996 law banned anyone convicted of a domestic violence offense from owning or using a gun.

Other proposed laws include:

Sharply increasing taxes on the sale of guns and bullets. Supporters say this will increase their cost and make them less available. Opponents say these laws will only affect law-abiding citizens who already pay high taxes on firearms.

Requiring gun owners to register firearms and to have a state firearms license. Supporters say that just as the state registers cars and licenses people who drive, the state should also license gun owners and register guns. They think such a system would help keep guns out of the wrong hands. Opponents believe this is the first step to outlawing guns, which will only keep guns away from law-abiding people. They also say the car comparison is faulty. Cars, they say, cause many more deaths than guns and, unlike gun ownership, car ownership is a privilege not a right.

Compel gun manufacturers to install safety devices. Proposals include requiring built-in locks and eventually "smart guns," which can be operated only by the lawful owner. Supporters believe these will prevent others

National Poll on Gun Control Measures	
Gun control measures	percent supporting the measure
Mandatory registration of handguns	85.3%
Keep handguns from criminals, even if harder for law-abiding citizens to purchase	75.3%
Mandatory registration of rifles and shotguns	72.3%
Ban possession of handguns, except by police or other authorized persons	38.5%
Total ban on handguns	15.6%

Source: *Sourcebook of Criminal Justice Statistics* 1998, Table 2.67, Bureau of Justice Statistics (1999)

Arguments on Handgun Control

Against Handgun Control	For Handgun Control
Gun control impinges on a basic right of all Americans—the right to protect themselves. This right is so important that the Second Amendment to the Constitution guarantees the right to bear arms.	The Second Amendment does not give an individual a right to own a gun. It guarantees a state's right to maintain a militia. The Supreme Court and federal appeals courts have never overturned a gun-control law on Second Amendment grounds.
With our society's high rate of violence and lack of adequate policing, guns offer citizens protection.	Guns are far more likely to harm members of the owner's household than offer protection against criminals.
"Guns don't kill people. People kill people." Switzerland, which has a low rate of murder, requires most adult males to keep automatic weapons at home for the army.	Guns make bad situations worse. Our murder rate is higher than other countries because handguns are so readily available.
"When guns are outlawed, only outlaws will have guns." Criminals will always find ways of getting guns or other weapons. Washington, D.C., and other jurisdictions with strong gun-control laws have the worst murder rates in the country.	Most of the crimes committed with guns in Washington, D.C., are committed with guns bought in nearby states with lax gun laws.
Instead of penalizing ordinary citizens, the proper way to keep criminals from using guns is to impose harsher penalties on criminals who use them.	We already impose mandatory sentences on criminals using guns.
Our country has too many guns in circulation for gun-control laws to be effective.	Canada had similar laws to ours until the 1920s. Gun control has worked there.
Even if gun control laws did reduce the use of handguns, criminals would simply shift to other weapons.	Guns are more fatal than other weapons. A person shot with a gun is five times more likely to die than a person stabbed with a knife.

from using the gun. Opponents believe these devices increase the costs and may cause the weapons to misfire.

Limit gun purchases to one a month per person. Much of the illegal gun trade is carried on by middlemen who buy guns from dealers in bulk and sell them to juveniles and criminals. Supporters say this law will stop the middlemen from buying guns. Opponents think criminals can easily get around this law by using groups of people to buy guns. Again, they say, only the law-abiding will be prevented from buying guns.

Ban handgun ownership. Under this proposal, only police and armed forces would be allowed to own handguns. Supporters think it is the only way to reduce handgun violence. Opponents believe it is an extreme measure that violates people's rights.

Supporters and opponents have long debated the merits of gun control. (See "Arguments on Handgun Control" for some of the most common arguments.) Both sides cite studies and cases to bolster their arguments.

Supporters of gun control point to other Western democracies, such as Canada, which have strict gun-control laws and far lower rates of violent crime. They cite a 1988 study in the *New England Journal of Medicine* comparing a Canadian city, Vancouver, with an American city, Seattle, which are about 100 miles apart. The risk of being murdered by a handgun was about five time higher in Seattle. And a person assaulted in Seattle was twice as likely to die as a person assaulted in Vancouver. Supporters of gun control argue that strict gun-control laws will reduce violent crime in America.

Opponents of gun control question the link between guns and violent crime. They cite countries, such as Switzerland and Israel, which mandate citizen-soldiers to keep guns at home and yet have low murder rates. Opponents say that gun-control laws have no effect on criminals. They point to Washington, D.C. It has in effect banned handguns and still has one of the worst murder rates in the country. Gun-control laws, they say, only make it more difficult for law-abiding citizens to buy firearms, which they believe is a citizen's right under the Constitution.

The Second Amendment to the Constitution reads as follows:

A well regulated Militia, being necessary to the security of a free State, the right of the people to keep and bear Arms, shall not be infringed.

Opponents of gun control argue that this amendment gives individuals the right to own firearms. They explain that this was considered a basic right when the Bill of Rights was written. Every able-bodied adult male citizen was part of the state militia and was expected to have his own gun.

Supporters of gun control read the amendment differently. They say the amendment only gives states the right to keep armed citizen militias. It does not, they say, give individual citizens a right to own guns that are not necessary for a state militia. According to supporters of gun control, this means that government can regulate private gun ownership.

The Supreme Court has made only one ruling on the Second Amendment in the last 100 years. In 1939 in *U.S. v. Miller*, the court upheld the federal government's 1934 gun law. Federal appeals courts have never overturned a gun-control law on Second Amendment grounds. In 1997 in *Printz v. U.S.*, the Supreme Court overturned portions of the Brady Act for other reasons. Justice Clarence Thomas in a concurring opinion noted that the law had not been challenged on Second Amendment grounds. He expressed hope that the court would someday be asked to make a definitive ruling on this amendment.

For Discussion

1. What do you think the Second Amendment means?

2. Do you think gun control can reduce violent crime? Why or why not?

3. Which of the gun-control policies mentioned seems the best? The worst? Why?

Class Activity: Gun-Control Policies

In this activity, students debate the merits of different gun-control policies.

1. Ask each student to read and decide which one of the following seven policies he or she thinks is the best:

    a. Get rid of all federal gun-control laws.

    b. Enforce the laws we have. They are enough.

    c. Require gun manufacturers to install safety devices.

    d. Limit gun purchases to one a month per person.

    e. Sharply increase taxes on the sale of guns and bullets.

    f. Register guns and license gun owners.

    g. Ban handgun ownership.

2. Have students meet in groups according to the policy they favor most. All who think policy "a" is best meet together, and so on for each policy.

3. Each group should:

    a. Create arguments favoring their policy.

    b. Develop a one-minute presentation to make to the class to convince others to favor the policy.

4. Regroup and have the groups make their presentations. Conclude by taking a class vote on each policy.

An Attack on Crime: The State Level

We must bear in mind that under our federal system of government, the states have primary authority for dealing with most crimes committed within their border, and that includes the vast majority of violent crimes.

—William French Smith, former U.S. attorney general

Like the federal government, state governments are divided into three branches—executive, legislative, and judicial. State legislatures define crimes and pass other crime bills, which the governor signs into law. State codes define all felony offenses and many lesser offenses, but local governments enact some misdemeanors and local ordinances.

In turn, state, county, and municipal police departments enforce these laws. The most visible of the state police agencies is usually the highway patrol, but the state also has narcotics, investigative, and other units. Almost every county has a sheriff's department run by an elected sheriff. By far the largest law enforcement agencies are the local police, which account for more than three-fourths of all those employed as police at all levels of government.

People accused of violating state or local crimes appear before state criminal trial courts. If convicted, they serve sentences in local jails or state prisons. They may also appeal their convictions in appellate courts. The highest appellate court in the state is usually called the state supreme court. It has the final word in interpreting state law and the state constitution. Defendants can appeal to the U.S. Supreme Court only on issues of U.S. constitutional law.

For Discussion

1. Why do you think controlling violent crime is primarily the responsibility of the states?

2. Under what circumstances could the U.S. Supreme Court overturn a state law? Explain.

Class Activity: A State Senate Committee

Passing anti-crime legislation is not as simple as learning the facts and holding a debate. In this activity, students learn some of the ins and outs of state legislation. They will take part in a role play based on a fictional state's attack on its crime problem. In the role play, students serve on a state senate committee discussing proposed Senate Bill 1715, an anti-crime bill.

1. As a class, read the background information on "The Fictional State of Columbia," plus the description of the anti-crime bill ("Senate Bill 1715") and the "Description of the State Districts." In the role play, each student represents one of the districts described.

2. Hold a discussion using the discussion questions on page 284.

3. Break the class into committees of five or 10 persons each.

4. Each committee should:

    a. Count off and assign either one or two persons (depending on the number of people on the committee) to represent one of the five districts.

    b. Select a chairperson.

       If the committee has an even number of members, the chairperson should be a non-voting member of the committee.

Police question young people hanging out on a street corner at night.

5. Each person should reread his or her district's description (on pages 282–284).

6. Before beginning committee deliberations, redivide the class into district caucuses for preliminary discussions. This means all the members representing a particular district, such as district 1, should meet in one group to discuss the district's reaction toward the three provisions of the bill (on page 282). Go over which sections the district favors, which it opposes, and discuss changes the district would like in the bill.

7. Have students return to the senate and meet with their senate committee. The committees should now carefully review all three provisions of SB 1715, discuss, and vote on the measure by following these steps:

First step. Committee chairperson or a designated member reads aloud the text of the first provision of SB 1715.

Second step. Chairperson calls on members to discuss this provision and how their districts feel about it.

Third step. Chairperson calls for amendments. Committee members can propose amendments to the provision. Members discuss any amendments and vote on them.

Fourth step. Chairperson has the committee vote on the provision, including any amendments the committee has added.

There are three votes possible:

> *Pass*, which will send the bill to the full senate with a recommendation to pass it.
>
> *Defeat*, which will send the bill to the full senate with a recommendation to defeat it.
>
> *Table*, which will delay consideration of the bill to a later date.

Fifth step. The committee repeats the steps for all three provisions of the bill and then writes a brief report on the committee's recommendations. (Break up the report so that different people on the committee work on different parts of the report.)

8. Reconvene the whole class as the full senate, and have each committee read its report. The whole class will vote on any amendments offered, and will then vote whether to pass or defeat the bill. Debrief the activity using the questions on page 284.

The Fictional State of Columbia

Columbia is a picturesque mountain and prairie state in the middle of the country far away from the coasts. It has almost 4 million residents, about half of whom live in rural areas on farms or in small towns. Columbia has many dairy farms and egg ranches. It also has a few large agricultural corporations that raise hogs, cattle, corn, and wheat.

Two million Columbians live in cities, almost a million in the biggest city, Athena. Industries in the Athena area mainly make textiles, clothing, and computer hardware. There is one auto assembly plant. A particularly rugged mountain range passes through the western part of the state, and tourists flock to the mountains summer and winter. Tourists also come to see Gold Canyon near the mountains, which is the site of the White Water mining district with many ghost towns and abandoned mines. Many Europeans come to see the mining areas and stay in one of the spas in the foothills. Tourism has become an important addition to a weak economy.

Although crime has fallen slightly in recent years, Columbia still has a major crime problem. It got national publicity last year when the daughter of the Danish ambassador was accidentally killed in a mini-market holdup. The crime problem grew serious in Athena when drugs were first imported by a West Coast gang 20 years ago. Since then, the problem has spread to most of the smaller cities in the state.

Senate Bill 1715

State Senator Alan Parsons introduced a bill designed to solve Columbia's crime problem. He incorporated many sweeping changes into his bill, which was assigned the number SB 1715, which stands for Senate Bill 1715. This is the bill:

Preamble:

We, the people of Columbia, declare that it is our inalienable right to live in a society free from the fear and threat of criminal attack upon our property and persons. We declare that the men and women who commit crimes are the enemies of our state, our society, and our general welfare. For this reason, we amend the Columbia Constitution and Penal Code to include the following provisions:

Provision 1: Any person who has already been convicted of two felonies shall, upon conviction of a third and separate felony, be sentenced to serve 25 years in state prison. This penalty is mandatory for all felons upon their third conviction and is to be served without possibility of parole.

Provision 2: Any citizen who wounds, disables, or apprehends a person committing or attempting to commit a robbery or burglary within the jurisdiction of this state shall be entitled to $4,000 upon the capture and conviction of said felon. In the event of the death of said felon, an award of $4,000 shall be made upon a finding of justifiable homicide by a duly constituted coroner's jury.

Provision 3: The legislature hereby appropriates $40 million from the general fund for use by county, municipal, or township governments for either of the following purposes:

a. The hiring, training, and maintenance of additional police officers.

b. The renovation of jails or the construction of additional cells in existing jails.

This fund shall be administered and distributed by the state attorney general's office upon application by local governments.

Description of the State Districts

In the role play that follows, you will represent one of the following districts in the state of Columbia. It will help you in the role play to be familiar with all the districts.

District 1

Most of the district is made up of the richer suburbs of Athena. There are two large modern malls to serve them and the state's only theme park, Prairieland. A lot of the residents are newly wealthy and have moved here to escape the troubles of the inner city. The state capital buildings in Athena are just across the district line, and many of the higher level state administrators live here.

The areas of district 1 nearest the city are often targeted for burglaries and there have been several brutal muggings and rapes on local streets. Recently there has been a number of carjackings, with new models taken from their owners at gunpoint.

The people in district 1 want someone to take action against crime immediately. Many of them, however, are against taxation and they are worried about the budget impact of new anti-crime measures. Also, several important people in district 1 have expressed concerns about the first provision of the bill. They do not want the bill to cover "victimless" crimes, such as drug use or gambling, and they don't want any attention given to white-collar crime, such as embezzlement or corporate fraud.

Rate of Violent Crime in Each State

Rate per 100,000 population

Alabama	564.5
Alaska	701.1
Arizona	623.7
Arkansas	526.9
California	798.3
Colorado	363.2
Connecticut	390.9
Delaware	677.9
Florida	1023.6
Georgia	606.6
Hawaii	277.9
Idaho	256.8
Illinois	861.4
Indiana	514.6
Iowa	310.0
Kansas	409.2
Kentucky	316.9
Louisiana	855.9
Maine	120.8
Maryland	846.6
Massachusetts	644.2
Michigan	590.0
Minnesota	337.8
Mississippi	469.0
Missouri	577.4
Montana	132.1
Nebraska	438.4
Nevada	798.7
New Jersey	492.6
New Hamp.	113.2
New Mexico	853.3
New York	688.6
North Carolina	607.0
North Dakota	87.2
Ohio	435.4
Oklahoma	559.5
Oregon	444.4
Pennsylvania	442.1
Rhode Island	333.5
South Carolina	990.3
South Dakota	197.4
Tennessee	789.7
Texas	602.5
Utah	334.0
Vermont	119.7
Virginia	345.2
Washington	440.7
West Virginia	218.7
Wisconsin	270.6
Wyoming	255.2

Violent crime includes murder and non-negligent manslaughter, forcible rape, robbery, and aggravated assault. Based on FBI's Uniform Crime Reporting Program.

Source: *Sourcebook of Criminal Justice Statistics 1998*, Table 3.119, Bureau of Justice Statistics (1999).

District 2

District 2 is on the opposite side of Athena from district 1, and it includes most of the blue-collar suburbs and the industries. It is mostly white, though some African Americans and Latinos have moved into the edge of the district. A recent recession and the closing of two electronics plants has hit district 2 hard. Almost 10 percent of the work force is unemployed. Even the auto assembly plant has cut production and laid off a quarter of its employees.

In the past, the main problems in the district were juvenile delinquency and fights outside several notorious bars. Now, however, the number of muggings and street robberies is rising. Also, the biggest industries report a number of suspicious fires and acts of sabotage. Gang graffiti has begun to appear on walls everywhere.

People in district 2 are very angry, but they are not sure what to do. Many of them talk about getting tougher on the criminals, and they blame the police. They feel that richer areas like district 1 get much better policing than they do.

District 3

District 3 is in the northwest part of the state. It includes Gold Canyon and was once the Whitewater Mining district. The minerals were played out long ago, and it is now mainly a picturesque tourist area in the foothills. The district features many resorts and spas. The biggest town is College Park, which contains Columbia State University, and most of the faculty and students live here.

Crime has decreased most in this district. The campus police have the university area under control, and a few extra units of the state police have managed to stop victimization of tourists.

People in the Whitewater area are worried that publicity about crime will scare off tourists. They want a well-publicized anti-crime campaign that will reassure potential tourists. Many other voters in the district, however, are opposed to what they see as repressive legislation like SB 1715.

The people near the university are largely opposed to handguns. They passed a local ordinance to require a long waiting period before purchasing any firearm. They would strongly oppose any state law that would encourage people to buy handguns.

District 4

This district is in the center of the state and largely agricultural. The largest town, Lone Pine, has just over 1,000 people and serves the surrounding farms. Three very large agricultural corporations employ hundreds of field hands and some administrators. People in the smaller towns run cafes and gas stations that are dependent on the tourists passing through to the mountains in the west.

A few years ago there was hardly any crime at all in district 4, except an occasional gas station holdup and a rare murder. Recently, gangs from the cities have made raids on the larger farms or on businesses on payroll day. There have even been a few midnight assaults and rapes in the small towns.

Many district residents blame Athena for the crime and they feel no one in the big city takes them seriously. Some are talking about taking the law into their own hands and forming vigilante posses.

District 5

District 5 includes all of the central city of Athena. The residents are mostly poor and many work at service industries in the city core that pay minimum wage. Those who do have jobs in the industries in the suburbs have to commute long distances. African Americans are about a third of the population, Latinos are another third, and the rest is made up of relatively new Asian immigrants and poor whites.

Crime rates have traditionally been high in district 5, but over the last two years they have actually dropped a little. Many people feel this is because of an active neighborhood-watch program and a well-funded federal jobs program for city youth.

Most urban residents oppose SB 1715. There have been many state cutbacks on welfare programs, and Athenians feel that the extra money proposed in the bill would be better spent combating poverty. They feel that is the way to fight crime.

Urban residents feel their neighborhood-watch and jobs programs are working, and they would like to see these expanded and reproduced in other population centers in the state. They want more money devoted to social welfare and anti-poverty programs. And they feel the second provision of the bill would just increase the level of violence and encourage dangerous vigilante action.

For Discussion

1. The preamble to SB 1715 declares that criminals are "enemies of the state." Are all criminals enemies of the state? What might be some problems with such an attitude?

2. Reread the provisions of SB 1715 one at a time. Answer the following questions for each:

   - What are some possible consequences if this proposition were enacted into law? Explain.

   - Which of these would have a positive impact on society? Which would have a negative impact? Explain.

Debriefing Questions

1. How does Columbia differ from your state? Which district described is closest to the one you live in? Why?

2. Would the people of your state support such a crime bill? Why or why not?

3. Do you think this exercise was a realistic representation of how your state senate would deal with a crime bill? Why or why not?

The New Role of State Supreme Courts

As the Supreme Court in recent years has restricted the rights of criminal defendants, defendants have increasingly looked to state supreme courts to protect their rights.

How can a state court offer more protection than the U.S. Supreme Court? The U.S. Supreme Court, after all, makes the final decision on matters of U.S. constitutional law. It decides whether the Constitution guarantees certain rights, and it determines the extent of these rights. A state supreme court could not, for example, declare that the *U.S.* Constitution gives people a right to privacy in the items they put out for trash collection, because the U.S. Supreme Court in *California v. Greenwood* (1988) has already ruled the U.S. Constitution grants no such right. The U.S. Supreme Court would reverse any contrary decision by a state court.

But a state supreme court could declare that its *state* constitution granted that right. The New Jersey Supreme Court did exactly this in its 1990 *State v. Hempele* decision. It ruled that under the New Jersey Constitution, residents have a right to privacy in items put in the trash. This right is protected independently by the state constitution. The U.S. Supreme Court cannot overrule this decision, because state supreme courts are the final judges of the meaning of their constitutions.

These constitutions can grant *more* rights than the U.S. Constitution. Thus criminal defendants appealing their convictions often ask state courts to find their rights have been violated under the state constitution. In many cases in the last 30 years, state supreme courts have ruled that their constitutions granted more protections than the U.S. Constitution. If the U.S. Supreme Court continues to restrict the rights of criminal defendants, more defendants will look to their state constitutions for protection. But one state, California, has put a stop to this practice. In 1982, the voters of California passed the Victims' Bill of Rights, which limited the rights of criminal defen-

Utah Supreme Court Justice Christine Durham poses outside the state capitol in Salt Lake City.

dants under the California Constitution to those granted under the U.S. Constitution.

For Discussion

1. On what basis can state courts grant greater protections for criminal defendants than those guaranteed by the U.S. Constitution?

2. Do you think state courts should do this? Why or why not?

3. Could a state court restrict or deny rights guaranteed by the U.S. Constitution? Explain.

The Color of Justice

In 1991 in Los Angeles, a bystander videotaped police officers beating Rodney King, a black man. People in the African-American community had long complained of cases of police brutality. At long last, they had clear evidence—a videotape. But at the trial in state court, the jury acquitted the four officers of using excessive force. A major riot erupted following the verdict.

Although two of the officers were subsequently convicted in federal court, many in the African-American and in other minority communities argue that this case shows how difficult it is for people of color to get justice from the criminal justice system. Racial discrimination, they say, permeates the system.

Critics who claim that racism taints the system have cited its treatment of African-American males. For example, statistics show that more than one-fourth of all black males and 16 percent of Latinos can expect to spend time in prison during their lifetime, while only 4 percent of white males ever go to prison. African-Americans make up 12 percent of the U.S. population, but they compose about half of all prison inmates and 40 percent of those sentenced to death. Even more startling, a third of all African-American males aged 20–29 are right now either locked up, on probation, or on parole.

The question remains whether these statistics come from racism in the criminal justice system or from other causes. Social scientists and politicians have argued about this question for decades.

In a controversial 1975 article, titled "White Racism, Black Crime, and American Justice," criminologist Robert Staples argued that discrimination pervades the justice sys-

tem. He said the legal system was made by white men to protect white interests and keep blacks down. Staples charged that the system was characterized by second-rate legal help for black defendants, biased jurors, and judges who discriminate in sentencing.

A dozen years later, sociologist William Wilbanks rejected the discrimination argument. In his book, *The Myth of a Racist Criminal Justice System*, Wilbanks reviewed scores of studies that showed statistical inequalities between whites and blacks in arrest rates, imprisonment, and other areas of criminal justice. He found that the inequalities came from factors other than racial discrimination, such as poverty and the defendant's prior record.

Other sociologists, too, have suggested that the apparent inequalities have more to do with poverty than race. Street crimes such as robbery and assault, prominent in the statistics, are usually committed by people from poor backgrounds. Today, even though significant improvements were made during the 1990s in minority employment, about one quarter of all African Americans and Latinos live below the official poverty line. This compares to only 10 percent of all whites.

The connection between poverty and crime has long been noted. During the 1930s, a much larger part of the white population was poor, and whites committed a greater percentage of street crime. Whites then accounted for nearly 80 percent of those in prison compared to 45 percent today. The question of poverty alone may well account for many of the apparent inequalities in the system.

A RAND Corporation study in 1983, however, unearthed some disturbing data. RAND compared the treatment of whites and blacks at key decision points in the criminal justice system. The researchers found that black defendants seemed to be treated more harshly at key points such as sentencing. But the researchers did not identify a cause for these inequalities. Later studies have provided more insight into this troubling data.

Arrest

African Americans account for about 40 percent of the arrests for violent crimes. This far surpasses their numbers in the population. Does this disparity come from racial discrimination? Those who say "no" point out that this percentage corresponds to reports from the National Crime Victimization Survey. This survey interviews thousands of victims of crime each year. The percentage of victims who say their perpetrator was black closely matches the percentage of African Americans arrested. A survey of arrest studies concluded, however, that "police are involved in *at least some discrimination* against members of racial and ethnic minorities."

In many jurisdictions, more blacks than whites are released after arrest. This is particularly true for less serious offenses such as prostitution, gambling, and public drunkenness. What this means is unclear. Some say it means that police and prosecutors are more likely to treat African Americans leniently. Others say it means that blacks are more likely to be arrested on insufficient evidence or harassed by police.

The release rate also varies according to neighborhood. If blacks are arrested in largely minority neighborhoods, they are more likely to be released than whites. But there is no difference in integrated neighborhoods.

Plea Bargaining

More than 90 percent of all criminal cases never go to trial. The defendant pleads guilty, often after the prosecutor and defense attorney negotiate. A 1990 study of about 1,000 cases by the U.S. Sentencing Commission found that whites did better in plea bargains. Twenty-five percent of whites, 18 percent of blacks, and 12 percent of Latinos got their sentences reduced through bargaining. The reason for the disparity was not determined.

The *San Jose Mercury News* conducted a massive study of 700,000 California legal cases over a 10-year period. The paper reported in December 1991 that a third of the white adults who were arrested, but had no prior record, were able to get felony charges against them reduced. Only a quarter of the African-Americans and Latinos with no priors were as successful in plea bargaining.

The *Mercury News* study did not blame intentional racism for these inequalities. It did, however, suggest that subtle cultural fears and insensitivity contributed to the problem. The study noted that more than 80 percent of all California prosecutors and judges are white, while more than 60 percent of those arrested are non-white.

Constance Rice, a lawyer for the NAACP Legal Defense Fund in Los Angeles, explained that when prosecutors and judges use their discretion, "we have always found evidence to support the notion that race plays a role."

Jury Verdicts

In 1985, Cornell law professor Sheri Lynn Johnson reviewed a dozen mock-jury studies. She concluded that the "race of the defendant significantly and directly affects the determination of guilt." In these studies, identical trials were simulated, sometimes with white defendants and sometimes with African Americans. Professor Johnson discovered that white jurors were more likely to find a black defendant guilty than a white defendant, even though the mock trials were based on the same crime and the same evidence.

And Professor Johnson found that black jurors behaved with the reverse bias. They found white defendants guilty more often than black defendants. Furthermore, the race of the **victim** in the case affected both groups. If the victim was black, white jurors tended to find a white defendant less blameworthy. In the same way, if the victim was white, black jurors found black defendants less blameworthy.

According to these mock-jury experiments, both white and black jurors seem to discriminate. Professor Johnson did not, however, think the juror bias was intentional. "Because the process of attributing guilt on the basis of race appears to be subconscious," Johnson says, "jurors are unlikely either to be aware of or to be able to control that process."

The mock trials did have one encouraging result. When white and black mock jurors met together, as many real juries do, the effect of race tended to disappear. This result seems to indicate that the best way to eliminate racial bias in verdicts is to select racially mixed juries. The U.S. Supreme Court has moved in this direction by prohibiting both prosecutors and defense lawyers from eliminating prospective jurors solely because of race. (See *Batson v. Kentucky*, 1986, and *Georgia v. McCollum*, 1992.)

An earlier study, however, pointed to less clear conclusions. Psychologist J.L. Bernard of Memphis State University examined a jury of six blacks and six whites deadlocked along racial lines over the guilt of a black defendant. According to Bernard, "black jurors as a whole may be more likely to acquit a defendant, regardless of race," because they are more suspicious of police motives and witnesses.

Sentencing

The 1983 RAND Corporation study found that convicted African-Americans were more likely than whites to go to prison. And their sentences were longer. "This disparity," the study concluded, "suggests that probation officers, judges, and parole boards are exercising discretion in sentencing or release decisions in ways that result in de facto discrimination against blacks." **De facto** means the discrimination exists in fact, but without legal authority. It may not be intentional.

Poll on Confidence in the Justice System		
"Please tell me how much confidence you, yourself, have in the criminal justice system."		
	Blacks	Whites
Very little	48%	28%
Some	22	39
Quite a lot	8	17
A great deal	17	11
Source: Gallup Organization / CNN / *USA Today* (1998)		

Unintended discrimination can occur at many points in the legal process. Probation officers often prepare pre-sentencing reports for a judge. The judge uses the reports to help make sentencing decisions. Reports include information on the criminal's prior record, family background, education, marital status, and employment history. Many African-Americans convicted of crimes come from deprived backgrounds. They may have things in their record—unemployment, trouble in school, family problems—that judges, who largely come from middle-class backgrounds, cannot relate to. This may sway some judges to treat them more harshly in sentencing.

In a 1999 survey of studies on discrimination in the justice system, researcher Christopher Stone found that much of the disparity in sentencing could be traced to differences in arrest charges and prior records of those convicted. He concluded: "There is no evidence of disparity that stretches across the justice system as a whole . . . . But studies of individual jurisdictions and specific parts of the court process do find some evidence of race bias in a significant number of cases."

Stone considered drug offences separately. Some federal mandatory sentences have come under fire for discriminating against minorities. Critics point to different sentences mandated for crack cocaine, a drug popular in poor minority communities, and powder cocaine, a drug used in wealthier communities. Under federal law, dealing five grams of crack cocaine gets a first offender a mandatory minimum sentence of five years. To receive a similar mandatory minimum sentence for trafficking in powder cocaine, an offender must possess 500 grams. Stone stated: "Whatever one believes about the rationality of the decision to create special, harsher penalties for crack cocaine, the concentration of these sentences on black defendants is striking."

States often have similar disparities in drug sentencing laws. In a 1996 study of California drug sentencing laws, researchers found that possession of crack cocaine and heroin, more commonly used by minorities, carried stiffer penalties than possession of methamphetamines, more commonly used by whites.

Death Penalty

A study was made of 2,000 murder cases prosecuted by the state of Georgia during the 1970s. It showed that defendants convicted of killing whites were more than four times as likely to receive the death penalty than those convicted of murdering blacks. The study also revealed that black defendants who murdered whites had by far the greatest chance of being sentenced to death.

A Georgia black man who had been sentenced to death for killing a white police officer used this study in his appeal to the U.S. Supreme Court. He claimed the study proved that Georgia's jurors and judges discriminated against African-American defendants. In a 5–4 decision, the Supreme Court accepted the results of the study, but ruled that it did not prove discrimination. Writing for the majority, Justice Lewis F. Powell concluded that the study failed to "demonstrate a constitutionally significant risk of racial bias affecting the Georgia capital sentencing process." (*McCleskey v. Kemp*, 1987.)

Studies confirm that racial disparities exist in the American criminal justice system, but they differ over the cause. Supreme Court decisions since 1960 have rooted out many overtly racist practices, such as in jury selection, but it is more difficult to address unintentional racist factors. Because these factors come from subtle assumptions and fears deeply ingrained in the wider society, only when society changes will they disappear.

Critics of the system, however, insist that inequalities, regardless of their basis, should not be swept under the rug. They must be paid attention to and any discrimination found must be eliminated. Many critics believe that the disparities in the system would be easier to accept as unbiased if more decision makers— police, prosecutors, judges, and juries—were people of color.

For Discussion

1. What are the disparities between white and black defendants at each of the following key decision points: arrest, plea bargaining, jury verdicts, sentencing, and capital punishment.

2. What do you think accounts for these disparities? Explain.

3. According to Andrew Hacker, author of *Two Nations, Black and White, Separate, Hostile, Unequal*, "The feeling persists that a black man who rapes or robs a white person has inflicted more harm than black or white criminals who prey on victims of their own race." Do you agree with this statement? Why or why not?

Class Activity: Toward a Colorblind Justice System

Various proposals have been put forward to prevent discrimination in arrests, plea bargaining, jury verdicts, sentencing, and the death penalty. In this activity, students evaluate a few of these and come up with suggestions of their own.

1. Break into small groups. Assign each group one of the four policy areas below.

2. Each group should:

    a.   Read its policy, evaluate it, and report back to the class.

    b.   To evaluate the policy, answer the following questions:

        (1) What problem is the policy designed to address? Does it

address the problem? Why or why not?

(2) Who might support the policy? Who might oppose it? Why?

(3) What benefits might come from the policy?

(4) What costs might result from the policy?

(5) What other policies might address the problem? Are they better? Why?

(6) What policy should be adopted? Why?

3. Have the groups report back. Conclude the activity with a discussion using the Debriefing Questions on this page.

I. Arrests

Policy: Police should collect data on the race and release records of every person they arrest.

Pros: This will enable departments to track officers who arrest minorities without sufficient cause.

Cons: Police have too much paperwork already and the statistics collected will be meaningless.

II. Plea Bargaining

Policy: Plea bargaining should be abolished.

Pros: It will do away with an informal process subject to abuse because the courts do not review it. It will ensure that all defendants have their day in court.

Cons: Doing away with plea bargaining will clog the courts with cases awaiting trial, resulting in increased court costs.

III. Jury Verdicts

Policy: Peremptory challenges should be abolished. (Peremptory challenges allow attorneys to exclude a limited number of prospective jurors for any reason except race and gender.)

Pros: Even though they are not supposed to, attorneys still use peremptory challenges to exclude jurors on account of race. This will end the practice.

Cons: It is already illegal to exclude jurors on account of race. Doing away with peremptory challenges is too extreme. These challenges help both the prosecution and defense exclude jurors who they feel might not be impartial.

IV. Sentencing

Policy: Federal law should not make first-time drug offenders face mandatory sentences. Judges should be allowed more discretion in sentencing these drug offenders.

Pros: Mandatory-minimum sentences cause first-time offenders, mostly minorities, to go into an already overcrowded prison system.

Cons: Mandatory-minimum sentences are needed to show we are serious in our war on drugs.

V. Death Penalty

Policy: Congress should reverse the decision in *McCleskey*. If statistical studies show racial disparities in a state's imposition of the death penalty, then minority defendants should not be sentenced to death in that state.

Pros: Race should play no role in whether or not a person receives the death penalty. The death penalty should be limited to aggravated cases where whites and blacks receive the same treatment.

Cons: Mere discrepancies in statistics should not invalidate the death penalty. A defendant should have to show discrimination in the particular case or that the state intended to discriminate.

Debriefing Questions

1. Which policies garnered the most support? The least support? Why?

2. What other policies did you think of that could prevent racial discrimination in the criminal justice system? Do you think they would work? Why or why not?

3. Why is it important that the criminal justice system not be perceived as racially biased?

CHAPTER 23
Crime and the Citizen

Getting Involved in Fighting Crime

[I]n Japan, you can walk into a park at midnight and sit on a bench and nothing will happen to you. You're completely safe, day or night. You can go anywhere. You won't be robbed or beaten or killed. You're not always looking behind you, not always worrying. You don't need walls or bodyguards. . . . You're free. It's a wonderful feeling. Here, everybody has to lock themselves up. Lock the door. Lock the car. People who spend their whole lives locked up are in prison.

—Michael Crichton, *Rising Sun*

Americans fear crime. Almost every year for the last 20 years, a majority of Americans have responded "more" to the Gallup Poll's question, "Is there more crime in your area than there was a year ago, or less?"

The fear of crime has spurred people into taking individual action against crime. They have built walls, bought guns, and installed security systems. A whole new security industry has blossomed. There are now more private security guards than police in the United States. But today and throughout our history ordinary citizens have banded together to fight crime—sometimes legally and other times illegally.

Vigilantes in American History

Violence and crime have been a major part of American history from the beginning. Vigilantes have been with us almost as long. Repeatedly, groups of citizens have banded together to take the law into their own hands and punish suspected criminals. These groups were usually well organized and had leaders and rules. Before illegally punishing their suspects, they often held some sort of trial. But the accused usually had little chance for a real defense.

Before 1900, vigilantism was relatively common in the United States. Episodes of vigilante justice occurred all over the country. Historians know of well over 300 vigilante movements in American history. Their size varied from small groups of about a dozen people to large organizations including thousands of citizens. Most numbered several hundred. Vigilante groups went by various names, including *regulators, slickers, stranglers, committees of safety,* and *vigilance committees.*

Vigilante organizations were usually formed for some specific purpose. Once the job was done, the vigilantes disbanded. Most operated for less than a year.

In the early years of our country, vigilantes ordinarily whipped, beat, or tarred and feathered those they believed guilty. But by the 1850s, hanging had become widespread. Those not hanged were usually forced to leave the area. Few escaped punishment.

Most vigilante groups were composed of normally law-abiding merchants, ranchers, and other prominent citizens. Their leaders were usually the wealthiest and most important people in the area. Why did these kinds of people resort to an illegal and often violent method of handling criminals? There are several reasons.

The most important reason was that the frontier lacked police, courts, and jails. Until 1900, many people lived in isolated frontier settlements far from established law and order. Faced with doing nothing about rampaging outlaws or taking the law into their own hands, respectable people chose the vigilante solution. Frontier Americans were used to relying on themselves to solve problems.

Another reason for vigilantism had to do with the determination of businessmen and the wealthy to maintain political control over the lower classes. When crime, violence, or political corruption seemed to tip the balance of power in a community toward the lower classes, a vigilante movement, led by merchants, bankers, or large landowners, was often organized.

In some cases, the reason for vigilance committees was simply to keep taxes low. It was much cheaper to take care of criminals by hauling them before a group of vigilantes than paying sheriffs, judges, prosecutors, and jailers to do the job.

The Earliest Vigilantes

The first vigilante movement in America was formed in the South Carolina backwoods in the 1760s. A newly settled frontier area, it had just undergone a costly Indian war with the Cherokees. Orphaned and homeless young people drifted into outlaw bands. These bands stole horses, kidnaped, raped, and robbed.

Since the area had no sheriffs and courts, a group known as the Regulators was organized in 1767. Composed of up to 6,000 normally law-abiding settlers, the Regulators attacked and broke up the outlaw gangs. The lawbreakers were given trials, whipped, driven out of the area, or forced to work on farms. Sixteen were killed.

The Regulators disbanded in 1769 when courts and sheriffs were established. But this group of vigilantes provided a model that many other vigilance movements throughout the country would later copy.

Vigilante movements were set up again and again before the Civil War to deal with horse thieves, counterfeiters, gamblers, and bands of robbers. Vigilantes were particularly active in Alabama, Mississippi, Louisiana, Iowa, Indiana, and Illinois.

Vigilantes from the West

Vigilante groups were more numerous and generally more deadly in the West. Between 1850 and 1900, about 200 vigilante movements were set up. They executed over 500 accused horse and cattle thieves, murderers, robbers, and others. Texas holds the record for the most vigilante killings with 140. But one Montana vigilante group in 1884 carried out 35 executions. Theodore Roosevelt, working as a cowboy in Montana at this time, wanted to join the vigilantes but never got the chance.

Some historians have attempted to classify vigilante movements as *constructive* and *destructive*. According to this viewpoint, constructive vigilante groups got rid of the criminal element quickly, restored order, and then disbanded. These groups usually had widespread public support. Destructive vigilante movements were often divided from within and frequently led to chaos and violence.

A good example of a destructive type of vigilante movement was the Regulator-Moderator War of Shelby County, Texas. In 1840, when Texas was an independent country, a group of Regulators formed to get rid of a corrupt ring of county officials. The county had attracted thieves, counterfeiters, and murderers.

The Regulator leader was killed and replaced by a man who took his role so seriously that he wore a military uniform. Soon an opposing group of vigilantes calling themselves the Moderators banded together. But criminals infiltrated both groups. Violence, revenge, and feuds erupted. The original reason for the formation of the vigilante movement was forgotten. An all-out battle broke out between the Regulators and Moderators in 1844 involving hundreds of men. Sam Houston and the Lone Star Republic militia finally stopped the violence.

The Johnson County Invasion is an example of what has been called constructive vigilantism. Some Wyoming big cattle ranchers, used to grazing their large herds on open range land, took exception when homesteaders began to fence off land. At first, the cattle barons accused the homesteaders of rustling. A few homesteaders were murdered, but no one was ever convicted of the killings. In April 1892, the large cattle ranchers brought in a trainload of heavily armed gunfighters supposedly to go after rustlers. In reality, they were

The San Francisco Committee of Vigilance prepares to execute one of its prisoners in front of its headquarters. The committee was organized to respond to lawlessness in the city during the 1850s.

hired to force out the homesteaders. The gunmen quickly went to work and killed two settlers. Enraged, the homesteaders formed a vigilante group, rounded up the invaders, and held them until federal troops arrived. Unfortunately, after being bailed out of jail by the cattle barons, the gunslingers disappeared. So they were never put on trial.

The San Francisco Vigilance Committees

Two of the most famous examples of vigilantism in American history occurred in San Francisco in 1851 and 1856.

In 1851, with the Gold Rush at its peak, San Francisco was wide open, rough, and dangerous. Its police could do little to stop a wave of crimes. A Committee of Vigilance was formed composed of over 500 leading citizens. William T. Coleman, a young merchant, led the committee.

The Committee of Vigilance announced that "no thief, burglar, incendiary, or assassin shall escape punishment, either by the quibbles of the law, the insecurity of prisons, the carelessness or corruption of the police, or a laxity of those who pretend to administer justice." Clearly, these San Francisco vigilantes had a low opinion of those responsible for law and order in the city.

Before the year ended, the committee had whipped one accused criminal, hanged four others, forced 15 to leave the city, and handed over another 15 to legal authorities. After cleaning up the city, the committee disbanded.

But five years later, San Francisco was in worse shape than before. Murders and other crimes were rampant. Even more frightening to San Francisco business leaders was the corrupt political machine that ran the city government. David C. Broderick, the Democratic Party leader of San Francisco, controlled the city. Kept in power by the votes of Irish-Catholic workers, Broderick stuffed his pockets and those of his friends with public funds. Businessmen resented that their tax dollars financed Broderick and his friends. By 1856, San Francisco was facing bankruptcy. Businessmen in the city, who depended on credit from Eastern banks, were worried.

SEAL OF THE CALIFORNIA VIGILANCE COMMITTEE.

Thousands of San Franciscans joined the Committee of Vigilance during its brief existence. Many other places in the West followed San Francisco's example.

James King, editor of the *San Francisco Daily Evening Bulletin*, wrote editorials attacking the crime problem and the corruption of the Broderick political machine. King, who had been a vigilante in 1851, also began to revive talk of vigilante justice. On May 14, 1856, he was shot to death on a San Francisco street.

The following day, William T. Coleman, leader of the vigilantes in 1851, formed a new vigilance committee. Within a few days, the vigilance committee arrested, tried, and hanged one of Broderick's political flunkies for the shooting.

During the next few months, perhaps as many as 8,000 San Franciscans joined the vigilantes. Most were merchants and skilled workers. Few were Irish. Coleman held almost dictatorial powers. With an executive committee of business men, he drew up a list of suspects. People were arrested and tried at vigilante headquarters, which was called Fort Gunnybags because it was protected with sandbags. In all, the committee executed four accused criminals. It put Broderick's henchmen on ships headed for Eastern and foreign ports and told them never to come back to the city. It called Broderick himself before the vigilance committee. When he was released, he left town.

In operation only three months, the vigilance committee disbanded on August 18 with a parade through the city. But the vigilance committee formed a political organization, the People's Party, that controlled San Francisco's city government for the next 10 years.

The San Francisco vigilance committees of 1851 and 1856 were widely publicized and copied throughout the West. Sometimes, however, it was difficult to tell the difference between a vigilance committee and a lynch mob. On July 4, 1851, for example, a bunch of drunken miners smashed into the shack of a Mexican woman in Downieville, California. Thinking she was being attacked, the woman stabbed one of the miners, who later died. The woman was quickly tried by a vigilante jury and sentenced to death. She was hanged from a wooden bridge over the Yuba River.

Was Vigilantism Ever Justified?

There seems to be a vigilante strain that has repeatedly surfaced in American history. Was vigilante justice ever warranted? One former Colorado vigilante thought vigilante justice worked better than legal procedures. "There were no appeals in those days," he said, "no writs of errors, no attorney's fees, no pardon in six months. Punishment was swift, sure, and certain." On the other hand, a New York City newspaper editorial criticizing the San Francisco vigilance committee of 1856 stated: "Better to endure the evil of escape of criminals than to inaugurate a reign of terror which today may punish one guilty head, and tomorrow wreak its mistaken vengeance on many innocent lives."

For Discussion

1. Why did normally law-abiding and well-to-do citizens turn to illegal vigilante methods? Do you think that people today could turn to vigilantism? Explain.

2. How are vigilante groups and lynch mobs different? How are they similar?

3. Do you think vigilantism was ever justified in American history? Do you think it would ever be justified today? Why or why not?

Crime in Schools

Crime and violence in schools is far greater today than the 1950s. A teacher from that decade would be astonished to enter some of our urban schools today and find police in the halls and metal detectors at the doors to keep out guns and knives. But the problems do not just belong to urban schools. The worst school shootings in recent years have taken place at rural and suburban schools.

The National Center for Education Statistics reports almost 3 million crimes a year on school grounds. More than 200,000 of these crimes are serious violent crimes (rape, robbery, and aggravated assault). Almost 10 percent of high school students reported carrying a weapon such as a gun, knife, or club to school. One in 20 reported being a victim of a violent crime at school or on the way to school. And each year about 16,000 teachers fall victim to serious violent crimes.

Schools have not always been so hazardous. From the 1950s through the middle 1960s, the main school problems were pranks, some ethnic rivalry, isolated fistfights, and occasional vandalism. For a brief time from about 1968 through the early 1970s, the massive college anti-war movement spilled over into the high schools. Demonstrations took place against the war and over local issues, such as integration or local school rules. But by the early 1970s, much more serious problems were occurring. Schools started to experience crimes of violence, drug offenses, rape, and even shootings.

Schools and Gangs

Schools, of course, reflect the communities they serve. In the early 1980s, crack cocaine and heavily armed drug-dealing gangs overran many urban communities. Gang members and gang "wanna-bes" adopted symbols such as colored head scarves and football team jackets. In some places, drug dealing and gang rivalries spilled over into the schools. Increased levels of violence in society as a whole affected the schools. Personal feuds over a girlfriend or an insult that would once have ended in a fistfight

turned into a gun battle. In New York City schools during the 1992 school year alone, five teachers, one policeman, two parents, and 16 students were shot.

By the late 1990s, crime had decreased in American society and in schools as well. In 1992, there were almost 150 crimes at school per 1,000 students. By 1997, this number had dropped to 100. Violent crimes had decreased as well but not as dramatically. The reason may be that the percentage of students reporting gangs at their school doubled from 1989 to 1995. Gangs are closely linked to school violence.

In the late 1990s, a series of shootings took place at non-urban schools. Out of the way places, such as Moses Lake, Washington; Bethel, Alaska; Pearl, Mississippi; Springfield, Oregon; and West Paducah, Kentucky experienced school shootings and killings.

In two instances, boys planned their shootings together. In 1998, two students opened fire on students gathered outside because of a false fire alarm at a middle school in Jonesboro, Arkansas, killing four girls and a teacher. In 1999 in Littleton, Colorado, two students went on a rampage killing 13 others and themselves at a high school.

These shooting shocked the nation. It seemed to many that if shootings could take place in these schools, they could happen anywhere. One parent summed up the fears of many: "It scares me to death that I'm sending my child to a school . . . and in light of getting an education, I may end up burying her."

Some commentators think these fears are overblown. They point out that lightning kills twice as many people each year as are killed in schools. They see no growing trend in school killings. They explain that school killings account for a small percentage of the homicides involving juveniles.

Even so, parents and students want schools as safe and orderly as possible. Schools in crisis cannot educate effectively. Disruptions and a sense of fear distract students and teachers from education.

Educators and schools across the nation are trying various measures to improve school safety. Although the goal of each school is the same, the problem varies from school to school. Some schools are safe and want to remain so. Others are plagued with problems and need to restore order. Different strategies are being tried. Among them are:

Increasing school security. Most schools now require visitors to sign in before entering the school, and about half monitor access to their buildings. Four-fifths of all high schools maintain "closed campuses," barring students from leaving for lunch. Almost nine out of 10 high schools have police stationed or readily available on the campus. About 20 percent report running drug sweeps. A few schools have resorted to metal detectors, but only 1 percent use them daily. Some schools have removed lockers to eliminate hiding places for guns or drugs. A few have done away with teachers' bathrooms, so that teachers have to visit the students' bathrooms regularly to discourage illegal activities.

Adopting "zero tolerance" policies. These policies mandate tough action, from suspension to expulsion, for certain offenses. More than 90 percent of schools have zero-tolerance policies for guns or other weapons. In the 1996–97 school year, about one out of 20 schools reported expelling or suspending a student for having a gun. About four-fifths of all schools also have zero-tolerance policies for alcohol, drugs, violence, and tobacco.

Running violence-prevention programs. More than three-fourths of all schools operate some type of violence-prevention program. Most of these programs are ongoing, but about a tenth of all schools have one-day programs only. The programs vary. Some offer conflict and peer mediation. Others are part of the curriculum. Service learning links classroom learning to activities in the community. Law-related education helps students understand the legal system and social issues through interactive classroom lessons. Character education teaches basic values.

Mandating dress codes or school uniforms. These policies aim to deter property crimes

Measures to Limit Violence on Campus	
A 1996 random survey of school administrators asked them to identify measures their schools had implemented to reduce violence.	
Measure	**% of administrators surveyed**
Taken by a majority of the schools	
Automatic suspensions for weapons violations	96
Revised disciplinary codes	81
Designation of school as a "drug-free" zone	74
Conflict resolution and mediation programs	71
Designation of school as a "gun-free" zone	66
Dress codes	63
Multicultural sensitivity training	60
Locker searches	55
Taken by fewer than a majority of the schools	
Non-police monitors in hallways or on school grounds	40
Photo IDs for staff and students	33
Video monitoring of school buses	31
Police on campus	27
Extra police patrols around school property	21
Police in school hallways	15
Rarely taken by the schools	
Video monitoring of hallways	10
ID checks at school entrances	6
Metal detectors at school entrances	2
Video monitoring of classrooms	2
Mandatory "see through" book bags	0

Source: "Controlling Violence: What Schools Are Doing," *Preventing School Violence*, National Institute of Justice (2000).

prompted when students wear designer clothing and expensive sneakers. They also prevent gang members from wearing colors and insignia and help school officials recognize intruders on the campus. Although many schools have adopted dress codes, only 3 percent of all schools have adopted uniforms—almost none at the high school level.

Making schools less impersonal. Many large schools are trying to break down their cold, impersonal atmosphere by creating "schools within schools." Some are hiring more teachers to minimize school violence associated with classroom overcrowding. Some schools are offering specialized vocational training, which young people can recognize as important. The National School Safety Center encourages schools to set up student committees to study school safety and even hold court on violators.

Schools across the country have set up committees to work on improving school safety. They are considering proposals such as these and others.

For Discussion

1. Describe how school conditions differed in each of the following periods: 1950–1968, 1968–1971, and 1972–present.

2. Does your school look different from a school of the 1950s? What is different and why?

3. Does your school have a crime problem? If so, what do you think are the primary causes of crime in your school? Explain. What do you think can be done about the problem?

Class Activity: Trouble at Coolidge High

What can be done about violence at school? One approach has been to ask members of the school community to find solutions to the problem. In the activity that follows, students role play members of a School Problems Committee.

1. As a class, read and briefly discuss "A Case Study" on page 298.

2. Divide the class into groups of five students. Each group will role play a five-member School Problems Committee. The committee will discuss and decide upon the various proposals to deal with the gang problem, including the proposal from Mr. Martinez. Assign each group member one of the following roles (if a group has more than five, assign the extra student a role as teacher):

   a. School principal

   b. Teacher

   c. Student representative, elected by the student body

   d. Student body president

   e. Parent

3. Before the School Problems Committees meet, have students get together with the other students who play the same role. For example, all the students assigned to be the school principal should get together. In these role groups, students should discuss how a person in that role would respond to the issue. How would that person view gangs in the school? What special interest would that person have in the problem?

4. Now regroup and form School Problems Committees. The principal should act as the chairperson.

5. Each committee should discuss the Coolidge High problems and the proposals. Before deciding on its recommendations, the committee should discuss the following questions:

   • What are the most serious problems facing Coolidge High?

   • Which proposals in the school plan will be effective in dealing with the problems? Which will be ineffective? Why?

   • What proposals should be adopted to form the school plan? Why?

6. After each committee has decided what should be done, the principals should report to the class on each committee's decisions. As a class, discuss the plans that the committees developed using the following questions:

   a. What are the strengths and weaknesses of the various plans? Which one is most likely to be successful?

   b. Would you like to see a School Problems Committee formed in your school? Why or why not?

   c. How should committee members be selected?

   d. How much authority should they have?

e. Do students in your school need a place to register complaints?

f. Are there better ways to deal with school crime and gangs than through this kind of committee? If so, what are they?

7. Ask students to make a list of issues they would take before a committee at your school. In a class discussion, decide which of these issues are the most important.

A Case Study

Coolidge High School is an old inner-city school. It has had trouble with gangs for many years. Three main gangs rival one another at school—the Dukes, the Rolling Nineties, and 35th Street. Most gang violence takes place off campus—at night and during weekends. But the school has suffered extensive vandalism, which appears to be gang-related. Gang names and symbols have been painted on the walls and carved on desks. Threats and challenges appear on the walls of the school entrance. A few fights have broken out, but no one has been seriously hurt yet.

Students are frisked for weapons at the school entrances, and the administration has tried to guard the halls to prevent more graffiti or fighting. Nothing has helped much, and school morale is low.

The following steps are being proposed to the School Problems Committee:

1. Teachers should periodically check classroom furniture and ask students to report any new marks.

2. Felt pens and magic markers should be banned from school.

3. Vandals who are caught should join work teams to clean or repair school property.

4. Parents should be told that they are liable for property destroyed by their children.

5. Teachers and administrators should frequently lecture students about vandalism.

6. The school should set up a school pride campaign.

There is one further proposal, a surprise that came at the last moment. Mr. Martinez is a social studies teacher who has worked well with all three gangs in the school. They respect him. He has given them special tutoring and helped them develop recreation programs. This is his proposal:

Mr. Martinez: "I believe the members of the Dukes, the Rolling Nineties, and 35th Street are now ready to sign a formal truce. Their leaders have told me they realize they have to live together here at Coolidge. They have offered to declare the school a safe zone, to leave their weapons home, and to set up a weekend patrol to guard the school from any outside gangs. In return, they would like a few designated areas on campus to paint their gang graffiti. They promise the graffiti will contain no threats or challenges. And they also want permission to wear their gang caps and jackets at school. I believe this could be an important opportunity, and I decided to bring this offer to you for discussion."

Activity: What Are Communities Doing About Crime in Schools?

At your school or community library or on the Internet, research about crime in schools. Choose one of the following problem areas: vandalism, burglaries, robberies, assaults on teachers and students, confiscations of weapons, rapes, or murders. Research to find the following:

1. What are schools across the country doing to attack the problem?

2. What are the latest statistics on this problem in schools?

Report your findings to the class.

Burglary Prevention

A **burglary** is an unlawful entry into a building or car with the intent to commit a crime, usually theft. It is the most common major felony in America. There are more than 2 million burglaries reported every year, and law enforcement experts believe an amount equal to that go unreported. That works out to more than 10,000 burglaries every day. The reported losses amount to a little more than $3 billion. To get an idea of how much money that is, imagine earning $1,000 a day. At that rate, it would take you more than 8,000 years to earn $3 billion. Only about 14 percent of these burglaries are ever cleared up by the police.

Burglary is a crime of opportunity. In about a third of all burglaries, force isn't used and nothing is broken. Many people fail to lock their doors or windows, and many others use inadequate locks. This makes the burglar's job easier. In many cases, it's just as easy for a burglar to pick a lock or break it as it is to open a door and walk in.

Perhaps more than anything else, burglars benefit when neighbors do not know each other. A neighbor is literally someone who lives nearby, but the word has come to suggest much more in our culture. Neighbors are supposed to be friendly and helpful. Before this century, neighbors traditionally banded together to help each other build houses and barns, sow and harvest crops, and protect their communities. But in our modern society, such tasks are taken care of by professionals, and people move so often that neighborly communities rarely develop. Because of the growing crime problem, many residents are afraid of talking to strangers—including their own neighbors.

These circumstances have made the burglars' task much easier. A stranger can often enter a community without being noticed and can go right up to a house without neighbors becoming suspicious.

Neighborhoods have responded in several ways to prevent burglaries. Some wealthier communities have hired private security companies to patrol their neighborhoods continuously. Other have turned themselves into gated communities, behind high walls and drive-in gates with 24-hour security guards.

One interesting experiment, modeled on the "Broken Windows" theory, was tried out in the 1980s in Virginia. In a high-burglary area, the community carted away trash and abandoned cars, filled in potholes, swept the streets, and painted out graffiti. The burglary rate dropped immediately by 35 percent. The people who ran the experiment argued that broken windows and other signs of urban decay "create fear in citizens and attract predators." They showed that simple attention to the look of an area can dramatically reduce crime.

Another response to the burglary problem has been the development of **neighborhood watch** groups or **block associations**. Police have often urged citizens to create neighborhood watch groups, especially in cities where community-policing programs are being set up. Neighborhood watch groups try to re-establish a sense of community. Members meet to discuss ways to make their area safer. They get to know one another, watch over one another's homes, and sometimes even clean up unsightly areas.

Neighborhood watch programs have proven successful in reducing crime, according to careful studies conducted in Seattle, San Diego, and Detroit. In one Detroit neighborhood, burglaries were reduced by 62 percent. The idea of neighborhood associations has even moved to the suburbs.

Ask an Expert

You can make a difference in fighting burglary in your own community. Most police departments have burglary-prevention units. Invite an officer from one of these units to come to your class and discuss the burglary problem in your community and practical steps for burglary prevention.

The Tierra Bonita Neighborhood Association

Tierra Bonita is an upper-middle-class hillside suburb on the West Coast. Because its houses are set back from the road, isolated by shrubbery and trees, burglars were having a field day there. In particular, burglars were breaking into homes when the residents went away on vacation. The police did what they could to increase patrolling, but only three officers were available at any one time to cover the whole area. The problem only got worse.

In desperation, a few energetic residents took the lead and called a meeting. More than 1,600 residents formed the Tierra Bonita Association of Neighborhoods. The association took on many tasks, but its top priority was an anti-burglary program. It formed an anti-burglary committee and invited the police to a public meeting to discuss the problem.

The police opened the meeting with a video that showed how burglars break in. It recommended some simple steps residents could take to safeguard their homes. The residents then set up a neighborhood-watch plan. Each block elected a coordinator, who was to be the primary contact with the police department. Block coordinators collected names and addresses so they knew who lived in their neighborhood. If anything suspicious happened, people could report it to the coordinator. And if someone went away on vacation, the coordinator could arrange to check the house periodically.

The association posted signs at every road leading into the area saying, "Tierra Bonita is a Neighborhood Watch Community." It set up a buddy system, so neighbors could watch one another's homes. Buddies also helped each other upgrade their locks and window latches. If one family in a buddy group went on vacation, the other could bring in the newspaper, open and close the drapes, and make the house look lived in. Finally, the association agreed to hold regular meetings to keep community spirit alive and to introduce new residents to the program.

Poll on Measures People Take to Protect Against Crime in the Home

"In the past 12 months, have you done any of these things to protect yourself from crime in the home ..."

Measure	Percent
You go to neighborhood watch meetings.	11
You and your neighbors have agreed to watch out for each other's safety.	61
You've installed a security system for your home.	18
You've asked the police department to do a home security check.	5
You have guard dogs at home.	15
You've engraved security identification numbers on all your belongings.	17
You've installed extra locks on windows and/or doors.	41
You keep weapons inside the home.	14
You've added outside automatic lighting (e.g. timers).	33
You've taken other precautions.	18

Repondents from 12 U.S. Cities: Chicago, IL; Kansas City, MO; Knoxville, TN; Los Angeles, CA; Madison, WI; New York, NY; San Diego, CA; Savannah, GA; Spokane, WA; Springfield, MA; Tucson, AZ; and Washington, DC. Responses of "don't know" and refusals to answer are excluded from the analysis. Totals exceed 100% due to multiple responses.

Source: *Sourcebook of Criminal Justice Statistics 1998*, Table 2.41, Bureau of Justice Statistics (1999)

In the first full year of operation, the burglary rate in Tierra Bonita dropped 54 percent.

For Discussion

1. Why do you think it's so difficult for the police to catch burglars without citizen help?

2. What are some easy ways to reduce burglary rates? What can homeowners do individually and with others?

3. How much responsibility should neighbors have for each other? Could neighborhood watches lead to an invasion of people's privacy? How could such problems be avoided? Explain.

4. Have you ever seen someone suspicious hanging around a neighbor's house? Did you call the police? Would you if it happened again? Why?

5. Is there a neighborhood-watch plan in your area? How is it working?

Activity: A Home Security Check

Walk through your own home and check how secure it is. While the following precautions will not guarantee protection from burglary, they will help deter it.

Door locks. A standard door lock has a slanted tongue only about a half inch long. It can be forced open easily by most burglars. The best protection for a door is a deadbolt. The bolt should extend at least an inch from the door, and it should have a hardened steel insert. Deadbolts with twist handles should not be within easy reach of a glass window.

Doors. A lock does little good if the door can be broken down easily. All outside doors should be at least 1¾ inches thick and made of metal or solid hardwood. The frames should be equally strong and fit the doors snugly.

Sliding glass doors. Burglars often enter houses through one of these doors. They simply lift the door out of its track. To prevent this, bolts or pins should be fitted into holes drilled through the track into the door frame. The bolt or pin can be easily removed from the inside when you want to use the door. A broomstick lying in the track provides some protection, but is much less effective.

Sash windows. For wooden sash windows, a bolt or pin should secure the two sashes to each other. For aluminum sash windows, buy a track lock that prevents the window from opening.

Sliding windows. Sliding windows can be secured in a similar way to sliding glass doors. A pin mechanism can be attached to the sliding window so it slides into a hole in the frame. Track locks are available, but many of these can be pushed aside with enough force on the window. If you use a track lock or a stick in the track, you should also fit a device on top of the window to prevent it being lifted out of its track.

Louvered windows. There are no easy ways to make louvered windows completely secure. Burglars can often slide the glass panes right out of their frames. On most louvered windows, the operating lever provides some locking protection if it is closed all the way. Make sure you cannot rotate the panes by hand when the lever is closed.

Window bars and grilles. If the house has window grilles, make sure they can be opened from inside in case of fire.

Shrubbery and lights outside. Shrubbery outside the windows should be trimmed so it does not give burglars a place to hide while they are trying to break in. Night lights should illuminate any dark areas where a burglar might lurk.

Valuables. You should have a list (or photos) of all the valuable items in the house and their serial numbers. Keep the list in a safe place, so it could be used later to help reclaim any stolen items or to catch a burglar or a dealer in stolen goods. As additional protection, you can engrave your name or Social Security number on all valuable items and then post a notice prominently in a window that all valuable items in the house are marked. Most police departments will lend an engraving tool to local residents.

Alarm system. If your home has an alarm system, test it to make sure it works. Test the window sensors or motion detectors to make sure they all work.

Activity: Organizing a Neighborhood Meeting

As you have learned, neighborhood cooperation is the real key to cutting down on burglaries. If your neighborhood does not already have a neighborhood watch or similar group, you can help organize one. People of all ages who live in the same neighborhood can work together to organize a meeting. You can also use this activity to plan a presentation to your local PTA or a community service club such as the Lions or Rotary. Use the following steps as a guide.

1. **Organize yourselves into teams of four or five students.** It is helpful if all team members live in the same general vicinity.

2. **Find a location for the meeting.** This can be someone's home, a clubhouse in a park, a multipurpose room in a library, a banquet room at a local restaurant, or a room at school.

3. **Schedule a specific time and date.** Evenings or weekend mornings are usually best.

4. **Plan a program for the meeting.** For helpful hints, review the Tierra Bonita group's meeting. Contact your local police department to see if it can send a burglary expert with a presentation. Some hardware stores and security firms are willing to send someone to demonstrate various locking devices and alarms. Prepare any visual aids you think might be helpful, such as charts of local burglary rates, local maps, or lists of burglary prevention steps. Prepare any handouts, such as maps and phone lists, and prepare name tags for people at the meeting. It can be a nice touch to plan simple refreshments, such as coffee and lemonade.

5. **Select a moderator for the meeting.** This can be one of your group or a community member who is willing to help.

6. **Write a one-page notice announcing the meeting.** Be sure to indicate clearly the purpose of the meeting and who is sponsoring it. Include the time, date, and location. A map or careful directions should be part of the notice. Make enough copies for the area and distribute them to residents in the area.

7. **Hold the meeting.** Be sure to arrive early to move chairs and to set up any displays and refreshments. Greet those arriving and make them feel welcome. For the first meeting, it is often best to wait an extra 15 minutes for latecomers. Don't be discouraged if the turnout is small. Even a few people can start a program. More will join later. The moderator should open the meeting, explain its purpose, and then introduce the presenters.

Before adjourning, some concrete plan should be made and people should take specific responsibilities. It is a common failing of new groups to decide that certain steps should be taken, but no one takes responsibility for them. At a minimum, you should have a phone list of those present for further contacts.

Remember that one of the main purposes of a neighborhood program like this is to get neighbors better acquainted with one another. This will help them watch out for one another and develop a sense of community. Allow some time at the meeting or after it for socializing.

Class Activity: A Citizen Task Force

In this simulation, students take the role of citizens of Athena, a city plagued by an upsurge in crime. The city has just received special federal funds to help solve its crime problem. A decision must be made about how the funds are to be used. The city council has created a special fund in the mayor's budget, and made the mayor responsible for distribution. The mayor has created a citizen task force to make recommendations on how the money should be spent. Many community members and organizations have a great interest in the task force's decision and some ideas on what should be recommended.

The simulation has two parts. In part 1, members of community organizations attend a reception and try to persuade task force members to fund their programs. In part 2, the task force members decide how the funds should be allocated in a public meeting.

1. As a class, read and discuss "The Mayor's Speech."

2. Break into seven groups. One group will be the task force and should have six to 10 members. The rest will be community organizations, which should have three to five students each. Assign each community group an organization to role play (e.g., Athena Police Department, Athena Chamber of Commerce, etc.).

3. Each group should:

   a. Appoint a chairperson.

   b. Review the mayor's speech briefly and then read the six proposals for 108F grants on pages 306–307.

   c. Rank the six proposals in order of which would be the most effective. Which proposal do you think would really help stop Athena's crime problem? Write a list with the most effective on top and the least effective on the bottom.

   d. Rank the six proposals again, this time in order of which would be the most effective *for the least amount of money.*

   e. Read and follow its group's instructions (See "Task Force Instructions, Part 1" or "Instructions for Community Organization" on page 305).

4. Hold the reception.

5. After the reception, the task force should meet in front of the whole class to discuss the proposals and make its recommendation to the mayor. The task force should read and follow "Task Force Instructions, Part 2," on page 307.

6. When the task force has reached a decision on the allocation of the funds, discuss the decision as a class using the Debriefing Questions on page 307.

The Mayor's Speech

A few days ago, Athena's mayor made the following remarks at a meeting of the Chamber of Commerce. The remarks were printed in their entirety in the *Athena Daily News*. The speech has aroused a great deal of discussion, particularly about how the funds should be spent. The text of the mayor's speech follows. Read it and think about recommendations you might make.

* * *

Good afternoon. I'm pleased to report today that Athena is bustling. Our population is growing, our standard of living is increasing, and in the last year alone three major new industries relocated here. These are high-tech corporations, and they brought in new jobs and created business for local suppliers. While I would like to take full credit for these developments, I know many of you have also worked hard to revitalize Athena. All of us here today deserve a warm round of applause for what we have done for our city.

But let's remember that Athena still faces many challenges. One problem in particular stands out. Because of this problem, we have faced deeply personal losses, even deaths of loved ones. Some of us can no longer afford insurance for our businesses or homes. Some of us have given up going out in the evening.

I am speaking, of course, of the upsurge in crime here in Athena. Before I address this issue, I want to make one thing perfectly clear. We do not believe the crime problem has been caused by weak laws, lenient courts, or poor police work. We have the best criminal justice system in the world. It is not my intention here today to try to fix blame for our problems or find a scapegoat. Our task is to find solutions.

Athena is not alone. Some communities throughout the state, indeed some communities across the nation, are experiencing the same increase in crime. The need to find solutions has been noted in the press and in numerous government studies. The federal government has heard the cries for help. It has created a pilot anti-crime program that will make some funds available to the cities. These funds are to be used at our discretion in attacking the crime problem. Under section 108F of the program we are entitled to $300,000 a year. At today's costs, that is not a very large amount, but it is a start and we must use it well.

Because of previous commitments to our Victim's Assistance Program, $120,000 of this money must be earmarked for crime victims. It will be used to cover the medical bills of victims, funeral expenses for their families, and to provide psychological counseling to those left disturbed and frightened. These are the forgotten men, women, and children who have suffered most from the rise in crime. It is altogether fitting that a share of the 108F funds be committed to them.

For the remaining $180,000, the money is to be spent at our discretion, as long as it is targeting crime control. Today I would like to solicit your opinions and suggestions for the use of these 108F funds. How should this money be spent? What programs would you like to see put into effect? To help make these decisions, I am going to appoint a citizens' task force. The task force will be made up of Athenans from all walks of life. It will review suggestions that have already been made by various city departments and citizens' groups, and members of the task force will make their

recommendations to me. I remind you that Athenans have solved many problems in the past by working together. If we stick together and share our wisdom with one another, we can take a major stride toward licking this problem, too.

* * *

An announcement of the new funds for Athena was made several weeks before the mayor's speech to the Chamber of Commerce. Community groups that thought they had a chance to obtain some of the funds began preparing proposals for programs to be funded by the money. As soon as the mayor let it be known that proposals were requested, several organizations were ready to deliver them. Within a few days, six proposals arrived at the mayor's office.

Not every proposal could be fully funded. Either all would be funded for less than requested or some would not be funded at all. Consequently, representatives of each sponsoring group were eager to influence those who would make the final decision.

This evening, the mayor is holding a reception in honor of the Anti-Crime Task Force. The mayor, staff, and the members of the task force as well as representatives of community organizations will be there.

Those attending the reception understand that this social event is an important opportunity for exchanging views informally, off the record. Both the members of the committee and the representatives of various community organizations know that the decision on who will receive the funds could be influenced by talking to the right people.

For Discussion

1. What is Athena's current problem? Why has the task force been called together?

2. What is the mayor's plan for $120,000 of the 108F funding? Do you agree with this commitment of part of the funds?

Do solutions to crime have to impinge on liberty?

Task Force Instructions, Part 1

As a member of this task force, your job is to consider the issues carefully and help the mayor decide on the best way to allocate the 108F funds. The mayor wants the task force to develop a consensus on its views before making its recommendations.

You know that citizen activists will be at the reception and that they will want to talk to you about the funding recommendations you will soon make. So at the reception, be sure to:

Give feedback. Inform citizens of your concerns about their proposals. Ask them to respond to these concerns by giving you arguments to take to the meeting. How they respond can help give you information to make a decision.

Speak to people from as many groups as possible. Those vying for your attention may resent your spending too much time with any one person or group.

Remember your political role. Be polite, listen carefully, but don't make any promises you can't keep. If you back out of a commitment, the committee and the mayor will look foolish.

Instructions for Community Organizations

You want to assure that your organization's proposal is fully understood by as many members of the task force as possible. Your goal at the reception is to convince them that your proposal should be fully funded. When talking with task force members, review the list of proposals and concentrate on the proposal for your organization.

Present your best arguments.

Stress the strengths of your organization.

Explain why the proposal a good idea for solving the crime problem in Athena.

Keep your presentation brief and to the point.

Ask for a firm commitment in support of your proposal.

Plan your strategy. Time at the reception is limited. Before it begins, consider the following:

- Should you concentrate on presenting the reasons why your proposal is best? Or on pointing out weaknesses in the other approaches and proposals? You may want to make use of your rankings of all the proposals.

- Should everyone in the group talk with as many committee members as they can? Or should each group member focus on a different person? Should you try to convince other groups to join with your group?

- Write a slogan for your group.

- Remember, this is a social occasion. Inappropriate behavior may prejudice members of the committee against you. Avoid arguing or interrupting conversations. See how subtle you can be.

Proposals for 108F Grants

Proposal 1: Police Aides
Sponsor: Athena Police Department
Cost: $108,000

This is a six-month program to provide each of the 14 two-officer patrols in the downtown area with one half-time aide. These aides would be students studying police science or public administration. They would take over clerical duties and allow officers to spend more time on patrol. The budget would pay for fourteen aides, at $15 an hour, for 20 hours per week. The program would last six months, providing an additional 7,000 hours of police patrol time.

Proposal 2: Force One Security Patrol
Sponsor: Athena Chamber of Commerce
Cost: $144,000

This six-month program would provide a two-person private security patrol for the downtown area, during non-business hours. The patrol would function from 5 p.m. to 8 a.m. weekdays and round the clock on weekends. The private agency would hire, train, and equip the patrol. The budget covers salaries, expenses, and transportation costs for six months.

Proposal 3: Self-Defense Classes
Sponsor: Urban Youth Association
Cost: $45,000

This year-round program would cover the fees for basic self-defense classes for up to a total of 500 Athenans. The basic course lasts four days a week for three weeks. Columbia Self-Defense normally charges $450 for this course, but by offering it for a large group, it will be charging the city only $81 per person. The Urban Youth Association has agreed to publicize the course and help select participants. Priority will go to low-income and elderly persons.

Proposal 4: Crime Prevention Seminars
Sponsor: Athena Police Protective League
Cost: $67,500

This is a year-round program that would provide four two-hour discussion seminars a week for one year. The seminars would be taught by police officers and would focus on ways private citizens and neighborhood-watch groups can help prevent crime. The budget would cover officer salaries, publicity expenses, and money for preparing pamphlets and visual aids for the seminars.

Proposal 5: Citizenswatch Patrols
Sponsor: Citizens for Public Safety
Cost: $33,000

This year-round program would help fund Citizenswatch patrols by business people and others. The patrols would cover the downtown and high-income residential areas. The patrol group is already formed and has made 46 citizen's arrests over the last six months. Unfortunately, only half those caught were brought to trial. In many cases, the untrained patrollers collected evidence incorrectly or violated the rights of those they detained. The budget will buy 40 citizen-band car radios and 20 hand-held walkie-talkies to improve communications with the police. Leaders of the group hope getting officers to the scene sooner will improve the conviction rate.

Proposal 6: Crimescope Hotline
Sponsor: Channel 14 Television
Cost: $75,000

This year-round program would provide a 24-hour telephone line, plus $70,000 in reward money to secret witnesses. Channel 14 has offered to raise half the reward money from private sources. Informants would be given code numbers, and their information would be passed on to the police. If the information resulted in a conviction, the informant would be paid a reward.

Task Force Instructions, Part 2

These are the instructions for the task force to use after the reception. The task force should meet in front of the whole class to discuss the proposals and make its recommendation to the mayor. The committee should review and modify, if necessary, its previous rankings. The committee must now decide on how to spend the $180,000.

Before convening their meeting, committee members should think about the following questions:

- Should the committee fund one or two of the programs it feels is most effective?

- Should it partially fund several programs?

- Should it fund the least expensive programs? Will the proposals rated highly serve a broad range of community interests?

- Will the proposals you fund serve more than one segment of the population?

The chairperson should run the meeting. This is an open meeting. The entire class will observe your deliberations. Write the following information on the board. Remember the committee cannot spend more than $180,000.

	Request	Award
1. Police Aides	$108,000	
2. Force One Security Patrol	$144,000	
3. Self-Defense Classes	$ 45,000	
4. Crime Prevention Seminars	$ 67,500	
5. Citizenswatch Patrols	$ 33,000	
6. Crimescope Hotline	$ 75,000	
TOTAL	$ 472,500	$180,000

Discuss each of the proposals and then decide how much to spend on each.

Debriefing Questions

1. Which proposals seemed weakest? Which seemed strongest? Why?

2. After hearing the task force's discussion, did you change your mind on any of the proposals? Why?

3. What seemed to make some groups more successful in persuading the task force?

4. What additional proposals can you think of that would help solve Athena's crime problems? Describe and summarize them on the board. What are the strengths of each? What are the weaknesses? Would any of these be better than those proposed to the mayor? Why?

To conclude the discussion, you may wish to conduct a class vote to find out which proposal discussed the class thinks would be the most effective.

Conclusion on Crime

The units in this book have covered crime, police, the criminal case, corrections, juvenile justice, and solutions. The book has revealed many debates over issues, but a few things are clear. America still has a significant crime problem. It also has a sophisticated criminal justice system.

Other things aren't quite so clear. Just how serious is America's crime problem? Is America's criminal justice system working and, if so, how well? What should be preserved? What should be changed? Americans—experts and non-experts alike—are divided on the answers to these questions. Differences of opinion on the exclusionary rule, tougher criminal laws, harsher sentencing, the death penalty, handguns, and the causes of crime often reflect and fuel the debates.

Public Perceptions

One thing seems more clear. Scientifically conducted polls indicate that people often believe the problem of crime is getting worse, even in times when the crime rate is dropping. Public attitudes also tend to favor harsher punishment for criminals, less judicial discretion in sentencing, and the death penalty as methods for reducing crime.

The news and entertainment media may be contributing to the perception that crime is out of control. Crime makes a good story. Newspapers and news broadcasts devote significant coverage to crime and criminal-justice issues. Much of the coverage is balanced and factual. Other times it borders on the sensational.

Many movie and television dramas also focus on crimes and criminals for their stories. By the early '90s, television had even developed several "reality shows" that follow real police officers on their patrols. The average viewer sees several murders a week on screen, plus dozens of other acts of violence.

Although the media seems to feed the public's fear of crime, much of that fear is based on reality. Despite declines in crime in the 1990s, America's rate of violent crime

---

Crime Prevention Programs

A 1997 report to Congress reviewed more than 500 crime prevention programs. Based on scientific studies, the report concluded that many programs worked to prevent crime, many others didn't work, and still others looked promising but needed more study. Here are a few of the findings.

What Works?

In communities—none as yet proved effective.

In schools
- Clear, consistent rules.
- Life skills training.
- Training in thinking skills for high-risk youth.

In places
- Nuisance abatement.

By police
- Extra police patrols in high-crime hot spots.
- Units that monitor high-risk repeat offenders
- Arresting domestic abusers who are employed.

By criminal justice agencies after arrest
- Incarceration of offenders who will continue to commit crimes.
- Rehabilitation programs for adult and juvenile offenders that focus on their risk factors.
- Drug treatment in prison.

Source: "Preventing Crime: What Works, What Doesn't, What's Promising," National Institute of Justice (1998)

---

remained far above rates in other developed countries. Almost everyone has some direct experience of crime—as a victim, friend of a victim, or even as someone who just has to pay high insurance rates. Under such conditions, what should be done?

Hardline Answers

Much of the public seems to favor getting tougher on criminals. Responding to this public demand, politicians over the years have made various proposals, such as:

- Build more prisons.

- Make prison sentences longer.

- Institute and carry out the death penalty.

- Restrict bail for dangerous suspects and for convicted persons waiting on appeals.

- Abolish parole.

- Give judges less discretion in sentencing.

- Make prison sentences mandatory for many crimes.

- Restrict the use of the insanity defense.

- Transfer more juveniles to adult courts.

- Hire more police.

States and the federal government have

already enacted many of these get-tough proposals. Some people believe that their implementation caused the crime rate to drop in the 1990s. They think that crime would drop even further if more states adopted them all.

Although many Americans favor get-tough measures, others disagree. Critics of the get-tough approach claim it doesn't work and it costs too much. They argue that crime dropped in the 1990s because the economy boomed and the crack cocaine epidemic ended—not because of the get-tough measures. They warn that the number of 15–24 year-olds in the population is increasing. This is the age group most likely to commit violent crimes. Critics also note that each year half a million prisoners go back into society. They worry that we may find our streets dominated by masses of hardened criminals as more and more prisoners are released.

The critics say that get-tough policies offer only a short-term answer to violent crime. In fact, they see the entire criminal justice system—police, courts, prisons—as incapable of affecting violent crime in the long run. The criminal justice system, they explain, reacts to violent crime after it has occurred. Locking up prisoners may prevent them from committing more crimes while they are imprisoned. But according to critics, it would be far better to prevent violent crime from occurring in the first place. One researcher has compared the criminal justice system to "operating an expensive ambulance service at the bottom of a cliff." In his view, it would be far more effective and cheaper to prevent people from falling in the first place.

This is not a new idea. Many experts have long believed the solution to violent crime is to attack its roots—poverty, racial discrimination, unemployment, lack of education, troubled families, and other social problems.

Searching for an answer to the violent crime of the 1960s, President Lyndon B. Johnson established the National Commission on the Causes and Prevention of Violence. In its final report in 1969, the commission stated that "the way in which we can make the greatest progress toward reducing violence in

---

Crime Prevention Programs

What Doesn't Work?

In communities
- Gun buyback programs.

In schools
- Individual counseling and peer counseling.
- Drug Abuse Resistance Education (DARE).

In places—none yet proved to be ineffective

By police
- Arrests of juveniles for minor offenses.
- Increased arrests or raids on drug markets.
- Storefront police offices.

By criminal justice agencies after arrest
- Boot camps.
- "Scared Straight" programs.
- Rehabilitation programs that do not focus on the offender's risk factors.

Source: "Preventing Crime: What Works, What Doesn't, What's Promising," National Institute of Justice (1998)

America is by taking the actions necessary to improve the conditions of family and community life for all who live in our cities, and especially the poor who are concentrated in the ghetto slums."

In 1990, the Milton S. Eisenhower Foundation, a non-profit created to follow up on the commission's work on violence, issued a report. It called for the federal government spend $10 billion a year to provide more early childhood education, reform inner-city schooling, create a youth investment corporation to assist inner-city youth, reform school-to-work programs, help repair urban areas, provide jobs for high-risk youth, and change the focus of the drug war to prevention and treatment.

In 1992, the RAND Corporation issued a report on the problems of urban America, including an in-depth focus on crime. Its report stated that "the impact of tougher sentences (particularly prison sentences) on crime rates is weak at best." It recommended focusing on imprisoning the most likely repeat offenders and diverting resources to non-penal strategies for crime prevention. The report concluded: "When the public debate focuses so heavily on punishment, it creates a false dichotomy between tough law enforcement and 'soft on crime' social programs. The choice is not one or the other—it must be both. . . . Our expectations of what justice agencies can do should be lowered, and our expectations of what social programs *must* do should rise."

With the current emphasis on deficit reduction and ending the "era of big government," social programs have fallen out of favor. Opponents tar them as "1960s programs" and "budget busters." Many argue that it's impossible to identify who will be a violent criminal or who won't. According to them, this means that prevention programs must target large segments of the population, wasting money on programs for people who don't need them.

Further, critics say that violence prevention programs do not work. Assuming we could identify future violent criminals, they argue, violence prevention programs cannot guarantee success. People can go through them and still commit violent acts. They conclude that the community cannot gamble its safety on violence prevention programs.

The root causes of violent crime, they contend, lie in the family. Government programs, they insist, cannot affect family life. If anything, they say, social spending over the last decades made people dependent on welfare and weakened families, causing more crime and violence, not less.

In 1996, the Council on Crime in America, a non-partisan conservative group, published its first report on crime in America. It strongly backed get-tough measures, arguing, for example, that "Prisons *do* cut crime." But its second report published in 1997 surprised many people. It advocated prevention programs to "monitor, mentor, and minister" to youth at risk of committing crimes. It favored non-profit and faith-based programs over government programs. It cited Big Brothers/Big Sisters and other church-based and volunteer programs as examples of programs that help prevent crime. These programs get caring, responsible adults involved in the lives of youth at risk. Professor John DiIulio, the author of both reports, emphasized that the criminal justice system alone cannot improve America's crime problem. He explained that

---

Crime Prevention Programs

What's Promising?

In communities
- Gang monitoring by probation and police.
- Mentoring by Big Brothers/Big Sisters.
- After-school recreation programs.

In schools
- "Schools within schools."
- Improved teaching and discipline techniques.

In places
- Adding a second clerk in already robbed convenience stores.
- Redesigning retail stores to reduce shoplifting.
- Improving training and management of bar staff.
- Street closures, barricades, and rerouting traffic.

By police
- Proactive arrests for concealed weapons.
- Higher numbers of police officers in cities.

By criminal justice agencies after arrest
- Drug courts that order and monitor rehabilitation and drug treatment.
- Intensive supervision of juvenile offenders.
- Fines in combination with other penalties.

Source: "Preventing Crime: What Works, What Doesn't, What's Promising," National Institute of Justice (1998)

"even at its best, the justice system cannot cost-effectively detect, arrest, convict, sanction, and supervise more than a small fraction of all criminals, adult and juvenile, suspected and adjudicated."

For Discussion

1. After studying the issues, has your opinion about America's crime problem changed? If so, how?

2. What do you think should be done about crime in the United States?

Class Activity: What Should Be Done?

Pretend you are a researcher drafting a study on crime in America. Prepare the concluding section of the report, "Recommendations on the Crime Problem." Use what you have learned from this book, class discussions, outside resources, and your own research. State your own ideas, opinions, and reasons. Prepare a presentation of your conclusion for the class.

Excerpts From the U.S. Constitution

Selected Sections of the U.S. Constitution, Ratified 1788

Preamble

We, the People of the United States, in Order to form a more perfect Union, establish Justice, insure domestic Tranquility, provide for the common defence, promote the general Welfare, and secure the Blessings of Liberty to ourselves and our Posterity, do ordain and establish this Constitution for the United States of America.

Article I

Section 1. All legislative Powers herein granted shall be vested in a Congress of the United States, which shall consist of a Senate and House of Representatives. . . .

Section 8. The Congress shall have Power . . . To provide for the Punishment of counterfeiting the Securities and Coin of the United States . . . To constitute tribunals inferior to the supreme Court; To define and punish Piracies and Felonies committed on the high Seas, and Offenses against the Law of Nations . . . To make all Laws which shall be necessary and proper for carrying into Execution the foregoing Powers, and all other Powers vested by this Constitution in the Government of the United States . . . .

Section 9. . . . The Privilege of the Writ of Habeas Corpus shall not be suspended, unless when in cases of Rebellion or Invasion the public safety may require it.
No Bill of Attainder or ex post facto Law shall be passed.

Article II

Section 1. The executive Power shall be vested in a President of the United States of America. He shall hold his Office during the Term of four Years, and, together with the Vice President, chosen for the same Term, be elected as follows . . . .

Section 2. The President shall be Commander in Chief of the Army and Navy of the United States, and of the Militia of the several States, when called into the actual Service of the United States; he may require the Opinion, in writing, of the principal Officer in each of the executive Departments, upon any Subject relating to the Duties of their respective Offices, and he shall have Power to grant Reprieves and Pardons for Offences against the United States, except in Cases of Impeachment.

He shall have Power, by and with the Advice and Consent of the Senate to make Treaties, provided two-thirds of the Senators present concur; and he shall nominate and by and with the Advice and Consent of the Senate, shall appoint Ambassadors, other public Ministers and Consuls, Judges of the supreme Court, and all other Officers of the United States, whose Appointments are not herein otherwise provided for, and which shall be established by Law: but the Congress may by Law vest the Appointment of such inferior Officers, as they think proper, in the President alone, in the Courts of Law, or in the Heads of Departments.

Section 3. . . . He shall take Care that the Laws be faithfully executed . . . .

Section 4. The President, Vice-President and all Civil Officers of the United States, shall be removed from Office on Impeachment for, and Conviction of, Treason, Bribery, or other high Crimes and Misdemeanors.

Article III

Section 1. The judicial Power of the United States, shall be vested in one supreme Court, and in such inferior Courts as the Congress may from time to time ordain and establish. The Judges, both of the supreme and inferior Courts, shall hold their Offices during good Behaviour, and shall, at stated Times, receive for their Services, a Compensation, which shall not be diminished during their Continuance in Office.

Section 2. The judicial Power shall extend to all Cases, in Law and Equity, arising under this Constitution, the Laws of the United States, and Treaties made, or which shall be made under their Authority;—to all Cases affecting Ambassadors, other public Ministers and Consuls;—to all Cases of admiralty and maritime Jurisdiction;—to Controversies to which the United States shall be a Party;—to Controversies between two or more States;—between a State and Citizens of another State;—between Citizens of different States;—between Citizens of the same State claiming Lands under Grants of different States, and between a State, or the Citizens thereof, and foreign States, Citizens or Subjects.

In all Cases affecting Ambassadors, other public Ministers and Consuls, and those in which a State shall be Party; the supreme Court shall have original Jurisdiction. In all the other Cases before mentioned, the supreme Court shall have appellate Jurisdiction, both as to Law and Fact, with such Exceptions, and under such Regulations as the Congress shall make.

The Trial of all Crimes, except in Cases of Impeachment, shall be by Jury; and such Trial shall be held in the State where the said Crimes shall have been committed; but when not committed within any State, the Trial shall be at such Place or Places as the Congress may by Law have directed.

Section 3. Treason against the United States shall consist only in levying War against them, or in adhering to their Enemies, giving them Aid and Comfort. No Person shall be convicted of Treason unless on the Testimony of two Witnesses to the same overt Act, or on Confession in open Court.

The Congress shall have Power to declare the Punishment of Treason, but no Attainder of Treason shall work Corruption of Blood, or Forfeiture except during the Life of the Person attainted.

Article IV

Section 1. Full faith and Credit shall be given in each State to the public Acts, Records, and judicial Proceedings of every other State. And the Congress may by general Laws prescribe the Manner in which such Acts, Records and Proceedings shall be proved, and the Effect thereof.

Section 2. The Citizens of each State shall be entitled to all Privileges and Immunities of Citizens in the several States.

A Person charged in any State with Treason, Felony or other Crime, who shall flee from Justice, and be found in another State, shall, on Demand of the executive Authority of the State from which he fled, be delivered up, to be removed to the State having Jurisdiction of the Crime. . . .

Section 4. The United States shall guarantee to every State in this Union a Republican Form of Government, and shall protect each of them against Invasion; and on Application of the Legislature, or of the Executive (when the Legislature cannot be convened) against domestic Violence.

Article VI

This Constitution, and the Laws of the United States which shall be made in Pursuance thereof; and all Treaties made, or which shall be made, under the Authority of the United States, shall be the supreme Law of the Land; and the Judges in every State shall be bound thereby, any Thing in the Constitution or Laws of any State to the Contrary notwithstanding. . . .

Selected Amendments from the Bill of Rights, Ratified 1791

First Amendment. Congress shall make no law respecting an establishment of religion, or prohibiting the free exercise thereof; or abridging the freedom of speech, or of the press; or the right of the people peaceably to assemble, and to petition the Government for a redress of grievances.

Second Amendment. A well regulated Militia, being necessary to the security of a free State, the right of the people to keep and bear Arms, shall not be infringed.

Fourth Amendment. The right of the people to be secure in their persons, houses, papers, and effects, against unreasonable searches and seizures, shall not be violated, and no Warrants shall issue, but upon probable cause, supported by Oath or affirmation, and particularly describing the place to be searched, and the persons or things to be seized.

Fifth Amendment. No person shall be held to answer for a capital, or otherwise infamous crime, unless on a presentment or indictment of a Grand Jury, except in cases arising in the land or naval forces, or in the Militia, when in actual service in time of War or public danger; nor shall any person be subject of the same offence to be twice put in jeopardy of life or limb; nor shall be compelled in any criminal case to be a witness against himself, nor be deprived of life, liberty, or property, without due process of law; nor shall private property be taken for public use, without just compensation.

Sixth Amendment. In all criminal prosecutions, the accused shall enjoy the right to a speedy and public trial, by an impartial jury of the State and district wherein the crime shall have been committed, which district shall have been previously ascertained by law, and to be informed of the nature and cause of the accusation; to be confronted with the witnesses against him to have compulsory process for obtaining witnesses in his favor, and to have the Assistance of Counsel for his defence.

Seventh Amendment. In Suits at common law, where the value in controversy shall exceed twenty dollars, the right of trial by jury shall be preserved, and no fact tried by a jury, shall be otherwise re-examined in any Court of the United States, than according to the rules of the common law.

Eighth Amendment. Excessive bail shall not be required, nor excessive fines imposed, nor cruel and unusual punishments inflicted.

Ninth Amendment. The enumeration in the Constitution, of certain rights, shall not be construed to deny or disparage others retained by the people.

10th Amendment. The powers not delegated to the United States by the Constitution, nor prohibited by it to the States, are reserved to the States respectively, or to the people.

Selected Later Amendments

13th Amendment, Ratified 1865. Neither slavery nor involuntary servitude, except as a punishment for crime whereof the party shall have been duly convicted, shall exist within the United States, or any place subject to their jurisdiction.

14th Amendment, Ratified 1868. All persons born or naturalized in the United States, and subject to the jurisdiction thereof, are citizens of the United States and of the State wherein they reside. No State shall make or enforce any law which shall abridge the privileges or immunities of citizens of the United States; nor shall any State deprive any person of life, liberty, of property, without due process of the law; nor deny to any person within its jurisdiction the equal protection of the laws.

Glossary

acquit To find not guilty.

affidavit A written statement made under oath.

affirmative defense A defense such as insanity, self-defense, and entrapment. If proved by the defendant, it makes the defendant not guilty of the crime even if the prosecution can prove the elements of the crime.

age of majority The age a person is considered an adult for legal purposes.

aggravated assault According to the UCR, an unlawful attack by one person upon another for the purpose of inflicting severe or aggravated bodily injury. Normally committed with a weapon.

appeal a request that an appellate court review a decision of a lower court.

appellate court A court that hears appeals; it is not a trial court. An appeals court.

attorney A lawyer; legal counsel; attorney at law. A person authorized to practice law.

arraignment A court hearing in which the defendant must enter a plea, e.g., guilty or not guilty.

arrest To take a person into custody for the purpose of charging the person with a crime.

arrestee The person arrested.

arson According to the UCR, any willful or malicious burning of another's property.

assault Technically, the immediate threat of attacking someone, but usually it means a physical attack on another person. See **battery**.

assault with a deadly weapon The crime of attacking someone with a weapon that could cause fatal injuries. See **aggravated assault**.

bailiff A police officer assigned to the courtroom to keep order.

battery The illegal touching of another person, usually an attack. When used in "assault and battery," the assault is the threat of attack and the battery the physical attack itself.

bench The judge's desk in the courtroom.

bench trial A trial held before a judge alone without a jury.

bill of attainder A legislative enactment that punishes a person in place of a trial. Banned by the U.S. Constitution.

Bill of Rights The first 10 amendments to the U.S. Constitution, which describe the rights and protections guaranteed to each citizen.

booking The official process of recording the arrest, which may include taking fingerprints and photographs of the accused.

Bureau of Justice Statistics An agency of the Department of Justice that collects crime-related statistics.

burden of proof The responsibility of proving facts in a case. In a criminal trial, the prosecution has the burden of proving its case beyond a reasonable doubt.

capital crime A crime punishable by death or life imprisonment.

capital punishment The death penalty.

case in chief One side's trial evidence. In a criminal trial, the prosecution presents its evidence first. After it rests its case, the defense presents its evidence.

case law Law made by judges interpreting constitutions, statutes, and other case law.

citizen review boards An official group, staffed by ordinary citizens, authorized to review complaints of police misconduct.

civil case A lawsuit between individuals or organizations, which normally seeks monetary compensation for damages.

civil court A court that handles civil cases.

civilian review boards See **citizen review boards**.

commissioner An attorney who acts as a judge.

common law 1. the unwritten law in England that evolved over centuries and is the basis for U.S. law. 2. Case law in the United States as opposed to statutory law.

crime An illegal act punishable upon conviction in a court.

crime rate The amount of crime per so many people in the population.

criminal procedure The rules for processing someone through the criminal justice system.

criminology The study of crime.

cross-examination The questioning of an opponent's witnesses at trial.

deadly force Force that poses a high risk of death or serious injury to its human target.

death row A separate section of a prison reserved for inmates awaiting execution.

defendant The accused in a criminal trial.

determinate sentence A prison sentence for a specific length of time, e.g., five years. A **fixed sentence**.

direct examination An attorney's initial questioning of his or her own witness.

discretion The power to choose.

discretionary jurisdiction The power of some appeals courts, such as the U.S. Supreme Court, to accept or refuse to hear particular appeals. See **writ of certiorari**.

due process In the Fifth and 14th amendments, the basic requirement that no person can be deprived of life, liberty, or property without a fair trial. This means both fair laws and fair procedures must be used.

en banc The full bench of justices. Each federal circuit court has from six to 27 justices, but for most cases the justices hear cases in panels of three. When all the justices in a circuit hear a case together, they hear it *en banc*.

evidence The means of determining facts in a trial. Testimony, physical objects, and exhibits are examples of evidence.

exclusionary rule A judicial rule that prevents the government from introducing illegally obtained evidence at a criminal trial.

fact finder The one responsible for deciding the facts of a particular case and coming to a verdict; either a judge or jury.

false imprisonment The crime of making a false arrest or unlawfully taking someone into custody.

felony A serious crime usually punished by one or more years of imprisonment in a state or federal penitentiary.

felony murder The rule that if any person is killed during a felony, the criminal can be charged with murder.

fixed sentence See **determinate sentence**.

forfeiture The confiscation of assets either used in or derived from illegal activity.

forgery The crime of falsely signing a document with the intent to defraud.

fraud The crime of obtaining another's property through lies and deceit.

habeas corpus, writ of A court order requiring authorities to release a prisoner because the court has found that the prisoner is being illegally detained.

hearing Any court proceeding, such as a trial.

homicide Literally, human killing. The crimes of homicide range from different degrees of murder to different kinds of manslaughter.

hypothetical A made-up example.

incarceration rate The number of prisoners per 100,000 population.

incorrigible Juveniles who cannot be controlled by their parents.

indeterminate sentence A prison sentence of an indefinite period of time, for example "one year to 30 years." Under this sentence, prisoners are released when the parole board determines they are rehabilitated.

interrogation Questioning.

jurisdiction 1. the geographical area over which particular courts have power; 2. state and federal government.

jurisprudence The philosophy of law, or the science that studies the principles of law.

lawyer See **attorney**.

magistrate A court officer who issues warrants; normally a lower-court judge who handles pretrial proceedings or presides over misdemeanor trials.

marshal A law-enforcement officer who normally performs duties connected with a court.

mayhem The crime of mutilating or cutting off a part of someone's body.

mens rea Guilty mind; the state of mind requirement for crimes.

Miranda **warning** A advisory statement about the rights of suspects that police must read to suspects in custody before questioning them. The Supreme Court first required this statement in its *Miranda v. Arizona* decision in 1966.

misdemeanor A crime less serious than a felony, usually punished by a fine or imprisonment up to one year in a local jail.

mitigate To make less serious. Mitigating circumstances are circumstances surrounding a crime that tend to make it less serious.

Model Penal Code A criminal code composed by legal experts at the American Law Institute as a standard that legislatures may want to adopt. Unless sections of it are adopted by jurisdictions, it has no legal authority.

motion A formal request made to a court.

motion to suppress A request that the court exclude particular evidence from the trial because it was illegally obtained.

National Institute of Justice The research agency of the U.S. Department of Justice.

nolo contendere plea A plea of no contest. (Latin for "I will not contest it.") It has the same effect as a guilty plea except that the person does not admit guilt. Thus if someone files a lawsuit against the person, the person has not admitted guilt.

organized crime A group that uses a business-like structure, with a boss and subordinates, to carry out crime on an ongoing basis.

pardon An act by the governor or president that forgives all or part of a prisoner's sentence.

parens patriae The idea that the state takes the role of parents to protect juveniles.

parole The conditional release of a prisoner before the end of a prison term.

parole board A board appointed by the governor that determines when prisoners may be released on parole.

penal Subject to punishment. A **penal code** is a list of laws defining crimes.

penitentiary A state or federal maximum-security prison.

peremptory challenge During jury selection, an attorney's rejection of a prospective juror that requires no reason be given to the court. Each side has a limited number of these challenges.

perjury The crime of lying while testifying under oath.

plaintiff The party in a lawsuit who sues the other party.

precedent An issue of law previously decided by a court that other courts follow.

probable cause Evidence that an independent, cautious person would have good reason to believe.

probation An alternative to prison. This sentence requires the offender to follow certain conditions, usually under the supervision of a probation officer.

prosecute To try someone for a crime.

prosecution The government's side in a criminal case.

prosecutor The government's attorney who presents the case against a criminal defendant.

prosecutorial discretion The prosecutor's authority to decide what charges to bring and how to pursue a criminal case.

prostitution Crime of engaging in a sexual act with another in exchange for money or other compensation.

rape According to the UCR, the carnal knowledge of a female forcibly and against her will.

recidivism The committing of further crimes by offenders after they have been punished for previous convictions.

redirect examination An attorney's requestioning of his or her own witness after cross-examination.

relevant Pertinent, appropriate, related to the subject at hand.

search In *Katz v. United States* (1967), the Supreme Court defined a search as any governmental intrusion into something in which a person has a reasonable expectation of privacy.

seizure Any taking into possession, custody, or control. Property may be seized, but so may people. An arrest is one form of seizure.

sentence A punishment for a crime.

sheriff A county law-enforcement officer.

sodomy Homosexual or oral copulation.

status offense An offense, such as truancy or running away from home, that would not be a crime if committed by an adult.

statute A written law; a law enacted by the legislature.

statutory law See **statute**.

sting operation Undercover police work that sets up a situation to catch criminals in the act.

street crime A class of crimes usually involving force or violence, such as murder, assault, robbery, or rape.

testify To make statements as a witness under oath.

testimony Statements made by witnesses under oath.

UCR Uniform Crime Reporting program. A nationwide program headed by the FBI that collects police reports of crime.

vandalism The crime of intentionally defacing or destroying another person's property.

venue The location of a trial.

verdict The decision of guilty or not guilty made by the jury or judge.

victimless crimes Crimes, such as prostitution and possession of illegal drugs, in which everyone involved chooses to be involved.

voir dire During jury selection, the questioning of prospective jurors.

warrant A court order issued by a judge authorizing a search, an arrest, or a seizure of evidence of a crime.

white-collar crime A class of property crimes that are usually job-related, such as embezzlement, bribery, and consumer fraud.

writ A written court order.

writ of certiorari An order from an appeals court stating that the court will hear a case. These writs are granted by appeals courts that have discretionary jurisdiction.

Table of Cases

Below are the titles of cases cited in the book followed by the legal citation, year, and the pages the cases are found in *Criminal Justice in America*.

Credits

All photographs, cartoons, and opinion polls are reprinted with the permission of the following:

Lalo Alcaraz, L.A. Weekly, p. 99

Kirk Anderson, St. Paul Pioneer Press, pp. 18, 265

AP/Wide World Photos, p. 33, 53, 116, 136, 196, 198, 219, 258, 285

Chuck Asay, Creators Syndicate, p. 50

Chuck Asay, 192

Jim Borgman, King Features Syndicate, p. 16

Steve Breen, Copley News Service, p. 245

Andrew Costly, CRF, pp. 91, 133, 271, cover (3)

Calif. Department of Corrections, cover (4)

Chris Britt, Copley News Service, p. 286

Callahan, Levin Presents, p. 139

Paul Conrad, Los Angeles Times, p. 106

Corbis, p. 28, 54, 89

CRF, 302, cover (6)

Culver Pictures, pp. 60, 170, 225, 227, 293, 294

John Deering, The Arkansas Democrat-Gazette, p. 49

Feature Photo Service, Microsoft Corp., cover (5)

The Gallup Organization, 46, 93, 218, 288

Herman®, © Jim Unger 2000 / Laughingstock Licensing, Inc., Ottawa, Canada, p. 119

Mark Ide, pp. 41, 58, 65, 70, 79, 82, 84, 94, 102, 154, 156, 168, 231, 242, 281, cover (1 & 2)

Gary Markstein, Copley News Service, p. 254

National Park Service, p. 202

Mike Peters, Tribune Media Services, p. 305

Bruce Plante, Courtesy of The Chattanooga Times, p. 206

Michael Ramirez, Copley News Service, p. 183

Rob Rogers, United Features Syndicate, Inc., p. 274

Tom Ryan, King Features Syndicate, pp. 43, 162

Steve Sack, Minneapolis Star-Tribune, p. 45

Walt Stewart, pp. 151, 152, 159

Signe Wilkinson, Washington Post Writers Group, p. 185

Index

Special Thanks to:

Cristy Lytal, proofreading and CJA Links

Esther Grassian, UCLA reference librarian

Charles Degelman, proofreading

Tina Esposito, proofreading

Katie Moore, proofreading